OXFORD
G N V Q

TRAINING AND
CTAD
DEVELOPMENT
LTD

Oxford University Press

Oxford University Press, Walton Street, Oxford OX2 6DP

Oxford New York

Athens Auckland Bangkok Bombay Calcutta Cape Town Dar es Salaam Delhi Florence Hong Kong Istanbul Karachi Kuala Lumpur Madras Madrid Melbourne Mexico City Nairobi Paris Singapore Taipei Tokyo Toronto

and associated companies in

Berlin Ibadan

Oxford is a trademark of the Oxford University Press

© Cambridge Training and Development Ltd 1996

First published 1996

A CIP catalogue record for this book is available from the British Library.

ISBN 0 19 832760 9 (Students' edition)

0 19 832759 5 (Bookshop edition)

Typeset and designed by Design Study, Bury St Edmunds and Chris Lord Information Design, Brighton, East Sussex

Printed and bound in Great Britain by Thomson Litho Ltd, East Kilbride, Scotland

Thanks go to the following:
Addenbrooke's NHS Trust, Cambridge; Cambridge and Huntingdon Health Authority; Gill Betts; Boots the Chemist Ltd, Cambridge; Centre 33 Young People's Counselling and Information Service, Cambridge; Emmaus Cambridge Community; The Evelyn Hospital, Cambridge; Howard Fried-Booth; Lilian Gates; Granta Housing Society Ltd, Cambridge; Dr J. David Greaves; Susan K. Greaves; Health Education Authority (physical activity team), London; Debra Howard; Joint Colleges Nursery, Cambridge; Lifespan Healthcare Trust; Alison Monk; Papworth Hospital NHS Trust; Mr Rankine's Dental Surgery, Cambridge ; Liz Redfern, education consultant (formerly assistant director of educational policy, English National Board); Sheila Stace, NVQ consultant; Sid Stace, senior social worker. Thanks also go to the many other organisations and individuals who contributed examples, case studies and other material.

Thanks for permission to reproduce photos/extracts go to:
Equal Opportunities Commission for Northern Ireland (Equal pay poster, p.12); © *Times Educational Supplement*, 1996 (Susannah Kirkham, author – The cost of imperfection, p.15; Gerald Haigh, author – Making an entrance, p.38); Department of Health (leaflet, p.18); Department for Education (leaflets, p.18); Equal Opportunites Commission (leaflet, p.21); Commission for Racial Equality (leaflet, p.21); Central Office of Information (leaflet, p.21); Reproduced with permission from Discrimination Case Law Digest, No:25, Autumn 1995, published by Industrial Relations Services, Eclipse Group Ltd, 18-20 Highbury Place, London, N5 1QP (Reinstatement recommended, p.9; £28,000 award in race case, p.22; Market forces no defence, p.22; Hulton Deutsch Collection (Suffragettes, p.24); Reproduced with the kind permission of the European Communities from the publication *Serving the European Union – A citizen's guide to the Institutions of the EC*, page 17 (European Court of Justice, p.25); Weidenfeld and Nicholson (extract from *The Eye of the Clock*, p.31); Josh Good (photos top row, middle row and bottom right, p.28; Elderly lady, p.72; Elderly couple, p.193; Disabled person, p.245 and 362); Joanne O'Brien (photo bottom left, p.28); Age Concern (Windsurfer, p.29; Doctor and patient, p.423; Service user and carer, p.319); The *Guardian*, 1996 (Generation gap chart, p.29; Raanon Gillon, author – Sometimes we have a duty of care not to intervene, p.53; Chris Mihill, author – NHS set to fund surrogate birth, p.54; Cash-strapped hospitals

plea for cancer patients, p.55 David Brindle, author – Schizophrenia drugs rationed, p.54; Keyhole revolution in coronary surgery, p.274); Crown copyright, reproduced by permission of the Controller of HMSO (Children Act leaflets p.30; Moving into a care home leaflet, p.324; Wintertime smog leaflet, p.338; The Children Act logo, p.346; Measles notifications graph, p.377 Drugs/solvents leaflets, p.386; Lily Savage leaflet, p.393; Balance of Good Health leaflet, p.392; Who Cares leaflet, p.398; Cot death leaflet, p.415; That's the limit leaflet, p.415); Justice Mary Hogg, Universal Pictorial Press (Female Judge, p.32); Forte plc (waiter, p.33; girl on computer, p.453; semi-structured interview, p.462;); National Extension College (Students and teacher, p.34); Age Concern (Men playing cards, p.41); Hospital Doctor magazine (22 February 1996 – Fighting fears on privacy, p.50; 14 April 1994 – Chief puts ops on funding blacklist, p.55); The *Guardian*, 1988 (Vieve Forward, author – A treat for Granny Bint, p.118); SECCHI–LECAQUE–ROUSSEL-UCLAF/ CRNI/Science Photo Library (rough endoplasmic reticulum, p.137); © Biophoto Associates (squamous tissue x 2, p.146); Manfred Kage/Science Photo Library (striated muscle tissue, p.146); CNRI/ Science Photo Library (compact bone, p.146); *Soft Exercise, The Complete Book of Stretching*, © 1983, by Arthur Balaskas and John Stirk, published by HarperCollins Publishers Ltd (Musculo-skeletal system, p.153); *Child development – a first course* by Sylvia and Lunt, published by Blackwell 1982 (Diagrams of Piagets experiments, p.198); The Ramblers' Association (Ramblers group, p.237);

Arthritis Care, 18 Stephenson Way, London NW1 2HD; Age Concern, Astral House, 1268 London Road, London, SW16 4ER; Avert, 11–13 Denne Parade, Horsham, West Sussex, RH12 1JD; Carers National Association, Ruth Pitter House, 20/25 Glasshouse Yard, London EC1A 4JS: (logos, p.248); The *Independent* (Glenda Cooper, author – How to mend a broken heart, p.274); Marie Curie Cancer Care (leaflet, p.319); Published by permission of the editor of Community Care (barcharts, p.280; Music therapy, p.321); Contact a Family (leaflet, p.326); Reprinted from *Promoting Health*, 3rd edition, authors – Linda Ewles and Ena Simnett, page 23, published 1995, by permission of the publisher, Academic Press Limited, London (Better Health diagram, p.333); Royal Pharmaceutical Society (Healthiest advice under the sun leaflet, p.338; Medicines are not child's play leaflet, p.409); Islington Council (Meals in the home leaflet, p.251; Poor housing leaflet, p.338; Croydon Social Services (leaflet, p.341); National Foster Care Association (Children's Life Story book, p.359); Department of Transport, BBC, Crown copyright, reproduced by permission of the Controller of HMSO (No Excuses leaflet, p.392); Boots the Chemist (Don't Burn, p.407); Durex Information Service (That's the Limit leaflet, p.415); Table 2 from PHLS AIDS Scottish Centre for Infection & Environmental Health, Institute of Child Health, London & Oxford Haemophilia Centre. Aids and HIV infection in the United Kingdom: monthly report, Communicable Disease Report. CDR wkly 1996; 6: p.252 (HIV-infected people chart, p.427); Stephen Lazarides (photo p.428).

Contents

ABOUT THE BOOK

This book contains the information you need to complete the eight mandatory units of your Advanced Health and Social Care GNVQ.

How it's organised

This book is organised in units and elements, like the GNVQ, so it's easy to find the information you need at any point in your course. Each element has several sections. They cover all the topics in the element, using the same headings as the GNVQ specifications. At the end of each element there are some key questions, so you can check your knowledge and prepare for the unit tests. There are also suggestions for an assignment, which will help you produce the evidence you need for your portfolio.

What's in it

The book presents information in several different ways so it's interesting to read. Some information is presented in the actual words of people who work in health or social care jobs, for example a child protection adviser, a social worker, a pharmacist and a doctor working in an NHS hospital, or in the words of service users, for example a young man who receives physiotherapy at home and a woman who is undergoing treatment for thyroid cancer. There are many definitions of terms you may not have come across before in this context, such as 'advocate', 'judicial review' or 'key worker'. Graphs illustrate things like the effect of immunising children against measles. There are illustrations, photographs and diagrams, extracts from people's diaries, examples from policy documents and health education leaflets. Case studies describe particular situations, the activities or views of health or social care organisations (such as the Health Education Authority), practitioners (such as a GP fundholder carrying out research) or service users (such as an elderly woman in residential care).

How to use the book

Decide which part you want to read. For example, you can go straight to any element and read through the relevant sections. You can find the information about any topic by looking at the list of contents at the front of the book and seeing which section looks most useful. Or you can use the index at the back to find a specific topic or organisation.

As well as information, the book has suggestions for things you can do to help you learn about health and social care in a practical way. Discussion points suggest topics that you can think about and discuss with other people – other students on your course, your tutor or teacher, friends, family, people who work in health or social care. Activities ask you to do things like: collect a range of health education leaflets and analyse the messages they are trying to put across; observe and record how people communicate verbally; develop a research hypothesis which links brushing teeth to dental health, and so on.

Doing the activities will help you to get a realistic picture of what it is like to work in the health and social care sector.

When you've finished an element, try answering the key questions at the end. You may want to make notes of your answers and use them when you're preparing for the unit tests. The assignment at the end of each element suggests what you can do to produce evidence for your portfolio. Some of the activities will also help you to build up the portfolio. You might want to make an action plan for each element to help you plan and carry out the work in the activities and assignment.

Other resources

This book is a valuable source of information for your GNVQ studies. But it also encourages you to use other resources effectively. There are suggestions for finding out more information about many topics, for example health education campaigns, legislation relevant to health or social care and theories about human growth and development, among others. You can get this information from health or social care journals, health or social care organisations, other books about health and social care, reports by the Office for National Statistics, or on-line information services. This book also asks you to investigate health and social care organisations or practitioners yourself, by reading about them in their literature, or talking to them about their professional views, activities and experiences.

Over to you

It's your GNVQ and your job to make the best of the opportunity to learn about health and social care. Use this book in whatever way helps you most. For example, you could:

■ look at the contents page to give you the whole picture
■ use the index to find out specific bits of information
■ read a section at a time to help you understand a topic
■ look at the activities and assignment before starting an element so you know what you have to do
■ turn things on their head and start with the key questions to see how much you already know about an element.

It's over to you now. Good luck.

UNIT **1**

Element 1.1
Legal rights and responsibilities

Element 1.2
Discrimination and individuals

Element 1.3
Ethical issues in health
and social care

Equal opportunities and individuals' rights

This unit is to help you understand legal rights
and responsibilities and their importance in
health and social care. You will consider how
rights can be affected by discrimination. This
unit and unit 6 also look at ethical issues in
health and social care practice.

ELEMENT **1.1**

Legal rights and responsibilities

In this element you will be looking at the legal rights and responsibilities as laid down in the main equal opportunities legislation, at the rights of different groups and at how equal opportunities legislation develops.

66 *The messages put across in equal opportunities training courses need to translate into what you do. It is easy to assume you are carrying out your duties with regard to equal opportunities. We have key structures in place through our recruitment and induction training but you have to consciously make the effort to consider situations in the light of equal opportunities and what the issues really mean on a day to day basis.* 99

child protection adviser

66 *One of the ground rules is absolute confidentiality. However, because of the legal and medical side of things, there are certain things I am legally bound to disclose. I make it clear to patients, at the stage of their initial assessment, what these things are. Things like suicidal feelings and difficult family dynamics which impair treatment would have to be shared with other professionals. So patients know where they stand, and can keep any area they wouldn't want discussed to themselves.* 99

head of medical counselling and family support

66 *Our equal opportunities policy aims to ensure that all the children are treated equally. It's something we're acutely aware of and all staff know that if they feel the policy is not being complied with completely in any area they can bring the matter directly to me or my deputy. We bring in multicultural activities as a matter of course so that the children understand that other people may be different in some way but they are still equal.* 99

head of private day nursery and childcare centre

66 *One of the organisation's stated aims is that everyone should be accorded equal respect, regardless of race, colour, creed, or sex. By the same token, we don't believe in positive discrimination. Everyone is judged on his or her own merits. We maintain the Declaration of Human Rights.* 99

community coordinator, community for homeless people

66 *Here at the Centre the emphasis is very much on the individual's right to decide: the young person has control over what action they take and the support they would like.* 99

senior worker (counselling), young people's counselling and information centre

The underpinning principles of the legislation

Principles are fundamental beliefs which guide the way people behave.

Individuals' principles form the basis of their personal code of conduct for life:

66 *I believe in animal rights, so I don't eat meat.* 99

66 *I don't think all women should have to have children – I'm not going to have any.* 99

In the same way, all societies have principles which control the way people behave towards each other. For example, two of the principles underpinning British society are that people shouldn't kill one another or be married to more than one person at the same time. Often these principles are enforced by laws – in this case, against murder and bigamy.

DISCUSSION POINT

How many principles can you think of which underpin the things you do – and don't do – from day to day? Which of these do you think are your own principles, and which have been passed on to you by the society you live in? Which of your principles are enforced by laws?

The principles of equality of opportunity have become increasingly important in Britain since World War II: immigration has created a more diverse, multicultural society; more women are working; disabled people's rights are more widely recognised. In line with this, a range of important equality of opportunity legislation has been introduced covering people's:

- sex – equality of opportunity for men and women
- race – equality of opportunity regardless of colour, race, ethnic or national origins
- disability
- pay – equal pay for men and women
- employment opportunities.

EMPLOYMENT
For example:
- Fair Employment (NI) Act 1989

SEX
For example:
- Sex Discrimination Acts 1975 and 1986
- Equal Pay Act 1970
- Employment Protection Act 1975

PAY
For example:
- Equal Pay Act 1970

Equality of opportunity legislation

DISABILITY
For example:
- Disabled Persons (Employment) Acts 1944 and 1958
- Chronically Sick and Disabled Persons Representation Act 1970
- Education (Handicapped Children) Act 1981
- Disabled Persons (Services, Consultation and Representation) Act 1986

RACE
For example:
- Race Relations Acts 1965, 1968 and 1976
- Public Order Act 1968

All of this legislation is underpinned by three principles which are essential in health and social care:

- equality of care
- individual rights
- individual choice.

Health and social care practitioners need to ensure that they implement these principles of equality of opportunity – following legislation when necessary – in every aspect of their work.

Equality of care

Equality of opportunity legislation is founded on the belief that people throughout society should be treated equally – a principle which is fundamental to health and social care services.

All health and social care organisations abide by equal opportunities legislation and, like the majority of organisations in other sectors, have their own policies on sexual harassment, race discrimination and other equal opportunities issues. In health care, practitioners would say that values are as important as the legislation. Felim, a ward nurse, explains:

66 *Illness and disease are great levellers and no particular respectors of background or race. As the NHS treats the illness or disease the personal circumstances of the patient comes second.* 99

Most health and social care practitioners come into contact with a wide range of people in the course of their work. All of these people have a right to receive care and treatment of an equal quality.

The first step towards achieving this is equal access, which is provided for by legislation. Health and social care practitioners can then put equality of care into practice by:

- encouraging everybody – regardless of sex, race, religion, age or disability – to make the most of the services on offer
- responding to every individual as a human being of equal value
- not discriminating against an individual on any grounds.

Individual rights

People brought up in a western country, like Britain or the USA, tend to hold the belief in their rights as individuals. They believe that they have the right to vote, to speak freely and to be educated. They also believe that they have the right to seek redress through the law, when they feel they have been wrongly treated.

Equality of opportunity legislation sets out the rights which should be shared by everyone in society. Health and social care practitioners need to recognise these rights, and help service users to understand and enforce them.

DISCUSSION POINT

If you were a GP, what practical steps could you take to ensure equality of care for the following people?

- an 85-year-old man with Alzheimer's disease
- a child with Down's syndrome
- a young woman with HIV
- a man who does not speak English.

A social worker explains the importance of promoting individual rights:

66 *The older people I support are often frail, sick and vulnerable – not in a good position to assert their rights. They feel that they are shuffled backwards and forwards from hospital bed to home, and their children see them as a burden rather than an individual. I try to talk to them as equals and individuals, to find out what they really want and need. However old and weak they are, they have fundamental rights to make choices, maintain their privacy and dignity, and, as far as possible, to think and act as independent human beings.* 99

Individual choice

Bound up with the concept of individual rights is individual choice – people's freedom to have their own beliefs and preferences, to make their own decisions, and to take responsibility for themselves and those around them. Both equality of opportunity legislation and health and social care services aim to support this by promoting individuals' rights to lead their lives in the way they want.

DISCUSSION POINT

Individual choice isn't always supported by legislation: many people argue that euthanasia – the right to bring about a gentle and easy death in the case of painful terminal disease – should be a matter of individual choice. Yet in Britain it is illegal. Do you think there is ever a case for individual choice to be limited by laws?

ACTIVITY

Divide the principles for care practitioners into three lists, depending on whether they relate mainly to:

■ equality of care

■ individual rights

■ individual choice.

Think of an example of each principle in action in the caring services.

THE CARE SECTOR CONSORTIUM

In 1991 the Care Sector Consortium – made up of representatives from across the caring services – set out the following principles of good practice to guide the actions of care practitioners.

■ The rights of all individuals within society should be promoted and supported so that equality and quality of life are available to each individual within the service.

■ Each individual should be treated as a whole person with a variety of needs.

■ Anti-discriminatory practice should be developed and promoted so that the confidentiality of information and its sources should be respected and disclosed only to those who necessarily require it and after agreement with the individual concerned.

■ All involved in the delivery of care are essential and integral to the care team (consistent with client choice) and therefore clients and their partners, relatives, friends and community should be involved at all stages.

■ The health and safety of workers, clients, their partners, relatives and friends is of paramount importance.

■ Every individual should be encouraged to be as independent as possible and to exercise informed choice.

■ Individual choice, wishes and preferences should be confirmed with the individual and respected in actions taken.

■ Communication (verbal or non-verbal) should be that most appropriate to the individual.

Responsibilities under equality of opportunity legislation

Sports association told to review employment policies

Liability for disability bar

Teacher victimised for bringing discrimination claim

'Not a job for a woman'

'We want to have a baby' mentally handicapped newly weds controversy

£34,000 award in race case

Woman demoted after having baby

Equality of opportunity legislation places responsibilities on both organisations and individuals to ensure the fair treatment of everyone in society.

Within health and social care organisations, equality of opportunity is important in two ways:

- to ensure the fair treatment of all employees working in health and social care services (e.g. in the way they are recruited and their working conditions)
- to ensure the fair treatment of everyone who uses health and social care services (e.g. in the quality of care they receive, free from discrimination).

To put equality of opportunity legislation into practice, all health and social care organisations – from regional and district health authorities to dental practices and residential homes – should have a policy for equality of opportunity. Managers should then make sure that staff know about this policy, and provide guidelines and training to help them implement it. In turn, individuals working within the organisations should make an effort to understand and promote equal opportunities in everything they do.

Legislation on equality of the sexes

The growing number of women in the workplace fuelled the drive for equal employment rights for both sexes in the 1960s and 1970s. The **Equal Pay Act 1970** (in Northern Ireland the Equal Pay Act [NI] 1970) was the first equality of opportunity legislation related to the sexes. Under the law, it became illegal for organisations to discriminate between men and women in pay and working conditions (for more on this, see page 13). This was followed by the **Employment Protection Act 1975**, which gave women the right to take paid maternity leave and then return to work after having a baby.

But the most far-reaching legislation was the **Sex Discrimination Act 1975** (in Northern Ireland the Sex Discrimination (NI) Order 1976). This states that it is unlawful to discriminate against people because of their sex or marital status in:

- employment (recruitment and promotion of both full-time and part-time staff)
- training
- education
- providing housing, goods, facilities and services
- advertising.

ACTIVITY

The Sex Discrimination Act 1975 set up the Equal Opportunities Commission (EOC) to promote and enforce equal opportunities for women and men. Write to the EOC for up-to-date information on the Equal Pay Act and the Sex Discrimination Act (their address is at the back of this book).

Then use this information to produce your own leaflet advising a hospital on its responsibilities to treat women and men equally. The leaflet should:

■ summarise the original Equal Pay and Sex Discrimination Acts

■ explain how and why the Acts have been amended (the Equal Pay Act in 1984, and the Sex Discrimination Act in 1986)

■ advise the hospital on its responsibilities towards clients under the Sex Discrimination Act

■ advise the hospital on its responsibilities towards staff under both Acts.

The Sex Discrimination Act recognises three types of discrimination:

■ **direct** discrimination – when one person is treated less favourably than another on the grounds of their sex

■ **indirect** discrimination – when unnecessary conditions are applied which disadvantage one sex

■ **victimisation** – when an employer treats an employee less favourably because they have made complaints of sex discrimination in the past.

Reinstatement recommended
Winn v Northwedge Ltd

A Bristol industrial tribunal (Chair: C F Sara) recommends the reinstatement of a female bouncer who was dismissed because of her sex.

Jacky Winn was the only female among five bouncers employed by Northwedge Ltd at a Trowbridge nightclub. In February 1995, the company took a policy decision not to employ female bouncers and Ms Winn was offered bar work. She refused the offer and was dismissed. The company admitted sex discrimination. The industrial tribunal awarded £2,416 compensation, including £1500 for injury to feelings. It also considered it appropriate to recommend reinstatement, to take effect from two weeks of the hearing date.

In the tribunal's view, although a replacement was already employed, this was a case where reinstatement was practicable. It took into account a number of factors including the employer's knowledge early on in the proceedings that the applicant would be seeking reinstatement; and and that there was no evidence that the replacement was "permanent", and even if he was, there there was no evidence of the difficulties which would arise if he were to be found other work. Another factor was the relationship between the parties. "Where an applicant has gone to a tribunal and the parties have given evidence, this is likely to sour relations between them and make the restoration of that relationship more difficult." However, in this case there were factors to the contrary, said the tribunal. "Firstly, perhaps unusually, the applicant herself wants to return to this job. Secondly, even after the application was threatened the respondents made it clear that they were willing to offer her bar work."

ACTIVITY

Based on your earlier research, decide whether each of the situations listed below is a case of direct discrimination, indirect discrimination or victimisation, or whether no discrimination has taken place. Explain your decision in each case.

1 A night club manager refusing to employ a woman because 'it's a man's job'.

2 A job advertisement asking for an 'experienced male actor to play the part of King Lear'.

3 A job advertisement asking for an 'experienced waitress'.

4 An interviewer asking a woman candidate about her childcare arrangements.

5 A male teacher being repeatedly passed over for promotion after giving evidence in a sex discrimination case.

6 A single-sex boys' school refusing to accept a female pupil.

Legislation relating to race

The first legislation protecting individuals against racial discrimination was the **Race Relations Act 1965** (amended in 1968). However, this left many loopholes in the law, and was replaced by the **Race Relations Act 1976**.

The Act protects individuals against discrimination when:
- applying for jobs
- at work
- buying a home
- renting accommodation
- buying goods or services (from banks, restaurants, shops and so on)
- in education and training
- joining a club.

The Act states that it is unlawful to discriminate on the grounds of colour, race, nationality or ethnic or national origin, and makes it an offence to incite racial hatred. The Commission for Racial Equality (CRE) was set up to enforce the Act and give advice on improving equal opportunities for ethnic minorities.

More recently, the **Public Order Act 1986** (in Northern Ireland the Public Order [NI] Order 1987) has strengthened the law by making it an offence to incite racial hatred by threatening, abusive or insulting words or behaviour intended to stir up racial hatred. This includes producing or possessing material in writing, on video or on tape.

As with sex discrimination, racial discrimination can be divided into:
- **direct** discrimination – when an individual is treated worse than others because of their race, colour, nationality or ethnic or national origin
- **indirect** discrimination – when people from a particular ethnic group are put at a greater disadvantage by conditions
- **victimisation** – when someone is victimised because they have complained about racial discrimination, or supported someone else's complaint.

Mr Singh, a Sikh, explains how he has been the victim of all three types of discrimination at different stages of his life:

66 *As a child, I was indirectly discriminated against by a school which refused to make an exception to the school rule of wearing a cap. As I had to wear a turban, this indirectly excluded me from the school. Since starting work I've suffered direct discrimination, being turned down for a transfer to a different (all-white) section because 'I wouldn't fit in'. I complained to the management, they apologised and the transfer went ahead. But since then I've been branded as a trouble-maker, and turned down for two promotions I know I should have got.* 99

ACTIVITY

Prepare a resource file of information on the Race Relations Act and the Public Order Act. Find out more about the following sources of information, and see how they can help:
- Commission for Racial Equality
- Institute of Race Relations
- your local Racial Equality Council
- Joint Council for the Welfare of Immigrants
- Liberty
- local Citizens Advice Bureaux
- local law centres
- libraries.

There are some useful addresses at the end of this book.

ACTIVITY

The Race Relations Act gives detailed guidelines on the legal responsibilities of employers when advertising jobs.

One of the following advertisements shows direct discrimination, another indirect discrimination, and the other is not discriminatory. From your research into the Race Relations Act, do you know which is which?

DOCTOR'S ○ RECEPTIONISTS

Busy doctor's surgery requires two new receptionists. Must have some secretarial experience and speak English as their mother tongue.

CHINESE WAITERS NEEDED FOR A NEW CHINESE RESTAURANT OPENING IN MAY

TELEPHONE 01824 426178 (ask for Mr Ling)

Youth Group seeks black coach for up-and-coming under 15 basketball team

A hospital realises that Asian and black nursing staff are under-represented, and decides to take positive action to encourage people from these racial groups to apply for jobs. Write an advertisement which does this within the law.

Legislation relating to disability

There are 6.5 million disabled people in the UK, and equality of opportunity legislation is currently changing with the aim of improving their rights.

A range of equality of opportunity legislation has been passed relating to disability. The **Disabled Persons (Employment) Acts 1944** and **1958** aimed to ensure employment rights for disabled people. The Act states that employers with 20 or more staff should employ at least 3% registered disabled people, and a register of disabled people was set up to help them do this. However, exemptions are allowed – companies which can show that work is unsuitable for disabled people, or that not enough disabled people have applied, can obtain a special permit. In practice, very few organisations have been prosecuted.

The **Chronically Sick and Disabled Persons Representation Act 1970** (in Northern Ireland the Chronically Sick and Disabled Persons [NI] Act 1978) required local authorities to identify people with disabilities in their area, and provide information on the services available for them. This was followed by the **Disabled Persons (Services, Consultation and Representation) Act 1986** (in Northern Ireland the Disabled Persons [NI] Act 1989), which states four main rights of people with disabilities:

- assessment of needs
- resources to help them live as independent a life as possible
- representation by another person or friend if they have restricted ability to speak for themselves
- monitoring and review of their needs over time.

Educational rights for those with disabilities were first enforced through the **Education Act 1944**, which specified that disabled children should be educated alongside their peers in primary and secondary education. More specific legislation is included in the **Education (Handicapped Children) Act 1981**, which sets out the requirements for integrating children with special needs (including learning difficulties, physical disabilities, ill health and emotional problems) into mainstream schools. Under the Act, all children are entitled to an assessment and statement of their educational needs, which local authorities must then try to meet.

However, in practice disabled people still face a struggle for equality of opportunity in their daily lives, as Clare, a young wheelchair user, explains:

66 *Apart from the day-to-day discrimination I face from people – the usual stuff of people assuming I can't speak because I can't walk – my life is frustrated by endless physical problems. I can't get on buses, I can't get on trains, I can't get into the bank, or the local Italian restaurant. When I do manage to get into buildings, there are rarely toilet facilities which I can use. Legislation at the moment isn't strong enough. I certainly don't feel as if I have equal opportunities.* 99

As a first step in tackling the discrimination still faced by many disabled people, a new Disability Discrimination Act includes measures to improve opportunities in the areas of:

■ employment
■ getting goods and services
■ buying or renting land or property.

A National Disability Council (and Northern Ireland Disability Council) has been set up to advise the Government on discrimination against disabled people.

ACTIVITY

Collect information about the new Disability Discrimination Act. Contact the National Disability Council, or the Royal Association for Disability and Rehabilitation (their addresses are at the back of this book).

Produce a summary for health and social care employers, outlining the legislation and identifying the new responsibilities of organisations and individuals.

Legislation relating to pay

The **Equal Pay Act 1970** (in Northern Ireland the Equal Pay Act [NI]) was introduced to eliminate discrimination between the rates of pay and terms of contract offered to men and the growing number of women in the workforce. Since being amended in 1984, the main focus of the legislation has become 'equal pay for work of equal value'. In the past, women had to prove that a man was being paid more for the same job to claim discrimination. But now, women doing jobs in which few men are employed (for example, sewing machinists and cleaners) can claim equal pay if they believe that men doing jobs which are similar in demand are paid more.

To assess whether jobs are of equal value, a job evaluation study is carried out, as in the following case.

MARKET FORCES NO DEFENCE

Ratcliffe and others v North Yorkshire County Council

This test case was brought by catering assistants (or 'dinner ladies'), a post almost exclusively carried out by women in North Yorkshire. Their work had been rated as equivalent to that of posts such as road-sweepers and refuse collectors under the local government job evaluation scheme. However, following compulsory competitive tendering, the council took the view that in order to compete with private contractors, it needed to reduce the catering assistants' pay. The catering assistants complained that this contravened the Equal Pay Act.

Their claim was upheld by an industrial tribunal, who found that the reduction in pay arose out of economic and social factors which led to the catering staff being almost exclusively women, who were prepared to accept lower rates of pay. However, according to the Court of Appeal the 'material factor' which led to the lower rates of pay was genuinely due to the operation of market forces and the need to compete with a rival bid, and was unconnected with the difference of sex.

The House of Lords restored the tribunal's decision and upheld the women's claim. Giving the decision for the Lords, Lord Slynn said: 'Though conscious of the difficult problem facing the employers in seeking to compete with a rival tenderer, I am satisfied that to reduce the women's wages below that of their male counterparts was the very kind of discrimination in relation to pay which the Act sought to remove.'

(from Equal Opportunities Review, Discrimination Case Law Digest)

ACTIVITY

Look at the information you collected from the Equal Opportunities Commission on the Equal Pay Act. Under the Act, what are the responsibilities of organisations such as North Yorkshire County Council in the case shown here? What are the responsibilities of individuals, like the catering assistants?

ACTIVITY

Draw out all the information relevant to employment from the research material on equality of opportunity legislation you have collected so far. Produce a poster, summarising the legislation relating to the employment of:

- men and women
- people of all races, colours and ethnic and national origins
- disabled people.

DISCUSSION POINT

In a situation at work where employees are likely to face abuse from their colleagues, what steps can employers take to prevent discrimination?

Legislation relating to employment

Equal rights to get jobs, and fair treatment at work, are a fundamental part of equality of opportunity legislation. In line with this, employment runs through most of the legislation, in particular:

- the Sex Discrimination Acts
- the Race Relations Act
- the Disability Discrimination Act
- the Equal Pay Act.

In Northern Ireland, where conflicts within the community have created special issues of discrimination, the Fair Employment Act (NI) 1989 makes it illegal to discriminate in employment on the grounds of religious belief or political opinion. The Act covers:

- applying for a job
- gaining promotion
- access to training opportunities
- dismissal
- redundancy.

In the past, Roman Catholics have been at a disadvantage in employment – only 40% of the population available for work in Northern Ireland are Roman Catholic; yet 65% of the long-term unemployed are Roman Catholic. The Fair Employment Commission gives a range of advice to employers, including:

66 *Create a neutral working environment. Prohibit the display of flags, emblems, posters, graffiti, or the circulation of materials, or the deliberate articulation of slogans or songs which are likely to give offence to, or cause apprehension among, existing or potential employees.* 99

ACTIVITY

Carry out a media search for two weeks, collecting news reports, features and advertisements related to equality of opportunity legislation. Organise the information according to whether it relates to sex, race, disability, pay or employment.

Consistencies and inconsistencies in the legislation

As the last section shows, a large amount of equality of opportunity legislation is in place in Britain. But how equal are people's rights under the law? And how consistently is legislation interpreted and enforced?

Rights under the law

Although equality of opportunity legislation is in place to safeguard equal rights, loopholes and inconsistencies within the laws can perpetuate, and even create, inequality. For example, the Race Relations Act covers colour, ethnic group and national origin, but not religion. Some religious groups – such as Sikhs and Jews – are protected under the law because they belong to an ethnic group. Other religions – for example, Christianity – don't have the same rights. The Sex Discrimination Act does not apply to employment in the armed forces. There are also special measures for ministers of religion, police, prison officers and competitive sport.

Many disabled people feel that equality of opportunity legislation does not give them the same rights under the law as other groups in society, and that although legislation exists, it doesn't make adequate allowance for the particular needs of those with disabilities. The following extract highlights the problems facing university students:

> ### DISCUSSION POINT
>
> The legal age of consent for homosexuals is higher than the age of consent for heterosexuals. Why do you think this inconsistency in the law exists? Whose principles is the legislation reflecting?

The cost of imperfection
Parents of students with disabilities are obliged to pay a high price for their children's university education, writes **Susannah Kirkman**

Against the odds, Tim Roberts, who was born profoundly deaf, gained a university place. But he and his parents were appalled to discover that the family would have to find an extra £16,000 immediately, on top of the £2,000 they were expecting to pay for his maintenance.

Tim's father, Malcolm Roberts, who is headteacher of Colden Common primary school in Hampshire, had always assumed that the Disabled Students Allowance to which his son is entitled would not be means-tested. "If a child has a disability, I don't think parents should have to continually fork out just to ensure that he gets the same chances as everyone else," Mr Roberts said. He and his wife, Brenda, who teaches at Rookwood infant school, Eastleigh, have already spent much time and money on extra support for Tim, who is now in the second year of a business studies course at Coventry University.

Tim needs someone to take lecture notes for him, and the cost – about £1,600 this year – is being borne by his parents. Last year he needed equipment worth £4,000 – a specially adapted computer

and software and a radio hearing aid. His parents also had to contribute £1,600 towards that expense before the local education authority would provide the top-up funding.

The Disabled Students Allowance is worth up to £7,280 a year over a three-year course. Unfortunately, because this is part of the maintenance grant, it is also means-tested, so that even

> **Disabled Students Allowance, 1995/1996**
> The three allowances are:
> - Up to £4,850 per annum for non-medical personal helpers such as note-takers.
> - Up to £3,650 over the whole course for major items of specialist equipment such as a computer.
> - Up to £1,215 pa for items which do not fall within the remit of the above or to supplement them if necessary.
>
> Parental contributions to maintenance grant and DSA:
> Joint residual income Contribution
>
> | Below £15,510 | £0 |
> |---|---|
> | £30,000 | £1,550 |
> | £35,000 | £2,244 |
> | £40,000 | £2,939 |
> | £60,599 or more | £5,800 |

families like the Roberts, who are not wealthy, have to make a substantial contribution towards the cost of essential "extras" for their children.

Tim is outraged by the unfairness of the system. "My parents didn't ask for me to be deaf," he said. "I would have been born a hearing person but for the fact that my mother contracted rubella when she was pregnant, and now the Government wants to penalise my parents."

Sophie Corlett, assistant director of SKILLS, the National Bureau for Students with Disabilities, agrees with Tim. "It is blatant discrimination," she said. "It's like asking parents with student daughters to fund the installation of ladies' lavatories at universities." She points out that £2,340 is usually the maximum which the Government asks even millionaire parents of a student without disabilities to contribute towards maintenance, while parents with a joint residual income of £60,599 could be asked to support their disabled child to the tune of £5,800 a year. Universities which have an unwelcoming approach to students with disabilities

may push up the cost of their education still further. Some universities offer free help to apply for the Disabled Students Allowance, make all the arrangements for note-takers and other helpers and provide free support and counselling, but others charge fees for providing advice and engaging personal helpers.

Other unhelpful practices include failing to make book lists and lecture notes available in advance and, in the case of one lecturer, refusing to use a radio microphone to enable a deaf student to follow a lecture. Sophie Corlett admits that any grants system is open to abuse but argues that the recent controversy over bogus "dyslexic" students claiming allowances which they didn't need is a red herring. "The problem is that there is no universally-accepted method of assessment of dyslexia," she said.

The Department for Education and Employment defends its operation of the Disabled Students Allowance by saying that means-testing should supply to everyone. Another problem is that the Allowance cannot be disentangled from the

means-tested maintenance grant without an Act of Parliament.

But Sophie Corlett thinks that the law should be changed to rectify the injustice to thousands of disabled students and their families. In any case, the total cost of their allowance, including parental contributions – £6 million in 1993/1994 – represents only 0.5 per cent of the total maintenance grant bill for students.

Meanwhile, Malcolm and Brenda Roberts are relying on their savings to pay for Tim's education. On a teacher's salary, Mr Roberts could not afford to take out a PEP or an endowment policy some years ago to fund the cost of his children's higher education, as his wife took a career break while their children were small.

"We can just about afford the extra, but many other families couldn't," Malcolm Roberts said. "It grieves me that many youngsters will be denied the chance of a university place, after struggling so hard to get there. The chances of employment must be even lower for someone who is disabled and also has no qualifications."

ACTIVITY

Focus on the same aspect of equal opportunities legislation for:

- people from different ethnic groups
- people with disabilities.

For example, you might look at rights to education, employment or obtaining goods and services. What are the similarities between people's rights under the legislation? What are the differences? Are there inconsistencies in the law, or do you think inconsistencies might arise from the way the law is applied?

As a result of differences in the legal systems in England, Wales, Scotland and Northern Ireland, there are also major inconsistencies between equality of opportunity legislation in different parts of the UK.

The structure of the law and the way in which services are provided is different in Scotland from England and Wales. Legislation often includes explanations of how the Act applies in Scotland, and sometimes a separate Act is passed.

Northern Ireland has its own legislation which is introduced by Order in Council. Acts which apply in the rest of the UK don't always have a related Order in Northern Ireland.

For example, the Education (Handicapped Children) Act 1981 focuses on the integration of children with special needs into mainstream schools in England and Wales. In Scotland the Education (Scotland) Act 1981 has the same function. But there is no comparable Act in Northern Ireland. In the same way, the Fair Employment Act (NI) only applies in Northern Ireland, and there is no comparable legislation in the rest of the UK.

ACTIVITY

Can you find other examples of inconsistencies in equality of opportunity rights between the four parts of the UK?

Interpretation of the law

Even when people's rights under the law are consistent, legislation is not always interpreted and applied consistently.

Some equality of opportunity laws are almost ignored. For example, the legal requirement for employers with a staff of over 20 people to employ 3% disabled people is rarely enforced. Since the legislation was introduced (in the 1940s), there has only been a handful of prosecutions.

In other areas people choose to ignore, or misinterpret, equality of opportunity legislation. Laws provide a starting point, but need positive action by organisations and individuals if they are to be put into action effectively. Employers may develop an equal opportunity policy supporting equal rights for women, but still not offer facilities such as crèches and flexible working arrangements to meet women's needs. Despite legislation:

- women's work tends to remain low-paid, and women are more likely to accept part-time work
- more women than men work in the health and social care services, but more senior managers are men
- 48% of secondary school teachers are women, but only 20% of head teachers are women.

DISCUSSION POINT

The figures below show unemployment among men and women in the UK, and rates of pay for men and women in the UK.

Economic activity by ethnic origin 1994

	Economically active (%)	Unemployed (%)
Females		
White	53%	7%
Non-white	49%	16%
Males		
White	72%	11%
Non-white	73%	25%

Earnings 1975, 1984, 1994

Average gross hourly earnings, excluding the effects of overtime, of full-time employees on adult rates.

	Pence per hour		
	1975	1984	1994
Females	98	309	688
Males	139	421	865
Differential	41	112	177
Female earnings as a % of male earnings	71%	73%	80%

source: Equal Opportunities Commission

How can these figures be possible with equality of opportunity legislation in place?

Seeking redress

Equality of opportunity legislation is only useful if individuals have routes through which they can seek redress – ways of complaining about, and getting compensation for, unfair treatment.

Routes for seeking redress under equality of opportunity legislation can be divided into four categories:

- organisational – procedures for complaints and comments in place within the organisation
- professional bodies – such as trade unions
- regulatory bodies – watchdogs which are independent from organisations and professional bodies, and offer an objective opinion on cases
- legal systems – from industrial tribunals to the House of Lords.

Organisational routes

Most organisations have internal policies to deal with employees' complaints, which are included in contracts of employment. In most cases, complaints of discrimination will be handled internally by the employee's manager or the human resource, or personnel, department. If the problem can't be sorted out informally, the employee can follow a more formal grievance procedure, which may involve a trade union representative.

Organisations also need policies in place to deal with complaints from outside the organisation. The Government has published a range of charters which set out what organisations should do to ensure high standards of service. For example:

- the Parent's Charter, which focuses on education and the rights of parents to choose a school for their children
- the Citizen's Charter, which aims to improve the quality and choice of public services.

National Health Service (NHS) organisations are guided by the Patients' Charter, which aims to improve the quality of health and social care services offered to the general public. The Charter sets out service users' rights and the standards of service they can expect to receive, including equality of care and individual choice:

66 *You can expect the NHS to respect your privacy, dignity and religious and cultural beliefs at all times and in all places. For example, meals should suit your dietary and religious needs.* **99**

Many health and social care services – from general practices to hospitals – are developing their own equal opportunity policies based on the standards laid down in the Patients' Charter. As an important part of this, they should include clear guidelines on how service users can complain when they feel they have been discriminated against. Complaints about the National Health Service are dealt with by Health Authorities and the Community Health Council.

Trade unions

Employees who have experienced discrimination in the workplace and are following internal complaints or grievance procedures can enlist the help of their trade union representative, if they have one.

A trade union is a group of people who work in similar jobs and join together to protect members' employment rights, welfare and working conditions. One of its roles is to protect against discrimination in recruitment, training, redundancy and dismissals.

Trade unions can provide information, support and often legal advice. Individuals making a complaint can ask their trade union representative to help present their case to their employer, and to attend hearings and meetings as a witness.

Regulatory bodies

Several regulatory bodies – independent from the Government or other organisations – provide support for individuals who have complaints about discrimination.

ACTIVITY

Collect a copy of your school or college equal opportunities policy, which will probably be based on the government charter for further education.

- What complaints procedures do the policies include?

Draw a flow chart, showing how individuals can seek redress for discrimination.

Regulatory body	How can it help?
Equal Opportunities Commission (EOC)	Ensures effective enforcement of the Sex Discrimination Act and the Equal Pay Act, and promotes equal opportunities between the sexes. It carries out formal investigations into complaints of sex discrimination, and in some cases helps individuals to prepare and conduct complaints in tribunals and courts.
Commission for Racial Equality (CRE)	Ensures effective enforcement of the Race Relations Act, and promotes equal opportunities for all, regardless of colour, race and ethnic or national origin. It has the power to advise and assist individuals taking cases to court.
Ombudsmen	Ombudsmen consider complaints from individuals who feel they have been treated unfairly in receiving a service. There is a Health Service Ombudsman who deals specifically with complaints about the NHS. The Ombudsman investigates complaints and seeks redress in cases of discrimination and wrongful treatment.
Citizens Advice Bureaux and law centres	Local Citizens Advice Bureaux and law centres provide information and advice for individuals on ways to seek redress for discrimination.
Advertising Standards Authority	The Advertising Standards Authority deals with complaints about discrimination in advertising on radio or television and in printed material.
Broadcasting Complaints Commission and Press Complaints Commission	The Broadcasting Complaints Commission deals with complaints about discrimination in television and radio programmes. The Press Complaints Commission handles complaints about material printed in newspapers and magazines.
Police Complaints Commission	If individuals have complaints about discriminatory treatment by the police, they can contact the Police Complaints Commission who will investigate the case and seek redress.

ACTIVITY

Natalie Harris, an administrative assistant, has been subjected to sexual harassment at work from a dentist at the health centre where she works. She has told him to stop, written down details of incidents which have occurred, and made a formal complaint to the management. But they refuse to take her claims seriously. She doesn't belong to a trade union, and needs advice on what to do next.

Write a letter to Natalie, advising her how regulatory bodies might be able to help her seek redress under the law, and giving addresses and details of relevant organisations.

Legal systems

If a complaint about discrimination cannot be resolved within the organisation, individuals have the right to seek redress through legal systems. This can mean taking a complaint to:

- a county court in England or Wales
- a sheriff court in Scotland
- an industrial tribunal.

Complaints about discrimination outside employment are dealt with in the courts. If the court finds that discrimination did occur, it can award damages.

Complaints about discrimination in employment are usually dealt with by an industrial tribunal. The employee alleging discrimination fills in an application form, and sends it to the Central Office of Industrial Tribunals. A copy of the form is also sent to the Advisory, Conciliation and Arbitration Service (ACAS), which was set up to settle industrial disputes. An ACAS official then tries to help the employee and employer reach an agreement without going to a tribunal. Time is an important factor in many cases – complaints under the Sex Discrimination Act should be presented to the tribunal within three months of the incident taking place.

If all else fails, the complaint is heard before a local industrial tribunal. A tribunal is made up of a panel of three people who listen to the case, and if they agree that discrimination has taken place they can:

- award compensation to the individual, including damages for injury to feelings
- recommend steps the employer should take to prevent discrimination occurring again.

£28,500 AWARD IN RACE CASE

Johnson v (1) Armitage (2) Marsden (3) HM Prison Service

From mid-1991 up to and beyond his industrial tribunal application in March 1993, Claude Johnson, a prison officer at Brixton prison, was ostracised by fellow prison officers following his complaint about the manhandling of a black prisoner by officers. He was also warned about his sickness absence, although a white officer with a poorer record was not warned; he was frequently detailed for particular work, but when he arrived at work was given non-detailed duties; and he was reported for leaving duty early, although it was customary to do so, and given a warning. The industrial tribunal found that Mr Johnson had suffered a 'campaign of appalling treatment', ruling that he had been unlawfully discriminated against on racial grounds. It awarded compensation of £28,500.

Noting that the campaign had gone on for 18 months, the tribunal considered that £20,000 'was a reasonable amount for injury to feelings over such a long period'. The tribunal also awarded £7,500 aggravated damages against the employer on grounds that whenever the applicant tried to complain, his complaints were dismissed and put down to defects in his personality.

£500 for injury to feelings was also awarded against the first two respondents, who were held to have victimised the applicant and knowingly aided the employer to discriminate. The tribunal said that 'where individuals are found to have committed unlawful acts of discrimination, they should be liable for their acts and not rely on their employers to bear complete responsibility.'

(from Equal Opportunities Review, Discrimination Case Law Digest)

DISCUSSION POINT

What are the advantages for an employee of taking a discrimination case to an industrial tribunal? Can you think of any possible disadvantages?

If an industrial tribunal does not agree that discrimination took place, the individual making the complaint can appeal to the Employment Appeal Tribunal, then to the Court of Appeal and finally to the House of Lords.

Factors which affect legislation

Government produces a Green Paper outlining issues under consideration or asks an organisation to produce a report

After discussion and consultation, the government publishes a White Paper outlining proposed legislation

A bill is produced, giving details of the legislation. This may be:
- a Government Bill
- a Private Member's Bill (sponsored by an individual MP).

This is then:
- debated in parliament
- passed by the House of Commons
- passed by the House of Lords
- given royal assent

ACT OF PARLIAMENT

Equality of opportunity legislation is contained in Acts of Parliament, which lay down the standards of behaviour expected by organisations and individuals. The chart on the left shows the different stages involved in the formation of an Act.

Different factors can influence the content and passing of equality of opportunity legislation at each of these stages.

Key groups

The following groups of people all contribute to the formation of equality of opportunity.

- **Pressure groups**, which campaign on issues such as rights for people with disabilities and rights for homosexual people. By raising awareness of issues and demanding action, they bring concerns into the public eye and onto MPs' agenda. Once a Green Paper or report has been drafted, pressure groups may be consulted for their opinions on the issues which concern them.

- **Publicly funded bodies**, such as the Equal Opportunities Commission and the Commission for Racial Equality (which both receive a grant from the Home Office). They review equality of opportunity legislation and make recommendations to the Government for changing it.

- **Political parties** which are represented in Parliament (such as Conservatives, Labour, Social and Liberal Democrats, Scottish National, Plaid Cymru and Ulster Unionist). Each has particular policies and concerns which they aim to promote by influencing legislation.

- **Members of Parliament** (MPs) debate and vote on bills introducing new laws, and have the final say in whether legislation is passed. They are influenced by the wishes of their political party, and the needs and concerns of their electorate (the people they represent).

- **European Union**. British law is now increasingly coming into line with European Union (EU) directives. European law, in particular the rights covered by the Treaty of Rome (1957), have had a major effect on British equality of opportunity legislation.

DISCUSSION POINT

❝ I believe deeply that all men and women should be able to go as far as talent, ambition and effort can take them. There should be no barriers of background, no barriers of religion, no barriers of race. I want . . . a society that encourages each and every one to fulfil his or her potential to the utmost . . . ❞

John Major, September 1991

Do you think this belief would be common to all political parties, or would different parties have their own particular equality of opportunity concerns?

Changes in societal values

Just 100 years ago women didn't have the right to vote; most people in Britain had never seen a black person; and some people with disabilities were still considered freaks. Events of the last 50 years – such as an increase in immigration and the growing number of women in the workplace – have accompanied enormous changes in society's values.

The experiences of a 90-year-old woman show just how much things have changed:

66 *When I was young, early this century, things were very different to today. I was one of seven children, although one of my younger sisters was deaf and put into an institution. The rest of us went to school, but left as soon as possible so we could earn some money. I worked in our local Woolworth's, which I loved, and I was made a supervisor by the time I was 20. My younger brother worked there too as a storeman, and was paid more than me – but then I suppose he was doing a man's job. When I was 21 and got married I had to give up my job, as married women weren't allowed to work when men were unemployed. I'm amazed when I see the things women take for granted today.* 99

As people's views of what is fair and how to behave have changed, equality of opportunity legislation has been introduced to reinforce the new principles. For example, as the number of working women increased, support grew for women's rights, leading to the formation of the Equal Pay and Sex Discrimination Acts.

Resource implications

Introducing new equality of opportunity legislation has resource implications for:

■ the government, which has to devote funds to developing and implementing the laws

DISCUSSION POINT

■ How do you think society's values might change in the future?

■ What effect would this have on equality of opportunity legislation?

ACTIVITY

Look back at your research into the new Disability Discrimination Act. List the possible resource implications of the Act on local government, organisations and individuals. Do you think these will have affected the final scope of the legislation?

- organisations, which have to spend money putting the laws into practice. Businesses and industry can put a great deal of pressure on MPs to change, hold up, or not pass legislation.

European Court of Human Rights

The European Court of Human Rights predates the EU. After World War II a number of bodies and institutions were set up to promote European reconciliation and recovery. In 1949 the Council of Europe was formed, and out of this the European Court of Human Rights was set up. It sits in Strasbourg and adjudicates in cases to protect individuals and groups from violations of their human rights. For example, its rulings have forced the Republic of Ireland to drop its constitutional ban on homosexuality and Germany to cease to exclude political left- and right-wingers from the civil service. In the UK its rulings have banned illegal telephone tapping, interference with the post and unfair curbs on the press.

Court of Justice of the European Communities

When the UK joined the European Community (now the European Union), it agreed to obey the authority of the Court of Justice of the European Communities. This is based in Luxembourg, and is made up of judges from each member country of the European Union.

The Court of Justice has passed several directives on equality of opportunity – including equal pay for men and women, equal pay for work of equal value, and free movement of workers from country to country – which have influenced the formation of equality of opportunity legislation in Britain.

DISCUSSION POINT

A woman who worked for SW Hampshire Health Authority appealed to the Court of Justice of the European Communities, claiming she was being discriminated against by being made to retire at 60 while her male colleagues didn't have to retire until they were 65. The Court decided this was discriminatory. Now most British companies are changing their pension schemes, and the Government has reviewed when state pensions should be paid.

Do you think it is right for the Court of Justice to intervene in issues like this?

The Court of Justice of the European Communities

Key questions

1   What three principles which underpin equality of opportunity legislation are most important to health and social care practitioners?

2   Name one piece of equality of opportunity legislation relating to each of the following: sex, race, disability, pay, employment.

3   Give three responsibilities of organisations under the Sex Discrimination Act.

4   List five situations in which the Race Relations Act protects against discrimination on the grounds of race.

5   Give three responsibilities of organisations under the new Disability Discrimination Act.

6   What is the main focus of the Equal Pay Act?

7   Explain why there are inconsistencies in equality of opportunity legislation in different parts of the UK, and give two examples.

8   Give two other examples of inconsistencies in individuals' rights under equality of opportunity legislation, and try to explain them.

9   How can government charters help people seeking redress for discrimination?

10 List five regulatory bodies which can help individuals seeking redress for discrimination.

11 What is an industrial tribunal?

12 What part do MPs play in the formation of equality of opportunity legislation?

13 Give two examples of how changes in societal values have influenced equality of opportunity in recent years.

14 Explain how resource implications can affect the formation of equality of opportunity legislation.

15 What is the Court of Justice of the European Communities?

Assignment

You work as an administrator at a health centre in an inner city area. Staff at the centre, and the people they work with, are from a range of ethnic groups and religions. The centre manager is concerned that not all staff are fully aware of their rights and responsibilities under equality of opportunity legislation relating to race, and has asked you to produce a staff information pack.

The manager has asked you to include the following information in the pack:

■   an introduction, explaining why the principles of equality of care, individual rights and individual choice are important to both equal opportunities and the work of the health centre

■   an explanation of three factors which affect the formation of equality of opportunity legislation relating to race

■   a summary of legislation relating to race

■   an explanation of responsibilities under the legislation, covering the health centre and the individuals who work there

■   an explanation of how service users and staff who experience discrimination can seek redress through
    – organisational routes
    – professional bodies (in the case of staff)
    – regulatory bodies
    – legal systems

■   a section for service users from other parts of the UK, summarising the consistencies and inconsistencies in equality of opportunity rights in the four UK countries.

Your information pack should be clear and concise, and include images where appropriate.

The manager is interested in producing further packs in the future on equality of opportunity legislation relating to:

■   sex
■   disability
■   pay
■   employment.

Make notes in preparation for writing these packs, summarising relevant legislation and explaining the responsibilities of individuals and organisations.

26

66 I have strong feelings about care of older people. They can be discriminated against. There is a tendency to write them off. If a resident comes forward with symptoms it's often a case of leaping to a conclusion: 'Well, what do you expect at their age?' Some GPs, especially fund-holders, see it as a waste of time and money to carry out investigations for older people. 99

project manager, residential care home for older people

66 We have evidence that gay young people are concerned about discrimination. Some feel they can't speak about it even with their families and friends. Its a common cause of concern. And obviously, unfortunately, we have black and Asian clients who have experienced discrimination or fear it. 99

senior worker (counselling), young people's counselling and information centre

66 There was a situation where some of the parents were worried because we were interviewing men for nursery nurse posts here. There has to be a consensus of opinion, but we can't discriminate. I would always recruit someone because they were the right person for the job. The other nursery nurses are absolutely fine about working with men. I would like to see it become an accepted part of everyday life for men as well as women to take care of children. If it doesn't we are not working towards equality in the wider world. 99

head of private day nursery and childcare centre

66 Basically, there is not equality of care in the NHS. 'Rationing' has been going on forever – it's just that the population are now aware of it. It happens because of age, social class and so on – the usual anti-social goings on. It's nothing new. 99

doctor in charge of health screening, private hospital

66 This project aims to focus on the whole person rather than the mentally ill person. Most people living here have come from a situation of not having had choices or responsibility for themselves. Residents have a right to choose about many things: where they go, what they eat, what they have in their rooms, and so on, and along with that they have things to do to look after themselves, like cooking, paying bills, tidying up and getting on with people. OK, they have mental health problems but they should still have a life. 99

project manager, supported housing scheme

Discrimination and individuals

In this element you will explore how people's rights may be affected by discrimination.

The bases of discrimination

Discrimination means treating people unfairly because of prejudice against them – anything from teasing someone because of their religion to beating someone up because they're black. So what causes discrimination?

From an early age, we make judgements about different groups of objects. For example, a toddler may try cabbage, hate it, and decide she doesn't like vegetables. In doing this she is making a judgement that all vegetables will be like cabbage, and that she won't like any of them. This is stereotyping – lumping a group of similar things together and assuming they will all have similar characteristics.

More dangerously, we form stereotypes about people. But people are all different, and don't conform to simple categories.

DISCUSSION POINT

Working in a small group, look at the pictures on the left and each think of three words you would use to describe the people in the photographs. Make a list of all your ideas.

What are your impressions of these people? What stereotypes are your impressions based on? How do you think you formed these stereotypes?

Children learn their stereotypes of people from the world around them – from parents, friends, television programmes, books, films, songs and comics. They learn to group people together and form opinions about them based on their colour, national origin, age, sex, job and so on. These opinions are **prejudices** – preconceived ideas of what a person, or a group of people, will be like.

Prejudices can be positive. For example, contestants on a TV programme like *Blind Date* who say they're a nurse get a spontaneous round of applause from the audience, based on the prejudice that all nurses are caring, self-sacrificing people.

But more often, prejudices, founded on ignorance rather than real knowledge of what people are like, are negative. A 16-year-old student describes how he came to recognise his prejudices:

DISCUSSION POINT

Most of you will have experienced discrimination at some time in your lives – whether it was being told you couldn't do something because you were a girl, or being teased or even physically abused because of your race.

In a small group, talk about occasions when you have felt discriminated against. Who discriminated against you? What do you think caused the discrimination?

Then think of an occasion when you have discriminated against someone else. What prejudice caused you to discriminate? And what stereotype do you think created your prejudice?

❝ *My mum and dad are quite racist and I suppose I took on board their values. When I was eleven we moved to a different area and I went to a new school with more black pupils than white. At first I was quite scared – I thought they'd be really aggressive and not interested in learning. I used to ignore the black pupils, and even got involved in some bullying at one stage. But as I got to know people I realised that the black kids were no different to the white – I liked some of them and not others. So instead of being prejudiced against them, I learnt to get to know them and then judge whether I liked them.* ❞

Discrimination is the outward result of **prejudice**. In this case, the student's prejudice led him to discriminate against black pupils by ignoring and bullying them.

So what type of people are discriminated against – what are the bases of discrimination?

Most discrimination is against groups of people who traditionally have low status in society, or who are in a minority group. The most common bases of discrimination are:

- age (in particular, elderly people)
- disability
- sex (in particular, women)
- health status (for example, long-term or mental illness)
- ethnic status (race, colour, national or ethnic origin)
- religion
- sexuality (for example, homosexuality).

Age

Discrimination based on age is widespread in developed countries like the UK. Here one 75-year-old man explains the frustrations of being pigeon-holed as an 'OAP':

❝ I was forced to retire from my job at 65, when I was perfectly healthy and happy. Since then, my life has gone downhill. I've got less money, and find it hard to fill my days. I don't like having to draw a pension – I see people looking at me when I go to collect my money, and am sure they feel I'm a drain on society. Even my family seem to think I've had a personality transplant since I hit 70 – they're always telling me to slow down and to 'grow old gracefully'! My daughter actually told me off for standing on a chair to change a light bulb the other day. I just wish they could see that I'm exactly the same person as I was 20 years ago, not some stereotype of a frail, semi-senile old man. ❞

DISCUSSION POINT

Recent research suggests that by 2025:

- the number of people in Europe aged over 60 will increase by 50%
- nearly a third of the population of the European Union will be pensioners.

How do you think this might change the position of elderly people in society? Do you think it will lead to more discrimination on the grounds of age, or less?

Generation gap

Relative percentage change in these three groups between 1995 and 2025: ■ UK only □ All European Union

Trends
Young and old: relative proportions of the population

0 – 19 years	20 – 59 years	Over 60 years
-8.2 / -10.6	-2.8 / -6.4	43.6 / 48.7

At the other end of the spectrum, children have traditionally been granted few rights in society. Children – seen but not heard – have been discriminated against as individuals without the knowledge or experience to make judgements and choices.

The Children Act, which came into force in 1991, aims to ensure that this is no longer the case, and that children have a say in what happens to them and how they are looked after. It aims to give them rights as people who must be:

- treated with respect
- protected
- listened to
- told their rights
- given an opportunity to talk about any worries, or complain if things go wrong.

ACTIVITY

Arrange for a practitioner to talk to your group about child protection, and collect information on the Children Act. Write a summary of the new rights it aims to give to children, and explain how you think the legislation will help prevent discrimination against children.

Disability

People with disabilities tend to be discriminated against on two levels:

- in terms of physical access to facilities and services
- in terms of people's attitudes.

Traditionally, those with disabilities have been on the edge of society, unable to play an active role in making decisions or shaping their world. As a result, society has not been set up to cope with disabilities. Housing, schools, shops and transport are often inaccessible, and the needs and feelings of people with disabilities are rarely taken into account when new facilities are built.

As well as being marginalised physically, people with disabilities are often seen as 'abnormal' – treated with a mixture of pity, fear and scorn born of prejudice and lack of understanding.

> Christopher Nolan nearly died at birth from asphyxiation, but survived with severe brain damage, mute and paralysed. He is now an award-winning author, and his writing gives first-hand insight into the discrimination which is an everyday part of life for people with disabilities.

> As day followed day in school, so too did daring sceptics voice loud their childish opinions. Joseph was now getting used to hearing himself discussed. Quite openly students discussed his defects, and certain as they were of his non-ability to understand, they decided to be as vociferous as if he were not really present. They wondered if the cripple wore a nappy and longed to be able to examine him and find out for certain. Then they discussed his lack of intelligence. They chose tags by which they would rate him. They bandied about the words weirdo, eejit, cripple, dummy and mental defective.

> from *The Eye of the Clock: the life story of Christopher Nolan*

ACTIVITY

Interview someone you know who has a disability (for example, a fellow student, someone in your family or an elderly person). Talk to them about the different types of discrimination they face. Do they feel they are pigeon-holed because of their disability? What problems do they face in their daily life?

Sex

Sex stereotyping has meant that there have always been different expectations and roles for men and women in society.

Back in 1792, Mary Wollstonecraft wrote in *A Vindication of the Rights of Women:*

> . . . the first object of laudable ambition is to obtain a character as a human being, regardless of the distinction of sex.

The struggle to achieve this, and for women to have the option to break out of their traditional role as wife, mother, housekeeper and carer, has been going on ever since. This century has seen enormous progress:

- taking on 'men's jobs' during wartime gave women an opportunity to show that they were capable of breaking traditional boundaries
- contraception has given women more control over their lives, and freedom to make choices between work and motherhood
- legislation (such as the Sex Discrimination Act) and organisations (such as the Equal Opportunities Commission) have been set up to establish and protect women's rights.

Yet prejudice about what women can and can't do still exists. Women working part-time and returning to work have problems getting training to move on or get promoted from low-paid jobs. Figures show the level of discrimination which exists:

- one in four young men employees aged 16 to 19 get job-related training, but only one in five young women
- 70% of language students are women, 86% of engineering and technology students are men
- women in full-time manual occupations earn 63.4% of men's average weekly earnings.

This discrimination is underpinned by a long tradition of stereotyping and prejudice.

DISCUSSION POINT

Read the following extracts from an article in the women's magazine Marie Claire on sexist men.

66 *Men are hunters so they are better at things like driving because they are naturally good with speed and good at handling danger. Women have a natural drive for chores, which they are better at.* 99 *(Richard Judd, 28)*

66 *They want to be equal, but that's stupid because they aren't competent enough. They can't cope with money and they can't deal with people. They should never be allowed in the army or navy because they can't fight either. Men are physically stronger and better suited for these things. Women should be seen and not heard because they've got nothing interesting to say.* 99 *(Peter Westham, 40)*

In a small group, talk about whether you have ever encountered views this extreme. What are the prejudices being expressed by the men? What stereotypes do you think underlie them, and how were they created?

It is important to recognise that it is not only women who are discriminated against because of their sex. Many men feel they have to live up to the traditional stereotype of hunter, fighter and breadwinner. If they don't, they risk ridicule and are made to feel they have failed. A recent report suggested that British men find it harder than their counterparts in the rest of Europe to break out of the traditional role and to take jobs such as waiting at tables, which they see as 'women's work'.

ACTIVITY

Interview:

- a man and a woman over 60
- a man and a woman under 30.

Ask each person to give you:

- five characteristics of the ideal woman
- five characteristics of the ideal man
- the first five jobs which come to mind as 'men's work'
- the first five jobs which come to mind as 'women's work'.

Record your findings, and use them to write profiles of each age group's images of men and women. What do the profiles tell you about how sex stereotypes have changed in the last 30 years?

DISCUSSION POINT

What prejudice or fear do you think causes the following examples of discrimination against people with health problems:

- a member of staff refusing to drink out of a coffee cup which has been used by a colleague who is HIV positive?
- a family campaigning against people with mental health problems being housed in their community?
- someone avoiding a visit to a friend with terminal cancer?
- a mother telling her child not to play with a pupil with severe eczema?

Health status

As well as having to cope with illness, people with long-term health problems and mental illness often face discrimination from the rest of society.

A young woman who is HIV positive describes the stigma attached to her health status:

66 *There's so much fear and lack of understanding surrounding HIV and AIDS. People struggle to pigeon-hole me – I'm not a gay man, I'm not a drug-user, I'm not a haemophiliac. I let them think what they want. The worst thing is seeing the fear in their eyes. The way they try not to touch me. Or sit too close to me. One person actually wore gloves the whole time she was in my house. In just ten years or so, society has built up dreadful prejudices against people with HIV and AIDS. It's thoroughly depressing.* 99

ACTIVITY

Talk to a health and social care practitioner about the prejudice faced by some of their clients. What type of physical discrimination do they experience? What discriminatory attitudes do they encounter?

33

Ethnic status

Ethnic status – colour, race, or ethnic or national origin – is one of the most obvious bases of discrimination. Ever since human civilisation began, tribes and races fought wars to try to achieve domination. Today the UK is a multicultural society, with people from many different origins living alongside each other. But prejudice and discrimination, particularly based on colour, are still commonplace.

Almost half the ethnic minority population of the UK was born in Britain, and nearly three-quarters are British citizens. Yet many are still treated as outsiders, facing discrimination in employment, housing and education, as well as day-to-day verbal and physical abuse.

Meena, a young Asian woman with eight GCSEs and three A levels, went for an interview at an insurance firm where her friend, Sally, worked.

❝ I didn't get the job. But Sally told me they said that, in the recession, it was important to give jobs to your own. Now, tell me, what does that mean? I was born here, I speak with a Brummie accent. My grandfather, like so many others, died fighting for this country – he was in Italy – we even have a letter from his commander about how brave he was. My mother works in the health service, my father in insurance. They've never collected a penny in benefits, and have paid taxes for 25 years. Dad won't even let me go on the dole. So what does 'your own' mean? ❞

from Race Through the 90s, *published by Commission for Racial Equality and BBC Radio 1*

Religion

Throughout the world, religion is one of the most common causes of discrimination and violence. From the Middle East to Northern Ireland, religious differences spark hatred and wars.

Unlike many forms of prejudice, religion is not usually based on appearances – with a few exceptions, you can't look at a person and tell what religion they are. But to many people their religion is a fundamental part of who they are, and they feel threatened and scared by other beliefs and customs. This fear creates prejudice, and leads to discrimination.

Sexuality

In the UK, many people are prejudiced against sexual relationships which don't conform to the conventional heterosexual pattern. Until the 1960s, homosexuals were treated as mentally ill, and homosexuality was illegal. People today are more tolerant, but discrimination still exists:

- the age of consent is higher for homosexuals than heterosexuals
- homosexuals miss out on job opportunities – for example, they are barred from military careers
- they may face verbal or physical abuse in everyday life.

The spread of HIV and AIDS – originally seen by many as a 'gay disease' – increased the suspicion and prejudice encountered by gay men.

Heterosexuals can also face discrimination if their sexual behaviour is seen as promiscuous or outside the 'norm'. But who decides what the 'norm' is?

DISCUSSION POINT

In 1986 a children's book, *Jenny Lives with Eric and Martin*, the story of a girl living with a gay male couple, prompted public outrage and was banned from schools. In the debate that followed, the BBC abandoned a drama for teenagers about homosexuality and bisexuality, and a teacher who discussed homosexuality with a group of Year 10 students was forced to move to another school. In 1988, Section 28 of the Local Government Act 1988 prohibited the promotion of homosexuality by local authorities.

In small groups, discuss the attitudes which you think underlie these events. How do you think sexuality should be handled in schools? How do you think children form prejudices and stereotypes about sexuality?

DISCUSSION POINT

In a small group, talk about whether you are prejudiced against any types of heterosexual behaviour. What do you think is promiscuous behaviour? Is there a difference between promiscuity for men and for women? What discrimination might be faced by someone who is considered promiscuous? By a prostitute? By a page-3 model?

The contexts for discrimination

Discrimination takes place on two different levels:

- Individual discrimination is when people treat individuals differently because of stereotyping and prejudice – for example, name-calling, or avoiding someone with a disability.
- Societal discrimination is when stereotyping and prejudice are so accepted that they become part of the framework for society – for example, lack of access to buildings for people with disabilities, or the higher age of consent for homosexuals.

Both individual and societal discrimination can be either direct or indirect:

- Direct discrimination is behaviour which shows open prejudice against an individual or group – for example, making it clear that only women should apply for a job, or bullying.
- Indirect discrimination is less open and easy to spot than direct discrimination. It involves showing prejudice against an individual or group by avoidance, body language, or exclusion – for example, avoiding someone who is black, or not providing a crèche for women workers.

ACTIVITY

Make a copy of the following chart, and tick whether you think each example of discrimination is individual or societal, and direct or indirect.

	Individual	Societal	Direct	Indirect
someone not telling a colleague who is HIV positive about a game of football after work	☐	☐	☐	☐
a museum not having disabled toilets	☐	☐	☐	☐
a gang of white boys attacking an Asian boy	☐	☐	☐	☐
gay men not being allowed to join the Army	☐	☐	☐	☐
a Jewish job applicant not being taken on because he would have to leave work early on Fridays in winter	☐	☐	☐	☐
a teacher asking boys in the class more questions than girls	☐	☐	☐	☐
a young person assuming an elderly person needs help crossing the road	☐	☐	☐	☐

Individual discrimination

Many people in the UK face individual discrimination as part of their everyday lives. A woman in a wheelchair explains:

❝ *I never have a chance to forget that I'm different. People try not to stare, and end up looking studiously in the other direction. Or else they make an effort to look me in the eye and smile – equally unnatural! Then there's the 'does she want a cup of tea?' approach, assuming that I can't talk for myself just because I'm in a wheelchair. Sometimes people's behaviour is conscious – they're well aware of what they're doing. They look at me, see someone in a wheelchair, and start teasing or patronising me. But sometimes I think discrimination is completely unconscious. People's stereotype of a person in a wheelchair is so entrenched that they automatically switch into 'talking-to-a-disabled-person' mode, without realising what they're doing.* ❞

DISCUSSION POINT

Although you may never consciously discriminate against someone, do you ever do so unconsciously? Do you think anyone can honestly say they never unconsciously discriminate?

DISCUSSION POINT

Do you agree with Ray? Or do you think individual discrimination through language reflects real prejudice? Is there a difference between an Australian calling an English person a 'Pommie', and an English person calling an Asian a 'Paki'?

Can you think of other examples of discriminatory language relating to:

- women?
- people with disabilities?

Many people are guilty of individual discrimination through language at some time in their lives. The words people use to refer to one another can be a powerful, direct way of expressing prejudice.

But to some people, language is a matter of political correctness rather than real concern. Ray, a 45-year-old salesman, gives his view:

❝ *I've got an Australian mate who calls me Pommie, and I don't take offence. To me, it's not a term of abuse, and neither are words like Limey, Honky, Chinky, Paki, Darky or Paddy, so I occasionally may use them without thinking much about it, although never in an offensive way . . . There's too much paranoia. You can't say 'coloured', you have to say 'black'. Now I'm told you can't even say half-caste or Red Indian; it has to be 'mixed-race' and 'Native American'. As long as people aren't physically hurt or personally attacked, does it really matter that much? I've got friends of all races and colours, and they're my mates because they're good blokes – their ethnic origin doesn't come into it.* ❞

(from Maxim magazine)

As individuals, health and social care practitioners must take steps to avoid both direct and indirect discrimination, by:

- thinking about the language they use
- making an effort to understand service users' religious practices, customs, diet and language needs
- not showing anger, frustration or dislike through their body language or tone of voice
- treating all service users equally, regardless of age, sex or specific health problems.

Health and social care practitioners are not clones, and all have their own opinions and feelings. However, they have a responsibility not to allow their personal prejudices to affect the quality of care they provide.

ACTIVITY

Talk to a health and social care practioner about how they avoid consciously, or unconsciously, discriminating against individual service users. Have they ever seen examples of direct discrimination in a health and social care setting? Have they ever encountered indirect discrimination?

Keep a record of your interview.

Societal discrimination

Within society as a whole, discrimination can occur on two levels:

- in structures – for example, access to buildings and transport
- in processes – for example, unequal pay for equal work, restricted access to promotion.

A form of direct societal discrimination which is a particular problem for people with physical disabilities is lack of access to buildings and services. Kamaldeep Singh is a primary school pupil with spina bifida, who uses sticks or a wheelchair, depending on his condition. He explains the problems he has faced at school:

66 *At my first school I was the only disabled kid and I had to leave at the end of Year 2 because I was leaving the infants and the junior school had lots of steps. When I first came here there were no ramps up to the huts, just steps. I could go up the steps on my sticks, but not in a wheelchair. Sometimes Mr Collins had to lift me up. There are ramps now, though . . . The toilets can be a problem too, you might have to go to one some way away if you need to use a catheter.* 99

source: Times Educational Supplement

ACTIVITY

All mainstream schools and colleges should be able to accommodate students with physical disabilities, but does reality live up to this ideal? Carry out a survey of facilities for disabled students at schools and colleges in your area. Find out whether students with disabilities attend, what facilities are available, and whether students are excluded from any activities or areas of the school because of their disabilities.

Present your findings in a short report. Why can't schools and colleges provide better facilities for students with disabilities? Do you think your findings show anything about society's prejudices? Or is it simply a question of finance?

Societal discrimination first experienced during childhood continues through employment. Society is built on a traditional view of job roles and who does them, and perpetuates these prejudices at work.

On the whole, society still sees women as secretaries, cleaners and nurses, rather than MPs, engineers and soldiers. In many cases, a woman's position in society still depends on that of her husband. Women often combine paid work with childcare, and neither employers nor the Government are obliged to help them by providing crèche facilities. As a result of this indirect discrimination, many women are forced to stay in part-time, low-paid jobs rather than seeking promotion.

Similarly, society tends to dismiss the importance of elderly people in the workplace. Unemployed people as young as 40 can find it hard to find work because of their age; employees in their 50s are overlooked for promotion; and people are forced to retire at 65. Awareness of the problems of age discrimination is growing, as the case below shows:

DISCUSSION POINT

■ Some regions of the NHS have been accused of denying certain treatments – such as physiotherapy – to elderly patients.

■ The death rate among Pakistani babies is twice the general British average.

■ One research report has shown that if you are born in Britain and your parents are Afro-Caribbean, you are twelve times more likely to end up diagnosed as schizophrenic than if you are white.

Do you think these facts are due to discrimination? What other factors might play a part? How could the health and social care sector try to tackle the problem in each case?

As well as individual practitioners needing to avoid prejudice and discrimination in their day-to-day work, the healthcare sector as a whole has to avoid societal discrimination.

DISCUSSION POINT

Can you think of other ways in which society discriminates against particular groups of people in the community? Are there restrictions on leisure and entertainment? Or on transport?

Carry out research into:

■ initiatives in your area to improve women's health

■ initiatives in your area to improve men's health

■ the uptake of the different services on offer.

Do your findings show societal discrimination in health care on the basis of sex? Can you collect any information on discrimination in healthcare on the basis of social class? People in the lower social classes tend to have less access to health care – why do you think this is?

In recent years the profile of women's health issues has increased. Women's health centres and well-woman clinics are now common, and most local health authorities employ someone to deal with women's issues. But has this resulted in discrimination against men in health care? Men suffer more serious illnesses than women and live, on average, five years less.

Stephen Firn, an adviser on men's health for the Royal College of Nursing, gives his opinion:

❝ *Not nearly enough is going on in men's health. They are at a huge risk from suicide, accidents and substance abuse. We commissioned MORI to survey all the directors of public health in the district health authorities and asked them to rank 13 different target groups in order of priority. Men's health was ranked twelfth. And not a single one could identify any initiative in improving men's health in their district . . . The Government says that it doesn't need a specific strategy for men and that it can leave it to the local areas to take their own initiatives.* **❞**

from Men's Health *magazine*

The effects of discrimination

Being discriminated against can create a range of reactions:

❝ *I feel furious at the injustice of being ignored because I'm a woman.* ❞

❝ *I feel frustrated that people don't see I'm just the same inside as I was when I was 30.* ❞

❝ *It really gets me down, being constantly told I'm not as good as my white colleagues. After a while it makes me start to wonder whether it's true...* ❞

❝ *At first I was angry at being passed over for promotion because of my disability. Now I'm just bored with my job, and can't be bothered to fight any more.* ❞

All of these emotional responses are a natural reaction to prejudice and discrimination.

In practical terms, individual and societal discrimination can also:

- affect individuals' rights
- restrict individuals' opportunities.

Effects on individuals' motivation

If people are constantly told they're not capable of doing something, they start to believe it. They lose their sense of control over a situation, feel powerless, and eventually give up trying.

Loss of motivation as a result of age discrimination is a particular problem. A care assistant explains how she tries to sustain people's motivation to live an independent life:

❝ *Quite often I visit elderly people who are letting their independence slip away from them. Once they're forced to give up work, they slowly fall into the stereotype of an 'old person'. Their family and friends start seeing them as frail and feeble, advise them to slow down, and tell them what they should and shouldn't be doing. The problem is often compounded by physical problems,*

DISCUSSION POINT

Think of occasions when you have been persistently discriminated against, bullied or teased – perhaps as a child. How did you react? Why did it happen? What long-term emotional effect did it have on you?

which make them lose confidence in their abilities. They are treated like an old person, and they start believing that is what they are. They feel helpless and weak, and lose their motivation to fight for their independence – in some cases, even their will to live. Part of my job is to help them rediscover their motivation by giving them small tasks to achieve from day to day – perhaps visiting a friend, or playing a game of cards. With achievable goals to strive towards, they regain some confidence and enthusiasm. 99

Effect on individuals' self-esteem

Self-esteem is a person's good opinion of themselves – their sense of self-worth. Loss of self-esteem is a common reaction to repeated discrimination. As one woman explained who suffered sex discrimination in the workplace:

66 *When my boss first ridiculed me for being an 'incompetent girl' I knew he was wrong and was angry. But as time went on, and he carried on putting me down, I began to lose confidence in myself. A nagging voice at the back of my mind started saying that perhaps he was right. Because I was nervous, I made more mistakes. Over the course of a couple of months I went from being a self-confident person to feeling helpless and worthless.* 99

ACTIVITY

Talk to someone you know who has been discriminated against, for example, a friend who has faced discrimination because they are black, gay, disabled or female. Ask them what emotional effect the discrimination had on them. Did it influence their motivation? Did they lose self-esteem?

With the permission of your interviewee, write a short case report focusing on the emotional effects of discrimination.

Effect on individuals' rights

People who have lost self-esteem as a result of discrimination are less likely to claim their rights in society. For example, the woman above who has been worn down by a long campaign of sex discrimination is unlikely to have the confidence or motivation to fight her case if she is unfairly dismissed. People who have a low sense of self-worth as a result of discrimination tend to believe that they get what they deserve.

In some cases, discrimination can have a direct effect on individuals' legal rights. Homosexuals have a higher age of consent than heterosexuals, and are barred from a military career:

As part of its report on homosexuals in the Armed Forces, the Ministry of Defence carried out a survey to find out the opinions of service personnel. Comments included:

66 *Men don't like taking showers with men who like taking showers with men.* 99

66 *I would not give first aid to a homosexual under any circumstances.* 99

66 *When I go to war, I would rather have alongside me a gay who shoots straight than a straight who shoots crooked.* 99

66 *People have an absolute right to be what they are . . . It is demonstrably not the case that homosexual orientation and military service are incompatible.* 99

In small groups, discuss the factors which underlie the ban on homosexuals in the Armed Forces. Do you think they are being denied the right to a career in the military because of discrimination? If so, whose discrimination?

Effect on individuals' opportunities

As element 1.1 showed, the UK has a wide range of equality of opportunity legislation to try to ensure that everyone in society has an equal chance to gain access to employment, services, housing and so on.

But often, the effect of individual discrimination is so strong that it overrides the influence of legislation. For example:
- a child who faces constant racial discrimination at school loses motivation, stops working, and misses opportunities to go on to further education
- a person with disabilities who is discriminated against loses self-esteem, and lacks the confidence to take opportunities to start work.

ACTIVITY

Look back at your work on equality of opportunity legislation for element 1.1. Choose one piece of legislation (for example, the Race Relations Act or the Sex Discrimination Act). List the main points covered by the Act, and give an example of how individual discrimination could affect someone's equality of opportunity, despite the law.

Key questions

1 Explain the difference between stereotypes, prejudice and discrimination.
2 Give six bases of discrimination.
3 List four rights given to children under the Children Act.
4 Why might people be discriminated against on the basis of their health status?
5 Give two examples of individual discrimination.
6 Give two examples of societal discrimination.
7 Give two examples of direct discrimination.
8 Give two examples of indirect discrimination.
9 What is the difference between conscious and unconscious individual discrimination?
10 Explain the difference between individual and societal discrimination in the context of health and social care.
11 Explain four ways that discrimination can affect individuals.

Assignment

Over a fortnight, collect as much information as you can about discrimination, for example:

■ articles from newspapers and magazines
■ leaflets produced by organisations like MENCAP and Age Concern
■ interviews with people who have experienced discrimination
■ reports in journals
■ extracts from books.

Use the information to produce your own report on discrimination, illustrated with the examples you have collected. Your report should include:

■ an explanation of the different bases of discrimination, including age, disability, sex, health status, ethnic origin, religion and sexuality
■ a description of how discrimination may appear in individuals' behaviour
■ a description of how discrimination may appear in society
■ a description of the effects of discrimination on individuals' motivation, self-esteem, rights and opportunities.

With other students in your group, you could use the material left over to create a display on discrimination for your school or college.

> 66 Confidentiality is the cornerstone of the Centre. We have excellent links with Social Services and the Health Authority Services. Social Services tell young people about us – for example if they receive disclosures of sexual abuse they know we are here if the young person wants to talk to us. It's their choice. 99
>
> senior worker (counselling), young people's counselling and information centre

> 66 I have to run an incredibly confidential practice. I see clients about very sensitive issues concerning their health and emotional lives, for example, people who are scared stiff they've got AIDS. They need a safe space to explore all that is troubling them and I can guarantee to them that this room is watertight. 99
>
> doctor in charge of health screening, private hospital

> 66 When dispensing prescriptions it doesn't matter who is seen – we would not divulge any detail of their prescription outside the company. 99
>
> pharmacist

> 66 Staff and patients do not always understand that counselling is about a free exploration of the issues rather than directive advice giving; so it is possible to be asked to persuade people to behave in a particular kind of way. Ethically, that is not my role – my role is to enable my patients to make their own choices. 99
>
> head of medical counselling and family support

> 66 In the cardiology unit at the hospital we prefer not to treat smokers with heart disease purely because they don't do so well. A person who smokes more than five cigarettes a day is more likely to have a recurrence of their symptoms. The effects of putting in new arteries lasts on average eight years in a non-smoker; for a smoker it could last less than five. It's a question of getting the maximum benefits from very scarce resources. 99
>
> doctor working in NHS hospital

> 66 Everything in child protection is a balance between the child's rights and the parents' rights. One example might be the dilemma of what action to take with a child whose parents have learning disabilities. Their neglect may be more by default than on purpose. Do we take the children away? It even raises the question of whether people with severe learning disabilities should have children at all. It's a major ethical issue. There are lot of different opinions about it. There are no easy or right answers, really. 99
>
> child protection adviser

Ethical issues in health and social care

In this element you will explore a range of ethical issues and dilemmas which health and social care practitioners may face in the course of their work, and some of the ways they are handled.

45

The responsibilities of care practitioners to act ethically

66 *We always called our doctor 'Sir' and wouldn't have dreamed of questioning anything he said. He was much cleverer than the rest of us, and we trusted him completely.* 99

89-year-old man

Although the general public's respect for the medical profession may not be as heartfelt as in the past, people still place enormous trust in health and social care workers.

People usually need health and social care support when they are vulnerable in some way – perhaps as a result of illness, frailty, financial problems or homelessness. They may be worried about the future, not understand what is happening to them and feel powerless to solve their problems.

In contrast, health and social care practitioners are in a powerful position. They have specialist knowledge, understand how the care system works, and often know personal details about the service user's health or lifestyle. The decisions they make can transform – sometimes even save or destroy – people's lives.

Because of this, people need to know they can trust health and social care practitioners to:

■ act in their best interests
■ only make decisions after assessing risks to individuals and groups
■ give them all the information they need
■ respect the confidentiality of information they provide
■ empower them – give them the freedom and knowledge they need to make decisions and maintain their independence.

These are health and social care practitioners' basic responsibilities to act 'ethically' – to behave in a morally correct way in their dealings with service users.

DISCUSSION POINT

What health and social care workers have supported you during your life (for example, doctors, dentists or social workers)? Who do you feel has had the power in these relationships? What responsibilities do you feel health and social care workers have as a result of the trust you place in them?

DISCUSSION POINT

Do you think it is always clear what the 'best interests' of service users are? Can you think of occasions when people – perhaps your parents, teachers or health and social care practitioners – have acted in what they thought was your best interests, but you disagreed? Who do you think knows best?

Acting in the best interests of service users

The fundamental goal of everyone working in health and social care is to act in the best interests of service users. For example:

■ doctors try to improve their patients' health, or at least their quality of life
■ nurses care for patients by meeting their needs
■ social workers try to improve the day-to-day lives of service users
■ care assistants give people the practical care they need.

ACTIVITY

The Patient's Charter defines many of the responsibilities of healthcare practitioners. Get a copy, and produce a chart to show the responsibilities included in the charter. Break your chart down into responsibilities to:

■ act in the best interests of clients

■ provide access to information

■ maintain the confidentiality of information

The right of service users to expect practitioners to act in their best interests is reinforced by professional codes of conduct, and legislation such as the Mental Health Act 1983 and the NHS and Community Care Act 1990. It is also reflected in equality of opportunity legislation such as the Sex Discrimination Act and the Race Relations Act, which aim to ensure that everybody has equal access to, and is offered equal care by, health and social care services.

The message at the heart of the Patient's Charter is: 'Patients must always come first.' The underlying theme is to ensure that everyone working for the National Health Service is committed to acting in the best interests of service users, whether this is:

❝ *the right to receive health care on the basis of your clinical need, not on your ability to pay, your lifestyle or any other factor* **❞**

or

❝ *the right to be referred to a consultant acceptable to you, when your GP thinks it is necessary, and to be referred for a second opinion if you and your GP agree this is desirable.* **❞**

Assessing risk to individuals and groups

The decisions which health and social care practitioners make can have far-reaching implications. Before taking action in a particular case, they have a responsibility to assess whether:

■ the person is at risk from their own behaviour (for example, a psychiatric patient who is suicidal)

■ the person is at risk from other people's actions (for example, a child who is the victim of abuse)

■ the person's family, friends or carers are at risk from their behaviour (for example, an exhausted husband caring for his wife with Alzheimer's)

■ the community as a whole is at risk from the person's behaviour.

Assessing risk to children is a particularly sensitive issue. The Children Act 1989 placed new emphasis on the importance of assessing children who might be at risk from physical violence, sexual abuse or neglect, and gave social services new duties to keep children safe.

A child considered at risk is interviewed by a social worker, and may be given a medical examination if physical or sexual abuse is thought to have occurred. A child protection conference is then held, at which doctors, social workers, teachers, parents, police (and the child if they want to) meet to assess the risk of the child being harmed. Possible outcomes include:

■ placing the child on a Child Protection Register (this is a list of children who are at risk of harm)

■ going to court to ask for a Care Order (committing the child to the care of the local authority)

■ going to court to ask for a Child Assessment Order (directing the child's parents to cooperate with further assessment of the child, before deciding what action to take).

ACTIVITY

The Children Act also establishes procedures for assessing children who may put themselves or other people at risk.

A 14-year-old boy has been missing school, staying out all night, and getting into trouble with the police for shoplifting and joy riding. His parents feel they have lost control, and are struggling to cope.

Using information about the Children Act, explain how health and social care workers might assess the risks involved in this situation and take action to help safeguard the child.

ACTIVITY

In recent years, the media have reported on a number of tragedies involving people with mental illness being cared for in the community. High-profile cases have included the murder of a man on a London tube platform, and a schizophrenic man who murdered his mother and young brother.

Carry out a media search to find reports on cases where care in the community has placed the community as a whole at risk. How did the community respond? Did their reaction influence the outcome? As far as you can tell from the reports, why do you think assessment of risk failed?

Like children, elderly people are often vulnerable and at risk from themselves and others. The NHS and Community Care Act 1990 aims to enable elderly people to continue being cared for (or caring for themselves) within the community. To achieve this safely, health and social care practitioners need to assess a range of risks, as a social worker explains:

66 *When assessing the needs of elderly people, we have to give careful consideration to the risks both to themselves, and to others. The possible risks to the client are physical and emotional – are they likely to fall? Can they undress themselves alone? Can they go to the toilet? Are they able to cope emotionally with living alone? When an elderly person is being cared for by family or friends, we need to consider whether the responsibility is placing too great a strain on the carers, putting them at risk. Sadly, we also have to be aware of any risk of the elderly person being harmed by those caring for them, which does sometimes happen.* 99

The NHS and Community Care Act also increased the number of people with mental health problems being cared for in the community rather than in a mental hospital. When deciding whether someone suffering from mental illness should be treated in the community, health and social care practitioners need to assess the possible risks to the person, the community and the person's family. If the risks are considered too great, the person can be 'sectioned' under the Mental Health Act 1983 – detained for treatment in a mental hospital.

Providing access to information

Health and social care practitioners have a duty to give service users information – from access to their medical records and explanations of procedures to information on hospital standards and clear guidelines on how to complain.

People can only make sensible decisions and choices if they have full, accurate information on a situation. For example, a parent asked to give permission for their child to have an operation needs to know the exact risks and benefits of surgery in order to make the right decision.

ACTIVITY

Get hold of a copy of last year's hospital league tables, which give the general public details of hospitals' performance in critical areas. List the different types of information included in the league tables. Do the tables compare like with like? How useful do you think the information is?

You have been asked to produce a summary of the performance of hospitals in your area. Choose what information to include in your summary, and think about how to present it in a way that would be useful and accessible for your community.

Table 1 Outpatients, assessment and operations (continued)

	Outpatient appointments % of patients seen within 30 minutes of appointment time			Accident and eme % of patients assess 5 minutes of arr	
National performance	88%			93%	
Andover District Community Healthcare NHS Trust	87%	★★★	▲	91%	★★★★
Avalon Somerset NHS Trust	100%	★★★★★		–	
Bath & West Community NHS Trust	94%	★★★★		100%	★★★★★
Bath Mental Healthcare NHS Trust	98%	★★★★★		–	
Cornwall & IoS Learning Disabilities NHS Trust	100%	★★★★★		–	
Cornwall Healthcare NHS Trust	91%	★★★★	▲	93%	★★★★
Dorset Community NHS Trust	91%	★★★★		100%	★★★★★
Dorset Health Care NHS Trust	93%	★★★★		96%	★★★★
East Gloucestershire NHS Trust	86%	★★★		97%	★★★
East Somerset NHS Trust	85%	★★★		94%	★★★★
East Wiltshire Health Care NHS Trust	99%	★★★★★		–	

League tables grade hospitals on their performance in a range of areas.

Practitioners' responsibilities to give service users access to information is laid down in two main pieces of legislation:

■ the Access to Personal Files Act 1987. This gives individuals the right to look at information local authorities (for example, social services departments) hold on them

■ the Access to Health Records Act 1990. This gives individuals the right to look at their NHS medical records.

Maintaining the confidentiality of information

To do their job well, practitioners need a range of information about service users – from facts about someone's physical well-being and financial situation to personal details about their feelings and relationships. Giving this information can be embarrassing and worrying, and people need to feel they can talk openly to their health and social care practitioners. This means trusting them to maintain the confidentiality of any information exchanged.

Establishing ground rules is an important part of building trust. Before asking questions and recording personal details, practitioners should explain why they need the information and how they are going to use it. In turn, service users should be able to insist that details are kept completely confidential, and not shared with their family, friends, other workers, and so on.

Fighting fears on privacy

ALARM over the security of the planned NHS-wide computer network has prompted an inquiry by a data safety watchdog.

The Data Protection Registrar last week took delivery of a preliminary investigation into the privacy of patient records on the network. It commissioned the report after the BMA strongly criticised Government plans for the protection of data.

The BMA says the Government's plans for a computer network could threaten the confidentiality of private medical records. It has urged doctors to boycott the plan until security issues have been properly addressed.

Results of the study should be released shortly. A spokesman said if there was cause for concern a more in-depth report might be commissioned.

She added: 'If we are happy with the security approach, we will leave it at that. If not, we will approach the NHS Executive or ask our computer security expert to look into it.'

Source: *Hospital Doctor* magazine

People's rights to confidentiality are reinforced by several pieces of legislation:

■ the Data Protection Act 1984 aims to ensure the confidentiality of information stored on computer. It sets rules on the personal information which can be held electronically, stating that information must be:
 – obtained legally
 – used in the way specified when it was collected
 – kept accurate and up to date
 – confidential, but available to those who have a right to see it
 In addition, organisations and individuals must register as holders of information.
■ the Access to Health Records Act 1990 and the Access to Personal Files Act 1987 establish procedures for handling confidential data.

Professional codes of practice also lay down standards of confidentiality, and it is an important part of the Patient's Charter.

Empowering service users

As already mentioned, it is easy for practitioners to assume a position of power in their relationships with service users. Obviously, in some circumstances – for example, if an individual is particularly vulnerable or ill – a service user may be dependent on practitioners. However, it is important that they are empowered to make decisions and take control of their lives as far as possible.

Empowerment means enabling people to make choices and promoting their rights as individuals. Even making simple decisions – such as what to wear, who to sit next to at dinner and what to watch on TV – helps a person to maintain their independence and dignity. In line with this, health and social care practitioners should enable service users to make as many choices as possible in their day-to-day lives.

Recognising people as individuals is a major step towards empowerment. Practitioners must:

- identify the personal beliefs and values of everyone they work with
- respect the individual needs and choices of every service user
- avoid stereotyping, which denies people's individuality
- consider people's feelings at all times.

DISCUSSION POINT

Read the following conversation between Joanna (a care assistant), and Mrs Clark (an elderly woman living in sheltered accommodation).

Joanna:	*Now come on, Mrs C. You know you like a nice cup of tea at 5 o'clock. Drink it up.*
Mrs Clark:	*Do you think I could have another spoon of sugar? I like two sugars in my tea.*
Joanna:	*(Sighs) We're getting confused again. Your son told me you had one sugar.*
Mrs Clark:	*Oh. (Takes a mouthful of tea and screws her face up)*
Joanna:	*Then when you've finished that, we'll get you into your nightie in time for Neighbours.*
Mrs Clark:	*But it's only 5! I wanted to pop next door to see how Jenny's feeling today. And I don't like that silly Neighbours anyway.*
Joanna:	*Look, the council's not made of money you know. I'm only here until 6, so we've got to get you ready for bed before I go. And I thought it would be nice for us to sit down cosily and watch telly together for half an hour.*
Mrs Clark:	*Oh well, if you say so.*

Talk about the conversation above. How many different ways does Joanna deny Mrs Clark her individual rights and choices? Could the organisation she works for do anything to help empower Mrs Clark?

UNIT

1

ELEMENT **1.3**

Often, information and knowledge are the key to empowerment. Without understanding their situation and the different options open to them, people can't make choices. People's rights to be given information in order to play an active role in their own health and social care are laid down in professional codes of practice and charters.

ACTIVITY

The Patient's Charter states that a pregnant woman has the right to choose: 'who will be responsible for looking after you; where you will have your baby; the type of care you wish to receive, for example whether you wish to have your care led by a midwife, GP or consultant obstetrician.'

Talk to someone who has had a baby in recent years to find out whether they felt they had these rights. What information did they need in order to make these choices? Where did they get the information from?

Recent legislation has been founded on the importance of empowering service users, in particular the NHS and Community Care Act 1990. This:

- places new emphasis on people's rights to choose their own health and care provision
- encourages people to live independently in the community, rather than in homes and hospitals.

ACTIVITY

Carry out research into the NHS and Community Care Act 1990, and make brief notes on how it empowers people using health and social care services. Then look back at your research into the Patient's Charter, and pull out the information on how it empowers service users.

From your notes, produce a short summary for service users, outlining their rights under legislation to make decisions about their own lives.

Ethical issues and dilemmas

ACTIVITY

In the case of Thomas Creedon, who do you think was in the best position to decide the child's best interests? What action do you think should have been taken in the child's best interests?

Choose one of the following dilemmas.

- Should an elderly person be taken into care? He is becoming increasingly frail and confused, but wants to stay at home. His family, who live 30 miles away, are concerned for his safety and think it would be in his best interests to go into care.

- Should the life-support system be switched off? A 16-year-old girl has been involved in a diving accident and is in a coma which appears to be irreversible. The doctors want to switch off the life-support system, but her family are strongly opposed. The girl's organs could be used for transplants, saving other people's lives.

Make lists of the different moral arguments for and against taking action. Remember to consider the dilemma from the point of view of legal issues, health and social care practitioners, the service user, their family and friends, and society as a whole. Talk to other people (including a health and social care practitioner if possible), to get their opinions. Then write a summary of the ethical dilemma facing the health and social care practitioners involved in each case.

An ethical dilemma involves making a decision when there is no clear-cut moral right or wrong. It may be that there is a conflict between different people's morals or beliefs. Or that an issue is so complex or difficult to understand that it raises moral questions which are almost impossible to answer.

DISCUSSION POINT

Have you experienced any ethical dilemmas in your life? Were your morals in conflict with someone else's? Or was the issue so confusing that you couldn't make your own mind up? How did you resolve the ethical dilemma?

With people's lives and well-being in their hands, many health and social care practitioners face ethical issues and dilemmas as part of their day-to-day jobs.

Agreeing the best interests of service users

As already discussed, the fundamental aim of practitioners is to act in the best interests of service users. However, is it always clear what these best interests are?

Everybody involved will have their own views on a service user's best interests, including:

- different health and social care practitioners
- the service user
- the service user's family and friends
- the community in which the service user lives.

When making decisions about the best interests of service users, health and social care practitioners need to reach an agreement with all of these groups of people. This can mean careful balancing of a range of highly emotive issues and views, as in the following case:

66 *Thomas Creedon, the severely brain-damaged two-year-old who died recently, had been kept alive by medical interventions, including artificial feeding and hydration. His parents had argued that life-prolonging interventions were against their child's best interests. The doctors disagreed, saying that food and water were every human being's basic rights.*

Had the child survived, the issues would have gone to court. Apparently, the doctors had also stated that were the infant to develop an infection, they would not prolong his life with antibiotics. Nor, presumably, was the child put on a respirator when his breathing stopped, nor efforts made to institute CPR – cardiopulmonary resuscitation – when his heart stopped beating, even though these might have prolonged his life. 99

The Guardian, *7 March 1996*

David, a 22-year-old who suffers from schizophrenia, has been extremely violent in the past, but appears to be stabilising and is desperate to move back home. His doctors are concerned, but are under pressure to reduce the number of people detained in mental hospitals in the area (in line with the NHS and Community Care Act). His parents love him and are torn between wanting him home and concern for the welfare of his younger brothers and sisters. The village they live in has raised a petition campaigning for David to stay in the mental hospital.

If you had to make the decision whether or not to let David go home, how would you balance David's needs, and the risks to his family, friends and community? Where do the needs of the NHS fit into the equation?

Balancing the needs of individuals against those of others

In many cases, it is not enough to consider only the best interests of the service user. Decisions can also have repercussions for their family and friends, and society as a whole.

As you have already seen, before making decisions about the best course of action, practitioners need to assess whether:

- the person is at risk from their own behaviour
- the person is at risk from other people's actions
- their family, friends or carers are at risk from their behaviour
- society as a whole is at risk from their behaviour.

A social worker describes the ethical dilemmas which arise when deciding how to deal with cases where children may be at risk:

66 *An important part of my job is making sure that children in need – who might suffer if they don't get help – are properly looked after. Whenever possible, I help families to bring up children in their own homes. I provide support in the form of home helps, nursery places for younger children, and sessions at a family centre. However, sometimes I believe children are in such danger that I have to go to court and ask for a Care or Supervision Order. This is always a terrible, heartrending decision to make. Even if they are at risk, leaving home is a dreadful experience for a young child. Parents may be very distressed and angry that their family is being broken up. Other brothers and sisters may be badly affected. But ultimately, I have to put the risk to the child first. My main responsibility is to keep them safe.* 99

Allocating resources

Schizophrenia drugs 'rationed'

David Brindle, Social Services Correspondent

Many psychiatrists are being prevented or deterred on cost grounds from prescribing drugs which can control schizophrenia, a survey suggests today.

The drugs cost up to £5.34 a day, or 66 times more than conventional medication — but that is dwarfed by the cost of in-patient treatment for a sufferer who breaks down and needs hospital admission.

Estimates put the lifetime costs of a schizophrenic needing long-term hospital care at £316,000, compared to £23,000 for a patient maintained in the community.

The results of the survey by the National Schizophrenia Fellowship and the Royal College of Psychiatrists are based on a questionnaire completed by 761 psychiatrists — some 59 per cent of those registered as working with patients in the community.

The aim of the survey was to establish attitudes to clozapine and risperidone — "new generation" generic drugs which are attracting growing, but not universal, endorsement for effectiveness in treating schizophrenia. Clozapine, which is typically given to patients who respond poorly to

other drugs, can have serious side-effects and requires regular blood monitoring. In contrast, risperidone is generally given as a first recourse and has fewer side-effects.

Although in Germany almost one in three people with schizophrenia is on clozapine, the survey found its use very limited in Britain.

Thirty-five per cent of the psychiatrists said they had no patients on Clozapine, and 25 per cent said they had none on risperidone. Most who prescribed it did so for fewer than five of their patients.

Forty-six per cent had been challenged about the cost of clozapine, £5.34 a day compared to 8p for a standard alternative, and 52 per cent had been challenged about risperidone, which costs £4.04.

Nine per cent said formal rationing was imposed on prescribing clozapine, and a further 14 per cent said informal limits existed.

Similarly 3 per cent said there were formal limits on risperidone prescription and 11 per cent cited informal curbs. One psychiatrist said: "I have 150 patients who would benefit from clozapine, but I am only allowed to prescribe it to 20.

Extract from the Guardian

NHS set to fund surrogate birth

Chris Mihill
Medical Correspondent

The first birth to a surrogate mother funded by the NHS could follow discussions between a health authority and a test tube baby clinic over the help to be given to the infertile couple.

Previous surrogacy arrangements — where a woman bears a child for an infertile couple — have been private. It is not yet known whether the health authority would restrict funding to in vitro fertilisation treatment, or if it would pay the expenses of the surrogate mother.

John Parsons head of the Assisted Conception Unit at King's College Hospital, south London, yesterday revealed that his clinic had been told by a health authority that it would meet the cost of a surrogate pregnancy, although

detailed discussions were continuing. Mr Parsons declined to give details of the couple who wanted the baby or the prospective surrogate mother. He also refused to identify the health authority, although it is believed to be in the south of the country.

The treatment involves taking eggs and sperm from the would be parents, mixing them in a laboratory and implanting them in the surrogate mother. IVF costs about £2,000 per course of treatment.

Expenses for a surrogate mother would normally include loss of earnings, travel costs and clothing. Most surrogate mothers receive between £7,000 and £10,000.

The announcement came as the British Medical Association issued revised guidance to doctors, saying they should help patients involved in surrogate

pregnancies, as counselling about the possible pitfalls would lessen the chances of arrangements going wrong.

Mr Parsons said he believed that surrogate pregnancies should be available on the NHS as a last resort for infertile couples. His unit received four or five requests a year for IVF treatment for surrogate pregnancies. Each case was decided by the hospitals ethics committee, after the couple and the surrogate mother had undergone psychological assessment and counselling.

Tim Hedgley, chairman of Issue, the fertility pressure group, said last night: "I think it is very good news. It is very forward thinking of the health authority. The authority is paying to alleviate stress and suffering in an infertile couple."

Extract from the Guardian

Since the introduction of the welfare state in 1944, people in Britain have come to expect the right to free health and social care on demand. However, resources today are limited, and 'health rationing' is becoming an increasingly high-profile issue.

Because of limited resources, most people can no longer choose when, where and how they receive treatment and help. However, those who can afford to do so will still be able to make choices by buying private medical support and care.

■ Do you think this is fair?

■ What ethical issues does this raise?

Health and social care organisations are given a limited amount of money, and have to work out how to balance the budget while providing as good a service as possible. This means making decisions about how to allocate resources.

To do this, they balance the needs of one group of service users against another, and decide who should receive priority. This may mean tackling ethical dilemmas such as:

■ Is a heart operation on a child more important than a hip operation on an elderly person?

■ Should resources be directed into buying vital new equipment which might save hundreds, rather than continuing the treatment of a young person with leukaemia who has a slim chance of survival?

■ Is it more important to take a child in danger of physical abuse into foster care, or to pay for home alterations for a physically disabled man of 30?

ACTIVITY

QALYs – quality adjusted life years – are a system to measure the costs and benefits of different healthcare decisions.

Carry out research to find out more about QALYs. Write a short report explaining how they work, and whether you think they are a good idea.

The following two articles show the type of decisions which health professionals have to make.

What do you think about the decisions made by the health authorities and hospital? What criteria do you think they used to decide how to allocate resources?

Cash-Strapped Hospital's plea for cancer patients

Chris Mihill
Medical Correspondent

A hospital which is sending home dying cancer patients with painkillers but no other form of treatment because of a cash crisis said yesterday it was seeking more money — but other services might suffer if the extra funding was found.

Bristol Royal Infirmary faces an overspend of £500,000 on its cancer treatment budget by the end of March, brought about by an unexpectedly high number of patients.

As a result, patients who are terminally ill are to be given a lower priority for radiotherapy treatment, which is to be mainly reserved for patients who can be cured.

A hospital spokesman explained there had been a continuing rise in cancer patients needing treatment. Over the past year 10 per cent more patients had been seen than had ben budgeted for.

The cancer centre is to close one of its five linear accelerator machines, used to deliver radiotherapy treatment and keep unfilled the vacant posts of four radiographers. It will mean about 40 to 50 fewer patients being seen each month.

Terminally ill patients will be told to see their GP for supplies of pain killers, rather than being given radiotherapy which can relieve pain.

Hugh Ross, the hospital's chief executive, said he was seeking more money from Avon health authority for cancer treatment, but if that was forthcoming it would mean other treatment areas being cut by the authority.

Dr Victor Barley, director of the hospital's cancer unit, said Bristol was not unique and cancer centres across the country were having to make the "judgments of Solomon" about who they treated because of lack of money.

An increase in the elderly population, who were more prone to cancer, and advances in treatment, were all increasing budgetary pressures, but extra funds were not being made available.

He admitted that failing to provide radiotherapy would diminish the quality of life for dying patients.

Extract from the *Guardian*

Chiefs put ops on funding blacklist

HEALTH authorities are sending GPs lists of treatments they are refusing to pay for in the latest round of rationing care.

South Essex Health Authority has said it will not buy largely cosmetic procedures.

In a letter to GPs, public health consultant Dr Mike Gogarty said: 'By taking this action we are certain resources can be directed into treatment of those whose needs are greatest and most likely to benefit from available interventions.'

The HA has said it does not wish to buy minor surgery for sebaceous cysts, lipomas, minor skin tags and seborrhoeic warts.

Varicose vein problems which can be adequately controlled by surgical support stockings will also not be funded.

But the authority stresses that it will allow exceptions where a good clinical case can be made.

Other authorities are also being explicit about rationing.

Dorset Health Commission has excluded vasectomy reversal and cosmetic surgery. And in Wessex a regional list has been drawn up to exclude a number of cosmetic surgery procedures.

Dr Andrew Vallance-Owen, head of policy at the BMA, said HA lists should be compiled by doctors and managers, with the public being involved and informed. The public should be aware that treatments were not being provided because there was not enough money.

Extract from *Hospital Doctor* magazine

What are people's views on health rationing? Compile a questionnaire to find out how your colleagues at school or college think resources should be allocated. For example, you might put together a list of different health problems, and ask people to rank them in order of importance. Or find out people's opinions on providing health care to the elderly and children, or to smokers with lung disease.

Write a short report on the results of your survey, presenting your statistical findings in bar charts and pie charts.

Giving information

A common dilemma faced by practitioners is deciding:

- what information people need to know
- who needs to know it.

Everyone has the right to enough information to make decisions about their treatment. For example, before signing a consent form for major surgery, a patient needs to know the pros and cons of going ahead with the operation. Their surgeon should explain the operation using simple language, and make notes and draw diagrams for the patient. But should they go into the full details of potential problems if this may be upsetting or confusing?

As well as deciding what information to give, health and social care practitioners often face ethical dilemmas when it comes to passing on knowledge to other people. They have a responsibility to keep information confidential, but may feel the service user's family has a right to know something. Or they may feel they can't cope with a case on their own, and decide to ask a colleague for advice.

DISCUSSION POINT

In which of the following situations do you think it is ethical for the health and social care practitioner to give information to people? What are the pros and cons in each case? What should the practitioner do next?

- A 14-year-old girl confides in the school nurse that she is pregnant, and the nurse has to decide whether to tell the girl's parents.

- An elderly man is suffering from a terminal illness, and has been given a month to live. His doctor tells the man's children, and they beg the doctor not to tell their father.

- A depressed and disruptive teenage girl confesses to her social worker that she was raped a year ago. She asks for the information to be kept confidential, but the social worker feels the girl needs specialist support which she can't provide.

Handling conflicting values and beliefs

Everyone has his or her own set of values and beliefs. Some of these are personal preferences, while others are religious beliefs or cultural practices.

Health and social care practitioners have a responsibility to recognise and respect these values and beliefs at all times – even when they are in conflict with their own values, or the organisation's practices.

A nurse who works in an area with a large Muslim population explains the importance of understanding the values of service users:

66 *When I first came to work in this area, I found Muslim beliefs and practices very strange. Now I have come to understand the significance of different customs and rituals, and do all I can to support the families and friends involved. For example, we recently had a Muslim patient who was dying. We moved him into a side room, where his many visitors could have more privacy, holy water could be given, and verses from the Qur'an could be read. When he died, I turned his face to the right, to symbolise turning to Mecca. I straightened his arms and legs, and closed his mouth and eyes. These simple things all helped to comfort the bereaved family. I'm a Roman Catholic myself, but don't have any problem following Muslim practice. It's a mark of respect for the patients and their families.* 99

DISCUSSION POINT

Jehovah's Witnesses don't believe in blood transfusions under any circumstances. Even if a child is about to die during an operation because they need blood, their parents won't give consent, and doctors can't intervene. How do you think this would affect the medical staff involved? Are there ever any circumstances in which you feel health and social care practitioners should be able to override the religious or cultural values of their clients?

Handling ethical issues

Every ethical issue and dilemma involves a unique set of circumstances, and has to be handled on its own terms. For example, it would be wrong to pass a blanket judgement that life-support systems should always be switched off after six months, or that all patients with mental health problems should be cared for in the community.

To help them approach the full range of ethical issues, health and social care practitioners have established different ways of handling dilemmas. These include:

- practitioners making individual decisions
- practitioners discussing issues with colleagues, service users and carers
- setting up organisational policies and practices
- taking advice from representative bodies
- following government legislation
- improving training for health and social care practitioners
- establishing codes of practice on how to behave in particular situations.

Individual decisions

Almost all health and social care practitioners make minor ethical decisions every day in their work. They have to make many of these decisions alone, relying on their own personal judgement and knowledge.

A care assistant explains some of the ethical issues she regularly faces:

66 My job involves making an endless string of ethical decisions – many of which I'm not even aware of at the time! Most of these are to do with empowering people by giving them the freedom and encouragement to do things for themselves, without putting their wellbeing at risk. For example, I have to decide whether to encourage someone with severe physical disabilities to make a cup of tea on their own, or whether to make an elderly person get up when she wants to stay in bed all day.

Sometimes I make an individual decision on the spot, and then inform the person's social worker of what has happened if I feel it is important. Recently, one of the elderly women I visit was crying because she didn't want to go to the day centre the following day. Even though it's part of her care programme, I felt her right to choose was more important, so I rang up the centre and told them not to pick her up. I then dropped a note to her social worker, as I felt he needed to be aware of the decision I'd made. 99

Handling ethical issues through discussion has advantages for all involved:

- it enables expert knowledge and understanding to be shared
- it gives the people involved a sense of ownership of the problem, and the decision reached
- it reflects the complexity of ethical issues by considering different viewpoints
- it gives people an opportunity to express their views
- it enables a range of different values and beliefs to be taken into account
- it means that decision making is shared, rather than being one person's responsibility.

DISCUSSION POINT

Think back to the ethical dilemmas you have faced in your life. How did you resolve them? Did you make a decision on your own? Or did you talk to other people or read information before making your decision?

ACTIVITY

Talk to a health or social care practitioners about some of the individual ethical decisions they make as part of their job. How do they reach these decisions? Are they comfortable with having to make decisions on their own?

DISCUSSION POINT

In most cases, important ethical decisions will only be taken after a discussion with one or more people. These discussions may be either:

■ informal – for example, talking to service users and their carers about what steps to take, or chatting to a colleague about a case

■ formal – for example, a case conference involving service users, colleagues and carers.

What might be the benefits and risks of each type of discussion?

ACTIVITY

Ten-year-old Christopher has been becoming increasingly disruptive at school, and his teacher has noticed some bruising on his body. Having talked to Christopher, the social worker has decided to call a child protection conference to discuss his case. Christopher does not want to attend the conference himself, but the following people will be present:

■ his social worker, who is coordinating the meeting

■ a senior social worker, who is very experienced in child protection work

■ his mother, who denies the allegations and is angry about the situation

■ his teacher, who is concerned about the signs of physical abuse and emotional disturbance shown by Christopher

■ a doctor, who has treated Christopher for a series of minor injuries in the past year.

In groups of five, roleplay the child protection conference, each taking on one of the roles. Remember that your overall aim is to assess the risks to Christopher, and make a decision about what action to take in his best interests. Think carefully about your character before you start, considering their feelings and what they want to gain from the meeting. If necessary, carry out research into child protection conferences.

After your roleplay, talk as a group about what you think each of the participants gained from the discussion. Do you think holding a case conference like this is a good way to make ethical decisions?

Organisational policies and practices

Many health and social care organisations, from hospitals and doctor's surgeries to health authorities and social services departments, have their own policies and practices for handling ethical issues. These may include:

■ charters which establish guidelines for acting in the best interests of service users, assessing risks, giving information and maintaining confidentiality and respecting personal values and beliefs

■ training programmes for staff, to help them handle ethical issues

■ guidelines on how to allocate resources between different areas.

The following extract is taken from the 1993–94 community care plan for Northumberland. It lays down clear guidelines on care priorities and how health and social care practitioners should allocate resources.

Category A:

help will always be offered to resolve problems in these areas if a solution is feasible and within the powers of the Authorities.

Getting into and out of bed; getting dressed and undressed; moving between your bed and a chair.

Washing your hands and face daily; looking after your body (e.g. getting your hair and nails cut, shaving); getting washed all over at least once a fortnight (more often if you need to for your health). Getting clean clothes and bedclothes, and keeping your home clean and well-maintained enough to avoid harm to your health.

Looking after your health by eating and drinking adequately, keeping warm, and taking medication appropriately. Carrying out bodily functions in a dignified and hygienic way; changing position often enough to avoid bedsores or other problems.

Avoiding preventable risks, such as risk of falls and burns; getting help in emergencies and letting people into your home safely.

Getting at least two hours a day free from care or self-care tasks. If you are a carer, getting at least two hours a week away from the person you care for.

Making your needs and views known; understanding your health condition; being properly prepared for the care or self-care tasks you carry out; knowing about your benefit entitlements.

Avoiding:

- Degrading treatment, extreme isolation or avoidable pain
- Harming yourself or other people
- The collapse of your relationships with the people you live with
- Significant harm to children, or children taking inappropriate responsibilities for care.

Category B:

social services or health resources should usually be available, if required, to resolve problems in these areas.

Living in your own home.

Keeping your home free from smells and grime. Basic money management.

Feeling confident about future support if current arrangements break down. If you are a carer, getting a few days each year away from caring.

Maintaining key friendships and contacts. Free from other people's rules about how you should live.

Sharing a bedroom with your partner if you wish to.

Reading, writing, watching TV, and listening to the radio (or equivalents if these are not possible). Finding satisfying and productive occupation if you are not able to work or study.

Avoiding:

- severe difficulty with basic tasks
- avoidable discomfort
- constant exhaustion
- difficulty coping with major crises such as bereavement.

DISCUSSION POINT

How useful do you think health and social care practitioners would have found this policy when faced with ethical dilemmas? Do you agree with the way needs have been prioritised? Can you think of circumstances in which such a clear-cut policy would not be helpful?

Advice from representative bodies

Health and social care practitioners can also seek the advice of representative bodies in the case of difficult ethical dilemmas, including:

■ the British Medical Association (which has a special ethics committee)
■ the Royal College of Nursing
■ the British Association of Social Workers
■ trade unions, such as Unison.

A major step forward was made in 1992, when the Care Sector Consortium established a Value Base of Care Practice. This lays down a set of values and principles which care practitioners should follow, and gives health and social care practitioners clear guidelines on ethical issues for the first time.

The Value Base is made up of five key areas.

■ Promotion of anti-discriminatory practice. Carers should:
  – identify and fight their own prejudices
  – never stereotype individuals
  – use language that service users can understand.
■ Maintaining confidentiality of information. Carers should:
  – respect service users' requests for confidentiality as far as possible
  – explain who will have access to information.
■ Promoting and supporting individual rights to dignity, independence, choice and health and safety. Carers should:
  – encourage service users to be independent
  – recognise service users' rights and choice
  – encourage individuals to express their needs and wishes.
■ Acknowledging individuals' personal beliefs and identity. Carers should:
  – recognise and support service users' rights to beliefs
  – encourage individuals to express personal beliefs and preferences, as long as they do not affect the rights of others.
■ Supporting individuals through effective communication. Carers should:
  – communicate in a way which is appropriate for individual service users (level of understanding, language and so on)
  – check that service users understand information
  – develop their listening skills
  – recognise the importance of non-verbal communication.

Government legislation

Some ethical issues which affect health and social care practitioners are considered so important that they are covered by government legislation. The main pieces of legislation include:

■ Sex Discrimination Act 1975, which covers
  – acting in the best interests of clients
■ Race Relations Act 1976, which covers
  – acting in the best interests of clients
  – handling conflicting values and beliefs
■ Mental Health Act 1983, which covers
  – acting in the best interests of clients

What do you think should happen if a service user's personal wishes or best interests conflict with legislation?

For example, a young woman with severe physical disabilities needs help undressing and washing. When she is sent a male care assistant she refuses assistance, becomes distressed and complains that she is being denied her rights to control her care. In turn, the care assistant claims that he is a victim of discrimination under the Sex Discrimination Act. What should the social services department do?

- assessing risks to individuals and groups
- The Children Act 1989, which covers
  - assessing risks to individuals and groups
  - acting in the best interests of clients
  - empowering clients
- Access to Personal Files Act 1987, which covers
  - confidentiality of information
  - access to information
- Disabled Persons Act 1986, which covers
  - empowering clients
- Access to Health Records Act 1990, which covers
  - confidentiality of information
  - access to information
- NHS and Community Care Act 1990, which covers
  - empowering clients
  - assessing risk to individuals and groups
- Data Protection Act 1984, which covers
  - confidentiality of information
  - access to information.

Professional training

Confidence in handling ethical issues usually comes through experience. However, professional training can help health and social care practitioners to:
- learn new skills in analysing and handling ethical issues
- reinforce their knowledge and understanding
- gain a wider perspective on ethical issues
- find out about professional codes of practice.

Initial professional training (before starting work) should give trainee health and social care practitioners an opportunity to explore ethical issues and learn the ground rules of handling ethical dilemmas. Continuing professional training should then support the practitioner's development of skills and understanding as they handle ethical issues in practice. Training may also be needed to explain and share ethical policies and procedures within an organisation.

At particular points in their careers, health and social care practitioners may need professional support to help them cope with the consequences of ethical dilemmas. Putting a major decision into practice – for example, switching off a coma patient's ventilator – can have a profound effect on the nurses and doctors who have been caring for the patient. In these situations they are given supervision, support and care to help them cope. Supervision is usually provided by an experienced member of staff, such as a doctor, nursing sister, hospital consultant, or care team leader.

Codes of practice

Codes of practice are issued by professional bodies to give health and social care practitioners guidelines for making ethical decisions. The idea of the

Talk to a health and social care practitioner to find out whether they have received any professional training on how to handle ethical issues and dilemmas. If they have, what did it cover? How useful was it in practice? If they haven't, what training would be useful?

modern code of practice is founded on the Hippocratic Oath – the traditional ethical code for doctors, which dates back to ancient Greece (although not taken by doctors today). The following version – known as the Declaration of Geneva – was drawn up by the World Medical Association in 1948, and then updated in 1968.

At the time of being admitted a member of the medical profession:

I solemnly pledge myself to consecrate my life to the service of humanity;

I will give my teachers the respect and gratitude which is their due;

I will practise my profession with conscience and dignity;

The health of my patient will be my first consideration;

I will respect the secrets which are confided in me, even after the patient has died;

I will maintain by all the means in my power, the honour and the noble traditions of the medical profession;

My colleagues will be my brothers;

I will not permit considerations of religion, nationality, race, party politics or social standing to intervene between my duty and my patient;

I will maintain the utmost respect for human life from the time of conception; even under threat I will not use my medical knowledge contrary to the laws of humanity.

I make these promises solemnly, freely and upon my honour.

ACTIVITY

Carry out research to find out more about modern codes of practice, such as those issued to nurses, social workers and residential homes. Choose one code, and compare it to the Declaration of Geneva for doctors. Summarise the different ethical issues covered by each code, and decide which you think would be more useful to health and social care practitioners.

ACTIVITY

During the next fortnight, collect as many reports as you can on health and social care cases involving ethical dilemmas. Look in newspapers, magazines and specialist journals, as well as watching out for news items on television and radio. At the end of the fortnight, compile a scrapbook on the different cases you have found, and choose one to focus on in more detail.

Write a short report on the case you have chosen, analysing the way the ethical dilemma was handled.

Analysing different approaches

To evaluate the success of different approaches to handling ethical issues and dilemmas, it is useful to stand back and analyse particular cases. This can help health and social care organisations to:

- assess how well policies and practices are working, and decide whether they need updating
- confront any complaints or allegations of mistakes
- identify where improvements could be made.

66 *There was a case last year with the very difficult death of someone's partner. During the bereavement follow-up it became clear that the surviving partner wanted to make a formal complaint about the patient's treatment. It also became clear that it was hoped by some staff that counselling would persuade him not to do so. But counselling isn't about calming situations down, or putting things right. It is about the patient exploring what is going on. During counselling he looked at what he had to gain and what he would lose emotionally if he went ahead. He came to the conclusion that it would help him to vent his feelings and he went ahead. It was his decision.* 99

head of medical counselling and family support

See also element 6.2, which looks at the ethical dilemmas which may arise when restricting the liberty of individuals.

Key questions

1 What are ethical issues?
2 When assessing the risks of taking a particular course of action, who do health and social care practitioners need to consider?
3 Name two pieces of legislation which establish service users' rights to look at information.
4 Give five of the main points made by the Data Protection Act 1984.
5 Explain some of the ways in which health and social care practitioners can empower service users.
6 Whose views should be considered when agreeing the best interests of service users?
7 What is 'health rationing'?
8 What are the main advantages of discussing ethical dilemmas?
9 Name three representative bodies which give health and social care practitioners advice on ethical issues.
10 What is the Value Base of Care Practice? What are the five main areas it covers?
11 List six pieces of government legislation which relate to ethical issues. Which issues do they cover?
12 List four factors you would consider when analysing examples of handling ethical issues and dilemmas.

Assignment

Prepare a presentation on two ethical dilemmas faced by health and social care practitioners. You may decide to collect information by interviewing practitioners or researching media reports and case studies. Consider whether it would be helpful to supplement your presentation by carrying out a survey of the general public's views on the issues you choose.

Your final presentation should be in four parts:
- an introduction – explaining the responsibilities placed on health and social care practitioners
- an overview of ethical issues and dilemmas – explaining what they are and giving examples of those faced by health and social care practitioners
- a detailed analysis of how your two chosen ethical issues were handled
- a suggestion of other ways the ethical issues could have been handled.

Make your presentation as clear and interesting as possible by using relevant visual images.

UNIT **2**

Element 2.1
Exploring interpersonal interaction

Element 2.2
Skills for interpersonal interaction

Element 2.3
Interacting with service users

Interpersonal interaction in health and social care

This unit is about the interpersonal skills needed for effective interactions in health and social care settings. You may find it helpful to look at unit 5 as well, especially element 5.3, which explains how health and social care is organised and the impact of the structure and organisation on the sector as a whole.

ELEMENT **2.1**

Exploring interpersonal interaction

In this element you will look at various forms of interpersonal interaction and gain an awareness of the importance of effective interactions.

66 *There has to be constant communication, so parents know exactly what is going on during the day. If people are working all day they must be reassured that their children are in the best of care. They also often feel guilty about leaving them. We aim to help them get over this, not only because it is worrying for the parents but also because the anxiety can communicate itself to the children.* **99**

head of private day nursery and childcare centre

66 *The counselling sessions provide a time and place for people to express their feelings in a safe environment. It's known as 'sustaining containment', because the boundaries of the set time (50 minutes, with ten minutes at the end to prepare to face the world again) and place (a room with a closed door and privacy) give people the support and structure they need to let off steam safely. They know it's their time. I'm not here to make them feel 'at ease'. It's not an 'easy' situation: they are trying to face up to very difficult events. While it can be very painful emotionally it can often be a very helpful experience.* **99**

head of medical counselling and family support

66 *I always check that I am clear about what a patient wants and that the patient has understood me. I do this by checking and summarising what the patient has said. I reassure patients that I am listening and have understood by echoing what they say. I also use touch, being very careful not to invade someone's personal space. I use it to gain someone's attention on a busy ward and to offer comfort. Touch can be useful with people with sight or hearing difficulties, but it should be used sensitively. These techniques may sound simple but they can make a huge difference in the quality of the exchange.* **99**

occupational therapy services manager

Forms of interpersonal interaction

Interpersonal interaction – communication between people – is the key to effective health and social care. Without good communication, health and social care practitioners will not understand service users' beliefs and preferences, and service users may not understand their individual rights and choices. In some cases, communication breakdowns can even result in people not getting the support they need and being put at risk.

The importance of good communication is recognised by the Care Sector Consortium's Value Base of Care Practice, which places emphasis on supporting service users through effective communication. It sees communication as central to promoting equality, helping care practitioners to learn about and understand other people. In line with this, the Value Base states that care practitioners should:

- recognise and overcome barriers to effective communication
- adapt the way they communicate to meet the needs of individuals
- develop good listening skills
- recognise the importance of body language (non-verbal communication).

As the Value Base suggests, one of the key factors in effective interpersonal interaction is recognising different forms of communication and using them appropriately. These different forms include:

- language – this may be spoken (such as English, Japanese or Urdu), a signed language (such as British sign language) or communication through technology (such as hearing aids and computers)
- sensory contact – any communication through the senses (seeing, hearing, smelling, touching)
- body position – including gestures, facial expressions, postures and distance from other people
- activities – interaction based on sharing activities like art and craft, sport, music and drama.

Language

People have been communicating with one another through language for about 30,000 years. When communicating through language, people use words, or signs, to express feelings, facts, beliefs, instructions, ideas or questions. In health and social care situations, conversation gives service users an opportunity to talk about their needs, concerns and attitudes. But to achieve this, the service user and practitioner must be speaking the same language.

Health and social care practitioners need to be aware of service users' different language needs, and enable them to use their first language whenever possible. This might be through:

- using an interpreter when working with someone whose first language is not English
- being aware when someone hard of hearing is lip reading, and making sure that they face the person and form words clearly

DISCUSSION POINT

Think of:

- one occasion when you had a positive encounter with someone, and came away feeling satisfied
- one occasion when you have had a negative encounter with someone, and came away feeling dissatisfied.

Do you think the quality of communication affected your feelings about the encounter?

Speaking and listening are often known as **verbal communication**.

Body position, touching and eye contact are often known as **non-verbal communication** or **body language**.

- signing, or using a signed language interpreter, with someone who is deaf or hard of hearing
- using low-tech communication systems, such as hearing aids, or an induction loop to relay sound in a lecture hall to an individual's hearing aid
- using high-tech communication systems – such as computerised control systems and electronic boards – to communicate with people who have severe disabilities.

Even if people are speaking the same language, jargon and technical terms can be barriers to communication. Health and social care practitioners need to make sure that they use words people will understand, and pitch their conversation at a level which meets an individual's needs.

ACTIVITY

Carry out an investigation into communication aids used by people with disabilities (you will probably find sales catalogues helpful). Produce a chart summarising the different aids available, who uses them, and factors that health and social care practitioners should be aware of when communicating with people using the aids.

ACTIVITY

Working in pairs, try modifying how you speak to express different emotions through the following phrases.

66 *Don't worry about me, I'm fine.* 99

66 *Can I go home now?* 99

Try saying each phrase in a way which expresses sadness, anxiety, happiness and anger. You might find it helpful to record your speech on audio or video tape. Analyse and make notes on how you use tone, volume, emphasis, speed, pitch and pauses to express particular emotions. If you have video you can also examine gestures and facial expressions.

Feelings and emotions are not only expressed by the words people say, but also by the way that they say them. This is called 'paralanguage', and includes:

- tone of voice (for example, harsh, bright)
- volume
- pitch (high or low)
- speed of speech
- emphasis of particular words
- pauses in speech
- gestures
- facial expression.

For example, a person speaking slowly, quietly and in a flat tone, with downturned eyes, gives the impression of being sad or depressed, whereas someone speaking quickly, loudly and with a wide variation in tone, accompanied by quick hand or arm movements, gives the impression of being happy and excited, or perhaps nervous.

Sensory contact

Sensory contact refers to any form of communication which involves the senses of hearing, seeing, smelling and touching. The activity most closely related to speech is hearing – or, more importantly, listening.

Good conversation depends on listening as much as talking. Unless people are deaf or hard of hearing, they can hear what other people say to them, but they may not listen. Although they may be registering sounds, they may not be thinking about what is being said and making an effort to understand it.

In the game Chinese Whispers messages are transformed as they are passed from person to person. It shows how easy it is for listeners to place their own interpretation on information they hear. A good listener:

■ makes eye contact with the speaker
■ lets the other person speak, and doesn't interrupt
■ hears the words the speaker says
■ concentrates on understanding them
■ encourages the speaker to continue, by nodding and giving encouraging signs, such as 'uh-huh' and 'yes, I know' at appropriate places
■ responds in an appropriate way.

Active listening is an important skill for health and social care practitioners. However well a health and social care practitioner can talk, if they can't listen well and understand what their clients are saying, they won't be good communicators.

Although the most obvious form of communication is through language, it has been estimated that up to 80% of interpersonal interaction takes place through non-verbal communication (not using words).

In sensory contact, important forms of non-verbal communication are:

■ eye contact
■ touch
■ presence.

People's eyes can express, or betray, a wide range of emotions – from wide-eyed fear or excitement, to dilated pupils and a long gaze showing attraction. Before beginning a conversation, people usually make eye contact as a signal that they are ready to speak or listen. Once a conversation is underway, regular glances lasting several seconds show interest and friendliness. Avoiding eye contact can show boredom or dislike, while staring at a person continually can make them uncomfortable.

DISCUSSION POINT

Think of someone you know who is a good listener. Can you recognise these characteristics in them? What makes a bad listener?

ACTIVITY

Work in pairs. Take it in turns to talk informally for 30 seconds to each other on any subject you like. The first time you observe your partner speak, gaze at them constantly. The second time, don't make any eye contact at all. Finally, while they are speaking for the third time, glance at them for a few seconds at a time, at regular intervals. Then swap roles.

How do you feel, as speaker and listener, in each of these circumstances? Which type of eye contact improves communication? Which makes communication most difficult?

People also communicate by touch and presence (how close they stand to each other). Practitioners can use touch as a way of showing warmth and understanding – children and people who are frail or vulnerable may particularly welcome the comfort of an arm around their shoulder or a squeeze of the hand.

However, although physical closeness can be reassuring and convey support and care, to some people it may seem intrusive and patronising. Practitioners need to be sensitive to different people's feelings; it can be helpful to gauge how someone reacts to a touch on the arm before giving them a hug. In addition, they have to be careful that physical contact is not misinterpreted, particularly if they are alone with service users.

In many cases, practitioners need to touch people in the course of caring for them. This may be when giving a medical examination, helping someone with tasks such as washing or dressing, or providing health care. In these situations, practitioners should explain what they are doing and treat people in a gentle, respectful way.

Body position

The way people position and move their body when interacting with others can give clear signals about how they are feeling – even if they're not aware of it!

So how do people communicate with their bodies?

DISCUSSION POINT

How do you react when you're not comfortable about someone touching you? What signs do you think health and social care workers should look for in order to assess whether people find touch comforting or intrusive?

ACTIVITY

Watch a video of a television debate or discussion, and make notes on people's use of:

- language (use of words when speaking)
- tone, pitch, volume of speech
- listening skills
- touch
- physical closeness to one another
- eye contact
- posture
- mirroring.

What do these show you about the people involved in the debate, and their relationships with each other?

Body language takes place through:

- gestures – such as shrugging, waving, nodding or shaking the head, giving a thumbs-up sign
- facial expressions – movement of the eyes, nose, mouth and brow can show every emotion from fear and grief to happiness and surprise
- posture – the way a person stands or sits; if someone has their arms folded and their legs crossed, they are said to be in a closed position (unwelcoming and defensive); if a person's hands are relaxed by their sides or in their laps, their legs are unfolded and they are leaning forward slightly, they are said to be in an open position (friendly and welcoming)
- body position – an upright body with clenched fists may suggest anger or nervousness; a slumped body with drooping head may suggest sadness
- body position in relation to others – sitting close to someone can suggest intimacy and affection.

If people are comfortable with each other and communicating well, they often copy each other's body language. This is called mirroring, and helps to create rapport. Practitioners may find that mirroring a service user's body positions – for example, tilting their head or positioning their legs the same way –

improves communication. However, it is important to draw the line between mirroring and mimicking – if someone thinks they are being made fun of, it is unlikely to have a good effect on their relationship!

Activity-based interaction

Taking part in activities often helps people to interact with each other in a natural, relaxed context. Activities such as art and craft, exercise and music can all be carried out by health and social care practitioners and service users, providing an opportunity to establish better relationships and understanding through shared experience.

An art therapist explains how she uses drama to help people interact:

66 *Drama can be an excellent context for carers and service users to work together in a relaxed, positive social context. We offer drama sessions to people with a range of emotional and physical needs, tailoring provision to meet their particular requirements. Sessions usually begin with relaxation exercises and games, which give everyone a chance to get to know one another and get comfortable. Then we suggest a variety of improvisations, roleplays and written pieces for groups to try. Improvisations and roleplays can be a particularly good way for people to express themselves and confront problems and concerns in their lives. Acting ability is not in the least important! What we're looking for is to encourage people to communicate through their words and bodies, and to work well together. At the end of the day, the reward comes from seeing people develop self-confidence, make new friends and build their social skills.* 99

DISCUSSION POINT

Think of occasions when you have taken part in activities with other people, such as sport, drama or music. Did you find this a good way of forming relationships and communicating with people? Why?

The influences of interaction on health and social wellbeing

Human beings are social creatures. People learn in groups, play with friends, live in families and work with colleagues. Most depend on interacting with others, and find living alone or being isolated from society depressing and disturbing.

Yet interacting with other people can be both positive and negative – people don't automatically come away feeling satisfied and happy.

Positive influences of interaction

From the moment they are born, children learn and develop through interacting with other people. They are given a sense of security through hugs and physical closeness, copy their parents' smiles and language, and mimic the behaviour of their brothers and sisters. As they grow up, teachers, family, friends, the media and many other people communicate information and ideas to them which shape their own beliefs and preferences.

Taken together, these different types of interaction help to create every child's unique character.

By the time they reach adolescence, most people like to feel that they are independent and can cope on their own – but in fact they still rely on interaction with a large network of family and friends throughout adulthood, to:

- make them feel cared for
- give them a sense of belonging to a group
- give them a feeling of value.

Mrs Hargreaves, an 86-year-old woman, explains how she misses the positive effects of interacting with other people:

66 *When I was younger, I had lots of friends. I came from a large family, my husband and I had two children of our own, and our house was always full of people laughing, talking and joking. I loved being around people, sharing stories and secrets, helping them out in the bad times and enjoying the good times. I was always the life and soul, and knew I was important to people. And I knew that someone was there for me if I needed help.*

Today my life's very different. My husband, brothers and sisters, and almost all my friends, have died. My children are living abroad, and I'm left living alone and feeling very isolated. It's funny, but without people to talk to you start thinking you're going mad. I get myself into a state over the silliest things, like the radiators making a funny noise, just because I haven't got anyone to talk to about it. When I get a cold it seems to drag on and on – it's almost as if there's no point in getting better. I can't stand feeling I'm of no use to anyone. When I think how confident and happy I used to be, it's hard to believe I'm the same person. 99

Negative influences of interaction

However, interaction with other people can also have a negative effect on an individual's health and social wellbeing.

If an individual is forced to interact with people who make them feel uncomfortable, or to join in with a group in which they feel they don't belong, this can increase their feeling of loneliness. Failing to succeed in interaction tends to make people feel inadequate, which in turn can lower their self-esteem, and in the long term lead to depression and loss of self-worth.

Interaction can also have a negative influence if people don't understand an individual's needs and feelings, and say things which upset or threaten them. Health and social care practitioners must be particularly aware of this, as many service users may feel vulnerable and react badly to insensitive communication.

ACTIVITY

Read through the following conversation between Moira, a family care practitioner, and Emma, a young mother who is struggling to cope with her baby.

Moira: *Hi, Emma. How are you feeling today? And how's this little one? (picking up the baby, who is crying)*

Emma: *Not too great actually. She won't stop crying and I just can't cope with her. Sometimes I have to walk out of the room because I'm afraid what I might do.*

Moira: *Look, we all feel like that sometimes. I know I did when my Darren was born and he was a real terror. Don't worry. We were fine in the end.*

Emma: *But I'm really worried we won't be.*

Moira: *Now don't get all upset, it's not going to help the baby, is it? Look, she's quietening down already with me. She's a lovely little thing. Have you been to the mother and baby group again?*

Emma: *No, it's not for me. They were really cliquey and all seemed to be such perfect mothers it made me feel even worse.*

Moira: *I'm sure it's in your imagination. You've really got to make the effort, you know. This should be the most wonderful time of your life.*

By the end of this conversation, Emma felt more miserable and inadequate than she had before Moira arrived. In small groups, discuss why you think this is. What did Moira say and do that upset Emma? Talk about what you think she should have said and done to have a more positive effect.

The effects of sex, age and culture

Although everyone interacts using verbal and non-verbal communication, sex, age and culture can create major differences in the way they do this.

The most obvious difference is in language – every culture has its own language or dialect, which immediately creates communication barriers between people of different cultural backgrounds. Even within the same culture, young and old often have their own words and ways of describing things.

ACTIVITY

Carry out an investigation to find out how your language has changed from generation to generation. Make a list of words you, your parents and an elderly person would use to describe:

■ something which is very good

■ something which is very bad

■ someone who is fashionable.

Could any of the different words cause confusion? Does the elderly person understand you if you use the words from your list? Do you understand all the words the elderly person would use?

As well as recognising these language differences, health and social care practitioners need to be aware of the way sex, age and culture can affect:

■ use of sensory contact (touch, eye contact)

■ distance between individuals (personal space)

■ body language

■ accepted forms of respect (ways of greeting and treating people)

■ what people are interested in

■ the way people like to communicate

■ personal strengths.

It is very easy for people to assume that their way of interacting is right, and to misinterpret other people's feelings and wishes by not being sensitive to their behaviour.

Use of sensory contact

Different cultures use sensory contact – such as eye contact and touch – in very different ways. In northern Europe people are taught that it is rude to stare, whereas in southern Europe it is considered polite to gaze (a sign of honesty). Many British people are disconcerted by the practice in other parts of Europe of greeting men and women by kissing on both cheeks, shying away from such close contact. In different parts of France there are strict rituals of kissing a certain number of times on each cheek, and getting it wrong can be taken as an insult.

Practitioners need to be aware of these types of differences, and take them into account before:

■ making assumptions about someone's feelings from their behaviour

■ using sensory contact to communicate.

DISCUSSION POINT

Within your group, are there any differences in attitude to sensory contact as a result of culture? Talk about the difference that your sex makes to what you consider acceptable sensory contact. How do you think older and younger people feel?

How large do you think your personal space is? Have a conversation with someone of the same sex, then someone of the opposite sex, and ask them to move slowly closer to you. When do you start feeling uncomfortable? How do you react? Is there a difference depending on the sex of the person you are talking to?

What steps can practitioners take to respect people's personal space?

Distance between individuals

Everybody has their own personal space – a distance they like to keep from other people. In the same way as sensory contact, personal space varies in different cultures. For example, in Western countries people tend to keep a fairly long way away from each other when talking, whereas in Arab countries they stand much closer. This can seem intimidating and annoying to Westerners.

Body language

Body language is constantly evolving, and as with other forms of non-verbal communication health and social care practitioners need to be aware of differences between cultures and age groups.

People in the UK use a fairly limited range of gestures compared to some cultures. Those that are used – such as nodding or shaking the head, or giving a thumbs-up sign – may mean something different to people from other cultures. Health and social care practitioners need to be particularly careful if the meaning of gestures can't be reinforced by a shared verbal language.

Body language is particularly important when interacting with young children, who can't rely on spoken language. Often children use gestures and facial expressions with less inhibition than adults, and are able to express their feelings more freely through body language. Health and social care practitioners need to be aware of this when watching a child's body language, and when using non-verbal communication themselves.

Watch people talking to each other in a natural situation – perhaps your family having a meal, or people having a drink in a pub. Focus on three people of different ages and sexes, and make notes on the way they use body language.

What differences do you observe? Check your findings by carrying out a more general observation of people you see every day. Do you think sex and age make a difference to people's use of body language?

Accepted forms of respect

Everybody likes to feel that their views and individuality are acknowledged and considered important. If practitioners show respect for their clients, this can be a major step towards good communication.

Jamie, a community nurse, describes how he tries to show patients that he respects them as individuals:

66 *I have many patients that I visit regularly, and I need to establish good relationships with them based on mutual respect. When I was training, I learnt an important lesson about respect for patients. I was examining an elderly*

woman, and without thinking called her by her first name, 'Daisy' I think it was. The woman gave me a dirty look, said 'Miss Carter to you', and I never managed to establish rapport with her. In fact, I felt she never trusted me. Now when I see a new patient, I always check what they like to be called, and make a note of it in their file. If they have a name which is difficult to pronounce, I spell it out phonetically in my notes and check how to say it before I go to visit them. It may sound petty, but it really does make all the difference. I know some colleagues who refer to all women clients as 'dear'. Not very respectful, and certainly lacking the personal touch! **99**

Items of interest

People of different ages and backgrounds are interested in different subjects. Noting and using these subjects as a starting point for conversation can help health and social care workers establish good relationships with service users.

Here is Jamie again:

66 *Everybody has their own interests and concerns, which vary according to their age, sex, family life and culture. It's no good talking to most elderly people about the latest computer game, but this can be an excellent way to establish rapport with a child. In the same way, if I remember that one of my elderly client's granddaughters was getting married and ask how the wedding went, they're likely to open up and chat to me straight away. It's always important to remember cultural differences such as religious practice and diet, and not to say anything which might offend or be misunderstood.* **99**

ACTIVITY

How good are you at observing forms of respect and people's interests? Think of two people you know slightly, perhaps a neighbour, or a younger student. One should be male and one female, and they should be in different age groups (for example, a young boy and an elderly woman). Write down:

■ what you think they like to be called (Are you sure about this? Should you check?)

■ subjects you know they are interested in, and which you think would be a good way to start communicating with them.

Next time you meet them, make an active effort to use accepted forms of respect and talk about items of interest. Does this make it easier to start a conversation with them? Why do you think this is a useful skill for health and social care practitioners to develop?

Preferred form of interaction

It is much harder for communication to succeed if one of the participants is uncomfortable with the form of interaction – for example, the language or

What would you need to consider when communicating with the following people for the first time? How would you go about establishing their preferred form of interaction?

- an elderly man who is hard of hearing but refuses to wear a hearing aid

- a family (mother, father and two children) who have recently arrived in the UK from India

- an adolescent girl with severe physical disabilities which prevent her communicating in spoken language.

body language – being used. Health and social care practitioners must be aware of this, and use service users' preferred form of interaction whenever possible.

If there is any doubt about how someone would like to communicate – for example, if English isn't their first language or if they are hard of hearing – the practitioner must ask. Making assumptions about someone's preferred form of communication can be patronising and insulting.

An Italian man who was in hospital for an operation explains:

66 *The nursing staff assumed that because I was Italian I would rather speak Italian, and kept sending Italian-speaking nurses to come and talk to me. The issue reached a head when a doctor came to examine me, and brought an Italian-speaking colleague to act as interpreter! I explained politely, but firmly, that I have lived in this country for five years, and that I understand, and would like to speak, English. I know they were only trying to be helpful, but they should have asked me first.* **99**

Personal strengths

Every individual has their own personal strengths and weaknesses. Some people react positively to, and cope well with, problems and illness; others quickly become depressed and unable to cope. Some may appear strong and cheerful, but are actually struggling in private.

Health and social care practitioners must be sensitive to the personality of every service user, and adapt their behaviour accordingly. This means recognising and reacting to people's individual needs and feelings when giving information and confronting emotional issues. Sometimes someone's personal strengths depend on their age – a doctor wouldn't usually give the same facts to a child with a terminal illness as they would to a middle-aged person. However, the key point is to remember that everybody – regardless of age, sex and culture – must be responded to as a unique individual.

How would you expect the following people to cope with serious illness:

- a ten-year-old boy?

- a successful 40-year-old businessman?

- a frail 88-year-old woman?

Then think of individuals you know who fall into these 'types'. How do you think they would react? Do you think health and social care practitioners can expect particular groups of people to have particular personal strengths?

Factors which affect interpersonal interaction

Every interaction between people involves a unique set of circumstances:

- different individuals
- in a particular place
- at a particular time
- with their own thoughts, feelings, interests, needs and concerns.

This combination of circumstances can either result in positive, productive interaction, or lead to communication breakdowns.

The factors you have identified can be divided into two types:

- **enhancers** – which improve the quality of interpersonal interaction
- **inhibitors** – which worsen the quality of interpersonal interaction.

DISCUSSION POINT

What factors affect how well, or how badly, you get on with someone when you meet them for the first time?

Enhancers

Being aware of factors that improve communication can help health and social care practitioners forge good relationships with service users.

A counsellor explains how he aims to enhance interaction with the people he meets:

66 *When people visit me, they are often nervous, embarrassed, angry or upset. I need to make sure I create a good atmosphere for them to talk in, putting them at ease and encouraging them to communicate. One of the first steps is to get the environment right – a warm room, comfy chairs, good lighting, no disruptive noise or disturbances, cups of coffee. I don't want to be seen as a figure of authority, so I try to sit alongside someone, rather than looking down on them from the other side of a desk. If I'm in my own office, I put the phone on divert and tell the receptionist only to interrupt me in an emergency.*

It's important to establish a good rapport with people – they have to like you if they're going to talk to you freely. If it's the first time I've met someone, we have a general chat so I can get to know them and their interests. Then the next time I meet them, I pick up on some of these points to show that I'm interested in them as a person and put them at ease. It can be helpful if we share a common interest – I've got one client who supports the same football team as my son, and we always begin with a quick discussion of Saturday's game.

During our conversation I listen carefully and try to increase their confidence in me as a listener, and in themselves as individuals with something valid to say. They will only speak to me openly if they feel I am paying attention and not sitting in judgement. 99

ACTIVITY

List the different factors which the counsellor finds enhance interaction with service users. From your own experience as a speaker and listener, can you add to this list?

Inhibitors

A range of factors – many of which can be avoided with consideration and planning – can inhibit interaction between health and social care practitioners and service users.

Environmental factors

A bleak, bare room containing technical books and equipment can be intimidating. People find it hard to relax and concentrate on the conversation if they are uncomfortable, too hot or cold, or blinded by a glaring light. Background noise – for example drilling or a banging window – can be particularly annoying.

Interruptions

A telephone call or someone else coming into the room in the middle of a conversation can make a client feel rejected, and cause a communication breakdown.

Social and cultural factors

Social and cultural differences can create language barriers, ranging from the service user and practitioner having different first languages, to problems with slang and dialect. Medical practitioners in particular must avoid using jargon and technical terms, as these can inhibit interaction.

Interpersonal factors

Practitioners must avoid stereotyping, and should treat and respect every service user as an individual. Communication is only effective if there is mutual respect and if the service user has the self-confidence to speak freely.

Psychological, physical and social problems

Service users who are anxious or distressed are unlikely to communicate well. Similarly, health and social care practitioners who are under stress find it hard to listen and respond constructively.

Body language

Without the right non-verbal communication, interaction is unlikely to succeed. If practitioners express boredom or lack of understanding through their body language, service users will pick up on these feelings and become angry, frustrated or silent. One yawn can end a conversation!

ACTIVITY

Interview a practitioner about the factors they think contribute to:

- good communication with service users
- communication breakdowns.

How do they try to enhance interpersonal interaction in their work?

Optimising effective interaction

As well as considering factors which enhance and inhibit communication, practitioners should be aware of how they can optimise interaction.

Optimising interaction means making the best of a meeting or conversation. Every time a practitioner meets a service user, they have an opportunity to:

- establish mutual trust and respect
- give and receive information
- give advice
- provide practical support.

So how can a practitioner make the most of these opportunities?

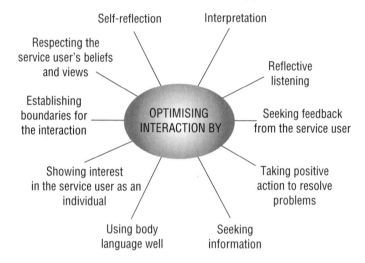

Respect for others' beliefs and views

Few people share exactly the same beliefs and views. Many health and social care practitioners meet and interact with service users from diverse age groups, cultures and backgrounds in the course of their work.

DISCUSSION POINT

People working in health and social care often have to care for people with conditions which are caused by their lifestyle (for example, smoking, or eating fatty foods). How easy do you think it would be to respect their views?

To optimise interaction with this wide range of people, practitioners must respect their beliefs and views as individuals. This involves:

- avoiding stereotyping because of age, sex or culture
- not passing judgement on the way people live
- not trying to impose their own views.

Only if people feel that their individual rights and values are respected will they develop the confidence to express themselves and make choices.

Establishing boundaries

People feel uneasy and tense when they don't know what to expect from a situation. Have you ever sat clock-watching, wondering when something will come to an end? Or sat in a lesson hoping that you're not going to be picked on? In both situations you probably felt uncomfortable, and didn't contribute well.

So that service users can relax and communicate freely, health and social care practitioners need to establish boundaries at the start of the interaction. These might include:

■ how long a meeting or interview will last
■ an explanation of confidentiality – what the service user can trust the practitioner not to disclose, and what might have to be shared with colleagues
■ a summary of the areas to be covered
■ an evaluation, at the end of the interaction, of what has been achieved
■ arrangements for the next meeting or interview (date, time, place).

Showing interest in the individual

Most people find it difficult to continue a conversation if the person they are talking to looks bored or uninterested. This is often particularly true of health and social care service users, who may lack self-confidence and need reassurance. To optimise interaction, practitioners must make a conscious effort to show interest in service users as individuals. This means establishing a rapport by:

■ remembering their name, likes and dislikes, and what they are interested in
■ listening carefully
■ asking relevant questions and not changing the subject abruptly
■ sharing personal information when it would be useful
■ using body language well – making eye contact, smiling, leaning forward, mirroring the client's body position and gestures.

ACTIVITY

Most of us know the feeling of talking to someone who isn't listening. Next time this happens to you, keep the 'conversation' going, and try to analyse how you know that the other person isn't interested in what you're saying.

Make notes on your observations.

Using body language

As already suggested, good body language can go a long way to optimising interaction in health and social care, particularly with people who have difficulties with verbal communication.

Practitioners need to be aware of their body language from the outset of interaction, greeting service users with a smile, eye contact and welcoming gestures. Once a conversation is under way, they should show:

- interest through eye contact
- emotion and friendliness in their facial expressions
- closeness through their body position in relation to the other person's
- empathy by mirroring the other person's gestures and body position
- openness by leaning forward slightly, with arms and legs unfolded
- calmness through relaxed muscles and posture.

Seeking information

Interaction involves practitioners gathering information from:

- service users
- other people, including colleagues, and the service user's family, friends and carers.

To do this, they need to develop skills in asking questions. There are five main types of question, all of which most people use automatically in the course of a conversation.

Type of question	What is it? When is it used?	Examples
Closed question	Can be answered in one or two words, often Yes or No. Useful for collecting factual information quickly.	■ Do you take sugar? ■ How old are you? ■ Can you make an appointment next Friday at 3?
Open question	Encourages a longer answer, giving an opportunity to explore detail. Useful for collecting information about feelings and emotions. Open questions usually begin with How . . . ?, What . . . ?, Why . . . ?, Where . . . ?, When . . . ?	■ How do you manage to make a cup of tea? ■ What are your views on that? ■ Why don't you want to move into sheltered accommodation?
Probe	Develops the response to another question. Useful for collecting more detail on a subject.	■ Open question: How are you feeling at the moment? ■ Response: I've got an awful headache, and I'm not coping too well with John. ■ Probe: How has John been the last week or so?
Prompt	Useful for collecting more information on a subject and keeping someone talking.	■ Open question: How are you feeling at the moment? ■ Response: I'm having a bad day today. Actually I'm feeling quite depressed. ■ Prompt: So you're feeling down at the moment?
Leading question	Gives help with the expected answer. Can be useful if a client is shy or lacks confidence.	■ You probably find it hard to get upstairs now, do you? ■ Its getting late – perhaps you'd like to stop now and come back next week?

At the start of a conversation and on first meeting a service user, a practitioner may use closed questions to collect factual information quickly. As closed questions are usually easy to answer, they can help to put people at ease.

Once the interaction is under way, open questions, probes and prompts can be used to encourage someone to express their feelings and expand on particular subjects. Used sensitively, they show that the practitioner is listening to the client and interested in what they are saying. Leading questions can be particularly helpful if someone is distressed or lacks self-esteem.

ACTIVITY

John, a social worker, used a range of questions to find out information from Mr Emberton, an elderly man who lives in sheltered accommodation. Write a conversation between the two men, based on John asking the following set of questions:

- *It's Mr Emberton, isn't it?*
- *How long have you lived here?*
- *And have you enjoyed your time here?*
- *Why has the last year been difficult?*
- *Perhaps you need more help with cooking and cleaning?*
- *What type of jobs would you like a home help to do?*
- *Well, I'll get in touch with the social services. Would you like another cup of coffee?*

Once you have written a conversation involving these questions, decide whether John is using each as an open question, a closed question, a probe, a prompt, or a leading question. (You may find that some could be categorised as more than one of these.)

Taking positive action

Sometimes a health and social care practitioner needs to take positive action to optimise interaction with a service user.

Joanna, a physiotherapist, explains:

66 *I work in the community, visiting people to give physiotherapy in their own homes. I try to make every encounter as worthwhile as possible, and to maintain a good relationship with all my patients. Often I need to take positive steps to optimise interaction, such as suggesting we move to a quieter room if there's a TV on in the background, or moving some comfortable chairs in from another room. Sometimes I have to make a conscious effort to avoid stereotyping and imposing my set of values and beliefs on people. If I walk into a home which seems dirty and uncared for, I remind myself to approach the person as an individual whose choices and way of living are as valid as my own.* **99**

Seeking feedback

Feedback is a response to what someone says. Giving and seeking feedback optimises interaction by showing that the listener is listening to, and has understood, what the speaker says.

When talking to service users, health and social care practitioners will both:

■ give feedback to show that they are listening and have taken in what the person has said by

 – saying things like Go on and Yes, and nodding while the person is speaking

 – summarising what the person has just said

 – asking prompt and probe questions about what the person has just said

 – repeating important points (see *Reflective listening* below).

■ seek feedback to check that the person has understood by

 – observing their body language as they listen

 – asking open questions related to a subject they have just explained.

Reflective listening

Reflective listening involves the listener reflecting back what the speaker has just said by:

■ repeating some of the speaker's words

■ paraphrasing what the speaker has said (summarising an important point in their own words).

The following conversation shows a counsellor using straightforward reflection and paraphrasing to persuade someone to say more:

Counsellor: *So why haven't you been going to school recently?*

Young person: *I don't know really. It's not worth it. I'm not going to pass any exams. And I don't like any of the people in my class.*

Counsellor: *You don't like any of the people in your class?*

Young person: *No. They were all in groups before I arrived at the school, and weren't interested in letting anyone else join in. I've never really made friends, and just have to hang around on my own during breaks.*

Counsellor: *So you're quite lonely at school?*

Young person: *Yes, I suppose I am.*

As this conversation shows, using reflective listening can help a health and social care practitioner to:

■ show that they are listening, and understand what the service user is saying

■ get the person to say more on a subject (in this case, why the student doesn't get on with people in his class)

■ help the person to understand their own feelings by reflecting them back ('So you're quite lonely at school?') – this may be the first time that the student has actually realised this.

ACTIVITY

Working in pairs, talk to each other for five minutes about what you did at the weekend. When you are listening to what your partner is saying, use the techniques of giving feedback and reflective listening. When you are speaking, seek feedback to make sure the listener has understood what you are saying. If possible, record your conversation on audio tape, and then play it back to analyse how you got on.

ACTIVITY

Carry out an investigation to find out the meaning of the following medical words, and write a definition that you could use to explain each term to a patient:

- thrombosis
- hyperglycaemia
- colitis
- anaemia
- osteoporosis.

Interpretation

Interpretation involves explaining the meaning of a piece of information in a way that an individual can understand. This may be necessary when:

- someone doesn't speak English as their first language (many local authorities and hospitals have lists of interpreters for health and social care practitioners to use)
- someone is deaf or hard of hearing, and needs information interpreted in sign language
- information is complex or involves a lot of specialist terms, and needs interpreting in a simple way for a member of the general public; this is particularly important for medical workers.

Self-reflection

Self-reflection involves a practitioner considering their own thoughts and feelings during an interaction. In doing this, they can:

- analyse and try to understand what they are doing
- deal with the feelings caused by working with a service user
- become more self-aware
- become more sensitive to other people
- improve their performance in the future.

Sometimes practitioners find that self-reflection with an experienced colleague or supervisor helps them to explore and learn from their experiences.

DISCUSSION POINT

Do you use self-reflection when interacting with people? Think of situations in which you might use self-reflection to help you develop your skills in interaction.

Closely linked to self-reflection is the practice of sharing information with a service user, often known as self-disclosure. Although health and social care practitioners must avoid taking over an interaction, by being open about themselves, their experiences and their feelings they can:

- encourage the service user to talk more freely
- help the service user to see them as a fellow human being, with similar needs and problems.

ACTIVITY

Watch a video of a television debate or discussion show in which the presenter has to try to optimise interaction between a number of people (for example, a studio audience or a panel of experts). Make a list of the different techniques covered in this section, and as you watch the video note down examples of how the presenter uses them.

Write a summary of your findings, including examples of each type of technique, and explain how well you think the presenter optimised interaction.

Data for evaluating interaction

As with any activity, it is important to evaluate the effectiveness of interpersonal interaction in order to:

- assess the impact of the interaction
- develop skills and techniques
- learn from mistakes
- make improvements in the future.

To carry out a focused evaluation of interaction, health and social care practitioners need:

- sources of data – information on, and responses to, an interaction
- evaluation criteria – measures against which the interaction can be judged.

Sources of data	**Evaluation criteria**
■ feedback from participants and observers	■ participation in the interaction
■ observation of the interaction	■ quality of contribution to the interaction
■ self-reflection on the interaction	■ improvements from previous occasions
■ the knowledge and understanding of participants gained as a result of the interaction	
■ tape recordings of interactions (with relevant permission)	

Feedback

Practitioners may gain feedback on an interaction from:

- the people involved in the interaction
- an observer (such as a manager or colleague), if there was one.

Feedback from service users or carers will usually be verbal. The health and social care practitioner may ask for their views on how a discussion went, what they felt they gained from the interaction, and how similar sessions could be improved in the future.

An observer may give either oral or written feedback. Assessment sheets and evaluation forms can be a good way to assess someone's performance while an interaction is taking place. This makes feedback more immediate, and often more relevant. Whether feedback is verbal or written, it should be given in a constructive, supportive way, so that practitioners can build on their skills in the future.

DISCUSSION POINT

You may have experience of evaluating your own and other people's work as part of your GNVQ or other courses. From your own experience, what are the important things to remember when giving someone else feedback on their performance? What should you avoid?

Observation

Making a video or audio recording of interaction – with the service user's permission – can be an effective way for practitioners to evaluate their own performance. Replaying and analysing a tape, either alone or with other people, provides an opportunity to focus on particular skills.

DISCUSSION POINT

Have you ever watched yourself on video, or listened to yourself on audio tape? What did it show you about the way you communicate with people?

Self-reflection

Self-reflection means reflecting on your own performance in an interaction. This can be done by:

■ watching a video
■ listening to an audio recording
■ making notes on what occurred.

The important point about self-reflection is to make it as honest as possible. It is often hard to be objective – some people tend to think they have done worse than they actually have, while others think they have done better.

DISCUSSION POINT

How could you ensure that your reflection on your own performance in an interaction was as fair and objective as possible?

Knowledge and understanding of participants

If one of the aims of a meeting or interview is to give information, the success of the interaction can be measured by checking how much participants have learnt and understood.

A community nurse involved in health promotion campaigns explains:

66 We sometimes run health awareness sessions on specific topics such as drugs, diet and fitness, which aim to promote healthy lifestyles among the general public. The sessions are designed to be fun, but also have a serious purpose of giving information and advice. To evaluate whether we have achieved this goal, we often give participants a short quiz at the end of the session to find out how much they have picked up. For participants, this is intended as a fun exercise with the chance to win a small prize. For us, it provides valuable data on whether the course has succeeded. 99

Information from all of these sources can be used as the basis of an evaluation report. A counsellor made the following notes after a group support session which she led:

GROUP MEETING, 12 MARCH

Session was recorded on video.

Participation

1) Video recording shows that everyone apart from David contributed at some point.

2) The general summary at the end, when participants talked about their achievements during the session, showed that all were concentrating and developing their knowledge and understanding.

Quality of contribution

1) During the meeting, I noted that Emma, John and Ruth contributed particularly well.

2) After the session, two participants approached me to say they had appreciated the detail of my introduction, but would have liked another factual input at a later stage.

3) Video recording shows that my body language deteriorated as the session progressed and I got tired. Must make an effort to improve this in the future.

Improvements from previous occasions

1) Looking back over records of previous meetings, levels of participation were much improved.

2) Feedback from participants suggests that this was a more productive session than in the past, and they appreciated coming away with some positive action points.

3) My feeling during the meeting was that there was a better general atmosphere on the whole, participants seemed more relaxed and open.

4) My role in leading the meeting was more clearly defined than in the past. I structured the session more tightly, and took a firmer lead in guiding the conversation. This approach seemed to work better (this has been supported by feedback from participants).

ACTIVITY

Organise a class discussion on a topic relevant to health and social care, such as the handling of the BSE scare, or the allocation of resources in the National Health Service or social services.

Before the discussion, plan the different sources of data you can use to evaluate the interaction.

After the discussion, write a short report evaluating participation, the quality of contributions, and how the interaction was an improvement on previous class discussions.

Key questions

1 Describe some of the different languages people with disabilities may use as their first language.
2 What is paralanguage?
3 Give five characteristics of a good listener.
4 Give five different types of body language.
5 What is mirroring?
6 Explain activity as a form of interaction.
7 Explain two positive and two negative influences of interaction.
8 How can age affect interpersonal interaction?
9 Explain some of the ways in which non-verbal communication is different in the UK and other cultures.
10 List five factors that enhance interpersonal interaction.
11 List five factors that inhibit interpersonal interaction.
12 How can health and social care practitioners optimise interaction with their clients?
13 Describe and give examples of four different types of question which can be used to seek information.
14 What is reflective listening? Give an example.
15 Give two examples of optimising interaction by using interpretation.
16 What is self-reflection?
17 Give four sources of data that can be used to evaluate interaction.
18 Give three evaluation criteria for interaction.

Assignment

For this assignment you need to carry out a detailed analysis of interaction taking place. If possible, try to spend time watching people interacting in a health and social care environment (for example, care practitioners with residents in a residential home). If this is not possible, analyse interactions in your class or family. You will probably find it helpful to make recordings (with permission), as well as making notes.

Try to collect as much information as possible on:
- the different forms of interpersonal interaction being used
- how age, sex and culture affect interaction
- how interaction is inhibited and enhanced in different situations
- the techniques people use to optimise interaction
- positive and negative influences of interaction on people (you need two examples of each).

Use this information as the basis of a report on interpersonal interaction.

At the end of the report, include a summary of the sources of data you could use to evaluate the interaction you observed.

> **"** When an elderly person comes here for the first time it is to look around to see if they might like to live here. All prospective residents are visited at home by the person who will be their key worker. Key workers are befrienders, really. Residents know they can go to them with any problems. **"**
>
> *project manager, residential care home for older people*

> **"** Last year we conducted a survey to assess the service we provide and ensure that the Centre was meeting the needs of our users. One of the things which emerged as being very important is the welcome they get on arrival. Before they cross that door they have made a big decision to come. I am sure that some of them get as far as the door and don't make it through. It's a big step. We do as much as we can to help them actually get into the building, by publicising our relaxed atmosphere and spelling out that it is confidential. Counsellors welcome our users warmly, and try to put them at their ease. Some of them are very withdrawn and can't cope with any eye contact to start with. The rooms are comfortable and warm. Distraction and noise is kept to a minimum. Once the young person understands there is no pressure on them, and that the counsellor is on their side and willing to listen, they can feel able to open up about what is bothering them. Often, it is a unique experience for a young person to feel they're being listened to. We aim to provide an atmosphere that will help them to communicate their needs. Sometimes they want complete privacy, but it is made clear that a friend is welcome to come with them at any time if they prefer. **"**
>
> *senior worker (counselling), young people's counselling and information service*

ELEMENT **2.2**

Skills for interpersonal interaction

In this element you will have the opportunity to apply the knowledge and understanding you gained in element 2.1 in one-to-one, small group and large group settings.

Establishing support

Effective interaction between a group of people doesn't just happen – meetings and group interactions must be managed. If ten people chosen at random were put in a room and told to talk, they probably wouldn't have a very productive conversation. They wouldn't know one another. They wouldn't know what they were supposed to talk about. There wouldn't be anybody to control the discussion. Nobody would take responsibility for making sure that people were comfortable.

To ensure that any discussion or activity is effective, participants need a range of support both before and during the interaction. It is usually the responsibility of the person organising the meeting to:

- make the environment comfortable and relaxing
- reduce stress as much as possible
- make sure that individuals' specific needs are met so that they can play a full part in the discussion.

This involves establishing participants' needs before the interaction, and being sensitive to their feelings throughout the discussion.

Before the interaction

Much of the support needed to ensure effective interaction takes place at the planning stage. Having a checklist of questions can be helpful:

- What are the aims of the interaction? What is to be discussed?
- What will participants hope to achieve?
- How many people will there be?
- Who is coming?
- Where will the meeting be held?
- Will the venue be large enough?
- Has the venue been booked?
- On what date and at what time will it be held?
- How long will the interaction last?
- Will there be enough chairs? Is a table needed?
- Will a flipchart, blackboard or overhead projector be needed?
- Will food and drink be needed?
- Do participants have any special dietary needs?
- Do participants have any other special needs (for example, wheelchair access, sign language interpreter, other language interpreter)?
- Are there adequate toilet facilities?
- Do participants know where to come, when, and how to get there?
- Do participants know what they will be discussing, and what the aims of the interaction are?

A volunteer counsellor who leads group sessions for an organisation for people with eating disorders explains why it is important to establish the support people need before the start of interaction:

66 *Careful planning is the key to good interaction. People who take part in group sessions often feel vulnerable, upset and depressed. As a result, it's vital to put them at ease right from the start by making sure that everything is exactly right. I begin planning a series of group sessions well in advance to make sure that I'm absolutely clear about what I'm trying to achieve. I find out how many people will be attending, then book a room which is big enough, but not so big that participants will feel lost. I make sure that it has comfy chairs, toilets nearby, and facilities for making tea and coffee. I also check that I'll be able to borrow any equipment I'm likely to need, such as an OHP or flipchart.*

Once I've booked the room, I write to all the participants. I introduce myself, explain how many people will be in the group and what we will try to achieve, give them an outline of what we will cover in each session, and then tell them where to be, when, and how to get there. At the bottom of the letter I include a tear-off slip for them to fill in and return to me, so I know whether they have any specific needs such as language difficulties or dietary preferences. I also ask them to summarise in one sentence what they hope to achieve from the day – this gives me a good idea of the areas to cover.

On the day of the session, I arrive early, make sure I have all the information and equipment I need, and that the room is set up well. Participants arrive to a warm and comfortable environment, already have an idea of what to expect because they've seen my introductory letter, and tend to settle down into a useful discussion very quickly. On the whole, I find that time and effort invested at an early stage is well spent. 99

Optimising the environment

It is easy to underestimate the importance of the environment in which interaction takes place, and to think that as long as the right people are present it doesn't matter where they are. However, many potentially useful discussions have been disrupted because participants were cold and uncomfortable, or unable to hear what was being said.

People organising an interaction can take steps to optimise the environment both before and during a discussion:

- Find out the number of participants, and arrange for the interaction to take place in a room large enough, but not so large that people will feel lost in it.
- Check that the room is at a suitable temperature.
- Make sure that there are enough chairs (comfortable ones, if possible). Chairs should all be the same height, so no one appears to be in a position of power.

93

What type of environment do your GNVQ lessons take place in? Choose one lesson to focus on, and think about how you could improve the room in which it takes place. How many people are involved in a normal lesson? Who are they? What are their needs? What types of activity take place? Then draw a floor plan to show how you would optimise the environment by rearranging furniture, changing lighting, and so on.

- Think about how to position group members so that they can all be seen. Arranging chairs in a circle or a horseshoe can encourage an open discussion in which everyone joins in. Rows tend to look intimidating, mean that people can't be seen, and can remind people of being at school!
- Leave space between chairs, so people don't feel their personal space is threatened.
- If there is a group leader, think about where they will sit. If they are behind a desk or on the other side of a table, this can create a barrier and suggest that they are going to dominate the discussion.
- Make sure that any equipment and furniture needed (tables, blackboard, flipchart, OHP and so on) is available.
- Check the lighting in the room. If participants don't need to write and the lighting seems harsh and glaring, consider bringing in small lamps to put around the room.
- Try to arrange for facilities for making tea or coffee – chatting over refreshments can help to put people at ease.
- During the interaction, deal with any unexpected disruptions – such as a noise outside the room, or a flickering light – as quickly and efficiently as possible.

During the interaction

Once the interaction is under way, it is important that someone takes responsibility for supporting and guiding the discussion. In group interactions, it is often useful to appoint a leader to do this.

The leader's role is not to dominate the discussion, but to create a positive atmosphere and enable everyone to participate fully. This may involve:
- giving everyone an opportunity to introduce themselves, so that participants feel they know one another
- introducing the subject to be discussed and explaining the aims of the interaction
- arranging for someone to take notes during the interaction, if appropriate, so that decisions and opinions are recorded
- using questioning and listening techniques to encourage people to talk (especially those who are too quiet)
- preventing everyone from speaking at once
- checking the meaning and clarifying what participants say, often by using reflective listening
- using body language well to promote an open and relaxed discussion
- moving the discussion in new directions
- asking for people's views on the interaction at the end of the meeting, to act as a summary of what has taken place
- making sure that the discussion doesn't go on for too long.

Even one-to-one discussions need this type of support to shape and direct the conversation.

DISCUSSION POINT

Who do you think would take responsibility for providing support during the following interactions:

■ a child protection conference involving a social worker, doctor, police officer, parents and child?

■ a nursing team's weekly meeting?

■ a conversation between a doctor and an elderly patient?

■ a conversation between two social workers about a service user?

Think of occasions when:

■ you take most of the responsibility for making sure a discussion goes well

■ you share the responsibility for making sure that a discussion goes well

■ you feel someone else is responsible for a discussion.

Who is involved in each case? How does your role affect the way you behave during the interaction?

Reducing stress

If people are feeling worried and under stress, they are less likely to take part in a discussion openly and honestly. An important part of providing support during an interaction is helping to reduce this stress, and put participants at ease.

A social worker explains how she aims to reduce stress in interactions with clients:

66 *Often people are already under considerable stress when they meet me – they may be depressed, upset, ill, nervous, or whatever. I try to reduce this stress as much as possible, so they feel relaxed enough to talk freely and honestly. I begin by explaining who I am and what we are going to talk about – in my experience no one relaxes when they're worried about what's going to happen next! Then I ask them some simple, closed questions to break the ice, before getting into a more in-depth discussion. I think about my body language at all times – making sure I sit in an open, relaxed position, maintaining good eye contact, and using facial expressions and gestures to show warmth and understanding. Perhaps most importantly, I'm constantly aware of how they are feeling. If they want to talk, I listen attentively and encourage them to work through their feelings. If they are feeling nervous and shy, I don't pressurise them into talking, but provide gentle encouragement through talking myself and asking questions.* 99

DISCUSSION POINT

Think of an occasion recently when you have felt under stress during an interaction. How did it affect your participation in the discussion? What could other participants have done to help reduce the stress?

Specific measures related to the needs of individuals

The people who take part in an interaction are all individuals with their own needs and preferences. Sometimes these may have a direct impact on the success of the interaction, and need to be supported through specific measures. For example:

- if a participant's first language is not English, an interpreter may be needed
- if a participant is hard of hearing, an induction loop or sign language interpreter may be needed
- if participants have different levels of knowledge and understanding (for example, if a group includes both children and adults), the leader needs to be aware of this and make sure everyone understands the views being expressed
- if a participant is in a wheelchair, they may need access to a toilet designed for disabled people
- if refreshments are provided, the organiser needs to be aware of any special dietary needs.

The person organising a group interaction should try to find out about individuals' needs in advance so there is plenty of time to make any special arrangements necessary. If the group isn't very large, they may be able to do this by talking to participants. However, if an interaction involves a large number of people, it is often easier to find out about their needs by sending them a short questionnaire.

ACTIVITY

You are organising a meeting on care support for the elderly in your area, to be attended by 30 people. The meeting is due to take place on 29 April at 2.00 p.m., and will be held in your local community centre. The session is expected to last for three hours, and refreshments will be provided during the afternoon.

Draft a letter to send to participants, notifying them of the place and time of the meeting, and outlining the areas the meeting will cover. Design a short questionnaire to send with the letter, to find out whether participants have any special needs that you should look after.

Meta, an Advanced GNVQ Health and Social Care student, planned an afternoon session for her group about equal opportunities, involving short inputs by a nurse, a social worker and a representative from a local Citizens Advice Bureau, followed by a general group discussion. She produced the following plan of how to support the interaction, to act as a reminder both before and during the session.

SUPPORTING PARTICIPANTS: EQUAL OPS SESSION

	Before interaction	During interaction
OPTIMISE THE ENVIRONMENT	■ Book a room which is a good size for 30 people (PX01?) ■ Check there's enough chairs - reasonably comfy? ■ Check the room's warm, but not too hot (PX01 gets stuffy) ■ Arrange the chairs to encourage everyone to participate - can rows be avoided? ■ Try to integrate speakers and students so everyone feels on even footing ■ Make sure any equipment needed is available and working ■ Check lighting - needs to be quite bright, as people will make notes ■ Organise refreshments	■ Be aware of, and solve, any problems such as flickering light, flapping blinds ... ■ Stand outside the room at lesson change, to keep the noise down
REDUCE STRESS	■ Work out what we are going to cover in what order, and make sure people know in advance ■ Talk to speakers about how long their inputs should be, and what to cover ■ Make sure everyone knows date, place, time ■ Tell everyone how long session will last	■ Give a short introduction, explaining who people are, what's going to happen ■ Give people a chance to introduce themselves ■ Ask questions during discussion session, get the ball rolling ■ Check with speakers the meaning of anything people may not have understood ■ Use body language well myself
MEET INDIVIDUALS' NEEDS	■ Ask speakers if they need any equipment (e.g OHP, flipchart) ■ Check whether there are any language needs for interpretation (don't think so) ■ Check whether anyone needs disabled access/toilets (Is Jason coming?) ■ Sandwiches to be provided - need to know how many veggies etc. Send out questionnaire with the information on the session	■ Provide any special measures, and make sure everything runs smoothly

ACTIVITY

The next time you are responsible for organising a discussion or meeting – whether it's a class debate, a meeting at a club you belong to, or a talk by a visiting health specialist – take special care to make sure that all participants have the support they need both before and during the interaction.

Keep a record of how you established and provided the support that the participants needed. You may find it useful to produce a plan like Meta's.

Appropriate forms of interaction

Interaction can take place in four main forms:

- through language – for example a spoken language such as English or Spanish, a signed language such as British sign language or using technology such as hearing aids and computers (for more about language, see page 67)
- through sensory contact – for example listening, eye contact and touch (see page 68)
- through body position – for example gestures, facial expression and posture (see page 70)
- through activities – for example drama, art, music and sport (see page 71).

When taking part in interaction, organisers need to decide what form would be most appropriate for participants. For example:

- a voluntary organisation may decide to run a discussion group for people with disabilities, making sure that forms of language were available to meet the needs of those with hearing difficulties
- a care assistant comforting an elderly person whose partner has just died may decide to rely mainly on touch and body position, rather than verbal language
- a nurse on a children's ward may decide to organise activities to help the children interact, such as games, art and music.

In practice, most interactions involve a combination of all four forms of interaction – it would be unusual to run an activity without using language at all, or to communicate with someone just through body language.

DISCUSSION POINT

Do you think the size of a group affects the success of different forms of interaction? What are the advantages and disadvantages of using each form of interaction with:

- one person (in a one-to-one meeting)?
- a small group (fewer than five people)?
- a larger group (more than five people)?

Language

Language is the main way in which people consciously communicate with one another, and almost every interaction involves the use of language.

Because of this, health and social care practitioners must be able to use language fluently, clearly and sensitively. A communications specialist, who provides training for care practitioners, explains:

❝ *All care workers need to be able to use language to communicate with service users. I advise them to remember three key points:*

- *Use people's first language whenever possible. If you can't communicate in the language yourself, use an interpreter.*

■ *Speak so that people will understand. Don't use jargon and technical terms to sound impressive – you'll only confuse them.*

■ *Be sensitive to the impression you're giving through your tone of voice, how loud you're speaking, how fast you're speaking, how you emphasise words, and whether you're speaking in a high-pitched or low-pitched voice.* **"**

ACTIVITY

As a whole class, decide on a health or social care topic for a class discussion. Ask your teacher to lead the discussion – your main aim is to concentrate on using language well. If anyone in the group has special language needs, make sure you take these into account.

Every student in the group should prepare a short talk (two minutes or so) summarising their views on the topic. Present these talks in turn, then take part in a general discussion of the issues raised. Avoid jargon, express yourself clearly and use paralanguage well.

Record the discussion on audio or video tape, and analyse your use of language. You may find an audio recording is particularly useful for this, as it forces you to concentrate on what is being said and how, rather than being distracted by body language.

Sensory contact

Sensory contact refers to using the senses – in particular, hearing, seeing and touching – to communicate. The chart below highlights some of the most important points to remember when using sensory contact.

LOOKING AND SEEING

■ Don't look away or avoid eye contact when someone's talking.
■ Glance at people regularly, every few seconds.
■ Don't stare at people when they are talking.
■ Try not to betray, through your eyes, emotions you don't want to show, e.g. shock, anger, boredom.
■ Remember to make allowances for cultural differences.

LISTENING

■ Make eye contact with the speaker.
■ Don't interrupt, let the other person speak.
■ Concentrate on understanding what the speaker is saying.
■ Nod, make encouraging sounds ('uh-huh', 'go on') to encourage the speaker to continue.
■ Respond appropriately.

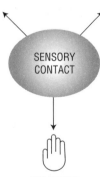

SENSORY CONTACT

TOUCHING

■ Use touch to show warmth and understanding, to convey comfort and reassurance.
■ See how people feel about being touched – don't use it indiscriminately.
■ Don't get too close to people if they seem uncomfortable – remember personal space.
■ If you need to use touch in caring for a client – for example to wash or dress them – treat them with respect and explain what you are doing.
■ Remember to make allowances for differences of sex, age and culture.

Body position

Body position – more often known as body language – is one of the most powerful forms of communication. Whether people are aware of it or not, they communicate an enormous range of feelings and information through the way they move and position their body.

Realising this, a college lecturer gave student nurses the following information sheet on body language, how to use it, and what it can show.

BODY LANGUAGE: dos and don'ts
Think about:
- What your **face** is showing: use your eyes, nose, mouth and brow to express emotion – smile if it's good news, look serious and sad if it's bad news, frown if it's unclear.
- Your **gestures**: nodding, shaking the head and shrugging can be useful ways to reinforce what you're saying in language -but remember, gestures can mean different things in different cultures.
- Your **body position**: try to look relaxed – if you look as if you're nervous, the patient definitely will be! Relax your muscles, sit with your hands loose in your lap, or stand with your arms by your sides; never clench your fists!
- Your **posture**: maintaining an open posture – with arms and legs unfolded, leaning forward slightly – gives the impression that you're friendly and welcoming; a closed posture – with legs crossed and arms folded – gives the impression that you're unwelcoming and defensive.
- **Mirroring**: if people are communicating well, they mirror each other's body language, so try leaning the same way as the person you're talking to, moving your head the same way, copying their gestures – it can create instant rapport! But don't make it too obvious what you're doing – they may think you're mimicking them.
- Your **position in relation to others**: don't intrude on their personal space – but remember, people from some cultures (such as Arab countries) stand much closer than Westerners.

ACTIVITY

A social worker is talking to a young person about problems at home and why they are playing truant from school. The girl is initially defensive and angry, and then becomes quite upset. The social worker concentrates on building a good rapport with the client using sensory contact and body language.

Working in pairs, roleplay the situation above, taking it in turns to be the social worker and the client. After each roleplay, discuss the social worker's use of sensory contact and body language. Make sure any feedback you give is constructive and sensitive, and try to be as honest as possible when evaluating your own performance.

Activity-based interaction

Taking part in activities can be a good way of promoting interaction between people. Activities can be enjoyable and relaxing, providing a natural context for social interaction whether:

- one-to-one
- with a small group of people
- with a larger group of people.

For example, watching a TV programme and chatting about it can be a good way to get talking; reading a story to a small group of children can encourage them to react and give their ideas; and taking part in group activity such as drama or sport can help a larger group of people get to know one another.

DISCUSSION POINT

Discuss the types of activity which might be useful forms of interaction for:

- a group of 30 elderly men and women
- a hospital patient who can't get out of bed
- five 13-year-olds.

As explained in section 2.1.5, there are many ways to optimise – make the best of – interaction. These include:

- using body language well
- seeking information by using questioning techniques
- taking positive action to improve interaction
- seeking and giving feedback
- using reflective listening
- interpreting what is being said, when necessary.

However, putting these techniques into practice is not always easy. To optimise interaction, you need to be aware of:

- everything you do
- everything you say
- what is going on around you
- how other participants are feeling.

Meta, the Advanced GNVQ Health and Social Care student who organised the equal opportunities afternoon for her GNVQ group (see section 2.2.1), made a particular effort to optimise the interaction between students and specialist speakers.

She arranged for one of the students to record the session on video tape. She then played this back several times, focusing on the different techniques she used to optimise effective interaction. The following extract is taken from her report on the event.

OPTIMISING EFFECTIVE INTERACTION

One of my main goals during the afternoon session was to optimise interaction between students and the speakers, to make sure that discussion was as useful and lively as possible. Because I was leading the session, and was the only person who knew both the students and speakers, I felt I was in a good position to do this.

The following section summarises the different ways I optimised effective interaction. It is based on watching a video recording of the session (the quotes are taken from the video).

BODY LANGUAGE

- I used facial expressions to express my thoughts and feelings. Most of the time, I was smiling and showing interest. I think this helped the other participants to relax and feel comfortable with what was happening. A couple of times, when I didn't understand something, I frowned and looked puzzled.

- I tried to maintain eye contact with whoever was speaking, to show that I was interested in what they were saying, but could probably use more eye contact.

- At one point, when one of the speakers had been going on for too long, I started to look worried. I must watch out that I don't give away my feelings through body language. This might have made participants feel uneasy.

- During the discussion I kept an open position, with my legs and arms unfolded. Hopefully this encouraged people to feel they could participate.

- When Jo was talking, I tried mirroring her body language to show I agreed with what she was saying. I think this looked a bit silly, it's probably something I need more practice with.

- Sometimes I looked a bit tense because I was quite nervous. Overall, I think if my body had been more relaxed it would have helped me to optimise interaction.

SEEKING INFORMATION

■ I used closed questions to collect basic information about the speakers. Example: 'Do you need a flipchart?'

■ I used open questions to get the speakers to explain points in more detail. Example: 'Why is equal opportunity particularly important in nursing?'

■ I used probes to get the speakers to develop a topic. Example: 'You said that your own experience has shown this, can you tell us how?'

■ I used leading questions to encourage other students in the group to participate. Example: 'Sam, you've probably found this during your work experience at the hospital, have you?'

TAKING POSITIVE ACTION

■ I tried to involve everyone in the discussion by asking questions I knew they'd be able to answer.

■ It got very noisy outside when people started going home from school, so I shut the windows.

■ Natalie said she couldn't hear at the back of the room, so I asked if everyone could move their chairs in a bit and asked the speakers if they could be a bit louder.

SEEKING FEEDBACK

■ I got feedback by looking at participants' body language. When they started looking bored, I tried to move the discussion on.

■ I tried to make sure that people had understood the main points made by the speakers by starting a discussion about different areas they had touched on.

REFLECTIVE LISTENING

■ I used reflective listening to encourage students to carry on talking during the discussion.

■ I used straightforward reflection. Example:

Jake 'I'm not sure there really is sex discrimination any more.'
Me   'You're not sure there's sex discrimination any more?'

■ I paraphrased what people said. Example:

Ali   'I've come across race discrimination in all sorts of situations. I've been teased at school and playing with friends. I didn't get a Saturday job and I think it might be because I'm black. My little brother got chased home from school last week by other boys in his class calling him names.'
Me   'So overall, you think race discrimination is still a serious problem?'

INTERPRETATION

■ There were no language difficulties within the group, so I did not have to organise any language interpretation.

■ Some of the information presented by the woman from the CAB was complicated, and I felt it might need interpreting. I tried to do this by summarising this myself. Luckily she realised that things needed explaining, and took over!

ACTIVITY

Working in pairs – to give you plenty of opportunities to practise techniques – arrange a discussion on a topic related to health or social care which interests both of you. Your main aim is to explore different ways of optimising interaction. Read Meta's notes before the discussion, to remind yourself of the different techniques you can use.

If possible, arrange for someone to video the discussion. Make notes about the different ways you optimised interaction (you may find it useful to follow the structure of Meta's report).

Evaluating interaction

Once you have taken part in an interaction, you need to evaluate:
- how effective the interaction was from the point of view of participants
- how well you contributed to the interaction.

You can then use the results of your evaluation to make recommendations for how the interaction could be improved in the future.

Whenever you carry out an evaluation, you need criteria against which to judge the interaction. For example:
- participation – how well people participated in the interaction
- quality of contribution to the interaction
- improvements from previous interactions
- how it relates to other aspects of individuals' lives
- the knowledge and understanding of participants as a result of the interaction.

One of the best ways to find out this information is to seek the opinions of the other people who took part in the interaction. To do this you might use feedback (oral and written), observation and self-reflection.

Verbal feedback

Verbal (or oral) feedback can be gained by asking participants what they thought of an interaction. This can be done:
- at the end of the interaction, during a general summing up of the session – this can be an efficient way to collect information from everyone involved, but participants may be constrained in what they say because of the other people present
- after the interaction, by approaching participants individually and asking for their views – feedback gained in this way is more likely to be honest and constructive, but it is time-consuming.

DISCUSSION POINT

You have been asked to collect verbal feedback from students in your group on how useful they found your last GNVQ lesson. What types of questions would you ask to get the feedback you need?

Written feedback

Written feedback provides a more formal record of participants' views on the success of an interaction. It is usually collected by distributing evaluation forms for participants to fill in, either:
- at the end of the session, before they go home – this has the advantage of the interaction still being fresh in people's minds; it is also easy to collect the responses
- after the session, once they've had time to reflect on the experience; however, this results in a less reliable response rate, and may mean that people forget how they felt during the interaction.

Meta, who organised the equal opportunities afternoon for students, gave every participant the following short evaluation form to complete at the end of the session.

EVALUATING THE EQUAL OPPORTUNITIES SESSION

Did you achieve what you wanted from the session?

_____

Did you find the talks by specialists helpful?

_____

How do you think this session compared with the last group meeting on care planning?

_____

_____

_____

_____

What do you think you have learned this afternoon?

_____

_____

_____

_____

How do you think sessions like this could be improved in the future?

_____

_____

_____

_____

ACTIVITY

Design a short evaluation form that you could give to fellow students to collect written feedback on a GNVQ lesson. Remember to cover the different evaluation criteria identified at the start of this section.

Observation

Observation can be one of the most effective ways to get participants' feelings about an interaction. Observation can be carried out either by:

- watching a video recording of an interaction (if all participants are happy for the session to be recorded)
- appointing someone to be an independent observer as the interaction takes place, who will watch and keep a record of people's responses as they take part in the discussion.

One of the main advantages of observation is that it gives an objective view that is not always gained through oral and written feedback. When people are

105

asked questions, their responses are often affected by what they think they are expected to say, or whether they like the person asking the questions. However, they cannot hide their reactions all the way through an interaction.

It is useful to have a checklist of things to look out for when carrying out observation, for example:

- What do people's facial expressions show?
- What does people's body language show?
- How well are different people contributing?
- Is everyone participating?
- Do participants seem to be developing knowledge and understanding?

Self-reflection

Self-reflection – for example, by keeping a diary of an interaction – is most useful when evaluating your own performance. But it can also be a helpful source of data when evaluating the feelings and contributions of other participants.

Meta kept a detailed record of her actions and feelings when organising the equal opportunities session, and then made notes during the interaction which she later wrote up as a diary of the afternoon. As well as covering her own contribution to the session, this provided some useful insight into how other participants reacted to the interaction, as the following extract shows:

3.45: Began general discussion about sex discrimination in health and social care I set the ball rolling by giving figures on men and women working in different roles in health and social care. Jo immediately stepped in and started talking about her own experiences, which was a good way to get more people involved. Anna, Natalie, Soraya and Tim all made good contributions and got a lively discussion going. All seemed interested in the issues, and everyone seemed to be listening, even if they weren't participating. Jake got bolshy, as usual, and started saying he doesn't think there's any such thing as sex discrimination. He didn't seem to have taken in what the speakers had said at all.

DISCUSSION POINT

Having read this extract from Meta's diary of the interaction, what problems can you see with using self-reflection to evaluate the perception of other participants?

Meta used four different sources of data to evaluate how effective the interaction was from the point of view of the other participants:

■ oral feedback – by allocating five minutes at the end of the session for people to give their views on the interaction, and by talking to participants individually after the session

■ written feedback – by giving people a short evaluation form to fill in at the end of the session

■ observation – by watching a video recording of the interaction

■ self-reflection – by keeping a diary of the session.

Using these sources of data, she made the following evaluation notes.

EVALUATING OTHER PEOPLE'S PERCEPTION OF THE EQUAL OPS SESSION

Participation

Everyone participated in the interaction at some point, apart from Clare. Verbal feedback from her showed that she found the session intimidating, and felt too nervous to contribute.

Other participants didn't seem to feel this way. The video of the session shows people looking relaxed, with open body language, and taking part in a lively debate. My own diary shows that levels of participation were good - I was ready to deal with awkward silences, but there were very few. People's verbal and written feedback suggests that all felt happy about participating and felt they joined in well.

Quality of contribution

Oral and written feedback on the contributions by the speakers showed that everybody felt the talks were excellent, particularly the one given by the social worker. The talk by Anne Halliday from the CAB was felt to be a bit long and technical, but included some useful information.

Observation and my own diary show that most participants made well thought out, useful contributions to the general discussion. Some people, such as Jake, Ali and Natalie, sometimes got a bit too involved in their own experiences and went on for too long.

Improvements from previous occasions

I included a question on the evaluation form asking students to compare this equal ops session with the last one on care planning. 18 of the 20 students who were at both interactions said they thought the equal ops session was more useful, 'more practical', 'gave more information', 'much more interesting'.

To check these views, I watched the video of the care planning session,

107

and compared it to that of the equal ops interaction. People seemed much less interested during the first interaction - they looked bored, there were lots of awkward pauses in the discussion, and didn't seem to pick up as much information. My diaries of the interactions also show this. My self-reflection during the care planning session was mostly 'I'm bored!'.

In the context of other aspects of individual's life

Most participants seemed to feel the equal opportunities topic was very relevant to aspects of their life outside the course. The girls were able to contribute personal experiences of sex discrimination (and a couple of the boys did too), and several of us had also experienced race discrimination. At the end of the afternoon, everybody seemed to feel that the session had made them more aware of why and how discrimination occurs in everyday life, and the importance of equal opportunities.

Knowledge and understanding of participants

Oral and written feedback showed that participants felt they had learnt some really useful information during the interaction, which would help them tackle Unit 1 with more confidence. As Jo said: 'At the start of the session I didn't think I knew enough to take part in a discussion. But after listening to the speakers, I felt quite confident about discussing equal opportunities.'

Observation of the interaction shows most people were able to contribute to the discussion with real knowledge. I definitely think the interaction was effective in helping people develop their understanding of equal opportunities.

Evaluating your own contribution

Evaluating your own contribution to an interaction is the best way to find out your strengths and weaknesses and improve your performance in the future.

As when evaluating other participants' feelings about an interaction, there are four sources of data which can help with self-evaluation:

- oral feedback
- written feedback
- observation
- self-reflection.

Verbal feedback

Verbal (or oral) feedback for self-evaluation can be collected from:

- independent observers who watched an interaction (for example, a teacher or assessor)
- other participants in the interaction.

Independent observers usually give verbal feedback after an interaction has taken place. The main advantage of collecting feedback in this way is that it provides an opportunity to talk things over sensitively and constructively. Meta explains:

66 *Our tutor likes to give us verbal feedback on our contribution to an interaction as well as written feedback. She chats with each of us for five minutes or so individually. She usually begins by picking up on good points about my contribution – perhaps my body language was good, or I used language well. Then she makes some constructive criticisms and suggests how I could improve in the future. Doing this face-to-face gives me a chance to respond, disagree or ask questions. If there's anything I don't understand, we can talk about it in greater depth. Sometimes when you just read something on paper, it can seem harsh and doesn't give you a chance to find out more.* 99

When collecting verbal feedback from other participants – in particular, fellow students – it is worth remembering that people's opinions are often subjective. Meta describes how she tried to make sense of verbal feedback from her colleagues:

66 *I found it quite difficult collecting verbal feedback from other students who took part in the interaction. For a start, it was a bit embarrassing, and I just didn't feel like they could look me in the eye and tell me the truth. Jo's my best friend, and she told me she thought I was absolutely brilliant in every way. Jake and I had had an argument, and he said he thought I was 'too bossy and always thought I was right'. Ben's feedback was probably nearest the truth, because I don't know him very well. He said that he thought I had guided the interaction well and made sure everything went smoothly, but that I should try to make sure I give everyone else a chance to speak.* 99

DISCUSSION POINT

Group discussion sessions in which participants give each other feedback on an interaction, can be a useful way to collect information about your own contribution. However, they can often turn into slanging matches, with people taking the opportunity to express personal grudges, or else other students are unwilling to give any feedback at all.

What strategies could you use to ensure a verbal feedback session was productive?

Written feedback

Written feedback on your own contribution to an interaction is useful because it acts as a permanent record. It can be collected from independent observers and other participants in an interaction.

Written feedback is usually collected on evaluation forms or assessment sheets. These may be completed during, at the end of or after an interaction.

Detailed feedback on particular aspects of an individual's performance – for example, use of body language and sensory contact – is best collected during the interaction by an independent observer (other participants won't have time). Meta was keen to improve her use of body language, and designed a special assessment sheet for her teacher to fill in during the interaction:

META AHMED - USE OF BODY LANGUAGE

ASSESSMENT SHEET

Please comment on my use of each of the following aspects of body language during the interaction

Listening skills:

- *Good concentrated listening. Able to paraphrase information provided by speakers and other students and responded appropriately*

- *Good use of prompts (nodding, 'uh-huh') to encourage people to go on*

- *Perhaps not quite enough eye contact – might suggest you're not listening even if you are (see below)*

- *Beware of interrupting! Let people speak*

Eye contact:

- *Not quite enough eye contact, particularly with speakers (perhaps due to nerves?)*

Touch

- *Not used - wouldn't have been appropriate*

Gestures

- *Good use of nodding and shaking head to show agreement / disagreement*

- *Could relax you hands and use them a bit more when speaking – gave a bit of a stiff impression*

Facial expression

- *Good use of smiling etc. You're good at showing warmth, openness, etc. through your face. Maintained facial expressions well throughout the interaction*

Posture

- *Open body position – arms legs uncrossed, leaning forward – good*

- *Bit stiff – muscles look tense. TRY TO RELAX!*

As with verbal feedback, it is important to:

- be sensitive when commenting on someone else's contribution – don't get personal
- take written feedback from others seriously – don't dismiss something because it's not what you want to hear.

ACTIVITY

Choose an interaction which you can use to carry out a detailed evaluation. You may decide to focus on a class discussion, a roleplay, or a meeting you attend while on work experience.

Your evaluation should be based on the following criteria:

- participation
- quality of contribution
- improvements from previous occasions
- knowledge and understanding of participants.

Using these criteria, carry out an evaluation of:

- how effective the interaction was from the point of view of other participants (look back to section 2.2.4 for help)
- your own contribution to the interaction.

Both parts of your evaluation should include:

- verbal feedback
- written feedback
- observation
- self-reflection.

Think about how to collect feedback and carry out the observation.

Based on your findings, make notes for a report evaluating other participants' views on the interaction, and your own contribution to the interaction.

ACTIVITY

Design an assessment sheet which an independent observer could use to evaluate your use of language during an interaction. Remember that the observer will need to know what to look for, or the assessment will be meaningless.

Observation

As already suggested, observation by an independent observer can be a good way to collect feedback for self-evaluation, if assessment sheets or evaluation forms are carefully designed.

Perhaps more useful still is a video recording of an interaction. This has the advantage of enabling you to observe and evaluate your own performance. Meta found this particularly helpful:

66 *Probably the most useful source of data on my own contribution was the video recording of the session. At first it was a bit strange watching myself on video, I kept being distracted by how my voice sounded and how big my nose looked! But once I had got used to this, I was able to collect some really useful information. I watched other people's reactions as I talked, and got a much better impression of what they thought about my performance. I was also able to play back particular sections and analyse my use of language and body language in detail. By the end of the video, I had a list of things I thought were my strong points, and areas I felt I could develop.* 99

ACTIVITY

Have you ever been recorded taking part in an interaction? If so, go back to the video or audio recording and use it to carry out a detailed analysis of your communication skills. What are the advantages and disadvantages of evaluating yourself in this way?

Self-reflection

Obviously, self-reflection is involved in every self-evaluation. Whether this self-reflection takes place through watching a video recording, keeping a diary or making notes, it should be:

- honest
- as objective as possible
- based on evidence, not just your own feelings.

111

Section 2.2.6

Making recommendations for improvement

Collecting information about evaluation forms, assessment sheets and reports

Pulling out the most important points

Deciding how improvements could be made in the future

Making a list of recommendations for improving future interactions

Ultimately, the aim of evaluating an interaction is to:

- learn lessons for the future, to ensure that interactions are as useful for participants as possible
- help individuals improve their own contribution to future interactions.

This involves working through four stages, as shown in the diagram.

These recommendations should be recorded in writing, so that they can be referred to in the future.

Meta wrote a report evaluating how effective the equal opportunities session was from the other participants' point of view, and assessing her own contribution to the interaction. She then looked through the report, listed all the criticisms made, and thought about how she could avoid being open to these criticisms in the future. This formed the basis of the following list of recommendations.

RECOMMENDATIONS FOR IMPROVING FUTURE INTERACTION

Improving the effectiveness of interaction from participants' point of view

- Make sure that speakers don't overrun or participants will become bored and stop listening.
- Make sure speakers are aware of participants' knowledge and understanding, so they pitch their talk at the right level.
- Don't let individuals dominate the general discussion too much. Make sure someone takes a lead in directing discussion and moving it on.
- If possible, give participants handouts summarising the main points covered by the speakers' talks. Many felt they were busy taking notes, rather than really listening.

Improving my own contribution to the interaction

- Don't be too dominant.
- Listen to what other people say, and never interrupt.
- Try to make sure everyone has a chance to speak.
- Improve eye contact (use it more).
- Try to relax more - don't let nerves show through my hands and posture.
- Watch the pitch of my voice. I tend to get squeaky when I'm excited or nervous.
- Practise mirroring, so it doesn't look too artificial.

ACTIVITY

Look back at the evaluation you carried out in section 2.2.5. Pull out the most important points from the evaluation, and make a list of recommendations for ways you could improve interaction in the future.

Key questions

1 List six ways of providing support to participants before an interaction.
2 List six ways of providing support to participants during an interaction.
3 How can you support participants by optimising the environment?
4 How can you reduce stress before and during an interaction?
5 What factors would you consider when deciding a form of interaction appropriate to participants and the context?
6 Give five ways to optimise interaction between participants.
7 List four sources of data you might use to evaluate interaction.
8 How could you collect written feedback?
9 Explain two ways of using observation to evaluate interaction.
10 Give four criteria you could use to evaluate interaction.

Assignment

For this assignment, you need to take part in three interactions:

- one with just one other person
- one in a small group (with less than five people)
- one in a larger group (with more than five people).

These may be interactions or activities you carry out as part of your work in other units.

One of the group interactions should be with people who aren't students, such as teachers, health and social care practitioners, children or elderly people. You could organise an interaction as part of your work experience or you could invite people into school or college.

One of the interactions should involve an activity, such as exercise, drama or music. If you want, this can also be the interaction involving people who aren't students.

For each interaction, keep records and notes to show how you:

- established the support needed by participants for effective interaction to take place
- used appropriate forms of interaction
- optimised the interactions
- carried out self-evaluation, and used feedback from other participants
- made recommendations for improvements.

ELEMENT **2.3**

Interacting with service users

In this element you will explore interaction in health and social care settings and look at ways they could be improved.

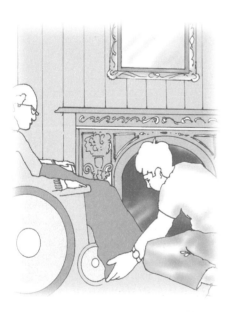

66 *You have to let patients know what is going to be happening to them and reassure them. We both have a role – the dentist and I both try to do our bit to put people at ease. The approach can be a bit different with children – you can often distract them and take their minds off it by talking to them about things they like. Today I had a child who was having his tooth out. I knew liked he football because in the waiting room I asked his Mum what he liked. So I asked him what team he supported and he was off. His mind switched away from his worry to his main passion and he kept calm. The treatment was a lot better experience for him than it could have been. By the time it was done he was surprised it wasn't so bad.*

You have to find a way to deal with people's fear. You can only carry out treatment with a person's consent. Children who are very worried often let us go ahead if they know they can hold my hand. I tell them to squeeze my hand when it hurts, which comforts them and gives them a feeling of control.

With adults it's not so easy because they are not so easily distracted. It's not the most pleasant of experiences but it can make a huge difference if there's a friendly face around. The dentist makes conversation, which helps them feel better. A calm and gentle atmosphere is important too, so although I have to do things quickly I don't rush about. 99

dental assistant

The effects of care settings

Many interactions between health and social care practitioners and service users are said to take place in a 'care setting', such as:

- the service user's own home
- a day-care centre
- a clinic
- a residential home
- a hospital.

The atmosphere, facilities and practices in this environment can have a major impact on the reaction to the care given.

DISCUSSION POINT

Think about how you felt on your first day at your current school or college. How is your memory of the day coloured by your reaction to the environment? Did you find the setting intimidating, or welcoming? Can you relate your experience to that of an elderly person spending their first day in residential care, or of a child being admitted to hospital?

ACTIVITY

Carry out a survey of your school or college to see how the environment would affect a student in a wheelchair arriving there for the first time. Think about whether it is clear where to go, the usefulness of the information about who people are, toilet facilities, the catering provision, the arrangement of rooms, the general atmosphere, and so on.

Care settings should:

- ensure the physical safety and security of service users
- provide emotional support, creating an environment which shows that service users are important and valued
- encourage social interaction
- give information about where to go and the roles of different members of staff
- have access and facilities for people with disabilities
- be functional, with appropriate toilet and washing facilities, catering provision, seating, lighting, heating and so on.

Health and social care practitioners need to be aware of the impact of the care setting, and do all they can to make the environment friendly and comfortable. However, the steps they can take are obviously limited by the financial resources and time at their disposal.

The service user's home

Since the NHS and Community Care Act 1990, which places emphasis on the benefits of caring for people in the community, a growing number of service users are being supported in their own homes. People who find it difficult to travel to clinics and out-patients departments may receive services such as physiotherapy and occupational therapy at home. More are now staying in their own homes – with appropriate support from care assistants, home helps, community nurses and meals delivery services – rather than receiving residential care.

In many cases, the service user's own home is a perfect care setting. They are in control of their own environment, and can decide where to sit, how warm

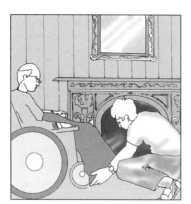

the room is, what to watch on TV, when to eat, and so on. The practitioner must fit in with this routine and environment, rather than imposing their own schedule and values. This may make the practitioner more aware of the service user's needs and preferences as an individual, and more likely to respect their privacy.

However, some people feel that practitioners coming in and out of their home is an intrusion – an invasion of their personal space. People who are used to looking after themselves may find it difficult to accept the help offered by home carers, and resent their presence. As a result, relationships with carers can become strained and this will affect the quality of care given and accepted.

This is particularly true for elderly people, who often find it hard to accept their changing lifestyle and loss of day-to-day independence. Unable to go out and see people, they may feel isolated in their own home, and would prefer to move into a residential care setting with other people around them.

For some people, living at home can entail actual physical risks – from burns and cuts while cooking to fire hazards from using electrical appliances. When deciding to care for someone at home, health and social care practitioners need to carry out a detailed assessment of risks to find out what level of support they need. As part of this, they need to ensure that facilities and equipment are in place to enable the service user to live safely and comfortably.

Day-care centres

For many service users, particularly elderly people, day-care centres offer a welcome opportunity to spend time away from home. In most cases, transport is provided to and from the centre, and people are able to spend the day talking, taking part in activities, and sharing a meal with others.

However, as with other care settings, day-care centres can have both positive and negative effects. Miss Crownley, who spends two days a week at a day-care centre for elderly people in her area, explains:

66 *I look forward to going to the centre because it gets me out the house. The minibus picks me up at 9.30 and I arrive at the centre at 10.15, after we've picked up other people who go. I don't really like travelling in the minibus – it's got writing on the side and you feel everyone's looking at you – but I'm sure they do the best they can.*

The centre's always warm and the helpers are very friendly. You can decide where to sit and I usually sit and chat to Mrs Burrows. She's my special friend. If she's not there, I don't really enjoy it very much. A lot of the old dears are going a bit senile, which gets me down. Four people who come on a Wednesday died over Christmas, which was horrible. You're always waiting to see who's going to be next.

We have a very good meal at dinnertime, although there's no choice and sometimes I don't like it and make myself a sandwich when I get home. All through the day there are things for us to do. I usually play whist in the morning and Scrabble in the afternoon. Sometimes the helpers persuade you to do something you're not very keen on. Last week I ended up knitting squares because Claire said she thought I should, and I've never liked knitting. 99

DISCUSSION POINT

Read through Miss Crownley's account of a day-care centre again. What are the positive effects of the centre? What are the negative effects? If you were an elderly person living alone, who found it hard to get out of the house, do you think you would want to go to a day-care centre?

ACTIVITY

Visit a clinic in your area, with the permission of its manager, and carry out an analysis of how you think the care setting would affect the people who use it. Look at the way interactions take place at the clinic, considering the different points listed above (you may find it helpful to take photographs, if the manager agrees). Write a short summary of possible positive and negative effects of the clinic on different user groups. At the end of your summary, suggest ways you think interactions at the clinic could be improved.

Clinics

Clinics – which provide medical services for the whole community – need to create an environment which is instantly friendly and welcoming to everyone.

People may only spend a matter of minutes in a clinic, and will want their visit to be quick and efficient. As a result, it is important that there is easy access to the building, including access for people with disabilities. When people arrive at the clinic for the first time, they will be unfamiliar with where to go and what to expect. Clear, accurate information can help reduce this sense of disorientation, as well as ensuring the appointments system runs smoothly.

People visiting a clinic will often feel vulnerable or afraid because they are unwell. A comfortable waiting area can go a long way towards putting people at ease by providing:

■ a bright, clean and welcoming environment
■ comfortable, good-quality seating
■ magazines for people to read (care should be taken to provide materials in appropriate languages)
■ toys for children to play with
■ leaflets and posters providing medical information
■ clearly signposted toilet facilities, with disabled access.

Residential homes

Moving into a residential home marks the start of a completely new phase in someone's life.

For some, it is an enormous relief. Emotionally, they may have been struggling to cope with living on their own, feeling lonely and isolated. Physically, they may have been put at risk by carrying out everyday tasks such as cooking, washing and cleaning. Residential care gives them the companionship of living with other people. It takes away the responsibility of having to cope with everyday tasks which may have become difficult or even frightening. It gives them the reassurance that if they fall ill or hurt themselves, they will be looked after.

To other people, moving into a residential home can mean a distressing loss of independence, privacy and hope. Elderly people, in particular, may feel they are being sent to a residential home to die. As a result, they often become withdrawn, depressed and lose their self-esteem.

The routines and rules of life in some residential homes can be dehumanising and depressing, as the following extract about a private nursing home shows.

A treat for Granny Bint

Life in a private nursing home gets tougher at bedtime

First Person

Viève Forward

• •

SHE MUST have been a lovely girl, Granny Bint. Twinkling blue eyes and a mischievous smile, now in her nineties, she sits chattering to herself. It is not cold and she is not alone but the company is poor: there's Margaret, who only speaks if you touch her arm: "That's my bad arm, you bloody buggers!" And Alice, who alternates between schoolmistressy beneficence and plaintive tears of woe, giving you a slap on the wrist when you try to undress her.

That's my job – undressing them, getting them into bed. First I give them their supper: eggs, or a sausage: Granny Bint giggles and gives me knowing looks when I put hers in her hand. I draw up a spare commode to put Alice's bowl on while I go to feed Margaret: jelly goes everywhere, as she ignores the spoon I give her and slurps straight from the bowl. Tea gets spilt down dresses and I have learned not to omit the sugar, or they won't drink it.

"I've got a treat for you, Granny Bint!" I say, handing her a digestive biscuit. Matron doesn't allow them any food with bran in it, as it gives them the runs. If they get constipated, they get a laxative.

Then comes the back-breaking task of getting them ready for bed, bending down over them, tugging away at sleeves and over heads with wet dresses as they set up passive resistance to my efforts, Alice whimpering pathetically, and Granny clamping both hands under her armpits: "Oh, Mother! Mother! No!" still clinging to her modesty through a fog of senility, as I undress her in full view of all the others: the single set of screens in the place will only be used when she is laid out.

Lyn lumbers flatfootedly in and helps me to fling them into beds like sacks of potatoes. Granny kisses me, then giggles at her daring. Alice is dying of cancer of the bowel, I discovered today, but only yesterday morning we lifted her crying with pain into the bath of lukewarm water Granny had just been lifted out of. Alice's pressure sores also give her pain, and Lyn peeks under the dressings with unwashed hands. Deciding the big one on her hip looks rather nasty, we put her into bed on her other side, where she will lie unturned in the inevitable pool of urine until the following morning. Already the skin on this hip is breaking up; if it breaks up completely before she dies, goodness knows which side we'll lie her on.

Next door we tie Ivy to the bed with a bandage, because last night she wandered into the shower and wrecked it. Ivy recently celebrated her hundredth birthday in hospital, having fallen on a heater and lain there undiscovered for some time. I hate tying her up; it would never be allowed on an NHS ward, but in these private homes they get away with murder . . . We find that she has cut her hand trying to escape to the toilet, and is sitting in a pile of excrement. "You bad girl," says Lyn, "not to tell me when you want to go. And don't laugh at me when I speak to you, or you'll get no breakfast tomorrow." Matron comes to bandage the wound once she's seen the end of Eastenders.

Downstairs, Flossie stands in the hall and refuses to go to bed until she's sure her Mother knows she's here: and Enid says: "Shall I die, Nurse?"

Lyn risks her back heaving them into bed without recourse to me because I'm away emptying commodes and filling the washing machine. She doesn't know any better. I do but I still can't find any soap to wash my hands. "You'd think they could afford soap, at least, on what they charge," says Lyn. "How much is that?"

"Over two hundred a week."

I do a quick calculation in my head. "That's 16 patients at two hundred a week . . ." My pay is £1.50 an hour; my spirits sink as I go to undress Vera, who has thrown up down her front during supper, who cannot help it, but is well aware of it. She is depressed because she overheard Lyn saying to me: "It makes me sick, doing Vera."

Lyn is very tired: she worked from 7.30 to 1.00 this morning, started again at 5.30 and now it's 7.30 again. Her hours are always as bad as this, and change at short notice. There's not much she can or will do about it, though, because she lives here and is afraid Matron might throw her out if she stands up for herself.

We finish with ten minutes to spare. We sip coffee as Matron makes her report to the RGN on night duty. Remembering my NHS days under the formidable Sister B, it strikes me as ironic to hear Matron discussing the residents, when all day she's been in her office or in here watching the telly.

Then at last: "Off you go, girls!" I strip off my soiled overalls and leave them for another auxiliary to put on the following morning.

As I walk up the drive, past Matron's Rover, her husband's Daimler and the BMW they bought their son for his eighteenth birthday, I m thinking of what Lyn said about Granny Bint: "They say she was a Suffragette, you know!" and meditate expensive sabotage.

The Guardian, *14 September 1988.*
Essential Articles, Carel Press, Carlisle.

Turning a poor residential setting into a good one is often a question of respecting people as individuals. Providing a comfortable environment automatically enhances people's self-esteem and sense of self-worth. Allowing people to make choices, rather than forcing them into rigid routines, helps them to maintain their independence.

Residential homes can show respect for individuals by:
- giving them a choice of having a room of their own (not making them share a room)
- respecting their privacy (staff should never enter someone's room without knocking first)
- letting them bring their own pictures, pieces of furniture, plants, crockery and so on
- letting them eat, wash, get up and go to bed when they want
- letting them sit where they want, in the type of chair they like
- providing them with any equipment they need to help them perform tasks independently
- letting them choose what they wear, and what they watch on television
- giving them a choice of menu, with options to suit particular diets
- letting them have access to the whole building.

DISCUSSION POINT

Sometimes residents' rights as individuals may be at odds with health and safety. If you were working in a residential care setting, what would you do in the following situations?

- A resident wants to cook his own meal, but has burnt himself badly when cooking in the past.
- Residents want the front door left unlocked at night so they can come and go freely, but staff are concerned about security.
- A resident wants to look after her own medicines, but there are concerns that she will forget to take important medication.
- A resident wants to be allowed to clean her own room, but is unable to keep it to hygienic standards.

Hospitals

The positive effects of going into hospital are obvious – medical staff there have the knowledge and skill to make patients better or improve their quality of life. This in itself can bring relief and comfort to someone who has been unwell for some time, or who knows they need help urgently.

But many people find going into hospital a frightening experience. Often they are admitted to hospital suddenly, as the result of an accident or emergency. As well as having to cope with the pain of injuries and illness, they have to deal with the shock of being in an unfamiliar, intimidating environment. Even if people know in advance that they are going into hospital, they have to cope with the fear of pain and sense of helplessness. They are separated from their family and friends, and have to form new relationships with other patients and medical staff.

In the past, the hospital environment has done little to relieve people's fears. Traditionally, hospitals have been imposing Victorian buildings, with gloomy corridors, peeling paint and large wards. Patients lie in bed in nightclothes while medical staff in uniform look after them, reinforcing the power relationship.

ACTIVITY

Visit a hospital in your area, and investigate the possible effects that the environment has on patients. Think about how it might influence different user groups, such as children, elderly people and adolescents. Watch interactions taking place between patients and staff. How do you think the hospital is trying to counter the negative effects of hospital care settings on interactions in the past?

Service users and the caring relationship

Caring for people is at the core of health and social care. Providing good care depends on building a good relationship with people through effective interaction.

People in need of health and social care often feel scared, embarrassed, inadequate or depressed. On the surface, their needs are usually for physical care, such as medical treatment or help with daily tasks, but they will also have emotional needs which can only be met through warm, supportive caring relationships. However effectively or efficiently a service is provided, if emotional needs are neglected then it cannot be seen as a complete success.

Matt, who receives physiotherapy at home twice a week, describes his experiences:

66 *Chris, a physiotherapist, comes to my house every Monday and Thursday to treat me, and he's very good. I'm slowly becoming more mobile, and the pain is less intense. I certainly can't complain about the service I'm getting. But he just doesn't seem interested in me, or want to offer anything apart from physical help. I'm stuck in the house all day and am lonely and bored until my girlfriend gets home from work. It would be great if we could have a chat – I don't expect us to be mates or anything, but it would be nice if I could look forward to him coming. Instead, I just feel like I'm being a nuisance – he makes me feel really useless.* **99**

Positive effects of caring relationships

The most obvious way in which people gain from a caring relationship is in their health and social wellbeing. Every health and social care practitioner should aim to act in the best interest of service users. In some cases, this may mean making people's everyday lives as pleasant and comfortable as possible. In others, it may mean actually saving their lives.

DISCUSSION POINT

What are the positive effects of the caring relationship between Chris and Matt? What are the negative effects? What characteristics do you think health and social care practitioners need to help them create good relationships with service users?

DISCUSSION POINT

In small groups, talk about caring relationships you have experienced in which you were the service user. What positive effects did the relationships have on you? How did the practitioner involved help to create these positive effects?

PROTECTION
■ by ensuring safety from dangers such as burns and falls
■ by safeguarding people who are at risk

PHYSICAL SUPPORT
■ medical treatment
■ physical care services such as help with washing, dressing and cooking
■ by providing care competently and efficiently

CARING RELATIONSHIPS CAN PROVIDE

EMOTIONAL SUPPORT
■ by helping people to cope with stressful situations
■ by promoting individuals' self-esteem and self-confidence
■ by making people feel valued and respected

INDEPENDENCE
■ by encouraging people to carry out tasks for themselves
■ by setting targets for users to achieve
■ by involving service users in their own care

SOCIAL SUPPORT
■ by giving users someone to listen and talk to
■ by encouraging users to develop communication skills and interact with others

Negative effects of caring relationships

As already suggested, even if their ultimate goal is to improve health and social wellbeing, caring relationships can have negative effects on service users. This may be because of lack of understanding and support on the part of the practitioner, or it may be because of the service user's particular needs and problems.

One of the most common negative effects of caring relationships is that they can create dependence. Clients who are forced to accept help – whether this is Meals on Wheels or hospital care – automatically lose some control over their lives. Some people find this difficult to accept, and become angry or lose self-confidence because of their loss of independence; others, particularly elderly people, can slip into a pattern of dependence easily, start slowing down, and become institutionalised.

To prevent this, practitioners must avoid over-protecting people and allow them to think and act for themselves. However, this is not always easy – care settings such as hospitals and residential homes often have rigid routines which service users must follow. These automatically threaten individuals' rights to make choices and maintain their independence.

Having to rely on a caring relationship – whether because of illness or social problems – can make people feel afraid and vulnerable. They may express this fear through becoming aggressive, upset or withdrawn. Health and social care practitioners need to be aware of this reaction, and counteract it by giving information and support to allay fears.

Sometimes fear in a caring relationship is created by practitioners themselves. Staff are often under enormous stress, and don't have the time or resources to give service users the individual attention they need. In extreme cases, service users may be neglected or even physically harmed (for example, by hitting or pushing). More often, harassed practitioners may lose their temper, show dislike or disapproval, or humiliate a service user in front of other people. All of these acts are abuses of the power which exists in the caring relationship. As a result, service users may become afraid, lacking in confidence, increasingly dependent, and eventually withdrawn and depressed.

DISCUSSION POINT

If you were a care assistant working in a residential home for people with disabilities, what practical steps could you take to encourage those in your care to make choices and maintain their independence?

ACTIVITY

Talk to a health or social care practitioner about how they try to avoid their caring relationships having negative effects on service users. How do they try to prevent users becoming too dependent? How do they deal with their fears and uncertainty?

Optimising interaction in care settings

As discussed in section 2.3.1, care settings such as hospitals, clinics and residential homes can have both positive and negative effects on service users. People working in health and social care need to be aware of this and act to ensure that interaction is as supportive and successful as possible.

Organisations can optimise interaction with service users by:
- giving them information about the organisation
- making changes to the environment (for example new furnishings, room layouts)
- providing interpretation services to help them communicate with practitioners
- arranging advocacy for service users who can't assert their own rights and wishes
- seeking feedback from service users to check their understanding and find out their feelings
- involving them in decision-making
- taking individuals' personal beliefs and preferences into account
- minimising constraints, such as introducing measures to reduce service users' stress or distress.

At a basic level, simply greeting people in an open and friendly way can help to ensure the success of an interaction in a care setting, as one woman explains:

66 I have recently accompanied my mother to hospital on several occasions. The most important factor which helped us relax and ask the right questions to meet our needs was that she was greeted by name, with a friendly smile, as if she was expected and wanted. The first five minutes in a care setting set the tone for the whole experience. **99**

Advocacy for service users

Many people find it hard to express and assert their needs, wishes and rights when they are in a care setting. Sometimes this is because illness or disability prevents them communicating clearly. In other cases language differences may create problems, or they may simply be too shy or frightened to speak up for themselves.

Practitioners in care settings need to be aware of this, and if necessary arrange for the service user to be represented by an advocate.

An advocate is someone who supports a service user and ensures that their needs, wishes and feelings are made clear to practitioners. The advocate is usually a carer, friend or relative – someone who understands their beliefs and feelings, and is able to communicate them to practitioners.

As far as possible, practitioners promote self-advocacy, encouraging service users to develop skills in expressing themselves, making decisions and asserting their own rights. Whether self-advocacy is possible depends on the particular needs and disabilities of the individual.

ACTIVITY

Arrange an interview with a practitioner who is based in a hospital, clinic, day-care centre or residential home. Talk through the list above with them, asking them to explain how they put each of the measures into practice. Either record the interview (with their permission), or make notes on what they say. Produce a chart summarising what you find out.

DISCUSSION POINT

If you were unable to communicate your own beliefs and feelings, who would you want to act as your advocate? Why? What factors do you think practitioners should consider when arranging advocacy?

Providing organisational information

In the past, care settings tended to be intimidating, mysterious places, with long corridors which all looked the same, unknown figures in uniforms and little information about where to go and what to do. This environment did little to dispel the fear of people arriving in the care setting for the first time.

Today, most hospitals, clinics and residential homes try to counter some of this fear of the unknown by giving people information about the organisation.

Many produce a leaflet or booklet that includes:
- maps or plans of the building and grounds
- organisational charts explaining who people are and what they do
- details of daily routines (for example mealtimes, menus, leisure facilities)
- information for visitors.

Others produce posters or wallcharts giving information about staff and the building. Whatever form it is produced in, information needs to be clear, easy to read, and available in different languages to meet the needs of everyone (including Braille, if appropriate).

In recent years, hospitals in particular have increased the amount of information available to service users. Most wards have a noticeboard with the names, and often photographs, of the staff who work there, and patients are given a card naming the nurse primarily responsible for their care.

Environmental changes

As already suggested in section 2.3.1, the physical environment of a care setting can have a major influence on the success of an interaction with clients. If people feel that the environment shows respect for their comfort, needs and wishes, they are likely to respond better to care.

Architects and designers building new hospitals, clinics, residential homes and day-care centres are aware of this, and aim to create light, airy environments. New care settings are usually bright, carpeted and comfortably furnished, with clear signs, good toilet and washing facilities, and pleasant reception areas. Modern hospitals have moved away from the long corridors and large wards of the past, and now have smaller rooms and central stations where patients and visitors can talk to nurses. Clinics and departments that care for children are bright and cheery, with posters, paintings and toys. Many residential homes for elderly people now invite new residents to decorate their rooms with their own furniture and pictures.

Practitioners based in older care settings may have to take an active problem-solving approach to improving the care environment – often on a small budget. Long, dark corridors can be cheered up by art and design projects with local schools. Television rooms can be improved by the addition of plants and rugs. Creating small garden areas for service users to sit in can improve the quality of life.

ACTIVITY

Collect examples of information produced by care organisations for service users. What types of information do you think are most useful? What would help to put people at ease?

ACTIVITY

Arrange a visit to an older-style care setting in your area, and investigate the problems associated with the environment. With permission, take photographs highlighting problem areas. Write a short summary of your investigation, explaining the problems and suggesting ways of solving them. Try to suggest both ideal solutions which would require a large budget, and short-term improvements which could be made with a small budget.

Interpretation

Care organisations need to be aware of the language needs of service users, and provide interpretation services when necessary. These may include:

- language interpreters for people who don't speak English as their first language
- sign language interpreters for clients who are deaf or hard of hearing
- leaflets, posters and booklets translated into different languages, or produced in Braille for people with visual impairments
- staff who are trained in explaining complicated, specialist information to members of the general public.

Seeking feedback from service users

Care organisations can improve interaction with service users by finding out what they think about the care provided.

All staff who interact with service users should be encouraged to communicate effectively by showing that they are listening, and seeking feedback to make sure that clients have understood what they are saying (see page 84). On an organisational level, care settings can carry out interviews or questionnaire surveys with service users to find out what they feel about the environment, staff, and the care provided, and how they think it could be improved. Some organisations provide a suggestions box, where people can leave ideas for improvements and changes.

Involving clients

In the past, care settings tended to reinforce the notion of service users as passive recipients of care. Practitioners were the experts, and knew what was best – individuals had little control over, or involvement in, the care they received. This has changed in recent years as most hospitals, day-care centres and residential homes now take steps to involve people in making decisions about their own care. This means giving people the information they need to make sound decisions, and respecting their needs and wishes as individuals. In some cases, their choices will be limited by their specific needs, in particular for medical care. However, practitioners can still ensure that people understand the situation and are aware of possible alternatives, so that they feel involved in the decision-making process.

As well as involving service users in making decisions, most care settings now encourage them to take as much responsibility as possible for their own care. Practitioners need to assess how much people can do for themselves, and then provide the time and equipment they need to do it. Residential homes in particular must make sure that they have the facilities and equipment to allow people to remain as independent as possible.

DISCUSSION POINT

What other methods could care organisations use to find out what users think about the service provided?

DISCUSSION POINT

Should children have the same rights to be involved in their own care as adults? When might practitioners have to treat children differently?

If a hospital patient is under 16, parents are responsible for signing a consent form for an operation to go ahead. Do you think this is fair? If you were a nurse or doctor, how could you involve the child in making the decision?

Taking account of individuals' personal beliefs and preferences

Successful interaction in care settings depends on people being treated as individuals with their own beliefs and preferences. This may be done:

■ on an organisational level – for example, by providing interpreting services and catering for different diets

■ on a personal level – by ensuring that individual practitioners avoid discrimination and respect people's needs and wishes.

A social worker explains how he and the social services department he works for aim to optimise interaction by taking into account service users' personal beliefs and preferences:

66 *Whenever I meet service users for the first time, I try to assess them as individuals. This means consciously avoiding stereotyping based on the way they look, where they live, what they do or their problems. Instead, I try to find out their opinions, beliefs, needs and preferences. This often takes all my communication skills – people may be unwilling to talk about themselves openly, be embarrassed or find it hard to express their feelings. Once I feel I've got a better handle on them, I put together a care package which meets their needs and respects their individual identity. As a department, we're aware of how important this is, and provide meals for clients with particular diets and interpretation services when necessary. Whether care is being provided in a hospital, a day-care centre or the person's own home, the important thing is to make sure that people are treated with dignity and respect.* 99

Minimising constraints

All interaction with service users is affected by constraints – factors which cause breakdowns in communication and care. Organisations and practitioners need to be aware of these constraints so that they can take steps to avoid problems, and solve them when they do occur.

Depending on the situation, constraints might include:

■ stress or distress, on the part of either the service user or the practitioner

■ language difficulties, caused by jargon, different first languages or disabilities

■ not having appropriate equipment to provide care

■ not having enough information about a service user's needs.

ACTIVITY

During work experience or a visit to a care setting, observe how the organisation and staff take into account service users' beliefs and preferences.

Write a short report giving examples of different steps taken and explaining how they help to optimise interaction.

DISCUSSION POINT

For each of the four constraints listed:

■ how could you recognise the problem?

■ how could you solve the problem?

Improving interaction in caring relationships

Health and social care practitioners can determine the success of interaction by their approach to, and skill in, providing care. The factors which affect interaction can be divided into three main categories:

■ characteristics of the practitioner
- skill and professionalism
- personal appearance
■ information
- supplying information
- empowering people through giving information
■ education and training
- education and training for practitioners
- counselling for practitioners.

Multi-skilled professionals

In recent years, there has been a new emphasis on health and social care practitioners being multi-skilled professionals, able to meet a range of their service users' needs.

Personal appearance of health and social care workers

Almost everybody judges the people they meet on the basis of their personal appearance. Whether it's fair or not, an initial impression created by the clothes someone wears, their hairstyle or how smart they are can mean the success or failure of a relationship.

Practitioners need to be aware of this, and dress in a way which is not going to offend or worry anyone. In general terms, they should:

■ be neat and tidy
■ consider health and hygiene
■ dress as particular service users would expect
■ dress appropriately for different situations – for example, a care practitioner might dress smartly for a formal meeting, but would probably wear casual clothes for an activity-based interaction with young people.

The main debate about health and social care practitioners' personal appearance focuses on whether or not they should wear uniforms. Some people find uniforms a reassuring sign of competence and authority. From a practical point of view, uniforms can be designed so that they are functional and hygienic, have pockets to hold any equipment the worker needs, and make them easy to identify. But some service users and practitioners feel that uniforms perpetuate the traditional power relationship, and make it harder to develop close and caring interaction.

Supplying information

People need information to understand what is happening to them, and practitioners need to be able to provide this information clearly and effectively. Practitioners may need to give people:

■ information about the organisation and building
■ details of care procedures

DISCUSSION POINT

What do you think are the advantages of practitioners being multi-skilled? Can you think of any disadvantages?

ACTIVITY

Carry out a survey to find out people's opinions on whether practitioners should wear uniforms. Present your findings in a short report, using pie charts and bar charts, and summarise your conclusions.

- facts about medical conditions
- practical details, such as menus and times of appointments.

Giving information about themselves can help practitioners to form good relationships with service users. Many workers now wear name badges so that people see them as individuals, and charts are displayed in care settings showing different members of staff and their roles. In some situations, practitioners may also exchange personal information with service users (known as self-disclosure). Used with care, this can help people see the practitioner as an individual they can trust, encouraging them to share their own feelings.

A nurse explains some of the skills involved in improving interaction with service users by supplying information:

66 *Giving patients information – anything from when they'll get dinner to details of their treatment – is an important part of my job. I have to decide when to give people information, taking into account confidentiality, the person's level of understanding, and their emotional condition. It's important to realise that patients feeling vulnerable or ill often see you as a figure in authority, and take what you say as gospel. So I make sure I only give them facts I'm certain about, and try to avoid giving my opinion if I'm not sure. I explain things as clearly as I can, avoiding medical jargon but trying not to sound patronising. In my experience, if patients understand their treatment and illness, it tends to relieve their stress and worry.* 99

Empowerment through giving information

People can only make sound decisions about their care and treatment if they have information. Therefore giving service users information is an important part of empowering them – increasing their independence and ability to make choices.

Many different types of information can empower service users. For example:

- someone arriving at a clinic feels in control of the situation if they are given clear information on where to wait and where to go
- a patient in hospital with a serious illness can be involved in decision-making about treatment if they are given clear information on the different options
- an elderly person in a residential home can structure their own day if they know when different activities take place.

Education and training for health and social care workers

To optimise interaction, practitioners need a range of skills in:

- communication (for example, reflective listening, seeking feedback, using body language)
- problem-solving
- providing efficient, effective health and social care.

ACTIVITY

People's rights to information are laid down in several pieces of legislation, including the Data Protection Act, the Access to Personal Files Act, and the Access to Health Records Act (look back to section 1.3.1 for more information on these). Carry out research into each Act, and compile a chart summarising the main points of each Act and how they help to optimise interaction.

DISCUSSION POINT

Have you ever felt powerless when receiving health and social care because you didn't have enough information? How could information have made a difference?

The education and training that practitioners receive before they begin employment aim to ensure that they have the fundamental skills they need. Further skills and knowledge are developed through:

- experience of different situations in the workplace
- learning from more experienced colleagues
- induction training, which practitioners receive when they start a new job
- training sessions within the care setting, which provide opportunities for colleagues to exchange ideas, skills and advice
- taking courses in order to gain more advanced qualifications, or to develop new areas of expertise.

Counselling for health and social care practitioners

Working in health and social care can be extremely stressful. Practitioners often have to work long, physically tiring days. They may work with distressed or seriously ill people, and have to cope with emotionally draining situations. Many have to make difficult decisions, and some even face dangerous situations every day. And often the help they can provide is restricted by lack of money, time and resources.

All of these factors create considerable stresses and pressures for practitioners. Without emotional support to help them cope, they may become depressed, frustrated, resentful, and unable to perform effectively in their job. Practitioners who are under stress find it hard to interact with service users and this can lead to breakdowns in communication. In extreme cases, they may even be driven to abuse people in their care.

To prevent this happening, practitioners need to be able to draw on the support of counselling services. Supervision by an experienced member of staff can help practitioners cope with difficult situations. Other counselling may be provided in-house by the occupational health department or through peer support.

ACTIVITY

Interview a health or social care practitioner about:

- their education and training
- counselling services available to them in the workplace
- how training and counselling help them to optimise interaction.

With your interviewee's permission, write a case study based on their experiences.

Recommending improvements

Every caring relationship, and every care setting, is unique. As a result, you have to analyse and judge each situation on its own merits before making recommendations on how a caring relationship might be improved.

It is easy to recommend how care settings and relationships might be improved in an ideal world. However, for recommendations to be effective they must be:

- realistic – capable of being put into practice
- valid – taking into account the context of the setting and the condition of the service user
- constructive – offering viable, useful suggestions rather than criticisms.

Mark, an Advanced GNVQ Health and Social Care student, spends an afternoon every week on work experience at a residential home for elderly people. As part of his assessment, his tutor has asked him to make recommendations as to how interaction could be improved in one caring relationship in the setting.

Mark's report

I observed the relationship between Mrs O'Hagan, one of the residents, and Kim Afzal, a care assistant who has special responsibility for caring for her.

Kim and Mrs O'Hagan have known each other for six months, and have developed a fairly close relationship. Mrs O'Hagan has her own room in the home which she has furnished with her own chairs and pictures. She has been in residential care for three years, and is quite settled and happy. But she is a bit of a loner, and doesn't mix very well with the other residents. She prefers to stay in her room watching TV rather than joining in activities in the communal areas. She has a small appetite, and often misses meals because she doesn't like coming downstairs for them.

I observed Kim's relationship with Mrs O'Hagan, with their permission, over two afternoons spent at the home. This included occasions when Kim was tidying Mrs O'Hagan's room, talking to her over a cup of tea, and trying to persuade her to come and eat dinner downstairs.

HOW COULD INTERACTION IN THE CARING RELATIONSHIP BE IMPROVED?

* *Kim went into Mrs O'Hagan's room without knocking. I think this is a bad start to interaction, as it doesn't show respect for someone's personal space. I would advise Kim to always knock before entering Mrs O'Hagan's room.*

* *Kim looks a bit of a mess! Mrs O'Hagan commented twice on her appearance.*

* Kim doesn't wear a name badge, and Mrs O'Hagan kept forgetting her name. I think all care assistants should be issued with name badges, as it would help the residents remember who is who. The name badges would have to be in quite large letters so that everyone can read them.

* Mrs O'Hagan sometimes found it hard to understand what Kim was saying, as she tended to mumble and spoke very fast without looking at her. I think it would be helpful for care assistants to go on a course in communication techniques.

* Kim didn't really listen to Mrs O'Hagan when she was explaining why she didn't want to go downstairs to dinner. Mrs O'Hagan doesn't like the woman she sits next to at the table, and didn't like the food on the menu. Kim just kept saying 'You've got to eat, you know', without trying to suggest any solutions.

* Mrs O'Hagan asked Kim when her next hospital appointment was, and Kim said she'd let her know a day in advance. I think this is wrong, and Kim should give Mrs O'Hagan this type of information. Mrs O'Hagan has a right to know about her own life, so she can plan her time and feel she has some say in what is going on.

* It would be better if there were twice as many care assistants in the home, then other people could share Mrs O'Hagan's care.

DISCUSSION POINT

Consider whether Mark's recommendations are realistic, valid and constructive. Which recommendations do you think would be most useful for the care assistant and the residential home?

ACTIVITY

Think of a caring relationship you are familiar with – perhaps through work experience, or people you know. Make recommendations as to how interaction in the relationship might be improved. All your recommendations should be realistic, valid and constructive.

Key questions

1   Give five examples of care settings.
2   What might be the positive and negative effects of being cared for in your own home?
3   How can residential homes show respect for their residents?
4   Explain five positive effects of caring relationships on service users.
5   Why might a caring relationship result in dependence and fear?
6   What is advocacy for service users? How does it optimise interaction in care settings?
7   What types of organisational information can optimise interaction?
8   Describe some of the ways in which people can be involved in their own care.
9   What are multi-skilled professionals? How can they improve interaction in caring relationships?
10 Explain how information can empower service users.
11 What types of education and training can help health and social care workers improve interaction?
12 Why do health and social care practitioners need access to counselling services?
13 What are realistic recommendations?
14 What are valid recommendations?
15 What are constructive recommendations?

Assignment

Choose two care settings, one domestic and one in an institution. These may be settings you know through work experience, visits or personal experience. Carry out a detailed investigation of each of the care settings and write a report explaining:

- the possible effects of the care setting on service users
- four ways of optimising interaction in the care setting
- two positive and two negative effects of caring relationships you observe within each care setting.

Confidentiality is important – remember to ask permission before carrying out the investigation and writing your report.

Then choose one service user–carer relationship to focus on in more detail. Carry out in-depth interviews with the practitioner involved and, if appropriate, the service user (again, remember to respect confidentiality). Prepare a presentation based on your findings, explaining four methods used to improve interaction in the caring relationship and recommending how interaction in the caring relationship might be improved further.

UNIT **3**

Element 3.1
Structures and systems in the human body

Element 3.2
The functions of the main organ systems

Element 3.3
Maintaining the healthy functioning of the body

Physical aspects of health and social wellbeing

This unit is about the physical aspects of health and social wellbeing. It explains how structures are organised in the human body, describes the functions of the main body systems and their relationships, and identifies how to monitor healthy functioning, focusing on the cardiorespiratory system.

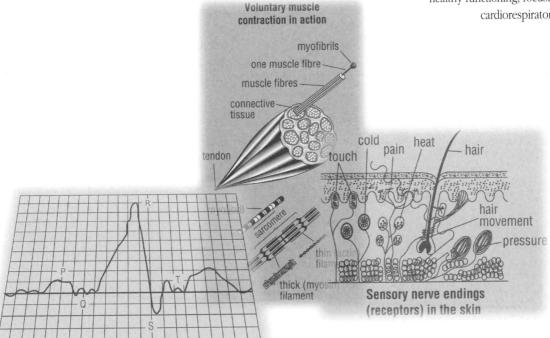

Voluntary muscle contraction in action

myofibrils
one muscle fibre
muscle fibres
connective tissue
tendon

sarcomere

thin actin filament

thick (myosin) filament

cold pain heat hair
touch

hair movement
pressure

Sensory nerve endings (receptors) in the skin

ELEMENT **3.1**

Structures and systems in the human body

In this element you will explore the organisation of structures within human body systems, focusing on tissue types and the process of cellular respiration.

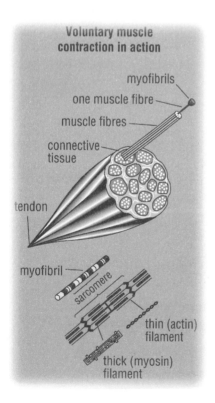

Voluntary muscle contraction in action

66 *If someone came to the counter with breathing difficulties but able to talk I would go through the WWHAM questions (who the medicine is for, what the symptoms are, how long they've had the symptoms, any action that's been taken and any medication they've taken for it or that they're already taking) to determine if they had taken anything which was causing the problem. Some decongestant tablets might be causing it. In most cases I would send them to their GP or to A&E, depending on the severity of the problem.* 99

pharmacist

The roles of major cell components

Cells are the simplest structural and functional units from which organisms – including human beings – are made. They were named by Robert Hooke, a British physicist who played a part in developing the microscope. Looking at slices of cork under a microscope in the 1660s, he observed honeycomb-like spaces which he called 'cells' from the Latin word *cella* ('store'). Although he actually saw dead cell walls, his observation led to other scientists discovering that all living organisms are made of cells.

Cells are much too small to be seen with the naked eye – human body cells are between about one hundredth of a millimetre and one tenth of a millimetre in size (the largest human cell is the female ovum). Since the development of the electron microscope, biologists have developed much greater understanding of the structure of cells.

As cells develop, their structure changes to allow them to fulfil special functions efficiently. Specialised cells act together to form tissues, which in turn make up organs. Similarly, organs work together to form body systems with a particular function. For example:

UNIT
3
ELEMENT **3.1**

Specialised cell (e.g. cardiac muscle cell)	Specialised tissue (e.g. heart muscle)	Organ (e.g. the heart)	Body system (e.g. cardio-vascular system)

Whatever their specialised function, all cells have the same basic structure, as shown in the diagram below.

The cell is held together by a thin boundary, often called the **plasma membrane.** Inside this membrane is the **cytoplasm,** which contains the different components of the cell suspended in a fluid called cytosol. These components – known as **organelles** – have their own structures and purposes. They include:

- endoplasmic reticulum
- ribosomes
- mitochondria
- nucleus.

ACTIVITY

Prepare a microscope slide from the cells lining a pig's trachea and examine it under a light microscope.

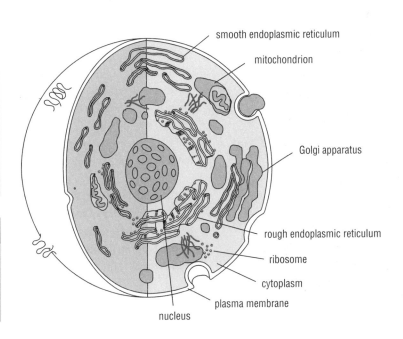

smooth endoplasmic reticulum

mitochondrion

Golgi apparatus

rough endoplasmic reticulum

ribosome

cytoplasm

plasma membrane

nucleus

The **plasma membrane** is the outer boundary of the cell. It:

■ holds together the cell's contents

■ stops the cell's contents mixing with substances outside the cell or in neighbouring cells

■ controls what substances enter and leave the cell.

The **endoplasmic reticulum** is a network of sac-like and tubular cavities held together by a membrane. It is the largest organelle, filling most of the cell's cytoplasm.

Plasma membrane

The plasma membrane is a complex structure which is made up of protein molecules and fatty substances called phospholipids.

Phospholipids have hydrophobic (water-hating) 'tails' of fatty acids, and hydrophilic (water-loving) 'heads' of phosphate. They are arranged in two layers in the plasma membrane, with their tails facing inwards and their heads facing outwards. Constant movement of the phospholipids means that the cell membrane is fluid.

Protein molecules are either contained within one of these layers, or cross the whole membrane. Many of them are carrier proteins, which transport substances across the membrane. Others are receptor sites, which receive information from outside the cell and neighbouring cells.

The outside of the plasma membrane has a cell coat made up of glycolipids, glycoprotein, mucopolysaccharides and byaluronic acid. This is sticky, helping cells to join together.

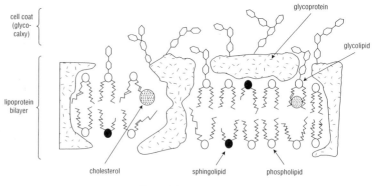

Diagram of plasma membrane

Different substances, such as nutrients, water, oxygen and waste materials, are constantly moving into and out of the cell by passing through the plasma membrane. The membrane is selectively permeable – it only lets some materials through. For example, water and gases can cross the cell wall freely, while ions (which carry an electron charge) and nutrient molecules have more difficulty. Some substances are transported through the membrane by carrier protein molecules. Others pass through by dissolving in the phospholipid layers.

Endoplasmic reticulum

There are two types of endoplasmic reticulum (ER):

■ rough ER (also known as granular ER). This is a series of flattened sacs covered with tiny granules – ribosomes (see below)

■ smooth ER (also known as agranular ER).

The ribosomes on rough ER make proteins which are used in the cell membrane and outside the cell.

DISCUSSION POINT

Can you identify the ribosomes in this micrograph of rough ER?

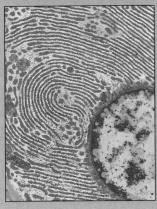

The smooth ER makes fatty materials, including the phospholipids which form part of the plasma membrane. In liver cells, the smooth ER contains enzymes which change dangerous chemicals into forms that can be excreted from the body safely.

Mitochondria

Mitochondria – the name means thread-granules – are small sacs which can be oval, spherical or rod-shaped. They have a smooth outer membrane and a folded inner membrane enclosing a space called the matrix, which contains:

- enzymes needed for the oxidation of glucose in the cell (see section 3.1.4); this process releases energy, which is stored in a compound called ATP ready for use by the cell
- DNA (deoxyribonucleic acid). Mitochondria have their own set of genetic material, which enables them to replicate when a cell divides.

Most cells contain hundreds of mitochondria. Very active cells which need lots of energy, such as liver cells, may contain up to 1,000 mitochondria.

ACTIVITY

Carry out research into the structure of mitochondria. From your research, and by looking at an electron micrograph, draw a labelled diagram showing the structure of a mitochondrion.

Ribosomes

Ribosomes themselves are made of protein and ribonucleic acid (ribosomal RNA).

Ribosomes are small granules which exist in cells in two forms:
- as free ribosomes, suspended in the cell's cytoplasm
- attached to the surface of rough ER.

Both types of ribosomes are vitally important because of their role in making proteins from chains of amino acids. Free ribosomes make proteins which are released directly into the cytoplasm and used in the cell. Ribosomes attached to rough ER make proteins which are transferred into a part of the cell called the Golgi apparatus, from where they are used in the plasma membrane or outside the cell.

ACTIVITY

Why is protein so important to human beings? Carry out research, and write a short explanation of the role of proteins. Include diagrams or images where useful.

The **nucleus** is a large spherical or oval body surrounded by a double-layered membrane. It contains protein and nucleic acids (DNA and RNA).

Nucleus

The nucleus is often referred to as the control centre of the cell – although a cell can live without a nucleus it can't divide and produce new cells. Instructions for making functional and structural cell proteins are carried in DNA (deoxyribonucleic acid) in the nucleus, which is wound up as a double spiral. When cells divide, the nucleus goes through a complex process (mitosis), which results in identical copies of the genetic material (DNA) being found in each new cell. When the cell is not dividing, the protein and nucleic acids appear as granules called chromatin. During division, the chromatin forms strands of DNA called chromosomes, which determine the structure of proteins in the organism. Information from the chromosomes is carried by messenger RNA through large pores in the nuclear membrane into the cytoplasm and ribosomes.

The nucleus is the easiest part of a cell to identify on a micrograph as it is more acidic than the cytoplasm and stains a darker colour. Within the nucleus there may also be darker round spots. These are the **nucleoli** where ribosomes are made.

ACTIVITY

Look at a micrograph of a human body cell, and identify:

- plasma membrane
- endoplasmic reticulum
- mitochondria
- ribosomes
- nucleus.

Calculate the actual distance across the middle of the nucleus using the information given about magnification.

Based on your observations, draw a diagram showing the main parts of a cell. To go with your diagram, write a short paragraph explaining the structure and function of each part.

The main tissue types

Examples of tissues found in the body are:

- muscular tissue, which controls movement
- connective tissue, which supports the body
- nervous tissue, which communicates messages around the body
- epithelial tissue, which provides protection and secretes substances.

Most cells don't function on their own in the body. Instead, cells with a similar form or function join together to make tissues.

Tissues consist of several different types of cells. The cells in tissue are surrounded by tissue fluid, which carries materials into and out of the cells.

The study of tissues is called **histology**.

Muscular tissue

About 40% of human body weight is made up of muscular tissue, which enables the body to move. Muscle cells have good contractility, which means they change in length easily. All movement depends on muscular tissue becoming shorter by contracting, and then becoming longer again by relaxing.

There are three types of muscle tissue:

- skeletal muscular tissue (also known as 'voluntary' or 'striated' muscle tissue)
- smooth muscular tissue (also known as 'involuntary' or 'unstriated' muscle tissue)
- cardiac muscular tissue (only found in the walls of the heart).

Skeletal muscular tissue

As its name suggests, skeletal muscular tissue is attached to the body's skeleton (bones), and controls its movement. It is made up of long cylindrical muscle fibres which are controlled voluntarily. This means that an individual can decide to walk, chew, smile, talk and so on, and control the contraction of the appropriate muscles.

Some muscles contain up to a thousand muscle fibres, each of which is a single muscle cell and may be as long as 30 cm. These are held together in a bundle by collagen (a protein which forms the basis of bones). In turn, each muscle fibre contains a bundle of smaller sub-fibres called myofibrils, made of tiny protein filaments. These lie in line with one another, and make skeletal muscular tissue look striped (striated) when it is viewed under a microscope.

Skeletal muscle fibres contain several nuclei, and also a large number of mitochondria (see page 137), which provide the energy to make the fibres contract. Electrical nerve impulses from the central nervous system trigger contraction and the muscle fibres shorten by pulling together the protein filaments. Muscle fibres can contract up to 50 times a second, shortening to about two-thirds of their usual length. Skeletal muscular tissue can contract quickly and powerfully, but soon tires.

Voluntary muscle contraction in action

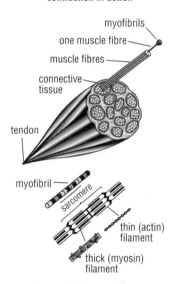

myofibrils
one muscle fibre
muscle fibres
connective tissue
tendon

myofibril
sarcomere
thin (actin) filament
thick (myosin) filament

ACTIVITY

Find out more about how skeletal muscles contract. Write a short explanation supported by diagrams, which explains how the structure of skeletal muscular tissue enables it to contract and create movement.

Smooth muscular tissue

Smooth muscular tissue is also known as involuntary muscle, because it isn't usually controlled consciously by the individual. Unlike skeletal muscular tissue, it doesn't have a striped appearance when viewed under a microscope (it is unstriated).

Smooth muscular tissue

Connective tissue   Central nucleus

Spindle or cigar-shaped
muscle cell

Smooth muscular tissue is made up of spindle-shaped muscle cells containing one nucleus, joined together in sheets. These sheets run in muscle layers around and down cylindrical organs such as blood vessels, the intestines, the bladder, the respiratory tract and the uterus. The muscular tissue enables the organ to contract and relax rhythmically on its own:

■ contraction of the muscle cells running around the organ causes it to become narrower

■ contraction of the muscle cells running down the organ cause it to become longer (and sometimes wider).

Cardiac muscular tissue

Cardiac muscular tissue is only found in the walls of the heart. Like skeletal muscle, it has a striped (striated) appearance, but like smooth muscle it can't be controlled consciously (movement is involuntary).

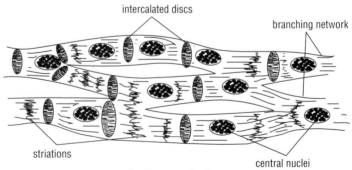

intercalated discs

branching network

striations

central nuclei

Cardiac muscular tissue

Cardiac muscular tissue is made up of branching muscle fibres which are interconnected and spread in a network across the heart. The fibres are divided into individual muscle cells by intercalated discs, made of several layers of membranes. These discs strengthen the muscle fibres, and help to conduct the electrical stimulus called the cardiac impulse which causes the whole heart muscle to contract and relax rhythmically. Each individual muscle cell has a central nucleus, and many mitochondria which provide the energy needed for contraction.

Connective tissue

The key feature of connective tissue is that it is made up of cells surrounded by a substance called the intercellular matrix. The composition of this matrix plays a large part in determining the function of different types of connective tissue.

All connective tissue apart from blood contains three main types of fibre in its intercellular matrix:

- collagen fibres (made of the protein collagen) – these provide good strength and structural support
- reticular fibres (made of the protein reticulin) – these support tissues containing many cells
- elastic fibres (made of elastin) – these can be stretched and then return to their normal length.

These fibres are present in varying proportions in the matrix, depending on the function of a particular type of tissue. For example, tendons and ligaments contain closely packed collagen fibres, which provide the strength and support needed to link muscle to bone and bone to bone. Connective tissue in the walls of arteries contains collagen for strength, and elastin to enable the blood vessels to dilate.

Blood cells are suspended in a fluid intercellular matrix called plasma – a straw-coloured liquid. This has a water base, and contains large amounts of proteins which contribute to the functioning of the blood. Some plasma proteins are involved in coagulation. Others carry substances such as vitamins, iron, antibodies, insulin and hormones.

Blood

Blood is a vital connective tissue, which:

- carries oxygen to every part of the body
- plays an important role in the body's immune system
- supplies glucose to tissues and organs
- carries away waste products.

As already mentioned, blood cells are surrounded by a fluid matrix called plasma, which comprises over half the total volume of blood. The following table shows the structure and function of different types of blood cells contained within this matrix.

Connective tissue supports, protects and holds together other tissues in the body. It is the most common type of tissue in the human body – blood, lymph, cartilage and bone are all examples of connective tissue.

ACTIVITY

There are three main types of cartilage:

- hyaline cartilage, which has a matrix containing a high proportion of collagen
- elastic cartilage, which contains a high proportion of elastin fibres in its matrix
- fibro-cartilage, which has a high proportion of collagen fibres in its matrix.

Carry out research into the function of these different types of cartilage. Write a short paragraph describing each and explaining how the composition of its intercellular matrix relates to its function.

Cell	Structure	Function

Red blood cells (erythrocytes)

Red blood cells (erythrocytes)

- no nucleus
- contain the red pigment haemoglobin
- don't contain ribosomes, so can't produce proteins, grow or repair
- survive in the blood for about four months

Collect oxygen from the lungs and deliver it to the body's tissues. There are over a thousand times as many red cells as white cells.

White blood cells (leucocytes)

Lymphocytes

- no granules in cytoplasm
- relatively large nucleus
- appear spherical

Produce and may carry antibodies, and play an important part in the body's immune system in response to infection.

Monocytes

- no granules in cytoplasm
- large cell
- kidney-shaped nucleus

Detect chemical substances produced by bacteria, move towards the bacteria, and engulf them in a process called phagocytosis.

Neutrophils

- granules in cytoplasm
- irregular nucleus, usually with three to five bumps

Locate and engulf bacteria (as monocytes, above).

Basophils

- spherical granules in cytoplasm
- kidney-shaped nucleus

Produce histamine.

Eosinophils

- granules in cytoplasm
- c-shaped nucleus

Involved in responding to allergic reactions. The number of eosinophils in the blood increases rapidly during an allergic reaction.

Compact bone tissue is made up of Haversian systems, which appear as a series of concentric rings (lamellae). At the centre of the lamellae are channels called Haversian canals, which contain blood vessels, lymphatic vessels and nerves. These connect with the periosteum (the tough membrane surrounding bones), and with the marrow (where red and white blood cells are produced). Within the lamellae there are small spaces called lacunae, where bone cells (osteocytes) are found. These secrete the bone matrix, and are linked by a series of fine channels.

Compact bone

Compact bone is dense and rigid bone found on the outside of all bones, and inside long bones of the skeleton (such as the femur). It has to:

■ bear the weight of the body

■ protect and support other tissues

■ withstand the stresses of standing and walking.

The intercellular matrix of compact bone contains:

■ a network of collagen fibres, which enable the bone to bear strain and ensure it is not too brittle

■ mineral salts (in particular, complex phosphates of calcium), which impregnate the collagen. These give the bone great strength and hardness.

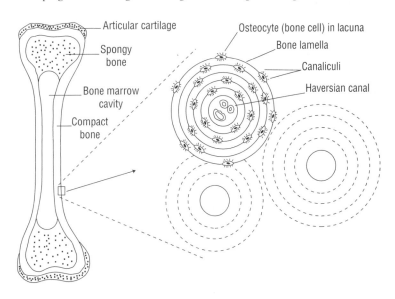

DISCUSSION POINT

As people get older, the amount of collagen and mineral salts in the matrix of their compact bone decreases. What effect do you think this has?

Nervous tissue

Nervous tissue is made up of nerve cells called neurons. The most important property of neurons is excitability. They:

■ are sensitive to stimuli, producing nerve impulses

■ transmit nerve impulses to other neurons or effectors (parts of the body which do things, or 'effect' action).

In doing so, they act as the body's rapid communication system.

Sensory neurons react to stimuli from the internal and external environment. Receptor organs – which control vision, hearing, smell and taste – are

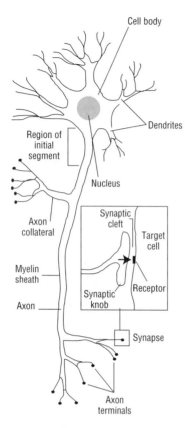

Cell body

Dendrites

Region of
initial
segment

Nucleus

Axon
collateral

Synaptic
cleft

Target
cell

Myelin
sheath

Receptor

Axon

Synaptic
knob

Synapse

Axon
terminals

A motor neurone

connected directly to the brain by short nerve tracts. Other sensory information is carried to the central nervous system (brain and spinal cord) from receptor nerve endings in the joints, skin, muscles, tendons and internal organs.

The central nervous system (CNS) processes the information it receives from sensory neurons. If action is necessary, motor neurons conduct impulses from the CNS to effector organs, triggering a response such as contraction of a muscle, or secretion in a gland.

Like other cells, neurons have a cell body containing a nucleus and cytoplasm. However, they also have dendrites and an axon, fibres which project from the cell body and give it its unique shape and excitability.

> **Dendrites** are fine branching fibres which receive impulses from other neurons and conduct them to the cell body. The **axon** is a long, single nerve fibre which conducts impulses away from the cell body. It is branched at the end, with small swellings called **synapses** which form the junctions with other neurons. Often, the axon is covered by a **myelin sheath,** a casing of fatty materials which insulates the fibre and increases the speed at which impulses are conducted. In human beings, most cell bodies are in the brain or spinal cord, and axons may be over a metre long in order to reach an organ.

Epithelial tissue

> **Epithelial tissue** lines internal and external body surfaces, and acts as a boundary between different tissues and organs. All epithelial tissue has a thin **basement membrane** containing reticular fibres (made up of the protein reticulin) and glycoprotein. This provides support and attachment.

Epithelial tissue can be divided into different categories depending on:
■ the shape of cells
■ whether it is simple epithelial tissue (with one layer of cells) or compound epithelial tissue (with many layers of cells).

Simple squamous tissue

This is simple epithelial tissue, consisting of one layer of flat, thin, irregularly-shaped cells,

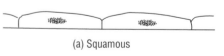

(a) Squamous

each with a nucleus in the middle. The bottom of each cell sits on the basement membrane; the top surface is free. Cells are packed together closely, with little fluid between them (simple squamous tissue is sometimes called pavement epithelium). This sort of tissue is found in, for example, blood and lymphatic vessels and lung alveoli.

> ### ACTIVITY
>
> Excitability depends on potassium ions inside the neuron and sodium ions outside it. Carry out research to find out more about:
>
> ■ how these ions enable neurons to receive and transmit impulses
>
> ■ how excitability enables neurons to communicate.

Cuboidal tissue

This is simple epithelial tissue, consisting of one layer of cube-shaped cells. Examples are found in kidney tubules and covering the ovaries.

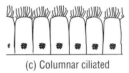

(b) Cuboidal

Columnar tissue

Also simple epithelial tissue, consisting of one layer of elongated, column-shaped cells. They often have cilia (small hairs) on the top surface. This type of tissue can be found in the lining of the digestive system.

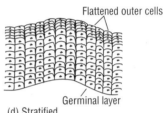

(c) Columnar ciliated

Stratified squamous epithelium

This is compound epithelial tissue, consisting of many layers of cells. The lower layers are cuboidal or columnar, the top layers are flatter (squamous). The lowest layer of cells sits on the basement membrane. Examples can be found in the lining of the mouth, tongue, vagina, oesophagus and rectum and in the skin (with an extra layer of dead cells for protection).

Flattened outer cells

Germinal layer

(d) Stratified

The main function of epithelial tissue is to provide protection by covering and lining tissues and organs. As a result, epithelial cells are regularly damaged, and have properties which enable them to repair well.

Some epithelial tissue is also secretory, forming glands which are specialised to secrete substances such as hormones and perspiration. These glands can be divided into:

- exocrine glands – which remain attached to the epithelial tissue they develop from and have a duct to the outside of the body (for example, mammary glands)
- endocrine glands – which are detached from the epithelial tissue they develop from. They are ductless and secrete hormones straight into the bloodstream (for example, the thyroid gland).

DISCUSSION POINT

Having investigated all four main tissue types, discuss how their features relate to their function. How is muscular tissue designed for movement rather than communication? Why is epithelial tissue protective rather than supportive?

Section 3.1.3	# Interpreting micrographs

Scientists examine cells and tissues using a microscope. To prepare a section of tissue for viewing under a light microscope, a piece of dead tissue is preserved in a fixing fluid and dehydrated with ethanol. It is then cleaned with an organic solvent and embedded in molten wax. When the wax hardens, a thin section of the tissue is cut and attached to a microscope slide. The wax is removed, and the tissue is stained to accentuate contrasts and make it easier to see tissue and cell structures.

So what is a micrograph?

- A micrograph is a photograph of a sample viewed through a light microscope.
- An electron micrograph is a photograph of a sample viewed through an electron microscope.

Micrographs of epithelial tissue

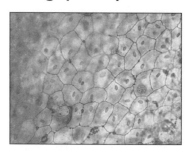 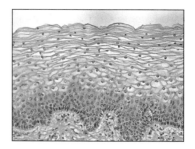

Micrographs of muscular tissue

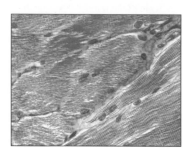

Micrographs of connective tissue

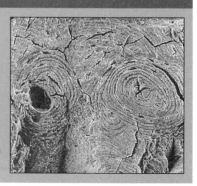

Cellular respiration

Cellular respiration provides cells with the energy they need to function – whether it's the energy a neuron uses to conduct an electrical impulse, or a muscle uses when contracting. Seen in wider terms, cellular respiration gives human beings the energy they need for life.

The original source of this energy is the sun. When plants carry out photosynthesis, they take the sun's energy, combine it with carbon dioxide from the air and water from the soil, and make oxygen and glucose. The energy is transferred into the glucose, and is stored in the chemical bonds holding together carbon, hydrogen and oxygen (the chemical formula of glucose is $C_6H_{12}O_6$).

Molecules containing energy enter the human body through the food chain. Digestion breaks down food into small units, but most of the energy is still trapped in the chemical bonds of glucose. Cellular respiration is the metabolic process by which this energy is released so that it can be used by the body.

Cellular respiration in the human body takes place either:
- aerobically – using oxygen to break down glucose and produce energy
- anaerobically – producing energy without using oxygen.

> The term **respiration** is often used to mean breathing – it is important to understand that this is not the same thing as cellular respiration. To make the distinction clearer, cellular respiration is also known as 'tissue respiration' or 'internal respiration'.

DISCUSSION POINT

Why do you think some foods provide more energy than others?

Aerobic respiration

When there are normal supplies of oxygen, cellular respiration takes place aerobically. In aerobic respiration, glucose is oxidised (combined with oxygen) to produce carbon dioxide, water and energy:

$$C_6H_{12}O_6 + 6O_2 = 6CO_2 + 6H_2O + energy$$

glucose + oxygen = carbon dioxide + water + energy

This process takes place through a series of small chemical reactions triggered by different enzymes within the cell. These can be divided into two key stages:
- glycolysis
- Krebs cycle.

Glycolysis

Glycolysis takes place in the cell's cytoplasm, and the enzymes needed for this stage of cellular respiration are contained in the cytoplasmic fluid.

Within cells, energy is stored in a compound called ATP (adenosine tri-phosphate). As its name suggests, ATP is made up of a substance called

147

adenosine attached to three phosphate groupings. These phosphates are joined by high-energy bonds, which contain a lot of energy. When one of the phosphate bonds is broken, the energy is released, and the ATP becomes ADP (adenosine diphosphate). The ADP can then rebuild itself by forming another phosphate bond to become ATP .

ATP supplies energy to start the process of glycolysis. Glucose enters the cell's cytoplasm, and takes phosphate from an ATP molecule to become glucose 6-phosphate. Phosphate from a second ATP molecule is then used to modify the glucose further, making fructose biphosphate, which is more reactive. Through a series of reactions, the six-carbon sugar molecule is converted into two molecules of the three-carbon compound pyruvic acid. From this point, two molecules are processed simultaneously. In the absence of oxygen (anaerobic respiration), pyruvic acid is converted to lactic acid.

During this process, energy is released from the glucose. Some of the energy is lost as heat, but the rest is trapped by ADP molecules and used to form ATP. The glycolysis of one molecule of glucose produces enough energy to create two new ATP molecules.

Glycolysis is often called the anaerobic stage of aerobic cellular respiration, as no oxygen is used during the process. Although it releases some energy, most of it remains within the pyruvic acid molecules.

■ If oxygen is available, this energy is released aerobically through the Krebs cycle (see below). This is the process which usually follows glycolysis.

■ If oxygen is in short supply, this energy can be released anaerobically (see *Anaerobic respiration*).

Krebs cycle

The Krebs cycle – also known as the tricarboxylic acid cycle – takes place in the mitochondria of cells.

The pyruvic acid molecules produced during glycolysis, which contain energy still to be released, are converted into an intermediate substance called acetyl coenzyme A and move into the cell's mitochondria. Here they combine with oxygen and are broken down into carbon dioxide and hydrogen atoms in a complex series of reactions. During these reactions the hydrogen atoms from the original pyruvic acid molecules are combined with oxygen to form water and so release energy, which is used to form ATP molecules.

At the end of the Krebs cycle:

■ carbon dioxide is removed as a waste product

■ the hydrogen atoms combine with oxygen to produce water

■ molecules of ATP have been formed (38 molecules for every molecule of glucose).

ACTIVITY

Draw a simple diagram showing the key processes involved in aerobic cellular respiration.

Because the Krebs cycle involves using oxygen, it is known as the aerobic stage of cellular respiration.

By breaking down glucose in this way, cells are provided with a large amount of energy – stored in ATP – which they can use to drive reactions.

Anaerobic respiration

Anaerobic (without using oxygen) cellular respiration only takes place when there is a shortage of oxygen in the body. ATP is used more quickly than the muscle cell's mitochondria can supply it aerobically through the reactions of the Krebs cycle. As a result, the muscle cell produces ATP without oxygen to meet its energy demands.

Glycolysis, which does not require oxygen, can still take place. However, instead of moving on to the Krebs cycle, the pyruvic acid produced remains in the cell's cytoplasm. Here it is converted into lactic acid, forming just two molecules of ATP for every glucose molecule (much less than is produced through aerobic respiration).

If muscle cells are forced to respire anaerobically for a long time, the lactic acid builds up and can cause cramp, forcing the individual to stop exercising. Even after stopping, the body is described as having an 'oxygen debt'. This is because all the lactic acid must be broken down through oxidisation before the muscles can return to normal.

ACTIVITY

Hold a heavy bag at arm's length in front of you for as long as you are able. Explain the results.

Carry out further research into anaerobic respiration, and write your own account of the processes which take place. Include diagrams to make your explanation as clear as possible.

DISCUSSION POINT

Why do you think warming up before strenuous exercise can help prevent cramp?

Having read the description of anaerobic respiration, can you explain why people who have exercised vigorously often pant and remain short of breath for some time after finishing exercising?

Key questions

1 What is the role of the plasma membrane?
2 How do substances cross the plasma membrane?
3 Explain the difference between rough endoplasmic reticulum and smooth endoplasmic reticulum.
4 What is the role of mitochondria?
5 Where are ribosomes found?
6 What is the main role of ribosomes?
7 Why is the nucleus often referred to as the cell's control centre?
8 Name the four main tissue types and summarise their functions.
9 How could you recognise skeletal muscular tissue, smooth muscular tissue and cardiac muscular tissue?
10 Name four types of connective tissue in the body.
11 Name and explain the function of five different types of blood cells.
12 What does the intercellular matrix of compact bone contain?
13 Explain excitability in terms of the structure of a neuron.
14 Describe three types of epithelial tissue.
15 What is a micrograph?
16 When might aerobic and anaerobic respiration occur?
17 What is glycolysis and where does it take place in the cell?
18 What is the role of the Krebs cycle in the metabolism of products of anaerobic respiration?

Assignment

For this assignment, your teacher or tutor needs to give you a set of micrographs of different tissue types. Look at the micrographs and identify what type of tissue each shows. Your teacher or tutor will keep a checklist to show whether you have been successful.

Using your observation of micrographs as a starting point, produce a booklet for human biology students on the organisation of structures within human body systems. Your booklet should:

■ describe the key features of the four main tissue types in relation to their functions (you may find it helpful to include labelled diagrams based on your observation of micrographs)
■ describe the role of major cell components in human body cells
■ explain the processes involved in cellular respiration.

Your booklet should be clear and pitched at an appropriate level for the target audience. Make sure you explain any technical terms, and use diagrams where appropriate.

ELEMENT **3.2**

The functions of the main organ systems

In this element you will explore the functions of the main body systems and how they work together, develop and age.

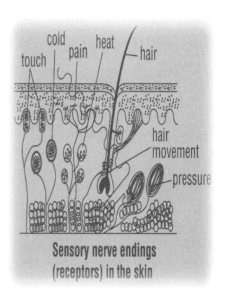

Sensory nerve endings (receptors) in the skin

| Section 3.2.1 | # How body systems interrelate to perform functions |

This looks at how body systems work together to perform the functions of:

- communication
- physical support and movement (locomotion)
- reproduction
- supply of energy
- excretion
- defence.

To stay alive the human body needs to deal with the environment – we need to breathe, eat, drink, get rid of waste products and to sense where we are and what's going on. The body's systems all interrelate to make these happen.

The skeletal structure provides:

- a support frame
- protection for delicate parts of the body such as organs, including the brain
- attachment for muscles
- opportunity for movement.

The muscles contract and relax as a result of nerve impulses pulling on the bones of the skeleton which act like levers to produce movement. The skeleton moves through a system of joints and muscle attachments. The muscles around the joints also help to protect the joints from injury.

The circulation system distributes blood to every living part of the body, including the muscles and bones. The nervous system and sense organs enable the brain to monitor conditions inside and outside the body.

These and other systems make up the complex and interconnected whole that allows the body to function.

Body systems for support and locomotion

Humans move, sit, stand, walk, talk, work, play, sing. In so many activities, the body is in motion. One feature of movement is the contraction and relaxation of muscles acting on bones at their joints. Muscles, bones and joints form the musculo-skeletal system, the largest and heaviest of the human body systems.

An osteopath expresses his view that:

66 *Everyone needs to learn how to care for their body's bony framework, its joints and the powers – muscles, tendons and other soft tissues – that hold it together, support it, position it, move it.* 99

Musculo-skeletal system

Most voluntary muscles act in pairs with one of the pair enabling movement in one direction and the other enabling movement in the opposite direction; each pair is known as antagonistic and usually, one muscle of the antagonistic pair is stronger than the other.

Voluntary muscles are elongated contractile fibres grouped in bundles and surrounded by sheaths of connective tissue. **Involuntary muscles** such as those in the arteries, the alimentary canal, the bladder and ureters are arranged in layers and made up of elongated contractile cells rather than fibres; they are usually controlled by the autonomic nervous system, although some are under conscious control. The heart consists of special muscle units which have groups of contractile tissues like the voluntary system but which are arranged and work like involuntary muscle.

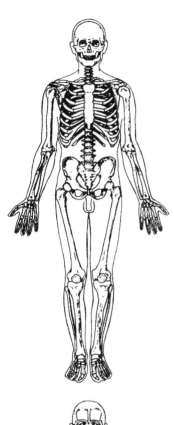

Each joint is moved by the two opposing sets of muscles – the flexors and the extensors. Basically, when one set is shortening, the other is stretching.

Interaction between the joints

Most joints (excluding sutures such as the joints in the skull) continually interact and are dependent on each other. For example, when you turn your head the entire spine moves subtly. Even breathing involves a wave of movement up and down the spinal column with all its joints. The joints of the feet interact with those connecting the neck and head during standing and walking. You are almost certainly not aware of it, but a fine adjustment between the different joints and muscles is happening all the time.

Nervous system

To move effectively, the contraction of many sets of muscles needs to be coordinated. Think of the motor coordination and balance needed by a dancer or a gymnast.

A system of stretch receptors in the muscles and joints sends nervous impulses to the brain via the spinal cord when the muscle is being stretched. These internal sensory organs are called proprioceptors. They send information to the brain about how the limbs are placed. The brain produces the information to enable the particular pattern of muscular activity needed in the movement, the proprioceptors feed back to the brain the information needed to monitor how the movement is proceeding and make any adjustments necessary.

Two types of nerve cell help protect muscles:
- muscle spindles
- tendon spindles.

When muscle groups are stretched, so are the muscle and tendon spindles. This helps to warn the brain well before the muscle is stretched too much, to the point of rupture. Signals are sent to contract the muscle. This helps to prevent injury.

Motor unit

A motor unit is made up of bundles of nerve cells with connections to the brain. Each cell branches off into fine filaments terminating in the muscle. The

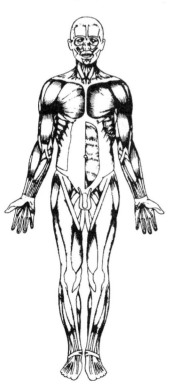

The musculo-skeletal system

number of cells in a motor unit depends on the degree of precision needed. The muscles responsible for the movement of the eye, for instance, have five to ten cells in each motor unit. The muscle forming the fleshy part of the buttock has several thousand cells in each unit.

When the motor unit is put to work, cells in the unit send impulses to the muscle to make it contract with maximum force. If the force of the muscle contraction needs to increase, more motor units come into operation.

A biomechanics lecturer explains:

66 *You need knowledge about the position and function of the muscles, forces, the movement of force, the centre of gravity and the moment of inertia if you are a gymnastics coach helping a performer to learn the skills of a new complex exercise.* **99**

Body systems for communication

Nervous system

Three main types of response are controlled by the nervous system:

- reflexes
- conscious response
- autonomic response.

Reflexes

A reflex is a quick automatic response to a particular stimulus – blinking, coughing, sneezing. Impulses from a sense organ (for example, the pain receptor in a finger) are carried along the sensory neurone to a dorsal root of the nerve cord. They move along a relay neurone, out of the nerve cord, along a motor neurone to the muscle. The muscle then responds to the stimulus. The example shows a pin pricking a finger and the muscles pulling the finger from the pin quickly and automatically. Such nerve connections are an example of a reflex arc.

Diagram of the main divisions of the nervous system

Autonomic system:
sympathetic
parasympathetic

Central system:
brain
spinal cord

peripheral
nerves

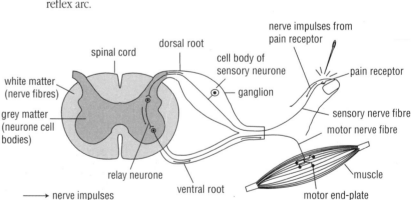

Sensory nerve endings (receptors) in the skin

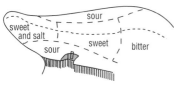

The position of taste receptors on the tongue

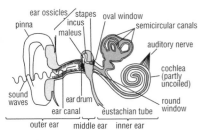

Sense organs

These are connected to the brain or spinal cord by nerve fibres. When a sense organ is stimulated it sends electrical impulses along the nerve fibre which supplies it. The impulses travel along the fibre to the spinal cord and on to the brain.

The sense organs include:

■ touch receptors – these are sensitive to light pressure and help us to distinguish one texture from another
■ pressure receptors – these are under the dermis and respond to heavy pressure
■ pain receptors – branched nerve endings in the epidermis and other parts of the body
■ temperature receptors – these help us to respond to hot and cold
■ nerve receptors at the hair roots – movements of hair
■ smell receptors – olfactory organs in the roof of the nasal passages
■ taste receptors – the four types of taste bud (salt, sweet, sour, bitter) concentrated in different areas of the tongue
■ sound mechanisms – the ear ossicles and cochlea which change sound waves into nerve impulses
■ balance mechanisms – the semicircular canals of the inner ear
■ image receptor mechanisms – the rods and cones which form images on the retina of the eye.

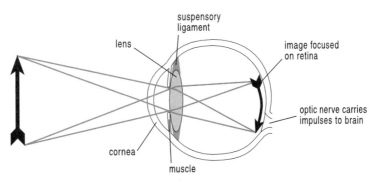

How images are formed in the eye

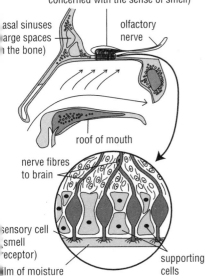

The olfactory system

ACTIVITY

Find out what happens when a region of the brain, which normally receives impulses from pain nerve endings, is suppressed by drugs such as aspirin. Write a brief summary on your findings.

155

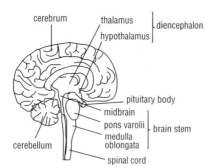

Main parts of the brain as seen in vertical section. The medulla, pons and midbrain constitute the brain stem.

Labels: cerebrum, thalamus, hypothalamus, diencephalon, pituitary body, midbrain, pons varolii, medulla oblongata, brain stem, spinal cord, cerebellum

The brain

Some theories say that because of the increasingly high level of effectiveness and specialisation of the sensory organs of the head (eyes, ears, nose) of animals more and more fibres entered the front part of the spinal cord. So in vertebrate animals, this region became very highly developed to form the brain. The more complex the lifestyle of the animal, the greater is this brain development.

Conscious response

This kind of response may begin with the sense organs or originate in the cerebrum of the brain.

Conscious responses are thought to be the outcome of activity in the cortex of the brain. But human beings can suppress a huge amount of sensory data which comes into the cerebral hemispheres and single out the aspects we want to concentrate on.

An example of a conscious response involving your sense organs and the brain is the command to move your arm. The stages of the process are:

■ you receive the command through your ear

■ the message, translated into nerve impulses, travels through auditory nerve to the brain

■ the brain processes the information

■ the brain then sends a motor impulse to the muscles of your arm.

A map of half of the cerebrum

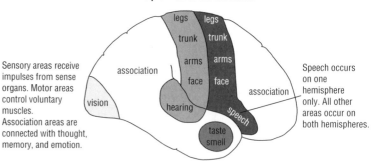

Sensory areas receive impulses from sense organs. Motor areas control voluntary muscles. Association areas are connected with thought, memory, and emotion.

Labels: legs, trunk, arms, face, association, vision, hearing, speech, taste smell

Speech occurs on one hemisphere only. All other areas occur on both hemispheres.

Autonomic response

Part of the nervous system coordinates internal, mainly involuntary, body activities such as:

■ digestion

■ blood pressure

■ vasoconstriction

■ the heartbeat

■ peristaltic contractions in the alimentary canal.

ACTIVITY

Find out the main effects of the autonomic nervous system. Draw up a chart with three columns. On the left side list:

- stomach
- sweat glands
- eye iris
- pancreas
- genitals
- saliva glands
- heart
- bronchii
- urinary bladder
- gut sphincter.

At the top of the middle column put the heading 'sympathetic effect'.

In the right-hand column put the heading 'parasympathetic effect'.

Define the sympathetic and parasympathetic systems. Then describe in the appropriate column of your chart how each system affects each item listed on the left.

ACTIVITY

The circulatory and endocrine systems also interrelate to perform the functions of support, movement and communication. Using an example (see the suggestion below) explain:

- the circulatory and endocrine systems
- how they are brought into play in communication and movement.

Your example could be a person on safari who strays from the main party and encounters a lioness anxious to defend her cubs; the person needs to return rapidly to the safety of the safari vehicle.

Body systems for reproduction

Sexual reproduction occurs when two cells, known as gametes (one from a female, the other a male) fuse together during fertilisation. The resulting cell is called a zygote.

ACTIVITY

Investigate and describe how the inherited characteristics of an individual develop from the zygote.

The main systems for reproduction are the reproductive organs and the endocrine and circulatory systems. In women the reproductive organs include the ovaries, oviducts, Fallopian tubes, uterus (or womb), vagina, cervix, labia majora and minora and vulva. In men they include the testes (enclosed in the scrotum), the epididymis, the sperm duct, the penis, urethra, prostate gland and Cowper's gland.

Within the endocrine and circulatory systems the chemicals produced by the endocrine glands enter the bloodstream as it circulates through the glands. The endocrine chemicals, called hormones, are circulated throughout the body. When they reach particular parts they cause changes. For example, oestrogen controls the development of female secondary characteristics at puberty, and the menstrual cycle, birth and lactation in women; testosterone in the male promotes development of the secondary male characteristics.

An oncologist (a doctor specialising in cancer treatment) explains the use of hormone therapy in treating secondary breast cancer and a possible effect on a woman's ability to have children:

66 *Hormones, especially the female ones, oestrogen and progesterone, affect the growth of some breast cancer cells. So drugs with hormones, or drugs that work against the effects of hormones, can be used to treat some types of secondary breast cancer. Hormones are usually quite safe, although there can be side effects, specific to the type of hormone therapy used. For instance,*

some can bring on a temporary menopause and it will not be possible to conceive at this time. But usually women start having their periods again when the treatment stops. **99**

Body systems for energy supply

Your imagination can affect the level of energy you experience. It is said that 'energy follows thought'.

Imagination is very powerful and can be a key to the energy you experience in your life. It also affects your body's systems.

All the functions the body carries out – movement, reproduction, excretion and so on – need energy. Human beings obtain energy mainly by eating food, but before the energy can be used by the cells it needs to be changed from the chemical form in the food store (fat and carbohydrate) into a form which the body can use (molecules of adenosine triphosphate ATP). The process of transferring energy in this way is called tissue respiration. It involves using oxygen and producing carbon dioxide.

Respiratory system

Oxygen enters the human body from the air through the respiratory organs, the lungs. A gaseous exchange takes place in the lungs: some oxygen from the atmosphere is absorbed and carbon dioxide from the blood is released into the lung cavities.

Our rhythmical breathing movements are usually done unconsciously. Adults inhale and exhale between 12 and 20 times a minute. It is thought that breathing rhythm is initiated by the brain. But the rate can be influenced by reflex action, the chemical composition of the blood and by conscious control.

Circulatory system

The circulatory system distributes food, oxygen and so on to all parts of the body. The movement of the blood in the vessels everywhere in the body continuously changes the fluid surrounding the cells so that:

- fresh supplies of oxygen and food are brought in
- toxins don't build up.

Oxygen dissolves in the blood in the lungs. Active tissues produce carbon dioxide and use oxygen. When the blood reaches these tissues, the raised acidity level caused by the carbon dioxide produced by the working tissues, and the low oxygen concentration, causes oxyhaemoglobin (haemoglobin combined with oxygen) to be broken down to produce oxygen that is released to the tissues.

> It takes about 45 seconds for a red cell to complete the circulation of the body.

ACTIVITY

Investigate how carbon dioxide is transported from the tissues into the lungs.

Then, using diagrams if appropriate, explain the connection between circulation, respiration and the effects on the body's energy.

Digestive system

Food is of little value unless its nutrients enter the bloodstream and are distributed to living tissues. Digestion and absorption take place in the alimentary canal. Food moves through the alimentary canal by:

- ingestion – bringing food in through the mouth
- swallowing – taking roughly six seconds for fairly solid food to reach the stomach
- peristalsis – the contracting and relaxing of the circular muscles in the walls of the alimentary canal
- egestion – expulsion of the undigested remains of food from the alimentary canal.

Digestion occurs in all the main parts of the alimentary canal:

- mouth
- stomach
- duodenum
- ileum
- colon.

The products of digestion pass across the wall of the alimentary canal and are carried around the body in the blood. Most living cells can absorb and metabolise glucose, fats and amino acids:

- Glucose is oxidised to carbon dioxide and water and this reaction produces ATP energy molecules which are used for the chemical processes in the cell. For example, in muscle cells it produces contractions and it aids the production of electrical changes in nerve cell transmission.

■ Fats are also oxidised by cells to produce the ATP energy for molecules needed for cell functions. Fats provide much more energy molecules than glucose.

■ Amino acids make proteins when absorbed by cells.

ACTIVITY

Explain what happens if the amount of food a person eats exceeds their needs. Describe what happens to glucose, fats and amino acids which are excess to needs.

Then explain the effects of these systems on the energy levels of a marathon runner:

■ digestive system

■ respiratory system

■ circulatory system.

Also think about how the other body systems affect the runner's energy level, for example:

■ the nervous system and sense organs

■ the endocrine system

■ the musculo-skeletal system

■ excretion (the next part looks at this).

Body systems for excretion

Excretion is the process of getting rid of unwanted substances from the body. These include:

■ toxic substances taken in with food or made from bacteria in the intestine

■ unwanted products from chemical reactions in cells

■ substances from food which are more than the body needs

■ chemicals such as hormones which have completed their work

■ drugs.

Excretory organs include:

■ the renal system, which controls the composition of the blood by eliminating
  – soluble nitrogen waste compounds which are above a certain level
  – excess water
  – excess salts above a certain level of concentration
  – excess hydrogen ions to maintain the right pH level.

■ the lungs, which mainly excrete excess carbon dioxide and water vapour

■ the liver, which removes bile products and adjusts the concentration of glucose in the blood.

The skin also loses fluid in the form of sweat made up of water with salts dissolved in it (mainly sodium chloride, urea and lactic acid). The skin helps to control blood temperature through the action of sweating.

ACTIVITY

Find out the cause of cramping pain in muscles which have been used a lot. Write an explanation of what it is, why it occurs and what can be done to prevent it.

Body systems for defence

The body's defence forces work together or separately, depending on the problem. For example, if the skin defence is broken, invading germs can be destroyed by defence cells in the blood or chemical 'weapons' (antibodies) from the immune system.

Certain substances regard the body as prey, for example bacteria, viruses and parasites. Other substances such as pollen and house dust need to be eliminated from the body to enable normal, healthy functioning, for example breathing. Human beings cannot survive without a complex, interactive and highly effective means of defence made up of:

- skin
- the immune system
- the circulatory system
- the lymphatic system.

A nutritionist in an NHS trust hospital explains:

66 *The body's way of repelling intruders sometimes makes it difficult to control the natural response to things like blood transfusions, organ transplants and skin grafts. Your body may need the thing that's being introduced, say, skin if you've been badly burned. But unless it's from your own body, you won't normally accept it straight away. Your immune system treats skin and other tissues grafted from another as foreign protein. It will do everything it can to get rid of it. That's why people with damaged kidneys need to wait for the right donor. It's also the reason why you can only accept blood from those with the same blood group as you.* 99

Skin

The most obvious defence is the skin. Every hole in the skin, especially bigger ones like the mouth, can be a weakness in the defence function. So the mouth, stomach and other exposed areas have their own defences, similar to the skin, called the mucosal area. For example, the mucosal lining inside the mouth including the gums and tongue is similar to that covering other vulnerable passages:

- the respiratory tract (nose, throat, bronchial passages and lungs)
- gastrointestinal tracts (oesophagus, stomach, small and large intestine).

The outer skin consists of dead cells which act like a defence wall, protecting us mainly against elements such as water, surface dirt, the wind and so on. The living cells are underneath. They have their own blood and nerve supply. They are also partly a defence, acting as a physical barrier to control:

- what passes in, for example ultraviolet light
- what passes out, for example sweat.

They also help the body to deal with excessive heat and cold.

Inside the body a mucosal layer acts as a defence in the same way as the skin outside the body. For example, the lining of the gastrointestinal tract helps with the digestion and absorption of food, so it needs special characteristics. Invaders attacking the defences of the mucosal layer trigger an attack by the defensive cells in the mucosal layer and from elsewhere in the body.

Immune system

The immune system and other defences are extremely complex. The skin, defensive cells and many kinds of body chemicals are all part of it.

Defensive cells

The white blood cells and other defensive cells are on constant alert. They detect and attack suspicious intruders (foreign proteins). There are two kinds of defensive cell:

- general cells, called macrophages, that deal with bacteria and particles
- specialist cells that concentrate on viral invaders the body may or may not have encountered before.

The invading particles have to be recognised and immobilised by special chemicals produced by the immune system – antibodies. The speciaslist cells include lymphocytes, which recognise the invading particles and communicate their presence to the immune system.

Chemicals

There are many different kinds of chemicals. Some, such as histamines, are produced by most cells in the body. Others, such as antibodies, are produced and discharged by the lymphocytes.

Different antibodies have different defence functions. The common ones are known by their initial:

- IgA – in the mucus produced in the nose, lungs and bowel. It offers surface protection. (IgA is also found in mother's milk and helps to protect babies from infection. It provides the body's first defence against bacteria and viruses.)
- IgD – identified but function as yet unknown.
- IgE – possibly involved in allergic reactions, otherwise function unknown.
- IgG and IgM – these are principle antibodies generated by lymphocytes, which initiate all secondary secretions.

Immunity to a particular disease is caused by the presence of antibodies. Antibodies will be present if they have:

- passed from mothers to babies through the breast milk
- developed following a natural exposure to infection
- developed after a deliberate exposure through vaccination.

ACTIVITY

Find out more about defensive cells – what are the different kinds and how do they operate when they are triggered by an intruder? Investigate the way certain types of defensive cells produce chemicals and how they 'remember' the identity of previous undesirables. Write up your findings in a brief report.

Circulatory system

Blood in the circulatory system defends the body by:

- preventing infection
- forming blood clots.

Preventing infection

If the skin defences are broken, bacteria can enter the body. In response, white blood cells from the capillaries in the area of the cut engulf and digest the bacteria or the damaged tissues which have been invaded.

The blood and circulatory system is part of the immune system – the antibodies are secreted into the blood, if they are not already part of it, and are carried to the site of the wound. Histamine is released by the damaged tissues and causes the capillaries around the site to expand. The arterioles around the site also expand so more blood can reach the site and the supply of antibodies and leucocytes can increase.

Water is extracted from the blood vessels around the wound, the site swells and the fluid is gradually drained into the lymphatic system. This flow is thought to help carry the bacteria away from the blood circulatory system.

Forming blood clots

Protein, called fibrinogen, in the blood plasma turns into fibrin when a blood vessel is cut or the vessel lining is damaged. The fibrin makes a clot of fibres which helps to prevent more blood leaking out and further bacteria coming in. Over time, the blood clot dries and shrinks and forms a scab. The scab itself is a defence, protecting the damaged area while the new tissue forms.

Lymphatic system

Fluid in the body's tissues returns to the circulation through:

- the capillaries
- the lymphatic system.

The lymphatic system consists of thin-walled vessels between the cells. The fluid in them, lymph, is similar to blood plasma but has much less protein. Lymph nodes, swellings on the lymphatic vessels, have fibres with white cells like macrophages attached to them. They can trap and ingest bacteria in the lymph; the bacteria can then be removed through the node before they get into the body's circulation.

163

Homeostatic mechanisms

The negative feedback loop

A change in the external environment causes a change in the body's internal environment

↓

Receptors – part of the nervous system – monitor the internal environment and detect changes

↓

Receptors send nerve impulses to a control centre (usually in the brain)

↓

The control centre sends nerve impulses or hormones to organs, which take action to bring conditions back to normal

Homeostatic mechanisms are the processes by which the body maintains homeostasis – a stable internal environment in which cells can function.

All chemical processes which take place within cells are controlled by enzymes. These are very sensitive to the conditions in which they work, and a slight fall in temperature or rise in acidity can slow down or stop a vital chemical reaction. To prevent this from happening, homeostatic mechanisms ensure that the composition of tissue fluid around cells remains stable despite changes to the external environment.

Homeostasis is controlled by the nervous system and hormones. A wide range of homeostatic mechanisms take place in the body. Most follow the same pattern, known as the negative feedback loop.

DISCUSSION POINT

Why do you think this is called a negative feedback loop?

Many homeostatic mechanisms take place in the body, including processes that concern the control of:

- body temperature
- blood sugar
- water
- respiratory rate.

Homeostatic mechanisms for body temperature

Human beings are homeotherms – like other mammals and birds. They maintain a constant body temperature (about 37 °C) whatever the temperature of the outside environment. Unlike animals such as reptiles, human beings can generate their own heat and don't have to rely on the sun.

The hypothalamus at the base of the brain acts as the body's thermoregulatory centre. It:

- checks the temperature of blood as it passes through the brain
- receives nerve impulses from receptors in the skin and around internal organs about changes in the temperature of the environment outside the body.

DISCUSSION POINT

What factors may cause body temperature to rise and fall?

ACTIVITY

Try to detect the cold sensitive receptors in the skin by running the point of a pencil slowly across the back of your hand.

If blood temperature is rising, the anterior hypothalamus sends nerve impulses to organs of the body which control mechanisms to prevent overheating. If blood temperature is falling, the posterior hypothalamus sends nerve impulses to organs of the body which control mechanisms to conserve heat. Action is taken to bring the body temperature back to normal.

This is the negative feedback loop for controlling body temperature. What action does the body take in each case?

If temperature is rising:

- blood vessels in the skin get wider (vasodilation) and more blood is directed to the skin, making the skin red and warm (the heat is then lost from the skin's surface by conduction, convection and radiation, causing cooling)
- sweat glands make more sweat, which is evaporated from the skin's surface using heat from the blood
- hairs on the skin lie flat, allowing air currents to pass across and cool the skin
- panting causes more heat to be lost as air is breathed out
- behaviour changes – clothes are removed and cold drinks taken.

If temperature is falling:

- blood vessels in the skin become narrower (vasoconstriction) and less blood is directed to the skin
- sweat glands stop producing sweat
- muscles beneath the skin contract, creating goose bumps and raising hair on the skin – this acts as an insulator, trapping warm air
- the body starts to shiver due to the contraction of skeletal muscles – this creates heat
- behaviour changes – clothes are put on and hot drinks taken.

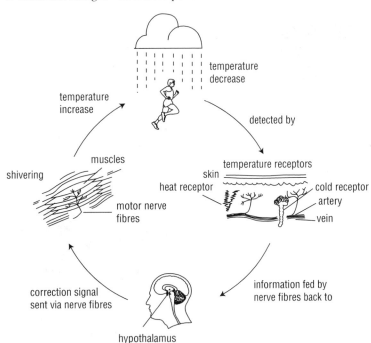

ACTIVITY

Carry out some experiments to demonstrate the changes which take place in the body when temperature rises and falls. How can you observe these changes physically? Explain why each of these changes occurs.

Homeostatic mechanisms for blood sugar

Blood sugar is the amount of glucose in the blood. This is usually about 1 mg of glucose for every cm^3 of blood.

As section 3.1.4 showed, cells need a constant supply of glucose to generate the energy they need to function. Because of this, the body uses homeostatic mechanisms to ensure there is a steady amount of glucose in the blood – a constant blood sugar level.

The digestive system breaks down carbohydrates eaten during a meal to produce glucose, which passes into the bloodstream. The pancreas (which is near to the stomach) detects that the blood sugar level has risen, and releases a hormone called insulin. Insulin:

- enables glucose to pass into body cells more easily by increasing the permeability of the cell membrane to glucose
- activates the enzymes inside the cells which make use of glucose
- converts glucose into glycogen, where it is stored for use in the future (this takes place in the liver).

If the pancreas detects that the blood sugar level is falling, it produces less insulin and fewer glucose reactions take place. The amount of glucose in the blood then increases, until levels are back to normal.

If the blood level sugar falls very low, the pancreas stops secreting insulin and produces another hormone called glucagon. This converts the sugar stores of glycogen held in the liver into glucose, which enters the bloodstream until the blood sugar level has stabilised.

During exercise or in response to stress, the adrenal glands produce another hormone – adrenalin – which helps to regulate blood sugar levels. Like glucagon, this converts glycogen stores into glucose, enabling the cells to generate more energy.

Homeostatic mechanisms for water

As well as needing glucose, cells depend on a constant, regular supply of water. To ensure that they receive this, the human body relies on a homeostatic mechanism involving the kidneys.

The negative feedback loop for water regulation begins with special receptors in the hypothalamus, called osmoreceptors. Rather than directly detecting the amount of water in the blood, these detect the osmotic potential of the blood. For example:

- if the blood is more concentrated than normal, it contains less water and so has a higher concentration of dissolved substances; in other words, the osmotic potential increases
- if the blood is less concentrated than normal, it contains more water so the dissolved substances are more diluted; in other words, the osmotic potential decreases.

ACTIVITY

Draw a diagram to show the negative feedback loop for maintaining blood sugar levels.

Carry out research into diabetes mellitus. What part of the loop doesn't work efficiently in patients with diabetes mellitus that began in childhood? How is it treated? How does this form of the disease compare with that associated with ageing?

If the blood's water content is low:

■ nerve impulses stimulate the pituitary gland to release more ADH to the kidneys

■ the collecting ducts become more permeable to water

■ more water is reabsorbed from the kidney nephrons (urinary tubules) into the blood

■ the level of water in the blood increases

■ concentrated urine is produced, and urinary flow decreases.

If the blood's water content is high:

■ osmoreceptors are not stimulated, and the pituitary gland releases less ADH to the kidneys

■ the collecting ducts become less permeable to water

■ less water is reabsorbed from the kidney nephrons (urinary tubules) into the blood

■ the level of water in the blood decreases

■ diluted urine is produced, and urinary flow increases.

DISCUSSION POINT

How do you think the body gains water? How does it lose water?

In response to changes in osmotic potential, the osmoreceptors send nerve impulses to the pituitary gland, which secretes antidiuretic hormone or ADH (also known as vasopressin).

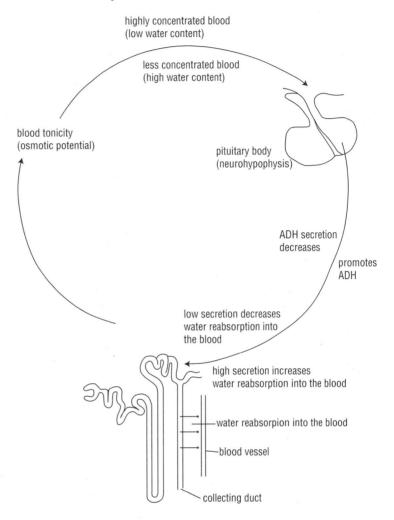

Homeostatic mechanisms for respiratory rate

Respiration – or breathing – is the process by which the body draws in oxygen from the atmosphere to the lungs, and pushes out carbon dioxide as a waste product. This consists of a cycle of inspirations (breathing in) and expirations (breathing out), which are controlled by homeostasis.

Skeletal muscles between the ribs and in the diaphragm bring about breathing. The movement of these muscles is triggered by nerve impulses from a respiratory centre in the brain. This centre consists of three distinct areas:

■ the medullary rhythmicity area – this controls the rhythm of breathing, producing nerve impulses which either cause inspiration and inhibit expiration, or vice versa

■ the apneustic area – this can produce nerve impulses which stimulate the medullary rhythmicity area to change the depth of breathing

■ the pneumotaxic area – this can produce nerve impulses which stimulate the medullary rhythmicity area to change the breathing rate.

The respiratory centre is sensitive to a range of signals from the body which show that breathing rate needs to change. For example, during exercise a rise in blood carbon dioxide causes an increase in the concentration of hydrogen ions in the blood, which is sensed by the respiratory centre. In addition, chemoreceptors (chemical receptors) in the aortic arch and the carotid arteries are sensitive to the levels of carbon dioxide and oxygen in the blood, and send nerve impulses to the respiratory centre. Breathing occurs at an increased rate and becomes deeper, in order to expel carbon dioxide from the body and take in more oxygen.

As well as being controlled by homeostasis, variations in breathing can be controlled at will. For example, an individual may choose to breathe at a different rate, or to hold their breath.

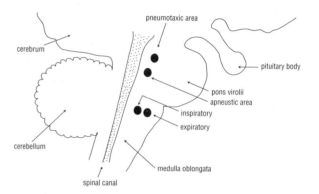

ACTIVITY

Explain, in a flow diagram, why the body hyperventilates (experiences an increased rate and depth of breathing) during exercise. What is the result of hyperventilation?

Normal body ranges

As shown in section 3.2.2, factors regulated by homeostasis include:

- body temperature
- blood sugar level
- the level of water in the blood
- respiratory rate.

Homeostasis maintains all of these factors at a 'normal', or average level. If levels deviate a long way from this norm, becoming very high or very low, they become 'abnormal' or 'pathological'.

Normal levels usually fall within a range rather than being a precise figure. Values not only vary between people, but also change in the same person depending on exercise, when they last ate, and level of excitement.

Body temperature

Normal body temperature can vary slightly for several reasons:

- the temperature in the rectum is usually slightly higher than in the mouth, which is slightly higher than the armpit
- a child's temperature is usually higher than an adult's
- temperature increases at ovulation during the menstrual cycle.

> Normal body temperature is around 37 °C. This is the temperature at which the body's enzymes work most efficiently.

Causes of an abnormally raised temperature may include:

- infection by bacteria or viruses
- damage to the thermoregulatory centre in the hypothalamus (for example, following a head injury or heat stroke)
- damage to body tissues (for example, caused by tumour growth, burns or scalds).

As the body temperature rises, the enzymes start to speed up. A patient with a high temperature is said to have pyrexia (or hyperthermia), and may show the following signs and symptoms:

- rapid respiration
- headache
- hot, flushed skin
- feeling cold and shivery
- dry mouth
- fast pulse
- aching limbs
- sweat
- delirium
- loss of consciousness
- convulsions.

It is considered a medical emergency if the body's temperature rises to 41 °C, when enzymes start to be destroyed by the heat and stop working. If body temperature rises above 44.4 °C to 45.5 °C, it causes death.

Conversely, if body temperature falls to below 35 °C, the person is said to be suffering from hypothermia. Elderly people are especially at risk from hypothermia, in particular if they are confused, have difficulty with mobility, or have limited money for heating and food. Someone with hypothermia may show the following signs and symptoms:

- slow respiration
- slow pulse
- shivering
- cold, pale, mottled skin
- mental slowness, loss of consciousness
- numbness of hands and feet.

It is considered a medical emergency if the body's temperature falls to 34.4 °C.

ACTIVITY

Carry out research into:

- the causes of pyrexia and hypothermia
- the signs and symptoms of pyrexia and hypothermia
- how to care for patients with pyrexia and hypothermia.

Produce a leaflet for families explaining normal ranges for body temperature; what might cause abnormalities; how to recognise high or low body temperature; and how to care for individuals.

ACTIVITY

Carry out research into:

- hyperglycaemia
- hypoglycaemia.

Write a paragraph explaining how each involves a variation from normal blood sugar levels.

Blood sugar

The normal level of glucose in the blood – blood sugar level – is about 1 mg of glucose for every cm³ of blood.

Water

This can be monitored by urinary output. On average:

- men produce between 30 and 50 ml of urine an hour
- women produce between 25 and 45 ml an hour.

If an individual is producing abnormally small amounts of urine, this may mean that there is not enough water in the body fluids or they are retaining fluid. If they are producing abnormally large amounts of urine, this may mean they have taken in a lot of fluid (for example, it is the natural response to drinking heavily).

ACTIVITY

Carry out research to find out the signs and symptoms of too much water in the body, and too little water in the body. When might each situation occur? Investigate the effects of drinking alcohol on the normal control mechanism described on pages 166–167. Write a brief report.

ACTIVITY

Devise a series of experiments to establish 'normal' respiratory rates, and to investigate what causes deviations from the norm. You may find it helpful to look at section 3.3.1 (see page 180).

Respiratory rate

During quiet breathing, inspiration (an intake of breath) lasts about two seconds, and expiration (breathing out) usually lasts about three seconds. An adult's normal resting respiratory rate is between 13 and 17 breaths per minute. During exercise, this may increase to as many as 80 breaths per minute.

Respiratory rate also varies with age – babies take between 30 and 40 breaths per minute.

ACTIVITY

Talk to a nurse or doctor in detail about how they monitor one of the factors described in this section. Ask them to explain:

■ normal body ranges for the factor

■ how they detect variations from the norm

■ what causes variations from the norm

■ what the possible implications are of variation from the norm

■ how they treat variations.

The main effects of ageing

DISCUSSION POINT

Think of people you know at similar stages of the ageing process – for example, two people in their 50s, two in their 60s and two in their 70s. How do you think ageing has affected them? Do people of the same age appear to be at the same stage of the ageing process? If not, why do you think this is?

From the moment human beings are born, they develop and change as part of a natural ageing process.

Until individuals reach about their mid-20s, most of ageing involves growth and development – becoming physically stronger and larger, reaching sexual maturity, and developing mental abilities.

From the mid-20s onwards, ageing involves a gradual decline – metabolism slows, joints stiffen, women reach the end of their fertile period during middle age and cells function less efficiently. Death occurs when cells stop working or are deprived of the substances they need.

Advances in medical science have resulted in longer life expectancy, but the ageing process still occurs. Some aspects of ageing are unavoidable and genetically controlled, such as menopause and hair loss. Others are affected by environment and lifestyle, and vary from person to person. For example, continuing physical exercise can help the circulation, keep muscles strong, prevent joints stiffening and increase metabolic rates.

Effects of ageing on support and locomotion

Human babies are born with little control over their movements, and are unable to support their body. As they grow, they develop the ability to walk and control locomotion, reaching a peak of physical strength with adulthood. However, this tends to diminish as the ageing process continues – many elderly people find it increasingly difficult to get around as they grow older.

The changing pattern of support and locomotion through life depends on the development and condition of the musculo-skeletal and nervous systems.

Growth profile

All human beings begin life as a zygote, a single cell about 0.1 mm in diameter. This contains all the information and material from which a unique individual grows. Before a baby is born, this cell increases in weight many millions of time, growing more rapidly than at any other time in life.

At birth a baby's head is about three quarters of its eventual adult size and a quarter of its total body length (an adult's head is only about one eighth of total body length). This is because most of the brain develops while the baby is still in the uterus.

After birth, growth is stimulated by growth hormones produced by the pituitary gland, which influence the rate at which tissues grow. Children who produce too much growth hormone before puberty may suffer from gigantism (excessive growth of the whole body). Underproduction of growth hormone may result in dwarfism.

Growth continues fairly constantly throughout childhood, with three growth 'spurts':

- from birth to the age of one, when most babies treble in weight and become 50% longer. All of the organs are complete at birth, but many are still structurally and functionally immature
- from five to seven years. A six-year-old's head is about 90% of the adult size
- at puberty, when the body grows rapidly. Feet grow first, then the legs, trunk and finally the face (as a result, the body often seems out of proportion at this time). Girls grow an average of 9 cm per year, while boys may grow up to 10 cm per year.

Most people's skeletal growth is complete by the age of 20. Body shape, as well as size, undergoes major changes during this time.

Elderly people – usually from their 60s onwards – may begin to hunch their backs and shrink in size as a result of contraction of discs between the vertebrae. This final stage in skeletal development is sometimes known as 'negative growth'.

ACTIVITY

Carry out research to find out how and when cartilage in the skeleton is replaced by bone, and how bones grow. Write an explanation of skeletal development, using diagrams where appropriate.

Joint mobility

Babies and young children are often incredibly flexible, able to bend and twist their limbs with ease. This is because young joints are mobile and ligaments stretch well.

As people grow older their joints become less mobile, and they tend to stiffen up and become less flexible. However, taking part in regular physical exercise can help to reduce this loss of mobility.

Many people in the middle or later years of life suffer from arthritis – an inflammation of the joints which reduces joint mobility. Two common types of arthritis are osteoarthritis and rheumatoid arthritis.

Osteoarthritis is a degenerative disease of the joints. It is probably caused by general wear and tear on the joints, and may be more likely if an individual is overweight or has poor posture. In osteoarthritis the cartilage in the joint which acts as a shock absorber becomes thin and worn, and there may be loss of fluid which helps the joint move. Bony outgrowths develop into the joint, resulting in thickening of bone and protruding ridges and bone spurs. As a result, the individual may experience stiffness, pain and difficulty in moving.

Rheumatoid arthritis is a chronic disease which most often affects people in their 40s and 50s, and is more common among women than men.

Inflammation and swelling of the synovial membrane and capsule in the joint result in the formation of scar tissue and adhesions. Joints become swollen, painful, red and stiff, and movement becomes increasingly difficult. In time, the inflammation begins to eat away the surfaces of the bones within the joints.

ACTIVITY

Contact the Arthritis and Rheumatism Council for Research (ARC) to find out more about how arthritis affects joint mobility in older people.

ACTIVITY

Draw a time line chart tracing development from birth to old age, highlighting:

- key stages in growth of the body
- when changes may occur to joint mobility
- when changes may occur as a result of degeneration of elasticity
- changes in the reproductive system.

You may find it helpful to use photographs or drawings on your chart, to help illustrate the points you are making.

Degeneration of elasticity

One of the most obvious signs of ageing is the lines and wrinkles which appear on the skin. Young people's skin is supple, and is able to return to its original shape when stretched or screwed up. However, elastic tissue in the skin loses its elasticity with age, causing the skin to wrinkle rather than bounce back into place.

In a similar way, loss of elasticity in lung tissue means that elderly people are more prone to respiratory problems and diseases like pneumonia. Even eyesight is affected by loss of elasticity – the eye lens becomes less supple with age, and is unable to focus as well. As a result, most people over the age of 45 are long-sighted (they find it hard to focus on things which are near to them).

Effects of ageing on reproduction

Human beings' reproductive organs remain undeveloped until they reach puberty (usually between 10 to 13 in girls, and 13 to 15 in boys). During puberty, physical changes take place which enable reproduction. Many men remain fertile for the rest of their lives, although sperm production may fall when they become elderly. Women's fertile stage usually ends between the ages of 45 and 55, with the onset of menopause.

Puberty

In girls, puberty is triggered when the pituitary gland produces a hormone which tells the ovaries to start ripening ova (eggs) and making oestrogen (the female sex hormone). As a result, a range of physical changes occur:
- breasts and nipples become larger
- pubic and underarm hair grows
- the pelvis widens
- fat is deposited under the skin of the hips, breasts and buttocks, creating a curvy shape
- the body sweats more
- menstruation begins.

Once ovulation has begun, the woman remains fertile until the menopause (usually between the ages of 45 and 55), although fertility often declines after the age of 35.

DISCUSSION POINT

Why do you think girls are reaching puberty at an earlier age than they were 50 years ago? What factors can delay puberty?

In boys, puberty is triggered when the pituitary gland produces a hormone which tells the testes to start making sperm and producing testosterone (the male sex hormone). As a result, a range of physical changes occur:

- the testes, scrotum, penis and prostate gland become larger
- pubic, underarm and facial hair grows (this may also be followed by hair on the chest and abdomen)
- the body grows stronger and more muscular
- the voice deepens (breaks) as a result of the larynx becoming larger
- the body sweats more.

Menopause

The menopause – usually experienced by women between the ages of 45 and 55 – marks the end of a woman's natural reproductive life. During the menopause, which may happen over several years or take place in a few months, the woman stops producing ova and oestrogen levels fall. As a result, she may experience a number of physical changes:

- hot flushes
- night sweats
- menstruation becomes irregular and finally stops
- the ovaries, uterus and cervix shrink
- Fallopian tubes become shorter
- mucus production decreases
- the bones become less dense, sometimes leading to osteoporosis.

Effects of ageing on homeostasis

The main homeostatic mechanism affected by ageing is control of body temperature.

Maintenance of body temperature

During most of people's lives, their body temperature is efficiently controlled by homeostasis. However, newborn babies and the elderly often struggle to maintain a consistent body temperature:

- a baby's brain may not be mature enough to react to changes in temperature. They also lose heat quickly because they have a large surface area in proportion to their body volume and are often bald (hair helps to insulate the body)
- an elderly person's cells may be unable to react efficiently enough.

As a result, babies and elderly people are particularly at risk from hypothermia. Sally, a care assistant who works with elderly clients, explains:

66 *I'm always on the lookout for signs of hypothermia in the winter. Clients who live alone, away from their families, are particularly susceptible – they're often too proud to ask for help, and try to pretend everything's fine. Some of my elderly clients are confused, and don't keep their homes warm enough or eat and drink properly. Others simply can't afford to. I take steps at the first sign of a client having a low temperature – older people are less able than we are to reverse the effects of hypothermia.* 99

DISCUSSION POINT

What is the difference between puberty and adolescence?

ACTIVITY

Find out about osteoporosis. Why does it occur after the menopause? Can it be avoided?

ACTIVITY

Find out what state benefits are available to help elderly people counteract the effects of a cold winter. What other practical steps do you think society could take to help elderly people? What steps could elderly people take themselves? Write up your findings and suggestions in a short report.

Key questions

1   List the features provided by the human skeletal structure.
2   Describe the three main types of response controlled by the nervous system.
3   What are the body systems for energy supply?
4   Describe the role of skin in the body's defence system.
5   How can immunity occur?
6   What is homeostasis?
7   What is a negative feedback loop?
8   Give five physical changes which take place when the body temperature is falling.
9   What is the role of insulin in homeostasis?
10 Describe what happens if the blood's water content is low.
11 Why does respiratory rate increase during exercise?
12 What are dangerously high and low body temperatures?
13 What is the normal blood sugar level?
14 How does joint mobility change as the body ages?
15 What are the physical signs of degeneration of elasticity?
16 List five physical changes which occur to the male body during puberty.
17 What physical changes does a woman experience during the menopause?
18 How does ageing affect regulation of body temperature?

Assignment

Produce a series of annotated diagrams – or one large diagram – explaining how body systems interrelate to carry out:

- communication
- support and locomotion
- reproduction
- energy supply
- excretion
- defence.

To go with your diagrams, devise an interesting, visual way to show how ageing affects the support/locomotion and reproductive systems.

Make notes explaining the homeostatic mechanisms which control body temperature, blood sugar, water and respiratory rate. Include a chart identifying the normal ranges for each of these factors.

ELEMENT **3.3**

Maintaining the healthy functioning of the body

In this element you will explore methods of monitoring the healthy functioning of the body, focusing on the cardiorespiratory system.

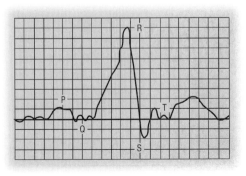

Monitoring the cardiorespiratory system

How efficiently the cardiorespiratory system is functioning gives an important indication of an individual's overall health. This can be monitored using a range of techniques which are simple, quick and non-invasive (they don't involve introducing anything into the body). They include measuring:

- pulse rate
- blood pressure
- breathing rate
- lung volumes.

Pulse rate

Pulse is the rhythmical throbbing of the arteries as blood flows through them. Contraction of the heart's ventricles forces blood into the main arteries, creating a wave of pressure. This wave – the pulse – can be felt wherever an artery is near to the surface of the body and crossing a bone or other firm tissue. An individual's pulse rate shows how often their heart is beating.

Pulse rate is usually measured in the wrist, where the radial artery crosses the bones. However, it can also be felt at:

- the carotid artery, on either side of the neck
- the brachial artery, on the inner arm
- the temporal artery, on either side of the forehead.

Monitoring pulse rate

1 Press two fingertips lightly against the wrist, just below the thumb. Make sure you don't press too hard, and don't use your thumb because this has its own pulse.

2 Feel the pulse where the radial artery crosses the wrist.

3 Using a clock or watch with a second hand, count the number of beats in 15 or 20 seconds.

4 Multiply your answer to find out how many times the pulse beats in a minute (if you have counted for 15 seconds, multiply by four; if you have counted for 20 seconds; multiply by three).

- For a resting adult, pulse rate is usually between 60 and 80 beats per minute.

- For a baby, pulse rate is usually about 130 beats per minute.

- For a young child, pulse rate is usually about 100 beats per minute.

DISCUSSION POINT

Why do you think medical staff usually measure pulse rate at the wrist, rather than another part of the body? When might it be difficult to feel a pulse at the wrist?

As well as measuring pulse rate to find out how fast the heart is beating, feeling the pulse can give other indications of an individual's state of health. While counting the number of beats, medical staff also check whether:

- the pulse's rhythm is regular
- the pulse feels strong or weak
- the artery feels soft or hard (hardness).

ACTIVITY

Carry out research to find out:

- possible causes of an irregular pulse
- possible causes of a weak pulse
- possible causes of an artery which feels hard.

Remember to think about these points when you monitor pulse rate yourself.

A pulse rate which is faster than normal can be caused by exercise; fear, fright or excitement; fever; or illness. A slow pulse rate can be caused by fainting and some heart disorders. However, it can also be a sign of fitness, showing that the circulatory system is functioning efficiently.

ACTIVITY

Working in pairs, measure your own and your partner's pulse rate when you have been resting, after gentle exercise (such as walking), and after vigorous exercise (such as running). After exercise, keep measuring the pulse rate every two minutes until it has returned to normal. Make sure that the exercise you choose is safe for both of you.

Record your results in a chart, and then draw graphs showing pulse rates against time. Explain why the pulse rate took time to return to normal after vigorous exercise.

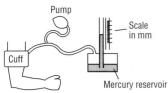

The raised pressure inflates the cuff and simultaneously pushes the mercury up the manometer.

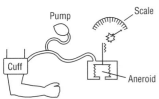

The raised pressure compressses the aneroid and moves the needle on the scale.

Blood pressure

Blood pressure is the pressure which blood exerts on the walls of the arteries as it flows through them. Maintaining normal blood pressure is essential, so that the blood can supply body tissues with oxygen and nutrients.

Blood pressure is measured using a piece of equipment called a sphygmomanometer. This consists of an inflatable cloth cuff connected to a pressure gauge. The pressure gauge may be:

- a vertical tube up which a column of mercury is pushed by the rising pressure (this is called a manometer)
- a cylinder with a dial attached (this is called an aneroid).

Measuring blood pressure

Safety point: only measure blood pressure if someone trained is with you.

1 Wrap the inflatable cuff around the upper arm, above the elbow.

2 Place the stethoscope bell over the brachial artery at the elbow, just below the cuff.

3 Inflate the cuff with air until the pressure gauge shows about 200 mmHg (millimetres of mercury). This should flatten the artery and stop blood flowing through it, and no pulse should be heard through the stethoscope. Don't leave the pressure this high for more than a few seconds, as there is no blood supply to the arm.

4 Gradually release the pressure in the cuff, listening carefully through the stethoscope.

5 When you hear blood rushing through the artery, with a loud knocking sound at every beat, write down the measurement on the pressure gauge. This is the systolic blood pressure (the pressure in the blood vessel as the heart contracts).

6 Carry on releasing the cuff pressure until you can't hear any more sound, and write down the measurement on the pressure gauge. This is the diastolic blood pressure (the pressure between heart beats).

7 Blood pressure is written as a fraction. Write the systolic pressure over the diastolic pressure to give the full blood pressure reading.

- In a healthy adult, blood pressure is usually about 120/80 mmHg.
- Readings up to 150/90 are considered healthy.

Blood pressure varies with every heart beat, and can be drawn like a wave showing the peaks and troughs of pressure.

Blood pressure wave

Abnormally high blood pressure is called hypertension. It can be caused by many factors, including anxiety, old age, pregnancy, exercise and smoking. It can also be a sign of renal disease, some tumours, and atherosclerosis (hardening and narrowing of the arteries). High blood pressure is dangerous because it often doesn't cause any symptoms, but the heart and major arteries are damaged by years of working at too high pressure. This can lead to heart attacks and strokes (cardiovascular accidents), so it is important to treat high blood pressure even if there are no symptoms. This is why doctors and nurses always check patients' blood pressure during routine clinical examinations.

Breathing rate

Breathing is the process by which the body draws in oxygen from the atmosphere to the lungs, and pushes out carbon dioxide as a waste product. This consists of a cycle of inspirations (breathing in) and expirations (breathing out). Breathing rate is the number of breaths taken in a minute.

Breathing is usually controlled by homeostasis, from the respiratory centre in the brain. However, it can also be controlled consciously.

Patients in hospital have their pulse rate, blood pressure and breathing (respiratory) rate taken regularly. During a visit to your local hospital or contact with nursing staff, ask for a copy of a chart they use to record this information. If it is unclear, ask them how they fill it in.

Then make a copy of the chart, and transfer the results of your own monitoring onto the chart.

Measuring peak flow

1 Take a deep breath, then blow into the mouthpiece as quickly as possible.

2 Repeat this twice, and take the highest reading obtained.

3 Repeat the process over a period of time, as peak expiratory flow varies at different times of the day.

4 Find the average result.

■ In a healthy adult, peak expiratory flow is usually between 400 and 600 dm^3 of air per minute.

ACTIVITY

The graph on the right shows normal peak expiratory flow rates for women of different ages and heights.

Investigate peak expiratory flow rates in your GNVQ group, relating your findings to height and gender. Ask your tutors to take part in the experiment, so that your sample includes people of different ages. Does anyone in your group have asthma?

Following the format of the graph above, produce a visual presentation of your findings.

Lung volumes

During breathing, the volume of the lungs changes – increasing as air is drawn in, and decreasing as it is pushed out. This changing lung volume can give a good indication of the health of the lungs, showing whether there is any obstruction to the respiratory pathway.

Measurements taken to test lung function include:
■ peak flow – the maximum rate at which air flows out of the lungs
■ tidal volume – the volume of air breathed in and out in a normal breath
■ vital capacity – the maximum amount of air which can be breathed in and out.

Peak flow

Peak expiratory flow estimation – measurement of the speed at which air flows out of the lungs – is carried out using a peak flow meter. This is a simple piece of equipment consisting of a calibrated meter attached to a mouthpiece.

People with asthma often have a low peak expiratory flow, as narrowing of the trachea and bronchi prevents air flowing out as quickly as usual. Some asthmatics use a peak flow meter to monitor their peak expiratory flow every day, and drugs are adjusted accordingly. If a patient uses a bronchodilator inhaler (a drug which widens the air passages) it is useful to measure the peak flow before and after using the inhaler.

Peak expiratory flow also varies with:
■ age – rising from childhood to adulthood, then falling after middle age
■ sex – men tend to have a higher peak flow than women
■ size – larger people have a higher peak flow than smaller people.

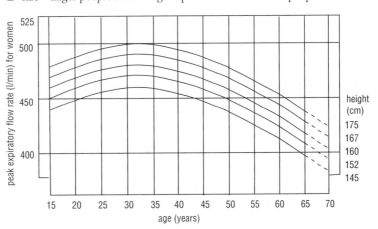

Measuring tidal volume and vital capacity

1 Breathe into the spirometer mouthpiece normally.

2 A drum containing a mixture of gases inside the spirometer inflates and deflates with the breaths. This moves a piston, which causes a recording pen to move on a chart, tracing the pattern of breaths. This trace shows the tidal volume.

3 Breathe out and in as deeply as possible.

4 The spirometer trace shows the vital capacity.

In a healthy adult, tidal volume is about 0.4 dm^3.

In a healthy adult, vital capacity is usually between 3 and 5 dm^3.

ACTIVITY

If possible, use a spirometer to measure your own tidal volume and vital capacity. You should only use a spirometer if there is a trained person present.

Keep a copy of your spirometer trace in your portfolio, labelling your tidal volume, vital capacity, inspiratory reserve volume, expiratory reserve volume and residual volume. Alongside the trace, give each measurement in figures and explain what it means.

Tidal volume and vital capacity

Breathing is described as tidal because air flows in and out of the lungs. The volume of air taken in and then let out during one normal breathing cycle is called the tidal volume. The maximum volume of air which can be taken in and let out, by breathing as deeply as possible, is called the vital capacity.

Tidal volume and vital capacity are measured with an instrument called a spirometer.

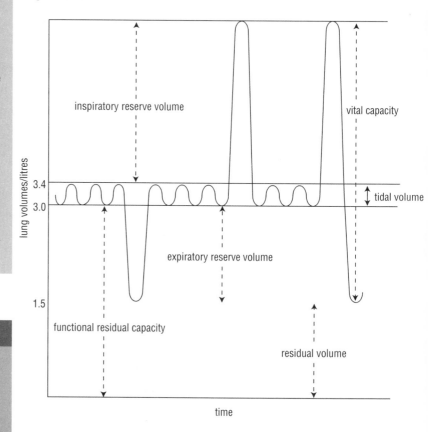

A typical spirometer trace

Using a spirometer can also provide other information about lung volumes, as the spirometer trace above shows:

■ inspiratory reserve volume – the extra air which can be drawn into lungs by breathing deeply

■ expiratory reserve volume – the extra air which can be forced our of lungs after a normal breath

■ residual volume – the amount of air left in the lungs after expiration. This is usually between 1 and 2.5 dm^3.

Physiological status and the cardiorespiratory system

By monitoring and then analysing the cardiorespiratory system, medical staff are able to draw valid conclusions about an individual's physiological status. This analysis may be:

- statistical – involving looking at the measurements as a set of figures in order to analyse an individual's status (for example, comparing the measurements with normal values)
- transformed – involving using formulae and graphical techniques to interpret measurements (for example, drawing a graph to analyse a patient's blood pressure over time)
- for clinical relevance – identifying physical dysfunction by monitoring the cardiorespiratory system (for example, identifying respiratory problems by measuring lung volumes).

UNIT

3

ELEMENT **3.3**

DISCUSSION POINT

What advice do you think the doctor might give Janet?

CASE STUDY: JANET'S CARDIORESPIRATORY MEASUREMENTS

The doctor examines Janet:

- Her pulse rate is 110 and her heartbeat is irregular.
- Her blood pressure is 190/110.
- Her respiratory rate is 25 breaths per minute.
- Her peak flow is 300 dm^3 per minute.

ACTIVITY

From the results of monitoring your own cardiorespiratory system in section 3.3.1, write up an analysis of your physiological status.

CASE STUDY: JANET HARVEY

Janet Harvey is 55 years old. She is 5'3" tall and weighs 85 kg. Janet has always smoked cigarettes and even now, although she has cut down, she still smokes ten cigarettes a day. Two years ago Janet suddenly developed a severe pain in the centre of her chest and down her left arm. In hospital, they told her she had had a heart attack. Ever since, Janet has experienced a similar but milder pain if she hurries or gets upset. It is particularly bad if she tries to walk up a hill. She is very upset about her condition as she has had to give up her job in a bank, and finds it difficult to do housework or go to the shops.

Janet is suffering from angina after having a myocardial infarction. Angina is a pain caused by the heart muscle not having enough oxygen. Janet has had hypertension for many years and this, and the smoking, are major risk factors.

Janet is seen regularly by her general practitioner because she says her angina is getting worse and she is getting breathless.

DISCUSSION POINT

How do these measurements differ from the normal values?

THE DOCTOR'S CONCLUSIONS

The doctor completes her examination of Janet. She draws the conclusion that a disturbance of the heart rate may have made Janet's heart beat less strongly and worsened her angina.

Sections 3.3.1 and 3.3.2 focused on primary source data – data you collected yourself. However, medical staff often rely on secondary source data – data collected by other people – to provide further insight into an individual's physiological status.

This secondary source data may include:

- electrocardiogram (ECG) traces
- blood cell counts
- electrolyte concentrations in body fluids
- spirometer tracings.

ECG traces

Each contraction of the heart muscle is stimulated by an electrical impulse called the cardiac impulse. This impulse starts in the sinoatrial node (SA node) of the heart, and travels across the muscle fibres of the atria, causing them to contract. It then spreads to the ventricles via the atrioventricular node and the Bundle of His (a conducting system of fibres), causing both ventricles to contract at the same time.

Electrocardiograms – or ECGs – enable medical staff to monitor an individual's heart activity.

The heart's electrical activity can be monitored using an ECG recorder. Electrodes connected to a monitor are attached to a client's wrists, ankles and across their chest. These amplify the electrical activity taking place in the heart, enabling it to be displayed on screen or as a trace on graph paper. The speed and rhythm of waves of electrical activity recorded can help doctors to diagnose a range of heart problems. Most modern ECG machines read the traces automatically, compare them with data stored on a computer, and print out a diagnosis.

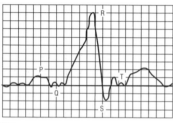

Key
P = Atria contract
QRS = Ventricles contract
T = Heart relaxes

The ECG trace above is normal for a healthy adult. The waves show the speed and rhythm of the electrical impulse passing through the heart:

- the P wave shows the contraction of the atria
- the Q, R and S wave shows the contraction of the ventricles
- the T wave shows the ventricles relaxing again.

This normal pattern of waves changes in individuals with heart disorders. Constant ECG monitoring of patients who have had a heart attack can alert medical staff to further problems. In some cases, for example patients with angina, an ECG is taken during exercise on a treadmill. This can reveal abnormalities not seen if the individual is resting.

CASE STUDY: JANET HARVEY'S ECG

Janet's doctor decided she needed some more information from tests which she could not do herself. She ordered:

- an ECG
- a chest X-ray
- a full blood count
- a urea and electrolytes profile.

This test confirmed that Janet's irregular heartbeat was caused by atrial fibrillation. This is important because it can be treated.

DISCUSSION POINT

The ECG trace on the right was taken from a patient with a heart disorder. Compare it with the normal ECG trace on page 184, and discuss the differences you can see.

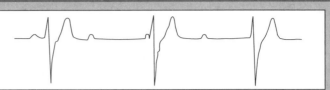

Blood cell counts

A blood cell count is one of the most commonly used sources of data on an individual's physiological status. A small sample of blood is taken and sent for laboratory analysis. The blood cell count may involve looking at:

- the number of red blood cells
- the number of grams of haemoglobin per dm^3
- the volume occupied by red blood cells when they have settled (packed cell volume)
- the number of white blood cells
- the number of different types of white blood cells
- the appearance and size of red and white blood cells
- the number and appearance of platelets.

Under normal conditions, blood is made up of each of these cells in particular proportions. Blood cell counts outside the normal range can provide important information about an individual's health.

Look back to the chart on page 142 to remind yourself of the structure and function of different types of blood cells. In a normal person, a blood cell count would show 5 million red blood cells in 1 mm^3 of blood – over a thousand times as many red cells as white. The different white cells would be found in the following proportions:

The study of blood and its diseases is called **haematology**.

Normal values for haematology tests

Haemoglobin (Hb)	Men: 13.5–18.0 g per 100 ml blood Women: 11.5–16.5 g per 100 ml blood
Red blood cell count	Men: 4.5–6 million per ml Women: 3.5–5 million per ml
Packed cell volume	Men: 40–55% Women: 36–47%
White blood cell count	$4.0–11.0 \times 10^9$ per litre
Differential white blood cell count:	Neutrophils 65% Lymphocytes 8% Monocytes 24% Eosinophils 2% Basophils 1%

Blood cell counts outside these normal ranges can indicate a wide range of illnesses and infection, including anaemias, blood disorders, and leukaemias.

Electrolyte concentrations in body fluids

The study of the composition of body fluids takes place in the clinical chemistry department of hospitals.

Electrolytes are substances which carry an electrical charge when dissolved. For example, sodium chloride (common salt) dissolves in body fluids to make positively charged sodium (Na^+) and negatively charged chloride (Cl^-).

Body fluids contain a range of electrolytes, including:

- sodium, potassium, calcium and magnesium (positively charged)
- chloride, phosphate, sulphate and nitrate (negatively charged).

These electrolytes need to be in balance for healthy functioning of the body. For example, too little potassium in the body can cause tiredness, faintness, abnormal heart rhythms, nausea, cramps, and even death in extreme cases.

The table on the left shows normal values for different substances in body fluid.

Na^+	134–147 mol/dm^3
K^+	3.4–5.0 mol/dm^3
Urea	2.5–7.0 mol/dm^3

CASE STUDY: JANET HARVEY'S LABORATORY TESTS

Janet Harvey has the following results from the laboratory.

Hb	125 g dm^{-3}
White blood cell count	6600 dm^{-3}
Na$^+$	145 m mol/ml
K$^+$	2.9 m mol/ml

ACTIVITY

Compare Janet's results with normal values. What is the abnormality?

Low blood levels of potassium can be caused by diuretic therapy with some drugs. Carry out research to find out what a diuretic is.

Janet has been having a diuretic to treat her high blood pressure. Her doctor knows that the low serum K$^+$ may have caused, or worsened, her atrial fibrillation. She prescribes oral potassium supplements.

Spirometer tracings

Spirometer tracings are often taken by one member of medical staff, and used by another as secondary source data to analyse an individual's physiological status.

For more information on spirometer tracings, see page 182.

ACTIVITY

Talk to a doctor or nurse about the importance and purpose of using both primary and secondary source data to monitor an individual's physiological status.

Imaging techniques

CASE STUDY: JANET HARVEY'S CHEST X-RAY

Janet has a chest X-ray. The lungs have normal shadows, but the heart is wider than normal. This suggests that the heart is swelling up and does not empty fully with each beat. This is a sign of heart failure.

Summary

Janet had worsening angina following her myocardial infarction. The doctor was able to note increased heart rate, hypertension and increased respiratory rate. She also noted the irregularity of Janet's heartbeat. This was enough to worry her, and she asked for further tests.

The ECG showed atrial fibrillation and a tachycardia. The laboratory results found low serum potassium. An X-ray showed that Janet's heart was beginning to enlarge due to heart failure. From all this evidence, the doctor organised the following treatment plan.

1   Janet had potassium tablets by mouth.

2   She was admitted to hospital for a day, and electric shock was used to return her heart to sinus rhythm.

3   Her blood pressure drugs were changed to give better control.

Three months on, Janet is much better. Her angina is less troublesome and she doesn't get breathless. Her blood pressure is 140/95 mm Hg and her heart rhythm is regular. She is trying to lose weight and give up smoking, as advised by her doctor.

Imaging techniques provide a picture of the body which can then be analysed. The first imaging technique, discovered at the end of last century, was the X-ray.

X-ray

Wilhelm Rontgen discovered X-rays while experimenting with passing a stream of electrons through a vacuum tube. When the electrons struck a plate made of tungsten (a heavy metal), invisible rays were produced. These were X-rays – short-wave, high-energy electromagnetic radiation. It was discovered that these rays could pass through opaque substances and create an image on a photographic plate, and they were quickly put to use in medicine.

Today, X-rays still play an important part in medical diagnosis. In hospital radiography units, X-rays are directed onto parts of the body which are being investigated, and pass through the tissue to produce an image on photographic film. Different body tissues absorb different amounts of X-rays – dense tissue, such as bone, absorbs more than softer tissue. As a result, some areas of the image appear darker than others. Bones appear clearly in white, making it easy to see any breaks, while other tissues are different shades from grey to black.

Plain X-rays of this type are particularly useful for investigating the bones and chest. On chest X-rays, the ribs can be seen clearly in white, with the heart and lungs appearing much darker.

X-ray machines are operated by radiographers in a hospital's radiology department. Like all doctors, they are able to interpret X-rays. However, specialists called radiologists are responsible for providing a final diagnosis. All medical staff who work in the radiography unit need to take special precautions to avoid over exposure to radiation, which can harm the body.

ACTIVITY

If possible, visit a radiography unit at a local hospital, or talk to a radiographer. Find out more about X-ray equipment and the safety precautions staff take.

Use of contrast media

Contrast media are radio-opaque dyes which are sometimes used to make X-ray images clearer. The dyes are introduced into the area of the body under investigation. When an X-ray image is taken, the dyes absorb the X-rays and produce a clearer picture of soft tissue than from using plain X-ray techniques.

The most commonly used contrast medium is barium, which can be swallowed (often known as a barium meal). In some cases, radio-opaque dyes are injected into the tissue being investigated, or into a vein. Contrast media are particularly useful for looking at hollow organs, such as the stomach and bowel, and are often used to diagnose stomach ulcers, cancer, and kidney disease.

Body scans

A major advance in imaging techniques came in 1971, with the development of the computerised tomography (CT) scanner. This takes a number of X-rays of the body from different angles. A computer then analyses the amount of X-rays absorbed by different tissues, and produces an image of a 'slice' of the body. This image is much clearer, and more detailed, than a plain X-ray. In some cases, contrast media may be used in conjunction with a CT scan.

CT scanning is a particularly good way to investigate the brain, and enables doctors to identify abnormal tissues and blood clots. However, CT scanners are very expensive, and are usually only available in large hospitals.

Magnetic resonance imaging

Magnetic resonance imaging – MRI – is a relatively new technique used to produce images similar to, and often better than, CT scans. However, unlike CT scanning it does not involve exposure to potentially dangerous X-rays.

Instead, MRI uses massive magnetic fields and radio signals to deflect hydrogen atoms, causing them to emit signals. The scanner interprets these signals, and produces a detailed computer-generated image.

MRI is particularly useful for soft tissue, and is used to investigate the eyes and ears, heart, urinary tract, spinal cord, brain and nervous system. It enables doctors to identify different types of tissue, and can help them detect tumours at an early stage and locate them accurately. However, like CT scanners, MRI equipment is expensive and is only available in large hospitals.

Ultrasound

As its name suggests, ultrasound involves the use of high-frequency sound waves (not audible to human beings). These waves are produced by hand-held equipment placed over the area under examination. The waves enter the body and bounce off structures, creating echoes which are recorded and analysed by a computer. From these echoes, a picture of internal structures is built up on the computer screen, which can then be printed off as an image.

The sound waves pass through liquids and soft tissues easily, without damaging the tissue. Ultrasound is widely used to monitor the development of the fetus during pregnancy – most pregnant women are given two ultrasound scans. By looking at an ultrasound image, doctors can identify the sex and age of the fetus, as well as detecting any abnormalities.

Ultrasound is also useful for detecting tumours and abnormalities in organs such as the liver, kidneys, gall bladder, heart and pancreas.

ACTIVITY

Talk to a doctor, nurse or radiographer and write a report about the importance of imaging and when different techniques are used.

189

Key questions

1   What causes the pulse?
2   What are the normal pulse rates for a resting adult, a baby and a young child?
3   Explain how you would use a sphygmomanometer, and what you would use it for.
4   What causes high blood pressure?
5   What is the normal breathing rate for adults, and what may it rise to after exercise?
6   Explain peak flow, tidal volume and vital capacity.
7   What equipment would you use to measure lung volumes?
8   What does an ECG show?
9   What is measured during a blood cell count?
10 What might a red blood cell count of 3 million cells per 1 mm^3 of blood suggest?
11 What are electrolytes?
12 Explain when you would use a plain X-ray, contrast media, and a body scan.
13 What does CT scan stand for?
14 Why is ultrasound used to monitor fetal development?
15 When would you use magnetic resonance imaging?

Assignment

Following safety procedures at all times, monitor the cardiorespiratory system of another member of your GNVQ group. You should take measurements during different levels of activity, and devise systems for recording the results clearly and accurately. Present your findings in a report, along with an analysis of the individual's physiological status.

Collect a range of secondary source data about an individual's physiological status – you may be able to get data from a hospital, or your tutor may supply you with typical results. Based on the data, write an analysis of the individual's physiological status, identifying whether measurements are outside normal parameters.

Finally, write a report on how imaging techniques are used to display anatomical features. You may find it helpful to visit a hospital and interview technicians. Illustrate your report with appropriate images.

UNIT **4**

Element 4.1
Human growth and development

Element 4.2
Individuals and society

Element 4.3
The effect of socioeconomic factors

Psychosocial aspects of wellbeing

This unit looks at the psychosocial aspects of human health and wellbeing. It includes concepts and theories from psychology, social psychology and sociology. Many of the ideas are developed further in units 5, 6 and 7.

ELEMENT **4.1**

Human growth and development

This element is about how humans grow and develop. It looks at physical growth and the development of linguistic and cognitive skills in infancy and childhood, and in later life. It also looks at emotional development throughout life. The element explores how people develop personalities and the influence of inherited and environmental factors on the way they behave. It also looks at the main changes and transitions in life, how people cope with them and what support is available when people need it.

> 66 Teaching is a challenge – but it is rewarding to see a child suddenly grasp an idea. I teach children who have physical disabilities and learning difficulties. We have one little girl of nine years old who was so overjoyed because she managed to lift a spoon to her mouth for the first time last week – we all could have cried with joy for her. 99
>
> *teacher in a special school*

> 66 It can get depressing here. We had a chap of 52 who had lost his job as a manager of an office a year ago. He had tried everything to find a new job, but felt as if he was on the scrap heap. His wife had left him, and he had got so short of money he had to lose the house. He had got so down he nearly committed suicide. I really feel the day centre has helped to bring him back from the brink but it is very distressing to see people who have got to such a state due to no fault of their own. 99
>
> *mental health nurse working in a day centre*

> 66 We have a lot of dependent elderly people here, but it is so homely and happy. The nurse in charge always seems to have a smile and a good word; we have old time music and singalongs most days and a lady who organises activities. The staff know what they have to do and matron is fair if she tells you off. She says it is better to have quality of life when you're old so we do everything to make today a good day, every day. 99
>
> *care worker in a nursing home for the elderly*

> 66 When people move in they are often giving up the home of a lifetime. All they can bring with them is some personal belongings and small items of furniture. It's a major bereavement for them and they need a lot of emotional support and care at this time. It is common for a new resident to be rude, unhappy or totally withdrawn. Staff here recognise that we have to spend a lot of time building up trust and reassuring new residents. 99
>
> *manager, residential care home for older people*

Key stages of growth and development

Key stages

child

adolescent

adult

elderly person

This section looks at the process of growth and development, from birth to old age. Health and social care practitioners need to understand how individuals change, develop and feel, so they can recognise and meet their needs effectively.

If you are familiar with babies you will know that they learn how to:
- recognise key people in their lives and respond in different ways
- recognise and respond to stimuli such as sound, movement or touch
- move and hold themselves up as they grow bigger and stronger
- understand and talk as their brains develop.

Humans continue to grow and change throughout their lives through a process of development that is partly genetic, partly social and environmental.

Many people grow up to be healthy members of society. They need relatively little professional health or social care for much of their lives. But sometimes, children are born with inherited or fetal development problems.

Other people may experience disease, accidents, or social problems later in their lives.

Because of improvements in living conditions and medicine, more people in the West are living longer. This affects individuals and society as a whole. There is a growing industry to support and care for the elderly, the disabled and those who are suffering from long-term illness, in their own homes and in sheltered or residential settings.

The rate of development varies according to:
- age
- health and disease
- nutrition
- genetic inheritance
- environment
- levels of stimulation and activity.

The key areas of development are:
- physical
- linguistic
- cognitive
- emotional.

DISCUSSION POINT

Why do you think it is important for practitioners to be able to make judgements about stages of development in adults as well as children?

Physical development

Physical development involves more than growth. It includes development or changes in:

- physical appearance
- sensory skills such as touch, hearing and sight
- motor coordination and balance which enable movement – for example catching a ball, or using a computer mouse to point to an object on the screen
- abilities and skills.

Children

The first years of life are a period of rapid physical development. Babies and small children are weighed, measured and checked for sensory development at child health clinics to ensure they are progressing 'normally'. The information is recorded on a centile chart (see the box below).

Normal development

Most babies and young children will:

- lift their head by three months
- sit unsupported by six to eight months
- start trying to crawl at about six months
- be crawling by nine months
- pull themselves upright holding onto furniture by ten to twelve months
- walk unaided by ten to 16 months
- learn to kick or throw a ball by 18 months to two years
- learn to pedal a tricycle by two to three years.

Measuring growth – centile charts

Centile charts are a means of assessing growth patterns. Centile charts used in the UK show growth within a 'normal' range, which covers 97% of the population of the UK. The exact average (mean) is 50%. The chart indicates the range within which children's weight and height are expected to fall, by a shaded curve. The range considered normal is quite wide. But it would cause concern if a child's weight declined from the

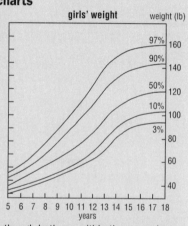

eightieth to the fortieth centile, even though both are within the normal range, because it might indicate a deterioration in health. Rates of growth need to be monitored for each individual, not just against the normal range.

DISCUSSION POINT

There are significant problems in conducting good scientific research into child development because of:

- the range of variables involved
- the length of time it takes to study one element of development in an individual
- the lack of variable control.

Physical development is the easiest aspect to study. Suggest ways in which you might determine the normal physical growth rate of children. What factors might affect the growth rate?

Adolescents

Puberty (the beginning of sexual maturity) begins between the ages of ten and 14 and may continue up until the age of 20 or 21, depending on the individual. Puberty involves the maturation of the primary sexual organs:

- ovaries in females
- testicles in males.

It also involves development of the secondary sexual characteristics:

- growth of hair around genitals and underarm for both sexes
- chest and facial hair in males
- changes in the shape of breasts and hips in females
- changes in depth of voice for males.

Adolescence signals a time of change in biological, social and cultural aspects of life. Physically, young people grow very rapidly and sometimes have an enormous appetite.

DISCUSSION POINT

In the UK, as in other Western countries, the age of puberty seems to be starting about 0.3 years lower each decade. Can you think why this might be?

Adults

The young adult is at the peak of physical functioning. The body develops quickly if physical activity is undertaken and heals quickly following injury. Performances of many tasks peak between the late teens and early thirties. Adults often 'slow down' as they get older, but it is possible to stay fit and healthy by eating sensibly and getting enough exercise. Loss of mental ability is compensated for by increased knowledge and experience, so that the peak of performance in mental spheres is usually in people's thirties, forties or fifties, rather than in their twenties. Adult life can be described in terms of stages and roles, shown in the box below.

Stages and roles in adult life

stage	description	roles
1	adult is newly married, with no children	role of partner is added
2	first child is born	role of parent is added
3	oldest child between two and six	role of parent has changed
4	oldest child is between six and twelve	role of parent has changed again as child enters school
5	oldest child is adolescent	role of parent changes again
6	oldest child has left home	sometimes called the 'launching centre' phase, as parents assist child to become independent
7	all children have left home	dramatic change in parental role; sometimes called the 'empty nest' or post-parental stage
8	one or both of the spouses has retired	sometimes called ageing family

Is there a biological clock?

The rhythm of the body's daily activities are regular and cyclical, revolving around a 24-hour day and night. There are also longer-term rhythms, such as monthly cycles. Research with animals shows that these rhythms persist even when the obvious sources of stimulation – food, other animals – are not present. These rhythms show themselves in patterns of electrical and chemical activity in nerve cells and ribonucleic acid (RNA) content. Is the slowing down of age a sign of a clock ticking slowly over the entire course of a person's life?

Language is an organised system of symbols used to communicate in speech, writing and signs. Language in all humans develops through the same stages, irrespective of culture.

Older people

In 1900, the average life expectancy in Britain was 49 years. Now it is usually considered to be over 70 years. The process of ageing can be considered as a gradual deterioration in function and capacity to respond to environmental stress. This process varies enormously between individuals, depending on their particular combination of genetic make-up, lifestyle choices, environment and experiences. Physical changes which occur to a greater or lesser degree in older people include:

- slowing of physical responses
- slowing of cognitive responses
- slower recovery times
- greater susceptibility to illness – particularly the diseases of age.

ACTIVITY

There are several theories suggesting reasons why humans age. One is the biological clock theory. Research this, or another theory on ageing, and explain it. If appropriate, include a series of diagrams in your explanation.

Language development

Babies can usually make noises from birth. A baby's development of language starts with cooing and babbling noises which are not affected by the language its parents or carers speak, whether people talk to it or whether the child is deaf. These noises are sometimes called 'pre-language'.

Between the ages of ten and twelve months, babies start to say their first recognisable words, and by 18 months they understand more than they can say. Parents help in the development of speech by:

- chatting to their babies, and to each other
- rehearsing phrases
- repeating them
- completing sentences.

To acquire language effectively, children need three types of competence:

- linguistic competence – such as adding on 's' to words to form a plural
- cognitive competence – the desire and ability to convey meaning or understand someone else's meaning
- communicative competence – relating to other people and a whole social environment.

Some elements of competence are built in, such as the ability to distinguish between subject and object. Others are learned, through listening and trying out and through a developing awareness of self and others.

People may lose the ability to speak or understand language because of illness, which can be most distressing for them and their carers. There are different ways of establishing and maintaining communication including:

- sign language
- technological developments
- touch.

66 *I am the only person who can understand my mother – she had a stroke last year and has not been able to speak since. But she can understand what I am saying if I speak clearly and don't use too many words. She makes me know what she wants by pointing to a large card we have made with different pictures – a cup for a drink, or flowers when she wants to go into the garden. It is difficult but we manage.* 99

daughter caring for her mother at home

66 *Karen used to babble happily as a baby – we did not realise she was deaf at first. She has special help. Her teachers are helping her to learn to communicate and she is able to make us understand most things.* 99

mother of a profoundly deaf child

Cognitive development

Cognition refers to the way people make sense of the world through what they know and learn about it. **Cognitive development** is the development of skills that make this possible.

Developmental psychologist Jean Piaget's findings on cognitive development in children, from experiments in the 1950s, are still are considered fundamental by some psychologists, though challenged by others. Piaget investigated:

- spatial awareness
- object permanence
- conservation
- hypothetical constructs
- abstract thinking.

Spatial awareness is important because many of the things people do require them to locate objects using their senses: seeing, hearing, touching and awareness of the movements and positions of their own bodies (kinesthesis). Some children have considerable problems in knowing where they are in space which may prevent them from understanding which is the left and right side of their body, or the geography of a building. It may also prevent them being able to dress easily or judge distances and directions. The box on the next page shows the normal development of sensorimotor coordination in children.

Age	Normal development
one month	follows objects with eyes and head
two to three months	predicts future position of moving objects; takes interest in close objects, including their arms
three months	directed arm movements, looks between grasped objects and hand
three to four months	watches how two hands work together
five months	controls actions of both hands/arms, reaches rapidly and grasps objects

Conservation experiment with beakers of liquid

Part 1 of experiment

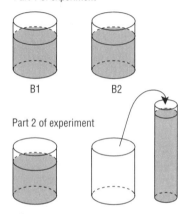

Part 2 of experiment

Conservation experiment with plasticine

Part 1 of experiment

Part 2 of experiment

Child development – a first course (K Sylva (1982), I Lunt, reprint (1984), Blackwell Pub.)

By the age of eight months children demonstrate curiosity about objects such as toys, but only if they can see them. If the toy is hidden, they lose interest. At about the age of twelve months babies start to understand that if the toy rolls out of sight it still exists behind whatever is obscuring it. This is what babies are exploring when they throw toys away from them for others to pick up and give back – they are learning that the toy still exists. Piaget called this 'object permanence'.

The ability to understand concepts of number, mass or volume seems built into humans, like the ability to acquire language. At around the age of six or seven, children learn to distinguish between different sizes, shapes and patterns which contain the same number, volume or mass of substance. This principle of conservation is needed for understanding maths and is important for the development of logical thinking.

Watching children play can be delightful: they have such vivid imaginations. A corner of the garden becomes their house, the stones are tables and the sticks are spoons. Scenes like these demonstrate that young children have the ability to think in the abstract and develop hypothetical constructs through cognitive techniques of assimilation and accommodation. As adolescents and adults this ability is used to build 'what if' scenarios, which enable ideas to be thought through and tested before implementation.

Assimilation is when perceptions are modified by what people already know. **Accommodation** is when existing structures of knowledge are modified by perceptions.

Piaget's work on egocentricity demonstrates how young children are only able to see things from their own point of view.

Modern research does not always agree with Piaget. Borke set three- and four-year-olds a perspective task using the character Grover from the children's television programme *Sesame Street*. He asked them to describe what Grover

ACTIVITY

Research Piaget's theory of egocentricity, set out the key points as a set of notes and describe one of his experiments.

DISCUSSION POINT

Piaget's original experiments were carried out in 1952, Borke's in 1975. It may be that the two sets of children had experienced different cultural environments, such as a greater experience of more sophisticated television programmes which present various perspectives. What do you think?

could see as he drove along in a fire engine. He found that children could decentre (put themselves in the place of Grover) to a greater extent than Piaget suggested was the norm.

Emotional development

The psychologist John Bowlby has helped to understand the behaviour of children and adults through his attachment theory. Bowlby paid particular attention to the bond between parent and child. He argued that babies are born with an innate tendency to create strong bonds with their care-givers to ensure survival. Attachment behaviour continues throughout people's lives. The formation of a bond is described as falling in love, maintaining a bond as loving someone, and losing a partner as grieving over someone.

Many mothers can identify five emotions in their one-month-old babies:

■ interest
■ surprise
■ joy
■ anger
■ fear.

DISCUSSION POINT

How do mothers recognise these emotions? Do you think other people might be able to identify them too?

Experimental evidence shows that very young babies respond to the shape of a particular face and quickly learn to distinguish their mother's face. A baby is able to recognise and bond with its mother soon after birth. A very young baby will turn its head to follow the sound of its mother's voice.

The state of mind of the mother can affect the state of mind of the baby. If a mother is upset the baby will sense her distress:

66 *When I am really tired and upset I give the baby to my partner or my mother. Because they are feeling calm this seems to settle the baby.* 99

mother of three-week-old baby

Role of interaction

Throughout life, people interact with others in various ways. The first and most important bond is with carers, but gradually friends also become important and influential. Researchers who interviewed children about their best friends identified three stages of friendship:

■ age five to seven – no real feelings of liking or disliking, no understanding of another's feelings (egocentric). Friendships easily started and finished, based on proximity and sharing things.

- age eight to eleven – mutual interests, responding to other's needs, tendency to form cliques
- age twelve and over – deeper, more enduring friendships, sharing thoughts, feelings and secrets. Friends give comfort and support, and act as confidants and therapists.

Positive close relationships enhance self-esteem and social skills. Friendships can offer close relationships in place of a family and are increasingly important with age. Negative close relationships, whether with friends or family, can have the opposite effect:

> 66 Although I loved my father, he was always saying that we were rubbish. I could never do anything right. I was convinced that I was stupid. But when Mum remarried, my new dad was very different. He had time for us and he even helped me with my school work. He showed me that I was really all right. I'm going to do my exams next year and have been put up a group at school. 99
>
> *15-year-old girl*

> 66 James always wears his emotions on his sleeves! You can always tell when he is upset, angry or bored. He doesn't have to say anything. 99
>
> *James's colleague*

Babies and young children usually show their emotions without restraint. The tantrums that are so common in children around the age of two are often due to an inability to cope with strong emotions such as anger and the forceful feelings they release. On the other hand, babies quickly learn the pleasure of amusement and become adept at evoking pleasure-giving responses from their carers.

As life progresses, social codes of behaviour begin to mould how people express emotions. Boys may still be taught that it is 'babyish' to cry. Girls may still be encouraged not to show anger. Children who cry a lot may be labelled 'cry babies', and this belittles their behaviour. People can be trained, encouraged or shamed into showing or concealing their feelings and emotions.

Different cultures have different ways of showing their emotions. Grief, for instance, is displayed in a variety of ways, according to the norm or tradition of the cultural group.

DISCUSSION POINT

Choose a cultural group that is different from your own and find out its traditional ways of expressing grief and happiness.

How might this behaviour be understood by people from other cultures? Why is it important that people should demonstrate their grief in a way that is comfortable for them?

Development of personality

DISCUSSION POINT

Are the patterns of behaviour which you see in yourself and other people there from birth, or were they learned?

Personality is a unique combination of each individual's bodily and mental characteristics, formed by experience and shown in their attitudes, interests, abilities and behaviour.

DISCUSSION POINT

What are the variables that usually make it difficult to reach conclusions about the relative importance of inherited and environmental factors on the development of personality?

The genetic make-up of an individual is called its **genotype**. The physical appearance of any given characteristic – such as colour blindness, height or personality – is called the **phenotype**.

Personality develops during childhood and adolescence and can continue to change throughout life. Social psychologists explain the development of personality in different ways. Some believe that inherited factors play the most significant role: others argue that environmental factors are the key. It is difficult to be sure either way because there are so many variables and some of them are impossible to control. Some elements of personality can be researched using identical twins who have not been brought up together. Other work focuses on children who have been deprived of stimulation because of illness or lack of contact with other people.

Inherited influences – genetics

The nucleus of each human cell contains 23 pairs of chromosomes, half from the female and half from the male parent. Each pair of chromosomes contains a set of genes which carry information about specific features of the offspring, one from each parent. Each gene is made up of two sets of information called alleles; one allele will have been derived from the mother, the maternal allele, and the other from the father, the paternal allele. Each allele may be in one of two forms:

- dominant: its characteristics show through in the physical appearance of the individual
- recessive: its characteristics can be masked in the physical appearance of the individual if a dominant equivalent is also prresent.

People inherit physical characteristics from their parents, such as hair and skin colour. Do they also inherit personality? There are two ways of studying the effects of genes on personality and behaviour. The first is to look at how genes specify the functions of the nervous system. This is done by finding out the pathways that link chromosomes to behaviour. The second is to look at the effects on behaviour of genetic changes, through selective breeding or mutations.

There is evidence that mutation in a single gene can have effects on behaviour. For example, babies who carry abnormal genes that make them unable to metabolise the amino acid phenylalanine have relatively low intelligence (which can be partly offset through diet). A study of one Dutch family with a history of violence discovered an inherited defect in the gene which makes monoathine oxidase (a chemical involved in metabolising adrenaline). The genetic defect on its own does not make members of the family more violent, but it does make them less able to deal with the social pressures that lead to violence.

Some diseases, such as colour blindness and haemophilia, are linked to the sex chromosome. These diseases will appear if a child fails to inherit a normal X chromosone from its mother. Boys usually show the symptoms of the disease, though girls can act as 'carriers' without being affected if their own sex chromosone has a normal corresponding set of information. Other diseases can be linked to specific combination traits in the parents, for example, cystic fibrosis.

DISCUSSION POINT

Look at the chart on page 206 giving Erikson's description of the stages of personality development. Why do you think Erikson devotes four stages to the early years of life?

DISCUSSION POINT

Geneticists can now identify genes which carry susceptibility to many diseases, such as heart disease, certain forms of cancer, sickle-cell anaemia and Huntington's chorea. It may be possible to eradicate genetically influenced disease. What practical problems might there be in doing this? What ethical problems are there?

Evidence that behaviours and personality traits, as well as physical characteristics, can have a genetic link comes from comparing identical twins who are brought up separately and identical twins brought up together. Both sets of twins have similar scores in intelligence tests. Aspects of their personality such as introvert or extrovert behaviours are also influenced by genetic factors.

In most of these cases, it is impossible to locate a single gene that is responsible for the similarities. They are probably a result of a combination of genes (known as 'polygenes'). As with the Dutch family, it is the interaction between individuals and their environment and its effect on the whole genotype that makes genetically inherited characteristics significant.

Psychological basis of personality

The founder of psychoanalysis, Sigmund Freud (1856–1939), suggested that behaviour is governed by unconscious processes. The most basic is an instinctive sexual drive he called 'libido', which he thought was present at birth and the motivating force behind virtually all our behaviour. Freud also introduced the concept of defence mechanisms – automatic, unconscious strategies for reducing anxiety. Examples are repression, denial and projection.

Another major influence on psychoanalytical theories about the development of personality was Erik Erikson. He shares most of Freud's basic assumptions, but argues that identity is not fully developed until adult life. Personality is seen to develop throughout life, in a similar, sequential way to physical development. Erikson identified eight stages, shown in the chart on page 206, during which the personality developed in different ways. The first four stages relate to the infant and child, the remaining four to adolescence onwards.

The psychologist Hans Eysenck, working in the 1940s and 50s, believed that personality is biologically based and lodges within the cortex of the brain. He proposed that personality could be looked at in terms of three ranges of behaviour:

- neuroticism versus stability
- extroversion versus introversion
- psychoticism versus intelligence.

Dimensions of personality

- neuroticism – describes people who have a tendency to worry, are temperamental, self-pitying, self-conscious, emotional and vulnerable

- extroversion – describes affectionate, talkative people who are likely to be active, fun-loving, passionate, and who join in

- openness to experience – this is characteristic of people who are imaginative, creative, original, curious, liberal and willing to explore inner feelings

- agreeableness – people who are soft-hearted, trusting, generous, acquiescent, lenient and good-natured

- conscientiousness – people who are hard-working, well-organised, punctual, ambitious and persevering.

DISCUSSION POINT

Look at Maslow's hierarchy of needs. What might be the result on someone's self-esteem if their need for love and belongingness were not fulfilled?

Eysenck suggested that introverts are more easily conditioned, more conforming, have a lower sensory threshold and therefore feel pain more acutely, whereas extroverts seek greater excitement and dangerous pastimes. Contemporary researchers have identified several aspects of personality which they say remain constant over periods of time and in a variety of situations. They are shown in the box on the left.

ACTIVITY

How are descriptions like these of people's personality types relevant to care? Find two or three specific examples showing how they influence health and social care today. You could find evidence in newspaper or journal articles, or by asking people you know who work in the care sector. Write up your examples in the form of case studies.

Environmental influences

How does the way a child is brought up, the type and method of education, expectations of society and other influences affect the development of personality?

Probably the best-known theorist to link development with environment was Abraham Maslow (1908–1970). He thought that individuals are born with a basic drive to fulfil their own potential and to achieve what he called 'self-actualisation'. Maslow was particularly interested in the developments of needs, which he divided into:

- physiological needs – food, warmth, shelter
- safety – physical and psychological
- love and belonging
- esteem
- self-actualisation.

Maslow argued that physiological needs must be met first, then safety needs and so on. Each stage was a foundation for the next and a weakness in fulfilment of a lower stage would have a negative impact on the stage above.

Inherited and environmental factors

66 *It's odd how the two sisters are so different: same parents, same school, same house: but they are like chalk and cheese!* 99

primary school teacher

How do inherited and environmental factors affect people's physical, linguistic, cognitive and emotional development?.

Physical development

The likeness of physical features in families clearly demonstrates that genes play a significant role in passing on certain characteristics from one generation to another. There is now clear evidence that some malignant diseases, heart disease and Down's syndrome are also carried in genes.

This discovery has increased the amount of screening done during pregnancy. It has also started to revolutionise the counselling services required to support people who are planning to have children. Potential parents need to know whether they are likely to pass on a genetically carried disease. The changing of gene patterns will allow children who previously would have died or been disabled to be born healthy.

The lifestyle of a child's biological parents and their carers also affects physical growth. For example, smoking during pregnancy is known to produce smaller babies and smoking around children is known to exacerbate certain conditions such as asthma.

Linguistic development

All children are born with the ability to learn language – grammar, vocabulary, sounds. Which language or languages and dialects they actually learn depends on the community that they grow up in. The first influence is the immediate family, and then as their social groups expand, other influences come into play. People continue to learn and develop language throughout their lives, as they move between different social groups or learn new things.

DISCUSSION POINT

Children from deprived backgrounds may suffer from poor language development. Why do you think this may happen?

Four main views about language development are summarised in the chart on the following page.

Theory	Name of theory	Person who developed theory
Language is learnt through practice or reinforcement and imitation. In families where parents talk more to the children, the children develop a wider-ranging vocabulary.	learning theory	Skinner (1957)
People are born with the ability to formulate and understand language. The brain is preprogrammed with the rules of grammar. Language is specific to a species, but almost all children learn language at the same age and in the same sequence.	nativist theory	Chomsky (1959)
Language depends on cognitive development, controlled by the development of the nervous system. Language develops as children interact with their environment. The child prompts the development.	cognitive theory	Piaget (1952)
Language is a means of social interaction. Children develop language for social reasons of their own, not just because they need it to survive in their environment.	social theory	Bruner (1983)

Cognitive development

Piaget (see page 197) believed strongly that cognitive development was due to an interaction between the environment, learning and genetic influences.

Piaget (see page 197)

ACTIVITY

Arrange to visit two schools or nurseries, one of which should be for children with learning difficulties. Observe for half an hour how the children are playing and interacting with others.

Describe what you see. Compare your findings with the two groups of children. Produce a table or chart showing:

- how their behaviours matched the expected developmental norms for children of that age
- the main differences between the two groups.

DISCUSSION POINT

Look at some case studies of children who have suffered from emotional deprivation and privation. Can you see a difference between the two types of suffering and their effects?

Emotional development

Family life, and in particular parental influences, affects the emotional state of children. Bowlby (see page 199) thought that maternal deprivation would result in an inability to establish relationships in later life, with a possible risk of anti-social behaviour. Other psychologists differentiate between two states where emotional needs are not met:

- deprivation, which has short-term effects
- privation, the effects of which are long-term.

Transition and change

ACTIVITY

What are the major events or stages in life? List ten or twelve. Then get together with three or four other people and look at each other's lists. How many can you add to your list from theirs?

Rank	Life event
1	death of spouse
2	divorce
3	marital separation
4	jail term
5	death of a close family member
6	personal injury or illness
7	marriage
8	fired at work
9	marital reconciliation
10	retirement
11	change in health of a family member
12	pregnancy
13	sex difficulties
14	gain of new family member
15	business readjustment
16	change in financial state
17	death of a close friend
18	change to a different line of work
19	change in number of arguments with spouse
20	large mortgage repayments

People experience similar broad changes in their lives. For example, most people experience loss (of parents, family or friends). Many of these events are expected, but they may still cause stress. Some are unexpected, like the onset of an illness or the death of a close friend.

How do people cope with the transition from one life stage to another, or with unexpected events? The answer is different for each person and depends on many factors, including their:

- age and maturity
- past experiences
- personality
- degree of support
- level of knowledge and understanding of the situation.

A lot of research has been carried out into the positive and negative effects of change. In 1967, two researchers published a scale indicating the impact of life events. It was based on research involving 5,000 people and aimed to identify what life events preceded illness. The events were then ranked. The top 20 stress-related events are shown in the margin.

Expected transition and change

Change can always be stressful, but when it happens at an appropriate time it is not so frightening, as a midwife explains:

66 *When mothers go into labour with a full term baby they are ready for the baby to be born. Although they are sometimes concerned that the process might be painful they are not usually frightened just apprehensive. If on the other hand it is a premature labour, they may be frightened for the new baby and for themselves.* 99

Things like weddings, twenty-first or fiftieth birthday parties and funerals help people to cope with the transition from one stage of life to another by formalising it as a social ritual.

More generally, life changes can be expected and planned for. Psychoanalyst Erik Erikson suggested that people's personalities develop throughout their lives in eight stages. The table below shows how the transition from one stage of development to another can be eased by activities and relationships.

Age	Transition	Activity	Important relationship
1	trust versus mistrust	consistent stable care	mother
2–3	autonomy versus shame	independence from parents	parents
4–5	initiative versus guilt	exploration of environment	basic family
6–11	industry versus inferiority	acquisition of knowledge	family, neighbours, teachers
12–18	identity versus role confusion	seeking coherent personality and vocation	peers, in-groups, out-groups
20–40	intimacy versus isolation	deep and lasting relationships	friends, lovers
40–64	generativity versus stagnation	being productive and creative for society	spouse, children
65+	integrity versus despair	review and evaluate life	spouse, children, grandchildren

Changes in childhood can be traumatic, and people working with young children need to be sensitive to the signs. The head of a childcare centre explains:

66 *With transitions like the birth of a brother or sister, or for example if mum or dad is ill, how they react depends on the character of the child. But it will nearly always show in some way or another. Small children may regress – a little one who is dry may start to wet again. Sometimes it comes out in imaginative play.* 99

Good, effective support can make a difference to their later development:

66 *Staff may observe children showing that they feel stressed. In these situations the carer must adjust accordingly and provide the extra support and reassurance needed. Children need to be made to feel special and that they have rights. If they come through difficult situations with the right support they learn how to empathise as they get older.* 99

Adolescence is a time when people change in many ways, physically and socially, and establish a sense of identity outside of the family. Parents and families must also come to terms with these changes.

The physical age of 40 years may be seen by some people as a 'mid-life crisis'. Hormonal changes for women may cause stress. Children may be growing into adolescence or adulthood at this time and facing emotional difficulties themselves. Some people see this time as a positive stage when they have accepted themselves and feel content with their lives.

Some life events involve individuals in loss, for example when a child leaves home. Even when the experience is mainly happy it can also involve loss, such as when first-time parents experience joy in their baby but also sadness at the loss of freedom. There is a common pattern of behaviour in situations where loss is experienced. Often the depth of the loss is marked by the length of time it takes to go through the pattern.

Psychologist John Bowlby distinguished five phases of grief and mourning:
- initial shock, denial, concentration on the lost person
- anger
- appeals for help
- despair, withdrawal, disorganisation
- resolution, reorganisation and new focus.

DISCUSSION POINT

Discuss the mid-life stage in terms of Maslow's hierarchy of needs (page 203).

Mr Graham was admitted to psychiatric care suffering from increasing bouts of uncontrollable anger. As a result of his behaviour he had lost his job, and his son refused to see him any more because he found his father's anger too difficult to handle. On admission to the ward, Mr Graham took out his anger on female staff and broke several windows.

After several weeks of therapy it was discovered that Mr Graham's wife had been killed in a road accident ten years previously. Mr Graham had not accepted this and never talked about it with anyone. He still laid the table for her at meal times and bought birthday and Christmas presents for her.

After treatment Mr Graham made a full recovery and was reunited with his son. The diagnosis was delayed grief syndrome.

Symptons of grieving

■ loss of appetite

■ anxiety

■ withdrawal

■ depression

■ guilt

■ sleep disturbance

■ panic attacks

■ crying

■ lack of concentration

■ difficulty in sleeping or excess sleepiness

■ poor memory

DISCUSSION POINT

Unexpected change is likely to cause higher levels of stress when compared with expected events Why should this be?

DISCUSSION POINT

Why do you think Mr Graham's condition might have arisen? Identify the stages in his grief pattern with reference to Bowlby's five phases.

Grieving ends when the person reconstructs their sense of self, comes to terms with the situation and accepts it, though they may always feel sad about it. Some common symptoms of grieving and adjusting are shown in the box on the left.

Positive changes such as promotion at work, moving house, and pregnancy also can be stressful and require coping strategies too.

Unexpected transition and change

Examples of this might include:

■ being a victim of crime

■ becoming disabled

■ serious illness

■ breakdown of significant relationships

■ death of a friend or relative.

Other stressful events which are becoming more common – though they are often unexpected – are redundancy and divorce.

Divorce is one of the most common unexpected life events. One in three marriages ends in divorce, mostly within the first seven years. Reactions vary according to what the marriage was like, and whether there are children involved.

DISCUSSION POINT

Studies in the United States found that more than 80% of children attending psychiatric clinics came from broken homes. Do you think that this could be related to the grief mechanism in some way? Should other factors be considered too? If so, what might they be?

Studies have shown that people who are unemployed experience more psychological difficulties and poorer health than when they were in work. Work is part of one's overall identity for many people. The loss of status, social contacts and sense of purpose can lead to a loss of self-esteem. For some people this can lead to an increased chance of depression, alcoholism or even suicide. Attempted suicides are eight times more common among unemployed people. They are most likely to occur during the first month of unemployment.

Methods of support

Most people turn to others to help them through a difficult time. Many support mechanisms are informal but some are more formal, including professional support.

Help is available from many sources, including:

- relatives and relationships
- networks
- organisations
- professionals
- resources.

Relationships

The first support often comes from immediate family. A death in the family may bring family members together. The funeral may assist the process of acceptance as it is a formal recognition of the death. It offers an opportunity to ask for help and support without embarrassment.

It is important to be able to talk about the problems. Close friends and family can often help to put the situation into context and give support. But family relationships are sometimes stressful in themselves and family members may not always be the best source of support.

Networks

A network is a collection of individuals or organisations linked in some informal way. When someone needs help they may be able to contact:

- friends – an informal network
- relatives – a formal network
- members of the community with an obligation to the person needing support – a semi-formal network.
- members of the community who want to help (volunteers) – a formal network.

Formal networks include religious communities. In some communities, neighbours act as a supportive network.

Organisational and professional support

There are many organisations that can help in times of crisis. Many are self-help groups set up by people wishing to share experiences and knowledge. There is more in element 5.1 about this.

The coordinator of a community for homeless people explains the nature of the support they give:

66 We get many situations where people come here from off the streets who are very run down physically and emotionally. We provide a firm foundation where people can heal themselves, with our support. During that period, they become physically stronger, they can cope with physical work and contribute to

ACTIVITY

Identify and list the support networks that would be available to you if you needed them. Ask a member of your family to do the same. Compare the two lists with those of other students. How similar are they? What are the benefits of each type of network?

Support organisations

- Citizens Advice Bureau
- Relate
- Victim Support
- Cruse
- British Red Cross
- Scope
- Childline
- Samaritans

the community. One guy had a massive drink problem and had been through ten years of various programmes of drying out at drinks clinics. On the first day here he couldn't even eat. Here we accept people as they are. As time went on he became more emotionally secure and physically stronger. Now he does the books for the community. The big difference here is that we don't focus on changing people. 99

Counselling can help physical and mental health following a major life change like bereavement, especially if there is little or no family support. A counsellor in a centre for young people explains that such support can also have long-term benefits:

66 *We have seen it happen many times before: a young person who can take advantage of counselling ends up knowing much more about who they are and can act more purposefully. They become self-confident and clear about their direction. It shows physically in their body language, eye contact and facial expression. It tends to improve their relationships with peers and parents. They also can become more creative as they gain in self-esteem. It is very rewarding to see these changes.* 99

Resources available

Some social security benefits are available for people who need support.

ACTIVITY

Choose one of the support organisations listed on page 209, or another you want to investigate. Find out what sort of support they provide and who it is for. Describe their main aims and role. Then design a leaflet which promotes their services and explains how to contact them.

DISCUSSION POINT

Why are so many different kinds of support needed? Give examples from your own experience or knowledge, drawing on the wide-ranging problems experienced by people of all ages.

ACTIVITY

Get information from a library or your local Social Security Office about the benefits aimed at supporting individuals through specific difficulties. List them in a table. Explain what they are for and why they may be needed. Suggest other possible resources for each type of support.

Key questions

1 What are the four main ways in which people develop?
2 What is the significance of interaction in human development?
3 What are the main stages of physical development in babies and young children?
4 What are the main stages of cognitive development, according to Piaget?
5 In Erikson's theory, what are the eight stages of the development of personality?
6 What do recent genetic discoveries add to our understanding of the development of personality?
7 How does the environment affect the development of personality?
8 How are people's responses different to expected change and unexpected change?
9 What is the difference between transition and change?
10 Why is it necessary to have a range of methods to support people when they are coping with change and transition?
11 What methods are there?

Assignment

This assignment is in two parts.

Part 1

Produce a diagram or a sequence of diagrams to represent the main stages of development in a human life, from birth to death in old age. At each stage, show what happens in terms of physical, linguistic, cognitive and emotional development.

When you have completed the diagram, think about factors that could alter the normal or expected pattern of development. At each stage, give an example of:

■ an inherited factor, such as a disease
■ an environmental factor, such as deprivation.

Describe how you would expect these two factors to alter the pattern or stage of development. Be as specific as you can, using your knowledge of real-life examples.

Part 2

Choose two of the stages on the diagram you produced in part 1. Think of two people you know who are at these stages of their lives. Give:

■ an example of an expected change or transition that might affect them at this stage
■ an example of an unexpected change that might affect them.

Write an explanation of how your two individuals might cope with these situations. Or, if you prefer, you could record your ideas on cassette.

Then think of three possible methods of support that may be available to your two individuals, to help them cope with the transition or change. Describe briefly why you have chosen these methods and how you think they might help.

ELEMENT **4.2**

Individuals and society

This element investigates why people living in the same society hold different values and beliefs. It looks at the process of socialisation that happens to everybody, through the primary influences of parents and family and the secondary influences of education, work and contact with other people. It examines how ideas about power, health and deviance are constructed by every society at a particular place and time, and how these ideas change. It also looks at the conflicts that might arise when people have different ideas and values, and how professionals in health and social care can deal with the conflicts in themselves.

66 *When I meet some forms of social behaviour which can seriously affect health I can't help but be upset. Alcohol is the one I get most upset about. It's the failure of people to realise that their habits are harmful to themselves and to those they live with.* 99

doctor in charge of health screening, private hospital

66 *One major change is that spectacles have become more of a fashion accessory, for children's frames as well as adults. There is not such a stigma to wearing glasses, even with the under-18s. At the moment, wire-rimmed ones are popular.* 99

optometrist

66 *Some people sometimes have different particular needs because of cultural or religious reasons. They often come to light during personal care assessments and are taken into account like any other needs.* 99

occupational therapy services manager

66 *We are hoping to influence people's choices about their lifestyles and give them information about how they could make positive changes. So we have to make sure that information is accessible and attractive to the right audience by thinking about how people see themselves in society. For example, we have found from research that many women don't take exercise because they don't see themselves as the 'sporty type'. But by no means all types of exercise have to involve sport – so we now know that many women need more information about how they can exercise without being 'sporty'.* 99

physical activity manager, Health Education Authority

The process of socialisation

As people grow up and grow older, many inherited and environmental factors combine to make them into unique individuals. Some of the factors are explored in element 4.1. These influences include the culture, values, ideas and attitudes of parents and other family members, teachers, friends and others in their peer group, employers and people they meet at work, religious institutions and the mass media – mainly newspapers, TV and radio.

The process of socialisation continues throughout life. Sociologists describe two main stages of socialisation:

- primary – the process of children growing up to become adults
- secondary – the process of adults interacting with the culture of a particular society at a particular time.

Family

Primary socialisation takes place within the family. Family, friends and neighbours are all strong influences. Young children learn firstly from their prime carer, usually the mother, and then from other members of the family. Family systems vary greatly, so there is really no standard experience. In a multicultural society, practitioners need to be aware of the variety of experiences and sensitive to the way these may affect people's behaviour.

Family life may be a mainly positive or mainly negative experience, physically and in other ways. If a child is abused or subjected to violent behaviour within the family, this is likely to have long-term negative effects which affect how they behave as an adult towards their own family. In terms of linguistic development, the social theorist Basil Bernstein showed how children growing up in middle-class families develop an 'elaborated' code of language in contrast to the 'restricted' code of children in working-class families.

As well as family members, other factors related to the family affect people's lifestyles and the process of socialisation. They include where the family lives, the economic status of parents or adult carers and the number and type of siblings (brothers and sisters).

Peer group

In today's society, more mothers work and many more children attend nurseries and day care. This provides opportunities to come into contact with their peers from an early age. Some group friendships last a long time, sometimes even a lifetime.

Peer group relationships tend to be more democratic than those between parents and children. They also open out important opportunities for new knowledge and experimentation. With their peers, young people:

- develop their own tastes and fashions, e.g. in clothes and music
- experiment with ways of challenging the values of their primary socialisation, such as families
- gain knowledge and experience of lifestyles different from their own.

Socialisation is learning the norms or rules of behaviour and acquiring (or rejecting) the belief systems of a family and society in general.

DISCUSSION POINT

You may know the term 'streetwise'. What does it mean to you? Does family influence play a role in whether someone is streetwise or are other processes of socialisation more influential?

Peer groups are people who have a similar status in some way, for example, in age or profession. The word 'peer' means 'equal'.

DISCUSSION POINT

What peer groups are you part of? How do these different groups influence your behaviour?

DISCUSSION POINT

Some people say of health or social care work: 'I could never do that type of work'. How might their socialisation make them not want to work in health or social care? How does your socialisation contribute to the interest you have in this type of work?

Work

In most cultures, work is one of the most important settings for socialisation. It is only within industrial societies that people 'go out to work'. In less industrialised societies, work is near or within the home or on the land associated with the home.

People's jobs affect their behaviour in many ways. Some people, such as hospital workers or police officers, work irregular hours. Many jobs have developed their own language and norms, as one staff nurse on an accident and emergency ward describes:

66 *The humour shared between hospital staff would be socially unacceptable at the dinner table of non-medical people. But it allows us to face traumatic and difficult situations with a sense of proportion.* 99

Education

Education plays an important role as a socialising influence. Every child in the UK must receive formal education until the age of 16. The great majority of children go to school but a few are educated at home. Schools are formal institutions with their own rules and codes of behaviour. All children attending state schools now follow a national curriculum so that there is a degree of uniformity to the knowledge and skills to which each child is introduced.

Education can be seen as a way of helping to equalise individuals in society, and this was the rationale for the comprehensive system introduced in Britain in the 1960s. There is an opposite argument which says that education in its present form ensures that inequalities in our society will continue. Bernstein's description of linguistic codes (see page 213) shows that children who have acquired an 'elaborated' code find it easier to cope with formal academic education. There is a tendency for children with a 'restricted' code to come from a lower socioeconomic background than those with an elaborated code.

DISCUSSION POINT

What did you learn at school, apart from the subjects you studied? What did you really take away from your years of schooling, into future life?

Socialisation in schools also takes place in more subtle ways. Sociologists describe a concept called 'the hidden curriculum', first described by Ivan Illich in 1971. He found that a lot of what is learnt in school has nothing to do with the formal content of the classes, but is about things like discipline and regimentation.

What are schools for?

Illich argued that schools have four main purposes. They:

- provide custodial care – keeping pupils off the streets and in a controlled environment
- help to distribute people between occupational roles – academic ability, skills developed and certificates awarded guide and restrict young people in terms of their future occupation
- teach dominant values – including moral and political values
- allow children and young people to acquire socially approved skills and knowledge – how to behave in a socially acceptable way, work as a team, listen and communicate, and so on.

DISCUSSION POINT

Formal education might reduce the influence that the family and peer groups have on the socialisation process. What do you think about this?

Religious institutions

Several values are common to many religions. Most religions use sets of symbols and are linked to rituals or ceremonies which are carried out by groups of believers. Some religions believe in a god or gods, others in a divine force. Many think with reverence about an important figure.

Three influential monotheistic (belief in one god) religions in the world today are Judaism, Christianity and Islam. The oldest of the world's major religions is Hinduism, which is a polytheistic religion (with a belief in many gods). Other religions such as Buddhism and Taoism relate to natural harmony, which is believed to unite all creatures and facets of the universe.

The strength of belief influences the behaviour of the believer. If the parents in a family are active believers, their children will be brought up in a religious environment. When people come to a religion later in life the effect may be different. In contemporary British society, many people do not take an active part in religion. The decline in the influence of religion is known as secularisation.

> **Religion** is 'the belief in, worship of, or obedience to a supernatural power or powers considered divine or to have control over human destiny'
>
> *Collins English Dictionary*

DISCUSSION POINT

Choose three of the main religions practised in the UK today. What are some of the similarities and differences between them?

The media

The modern world is dependent on communications. The mass media – newspapers, magazines, cinema, radio and television – are all influential channels which have a powerful effect on the information audiences receive and the way in which it is interpreted.

The media help to shape people's cultural identity. For example, many TV soaps confirm how we live or make us behave in a different way because we like or have learned from the way the characters behave. Often these programmes highlight important issues of the day. Examples include dealing with a friend suffering from HIV/AIDS, the breakdown of a marriage and how it affects children in the family.

Some media messages may concern anyone working in health and social care. For example, the media have been blamed for portraying an image of models as 'waifs': girls seeing these images strive to match them and may enter the spiral of strict dieting that leads to anorexia nervosa.

The media are a method of control as well as a channel of information. An important aspect of secondary socialisation is learning to ask the questions:
- Who is passing on this information?
- Why are they doing it this way?

DISCUSSION POINT

How do you think communication through the Internet is likely to change the way in which people receive information? How could it reduce cultural uniformity?

A **social construct** is a set of behaviours which society ascribes to a social role or function. For example, one social construct of the family is the idea of a 'nuclear' family.

DISCUSSION POINT

What sort of things would you expect society to have a shared view about? List half a dozen broad topics or themes.

DISCUSSION POINT

Think about the roles of mother and father. Discuss how changes in society over your lifetime have affected the social constructs of these two roles.

DISCUSSION POINT

Do you think it is acceptable for a man to be a midwife? Do you and others around you have a gender construct of this role?

Element 4.1 describes how people develop a personal concept of themselves, others or things that is not necessarily shared by other people. Social constructs reflect a shared view held by society as a whole.

Social constructs are not fixed. They are open to re-evaluation and review in the light of new information and changes in the way people think. But with social constructs, just as with personal constructs, it is possible to have stereotypical ideas about people or roles.

Some of the most powerful and influential social constructs are made about:
- people's roles – especially in relation to their gender and their family role
- power – the relative power of individuals to one another and the power of social structures, such as the idea of the free market
- deviance – behaviour that is not normal or socially acceptable, including criminal behaviour
- health and illness.

Gender

Gender socialisation starts as soon as a child is born. Even parents who believe they treat children equally probably act differently with boys and girls. These differences are reinforced by many other cultural influences. On the whole, society has different expectations of boys and girls.

66 *We still comment when a girl is admitted to the ward with a football injury – we are surprised.* 99

orthopaedic ward sister

Feminists say that the role of women in relation to men is a result of socioeconomic factors and can be changed. In the last 25 years, they have challenged many of the gender constructs affecting women, especially in their demands for equal pay, equal opportunities at work and abortion on demand. Since the 1960s, women have become more active in the workplace. During the last 20 years there has been an increase in:
- the number of women in management
- female doctors
- men in secretarial work
- men as child carers in the home.

But research shows that women still face gender barriers and stereotypes at work. They are lower paid, more likely to be in part-time, low-paid or repetitive low-skill work and still face a 'glass ceiling' – an invisible barrier to progression in a career. At home, they still undertake the bulk of household tasks.

Family

Virtually everybody in the UK is brought up in some type of family context. The most common type of family in our society is still the 'nuclear' family, which consists of two parents living together with their children. The

DISCUSSION POINT

Some people have a different attitude to lone parents who are in that position through divorce or voluntary separation, to those who have become lone parents through the death of a partner. What attitudes have you encountered in these cases? What do the differences in people's attitudes say about the modern family as a social construct?

To what extent are changes in family relationships influencing the social construct of the family?

There are alternatives to the traditional family. **Communes** such as the kibbutzim in Israel have existed for a long time. A kibbutz is a community of families and individuals which cooperates in raising children.

Power is the ability of an individual or group to carry out its wishes or policies, and to control or influence the behaviour of others, whether they wish to cooperate or not.

ACTIVITY

The use – and sometimes abuse – of power is an important aspect of care. Identify specific examples in the health and social care field where each type of power listed in the table above is demonstrated. Explain whether you think the use of power in each case is good or bad.

'extended' family, perhaps a group of two or three generations living either together in the same dwelling or in close proximity, was widespread up to the beginning of the 20th century and is still fairly common today.

Throughout this century there have been constant changes in what constitutes the family. In recent years there have been many changes in the structures of family groups. The main cause for this is the increase of single-parent households. Since 1971, the marriage rate in the UK has more than halved, from 69 per 1,000 unmarried people down to 34 in 1994. Some people choose to be lone parents or to live with rather than marry the other parent of their children. Others may be alone because of marriage breakdown, through divorce, separation or the death of one of the partners. Remarriage and step-parenting is becoming increasingly common.

Cohabitation is the name given to the state in which a couple live together in a sexual relationship without being married. This is increasingly common in the UK and many other countries: figures from 1994 suggest that ten per cent of men and women aged between 18 and 49 were cohabiting. Many cohabiting couples who choose to have children no longer feel compelled to marry. In 1995, 34% of babies born in England and Wales were to unmarried women.

Families in which the parents are gay or lesbian are also increasing, although many people still do not accept this concept. Some gay or lesbian couples have entered into 'marriages' and are bringing up the biological children of one of the partners.

DISCUSSION POINT

Will the family survive as a social construct? What do you think families might be like in the UK 50 years from now?

Power

Whoever possesses power has resources to impose their will on others. These resources often stem from social relationships and the individual's position in a group or society. The terms power, authority and influence are sometimes called 'authority terms', implying the ability of one person or group to change the behaviour of a weaker one.

In the care sector, the use of power changes from one agency or group to another with time and the development of society's expectations. An example is the change brought about by the Children Act 1989. (Sections 6.2.3 and 6.2.4 look at the Act in more detail.)

One of the most important aspects of power is how vulnerable people can be given power and protected from the misuse of power. The value base of care work is designed to protect the individual. Section 6.2.4 looks at this in more detail. Links between advocacy and empowerment are explored in units 1, 2 and 6. Section 6.3.4 considers ways in which service users may be enabled to assume greater power over their lives.

types of power	name
When the actions of a weaker individual or group are restricted by the threat of physical force. This can be acceptable if people believe it is administered by appropriate office-holders, such as the police.	coercive power
When one person or group believes that someone else, or another group, has superior knowledge and ability.	expert power
Power that results from an individual's position within a social system or social group. It stems from the moral authority of a particular position in the group.	legitimate power
Power derived from to the prestige of individuals and the status of a person in the social system or social group.	referred power
Power derived from the influence some people have by their ability to control rewards or resources.	reward power

Deviance

> **Deviance** is the non-conforming by an individual or group to the social rules (or norms) accepted by the majority of people in a community or society.

Deviance is usually seen by society as a whole as unacceptable, immoral or criminal. But deviant behaviour does not always harm others.

Society's view of what is deviant behaviour changes. For example, it is now generally acceptable to cohabit, whereas 50 years ago it was considered deviant. Behaviour thought of as normal in one cultural setting may be considered deviant in another. Some sections of society apply formal or informal sanctions to ensure that people follow their norms. Cultural differences and generation gaps can cause some people to label others as deviant. The sociologist Erving Goffman (1922–1982) has shown that everyone is deviant some of the time, because they never conform to all of society's norms.

DISCUSSION POINT

Why are certain behaviours labelled as deviant? Find two or three examples of such 'labelling' and think about the possible reasons for these attitudes.

Health

The word 'health' comes from an Anglo-Saxon term meaning wholeness. The religious idea of being spiritually holy has a similar origin to the medical notion of being physically healthy. Many cultures associate spiritual or emotional health with physical health.

Health is 'a state of complete physical, mental, and social wellbeing . . . not just the absence of disease or infirmity' (World Health Organisation, 1948).

There is general agreement that to be in the ideal state of health, people should:

- live in good social, political and economic conditions
- be able to love, work, create and be physically whole.

This is not always very realistic. For many people, life is about getting by rather than a state of complete wellbeing. For a practical definition of health, it may be better to think about a 'wellness continuum'. This acknowledges that while generally being healthy, people may improve on the continuum towards optimum health, or conversely may deteriorate.

premature death ←————————————————————→ optimum wellness

There are different models (ways of thinking) of health. In the medical and healthcare professions, a biomedical model of health is most common. Practitioners who base their practice on this model tend to :

- reduce the explanation of illness to the simplest possible process
- look for one cause rather than a range of contributing factors
- make a distinction between the mind and the body
- focus on treating the illness rather than promoting health.

The biomedical model, although still dominant in the medical profession, may not be the best single approach to contemporary Western patterns of mortality and morbidity, which reflect the impact of 'lifestyle diseases' such as heart disease and strokes. Increasingly, health professionals are recognising the links between biological, social and psychological factors.

Identification of illness

Defining illness is no easier than defining health. People normally consider several factors before deciding that they are ill:

- how they normally feel
- how they could feel
- what the cause of their present condition is
- how they think other people feel
- how other people respond to them
- how friends, family and culture describe their symptoms, behaviour and feelings.

Mental illness used to be considered deviant behaviour. The term 'mentally ill' has only been used during the last 200 years and even in the first half of this century treatment for those thought to be mentally ill was similar to that for criminals – they were locked up and restrained, away from society. Less than 100 years ago unmarried mothers were detained in psychiatric hospitals as they were considered to be of unbalanced mind and immoral.

Today, many psychological conditions are treated without the use of physical intervention – drugs or surgery. Counselling, psychotherapy, self-help, and support groups are often used instead.

Many cultures do not perceive mental illness in the way that our society does. Schizophrenia is seen by some cultures as bizarre behaviour, but not an illness. Sociologists point out that some people learn to become mentally ill through the very process that is supposed to treat them. Many people who were on long-stay psychiatric wards have now returned to the community and are living active and independent lives. With illness, as with other social constructs, labelling plays an important part in how people behave and how their behaviour is seen by others.

ACTIVITY

Find out how treatment of people with mental health problems has changed since the Mental Health Act (1983). If possible, arrange to speak to a mental health practitioner about it. Write notes on:

- how attitudes to mental health problems are changing
- some of the difficulties that are still being faced.

Potential conflicts between groups

Treating people as individuals means recognising that they may:
- come from a different social background and culture from your own
- have different explanations for the same situation
- have different roles and responsibilities
- have individual expectations and values.

Cultural diversity makes a society rich and interesting. It can also be a source of potential conflict. In some circumstances conflict is part of life, as most families know very well. Health and social care sector practitioners need to be aware of areas of potential conflict and work towards supporting individuals and minimising the risk of conflict.

Common areas for potential conflict are:
- role status
- cultural norms
- how society expects people in certain roles to behave
- authority
- deviant behaviour
- attitudes to pain.

Role status

Each individual takes on many roles. For example, a woman might be a mother, wife, business manager and employee, voluntary worker and a member of an art evening class. Within each role, she will experience a particular identity and have different expectations of how others will behave towards her.

66 *When I am in the surgery and the last patient wants to talk I find it very hard to concentrate if I'm late for picking up the children from school.* 99

GP and mother

66 *People are sometimes surprised when they see me at the mother and toddler group with the twins.* 99

John, father

Status refers to differences in the social honour or prestige individuals are accorded by others. Divisions in status often vary independently of social class, and social honour may be positive or negative. The low status of some groups, such as the 'untouchables' in India, may prevent them taking advantage of opportunities which are open to others.

Cultural norms

Different cultures have similar and different norms to your own. The differences may be very important to an individual, such as not eating what they perceive as sacred or unclean food, the procedure to be followed when somebody dies and the type of burial or cremation that has to be carried out. In a multicultural society there is often conflict between the generations, particularly when the younger generation has become more part of UK culture than their parents.

Cultural norms include:

- dress and appearance
- marriage customs and family life
- patterns of work
- religious beliefs and practices
- leisure pursuits
- rules of public behaviour.

They also include the goods and artefacts which are meaningful to the society, such as books, work places, living spaces, artistic expression – and much more.

DISCUSSION POINT

More women are delaying having their first child until they are over 30 or deciding not to have children – ONS forecasts suggest that over 20% of women now aged between 27 and 32 will never have children, compared to less than ten per cent 30 years ago. What roles are they rejecting? What other roles are they taking on? How might their parents and friends react?

DISCUSSION POINT

Think about the potential for conflict when a young person in a Catholic family wishes to take the contraceptive pill. What happens to the role of authority in such a case?

ACTIVITY

Identify four cultural norms that could cause conflict for an individual in one culture in the UK. Write short case studies:

- explaining the potential conflicts
- describing how they might be dealt with supportively and with the aim of minimising conflict.

Expectations of roles

Society confers roles on individuals. Sometimes there are stereotypical expectations of how people should behave in their roles, as a registered nurse working with people with learning difficulties explains:

66 *When I say I am a nurse people expect me to have a smart uniform and mop people's brows as they lie in bed. In fact my job involves supporting people with learning difficulties in their own homes. I help them to prepare for and cope with everyday life and decisions. People usually look surprised and say that they didn't know that job existed.* 99

Inexperienced staff may find some service users intimidating if they are in awe of the person's position or role outside the care setting. A medical student in the final year of studying gives an example:

66 *One of my first patients was a former teacher of mine: I found examining him very embarrassing, and did not feel I could explain things to him without being condescending. He, on the other hand, had an expectation of my capabilities that I felt sure I could not live up to.* 99

Conflict can occur when individuals fail to fulfil the gender or family roles expected of them. Their own values, wishes or expectations may be different from those expected of them by society or more specifically their family. For example, some families criticise members who choose to live together rather than marry. Sometimes, men who choose jobs that are traditionally done by women are still likely to be subject to criticism.

Authority

There are three main characteristics associated with authority:

- the right to make certain decisions or to act in particular ways within defined limits or restraints
- the ability to confirm or agree that people can take certain actions
- actually giving people instructions or orders.

The right to use authority is often linked with status. Authority might be held by a person or an organisation such as a health authority, social services department, school or religious institution.

Deviant behaviour

As explained on page 218, deviant behaviour is likely to cause conflict. An example is the conflict between meeting the needs of those with mental health

DISCUSSION POINT

A family of travellers arrives in town. Their children go to the local school to attend for the next few weeks, until they move on. What is the potential for conflict in this situation?

problems or learning difficulties within the community, and how people in the community perceive mental illness. The manager of a small residential home describes a situation like this:

❝ *When we moved here our residents wanted to join in the local community. Some went to the local church, but after a few weeks they were asked to leave as they were upsetting a few churchgoers. This made them unhappy. They were not sure what they had done wrong. As it turned out, the residents discovered the local pub where they were made very welcome, and this has become a regular social activity.* ❞

Attitudes to pain

Pain is not all negative. It can:

- act as a warning to prevent further damage – for example, picking up a hot saucepan handle causes you to drop it in order to prevent further burning
- aid learning and help people avoid harmful situations in the future
- limit mobility, so aiding recovery and preventing further damage.

Sometimes people suffer pain which serves no purpose. Pain can become the problem itself rather than a sign of the problem. The control of pain can cause conflicts for doctors. Sometimes the drugs needed to control it may shorten the individual's life, or might cause tolerance of the drug so that increasingly larger doses are required.

People from different cultures may react differently to pain, as a doctor in charge of health screening explains:

❝ *Sometimes, with patients from certain cultures, it can be very difficult to get them to stop worrying and recover fully. Some have a difficult convalescence because they worry about every pain, thinking it is a recurrence. Sometimes this happens due to lack of family support.* ❞

DISCUSSION POINT

There is a lot of debate about whether it is right to help a person to die when they are suffering from a painful terminal illness. What are the potential conflicts of euthanasia for practitioners, the individual and their family and friends?

Pain is recognised to be more severe when a person is frightened, or does not understand what is going on. Doctors have only recently acknowledged that premature babies suffer pain and that care must be taken when carrying out clinical procedures on them.

ACTIVITY

Make arrangements to talk to a midwife about pain control in childbirth. Find out the alternative methods and why women giving birth might choose one rather than another. Compare those popular with mothers with the preferred methods of the medical staff and midwife. Why might they be different?

Different values

The value base of care work tries to ensure that the beliefs, culture and needs of all clients are taken into consideration and respected (see unit 6). These values may be personal or stem from professional judgement and knowledge.

Differences in beliefs

Health practitioners have personal beliefs and values which are important to them as individuals. When they work with people these values may come into conflict. For example, a practitioner may believe that terminating a pregnancy is wrong but they still have a duty to care for the patient undergoing such a procedure without expressing their views to the patient. In situations like this, practitioners may opt out of the actual procedure on grounds of conscience, but they must care for the patient before and after the procedure has been carried out.

Some groups in society, such as Jehovah's Witnesses, do not believe in blood transfusions. This might lead to conflicting values of healthcare practitioners and parents of a child requiring a blood transfusion.

> ## DISCUSSION POINT
>
> Think about whether healthcare workers should lead lifestyles which they think are setting good examples to others. What are the dangers in such an approach?

Differences in cultural background

Some of the values that healthcare practitioners put forward to support a healthy lifestyle are based on a western culture or lifestyle. One of the priorities identified in *The Health of the Nation* is to support the health needs of the African and Asian groups who have been found to have higher rates of coronary heart disease and strokes. While it is possible to suggest a change to increase exercise and change the diet, the form of exercise needs to be acceptable to the culture. For example, some Asian women do not like to exercise where they could be seen by men.

> ## DISCUSSION POINT
>
> Can care practitioners give messages that are equally acceptable to all cultures? What are the implications for health promotion if they can't (see unit 7 for more on this)?

The use of drugs such as cannabis is seen as a normal part of some cultures. (In some medical conditions it is also considered to have a beneficial effect.) There are difficulties here for the personal values of the service user and healthcare practitioner, and there are also legal factors to consider.

To cut down on the likelihood of conflict it is often appropriate for a practitioner from a similar cultural background to work with service users.

Differences in context

Values held by health and social care practitioners in their professional lives may not be the same as values held by them, or other people, in private.

Health and safety advice, or how to deal with personal relationships, may differ from one context to another.

Practitioners may have to visit people in their own homes, for example to advise on hygiene or how to keep a child safe. They do not have the right to enforce their own values, but they should advise about good health. Service users have the right to choose not to follow the advice.

Differences in perspective

In care, the duty to find out about and understand the user's perspective rests with the practitioner. It is important for practitioners to discover why a person believes or acts in a certain way. Then the practitioner has to make a judgement whether or not it may be possible to work together to see if the values can be changed or adapted. Where this is not possible, practitioners must continue to support the individual in their choice.

Mrs Jones has requested help in her home. The care manager has agreed that this is needed and Mrs Thompson is assigned to carry out the work. After three days Mrs Jones telephones the care manager to say that she wants Mrs Thompson removed and someone else instead. At first the care manager was concerned that the help arranged was not up to standard, but discovered that this was not the case. In fact Mrs Jones says that the reason is that she does not want a black person in her home.

ACTIVITY

Read the case study again. What are the conflicts here, and how should the care manager deal with the situation? In groups of three, roleplay how this situation could be resolved.

Key questions

1 Who are the main influences in primary socialisation?
2 How does secondary socialisation affect primary socialisation?
3 In what ways do work and religious institutions contribute to socialisation?
4 How can the political and cultural effects of the mass media be described?
5 What are social constructs?
6 Why do social constructs change over a period of time?
7 What are the links between power and deviance?
8 What are the links between health and illness?
9 How are cultural norms constructed?
10 What potential conflicts are there between an individual's needs and the culture they live in?
11 Why do these conflicts arise?
12 Who is responsible for recognising potential differences in values between service users and carers?
13 How can health and social care practitioners minimise the impact of their own values on service users?

Assignment

You may be able to combine this assignment with the research assignments in elements 8.2 and 8.3.

Identify someone you can talk to who comes from a different cultural background from your own. For example, they may be of different ethnic origin or religion, or their family structure might be different.

Design a set of questions that will allow you to compare the socialisation that you have both undergone. Obtain answers from the person you chose and also write down your own responses to each question.

Analyse the results and discuss them with the subject of your research. Identify:
■ differences in values and beliefs between you
■ how these values and beliefs developed, through primary and secondary socialisation
■ how the different norms of your two cultures affect the way you behave
■ any potential conflicts that might arise from the norms and values.

Produce a report explaining what you have discovered, and how it has developed your attitude to one another. Conclude the report by:
■ explaining how two of the social constructs you identified have changed over time
■ saying how your investigation and the results might be useful more generally for good practice in health and social care work.

You may write the report or record it on audio cassette.

> 66 Parents can put a lot of pressure on young people to perform well. Parents are often trying to persuade their children to gain what they see as a better life, but the students may not know why they are doing it. 'Who am I doing this for?' is a question we often hear. Even going down one grade can be hugely stressful – there is a pressure to maintain their position within the group. Also, if they're studying all the time it can create direct conflict with their need to be with their peer group, which when you're young is especially important. There are conflicting loyalties – they worry about who they should align themselves with. 99
>
> *senior worker (counselling), young people's counselling and information centre*

> 66 It's surprising how common it is for children to think they are to blame for their parent's illness. They need to be convinced that it certainly isn't their fault. I work at the pace of the child to help them prepare for the death. For example, they can prepare a memory box about the parent. It's often long-term work, which requires a lot of resourcing. But pre-bereavement work makes it easier for the whole family to cope and post-bereavement trauma is often less. 99
>
> *head of medical counselling and family support*

> 66 There should be greater access to public buildings for disabled people, and not only for the physically disabled, but for people whose sight or hearing is impaired and so on. It is often difficult or impossible for people with disabilities to get around. 99
>
> *occupational therapy services manager*

> 66 Society as a whole should accept that the people who can afford to pay should support people in real need. To have an effective, well-run NHS system takes money, and revenue from taxes should be diverted this way. 99
>
> *coordinator, community for homeless people*

ELEMENT 4.3

The effect of socioeconomic factors

This element examines the effects of socioeconomic factors on health and social wellbeing. It looks at demographic characteristics such as the incidence of disease and disability, trends in marriage and divorce, suicide and crime rates and life expectancy. It shows how these characteristics are related to socioeconomic factors such as housing, people's jobs, social class and the environment. It also shows how socioeconomic factors influence lifestyle choices, which have an impact on people's health and wellbeing. Finally it explains how current social policies are changing the way health and social services are provided.

Demographic characteristics

The *Health Survey for England* monitors trends in health. It includes information on:

- the proportions of people with specific conditions
- the prevalence of risk factors associated with these conditions
- how likely different groups are to have these conditions
- progress towards *The Health of the Nation* targets.

Social Trends is an annual report which presents and analyses figures on:

- employment
- leisure
- transport
- housing
- health
- crime . . .

. . . and many other issues. It is supplemented by a new *Social Focus* series which focuses on particular groups of society, such as children, women and ethnic groups. This series also provides information on lifestyles and health. A CD-ROM called *25 Years of Social Trends* presents statistics and trends from 1970 to 1995.

DISCUSSION POINT

What data might be useful if you were comparing the health needs of your peer group with that of a similar group ten years ago, and the likely needs of another group ten years in the future?

Demography is the statistical study of populations in terms of their size, structure and compositions, and changes in these things over time.

Demographic data is in the form of quantitative data which can be presented in a numerical or statistical format. The data may describe characteristics such as:

- age
- sex
- income
- employment
- housing tenure.

The Government and other agencies such as health authorities and social services departments use statistical information for their annual plans and long-term strategies. They tend to use quantitative data as a basis for planning services and setting targets as it is considered more objective than qualitative data. (Unit 8 describes the differences between quantitative and qualitative data.) Quantitative data can be used to measure and evaluate the effectiveness of the strategies over time.

66 *If we look at the changing demographic picture, we can see that we will need more care in the community as there will be more people over the age of 75 in the next decade than is the present case. We make educated estimates of the cost to the area. We also have to look at ways of cutting costs in other areas. Without demographic information, we could not plan.* 99

director of social services

The Office for National Statistics (ONS) publishes many sets of government statistics on health and social issues. Two of them are described in the box on the left and others are described in the appropriate place in this section. The ONS has a catalogue and a site on the World Wide Web: http//www.emap.co.uk/ons/

ACTIVITY

The major concepts in population analysis are:

- birth rate
- death rate
- infant mortality rate
- neonatal mortality rate
- standardised mortality rate
- morbidity
- fecundity
- fertility.

Find out what each of these terms means and write short definitions of them.

DATA ON HEART DISEASE

Deaths from ischaemic heart disease, also known as coronary heart disease, have dramatically increased during this century. Ischaemia means bloodlessness of a part of the body, due to contraction, spasm, constriction or blockage of the blood vessel. It is the main cause of death in the UK. Coronary heart disease affects all sections of the community but the highest mortality is in the men and women of lower socioeconomic groups and in men and women of Asian origin.

There is also a marked difference between the death rate and incidence of ischaemic heart disease in men and women of middle age. The rate in men is five times greater than that of women. From the menopause onwards, the death rates in women rise progressively, until at the age of 70 the rates in the sexes are roughly equal.

Data commonly used in health and social care provide information about the incidence of:

- disease
- disability and dysfunction
- suicide
- crime
- divorce
- life expectancy.

Disease

Diseases can only be effectively prevented or controlled if the various factors which relate to them (listed in the box below) are fully known and understood. The study of these factors is called epidemiology.

Epidemiological factors

- variations of the incidence of disease over a period of time and geographical area
- present-day incidence of the disease
- associated social factors
- mortality rates
- estimated chances of an individual developing the disease
- methods of prevention.

ACTIVITY

Look at a copy of the World Health Annual Statistics (published by WHO) and prepare a chart comparing deaths from ischaemic heart disease in one country from each continent. Summarise your findings and write a short report suggesting why the differences might exist.

The second most common cause of death in the UK is cancer. This term describes a group of conditions which feature malignant tumours, groups of cells capable of growing without the normal control of their site or tissue type. Cancer is also capable of being carried to other areas of the body through the lymphatic system or bloodstream. The different forms of cancers have differing prognoses or outcomes – some are treated more successfully than others. Just over 60% of all cancers are attributed to two main causes:

- smoking
- unhealthy diet.

❝ *If there were one thing I would recommend for the improved health of everyone it would be to make cigarettes a legally controlled drug. It kills more people than any other action. It affects everything – the whole arterial system:*

UNIT

4

ELEMENT **4.3**

ACTIVITY

Using the WHO statistics again, compare the incidence of lung, stomach and skin cancers across countries from the five continents of the world. Present your findings in a bar chart. Write a brief report on the factors that might cause the differences in the incidence of one type of cancer between the continents.

heart, lungs, legs. It is implicated in every cancer. There is a gene in our bodies which defends us against cancer, the nicotine in cigarettes 'turns off' this gene. It's as simple as that. **99**

doctor in charge of health screening, private hospital

Relevant ONS publications include *Morbidity Statistics from General Practice* – patterns of diseases seen by GPs, with analysis by age, sex and socio-demographic characteristics, and indications of the care provided.

Disability and dysfunction

The term **disability** covers a wide range of problems, including:

- physical disability
- learning difficulty
- sensory impairment.

Social service departments are responsible for registering disabled people. The number of people on the register has steadily increased over many years. This may be because more disabled people are registering, so that they can receive the benefits they are entitled to, rather than an increase in the incidence of disability.

ACTIVITY

People registered as substantially and permanently disabled by type and degree of disability, England, 1987 and 1990 (thousands)

	1987		1990	
	All ages	65 years and over (%)	All ages	65 years and over (%)
Very severely disabled	76.1	42.9 (56.4)	75.9	42.5 (56.0)
Severely disabled	516.1	338.5 (65.6)	544.5	364.0 (66.8)
Other registered	638.5	425.2 (66.6)	645.0	438.8 (68.0)
Blind people	133.9	104.5 (78.1)	–	–
Partially sighted people	79.0	60.1 (76.1)	–	–
Deaf people	37.9	12.3 (32.6)	37.9	12.3 (32.6)
Hard of hearing people	70.9	55.6 (79.1)	70.9	55.6 (79.1)

The table above shows that the incidence of disability and handicap rises significantly as the age group rises, and that at least 65% of all disability occurs in those aged 65 years and over. Find out how many people aged 65 years and over are forecasted to be living in your area in 15 years' time. Using the figures in the table, suggest how many of them might be registered as disabled. Present your findings in graph form.

230

Types of disability

- locomotion
- behaviour
- disfigurement
- dexterity
- hearing
- seeing
- continence
- personal care
- communication
- reaching and stretching
- eating, drinking and digestion
- consciousness
- intellectual function

UNIT

4

ELEMENT **4.3**

Disability registration figures are based on diagnosis rather than assessment of function, so they do not give a full indication of the problems which a disabled person needs to overcome to be able to live as normal a life as possible. A survey carried out between 1985 and 1988 identified 13 main types of disability, listed in the margin. Most adults with disabilities were found to have more than one type of disability. The three most common are:

- locomotion
- hearing
- personal care.

Relevant ONS publications include:

- *OPCS Surveys of Psychiatric Morbidity* – eight reports focusing on different types of mental disorders and their effects on people's lives
- *Causes of Blindness and Partial Sight in England and Wales 1990–91* – figures broken down by age, sex and cause.

DISCUSSION POINT

Suicide rate figures may not be accurate. What social pressures might increase the likelihood of inaccurate figures?

Suicide

Suicide is defined as the act of killing oneself intentionally. The term 'paracide' is sometimes used to label attempted suicide.

Suicide statistics are based on the recording of the cause of death as suicide by the coroner. The Government uses the suicide figure as a measure of mental health. In 1992 there were almost 5,000 suicides by those aged between 16 and 74 years of age. There is a trend showing an increase in the number of males committing suicide, from two-thirds of the total in 1982 to three-quarters of the total in 1992. Targets set in *The Health of the Nation* include a reduction in suicide rates.

ACTIVITY

Research the suicide rates of teenagers. Discover whether males or females have the higher rates of suicide and depression. Can you think of any possible explanations for the difference? Present your findings in a table and write a short report on your interpretation of the figures.

Relevant ONS publications include *Mortality Statistics* – which gives annual reports for deaths by cause.

Crime

There is much debate about the level of crime in society today, compared with the past. Official crime statistics only include crimes recorded by the police and the majority of petty crimes are never reported. Some surveys estimate that at least half of all serious crimes, including rape, robbery and aggravated assault are not reported to the police.

There is an opposite phenomenon known as 'crime inflation'. Newspapers notice that a particular crime is on the increase and publicise the need for increased police action. The Government responds with special action or a higher allocation of police resources. As a result, more crimes are recorded and the process is repeated.

Relevant ONS publications include *Social Trends*, which contains figures on crime.

Divorce

Divorce is becoming increasingly common in our society. In 1994, there was more than one divorce for every two weddings. The divorce rate was 13.4 per 1,000 marriages compared to 5.9 per 1,000 in 1974. This means that in 1994, 13.4 out of every 1000 marriages were ended by divorce proceedings, over twice as many as 20 years before. Changes in legislation have made it easier to dissolve unhappy marriages: 'no-fault' divorce laws were first introduced in 1971 and revised in 1996.

Divorce statistics present only part of the picture: legal separations and couples living apart are not included in the figures. However, lone-parent families often face particular problems of health and social wellbeing. Accurate information is required so that the needs of these groups can be identified and plans made to support them.

Relevant ONS publications include *Marriage and Divorce Statistics*, which has figures for the regions in England and Wales and details of the grounds for divorce.

Life expectancy

Estimations of life expectancy are made by life insurance companies to gauge the financial risk. The infant mortality rate is one of the most useful measures of living conditions. This is because the main factors influencing any infant's life are most likely to be connected with the home environment. Until 1979 the expectation of life was lower at birth than at one year, reflecting the high infant mortality rate of previous years. Since then the trend has reversed. The factors making this possible are both social and medical.

Although recent measures of life expectancy show a slow but constant increase, this is only part of the social picture. For example, the figures do not show how the increase in life expectancy is also bringing with it an increase in disability. It is essential to synthesise all the relevant demographic information to gain a useful picture. There is more about this in element 5.2.

Socioeconomic factors and demographic characteristics

Demographic characteristics (explored in section 4.3.1) give part of the picture, but not the whole picture. They should be viewed together with socioeconomic factors such as:

- housing
- employment status
- relative wealth
- environment
- social class
- age profile.

Housing

Improved, affordable housing was one of the main aims of Beveridge's welfare state. Many studies have indicated the close link between poor housing conditions and premature death or chronic illness.

> Many of the people I see live in poor, damp surroundings. It is hard for them to improve things without help from outside agencies. I am sure that many of their children's health problems are caused by the damp conditions.
>
> *health visitor*

In 1992, the official figure showed that approximately 480,000 people were homeless. Living in accommodation that is unfit for human habitation, overcrowded or even dangerous does not automatically give people the right to be classified as homeless. If the figure had included the numbers of young people living away from home, the housing charity Shelter estimated that the real figure was about 3,000,000.

Being homeless also affects a person's health. A person is classified as homeless if they are without a home and have no legal right to housing, or if threats of violence prevent them from exercising this right. If the homelessness is intentional, the local authority has no legal duty to rehouse the person.

> Basically, being homeless creates problems of being unable to function as part of the system anything like people with homes are able to do. It affects your health, mental and physical. The situation has created a whole sub-society that exists below the poverty line. There's also the issue of what the term 'homeless' really means. There are families in B & B accommodation who are afraid to stay in it because of the severe overcrowding and, sometimes, danger – you see them on the streets. I would call this homeless, but they don't qualify.
>
> *coordinator, community for homeless people*

Employment status

At any one time only a minority of the adult population are in paid employment. The young, the elderly, a high proportion of women, those living off unearned income and unemployed people are all outside the adult work force. But many of these people work just as hard as those in paid employment.

> I had to give up my job. Now I have both my parents living with us. My mother has arthritis and can't get around much. My father used to look after her, but now he has Alzheimer's disease.
>
> *42-year-old woman*

DISCUSSION POINT

Poor health may sometimes result in unemployment. Do you think that sometimes unemployment can lead to ill health?

In our society, as in most, having a job is important for wellbeing. It provides:

- money – without the income from work, anxieties about coping with day-to-day life tend to multiply and problems of housing, nutrition and other health-related factors multiply

233

ACTIVITY

Various demographic characteristics can be linked to employment rates.

Look at recent statistics for one of these:

- disability
- chronic ill health
- suicide
- a specific disease, e.g. stomach ulcers

Can you link them to employment or unemployment rates? Analyse your findings in a report.

DISCUSSION POINT

Education raises people's expectations of life and their standard of living. Does it also improve their health?

The term **wealth** covers economic resources including property, vehicles, investments and pension rights.

- activity level – employment often provides the opportunity to gain and exercise skills and capacities; it also offers a structured environment in which people's energies may be absorbed
- variety – a job provides access to contexts that contrast with domestic surroundings even when the tasks involved are relatively dull
- structure – for people in regular employment the day is usually organised around work; those who are out of work may get bored or apathetic
- social contacts – friendships and opportunities to participate in shared activities with others
- personal identity – employment is usually valued for the sense of stable social identity it offers, and self-esteem is often bound up with the economic contribution people make to the household.

Education

In countries where the level of literacy is low, there may be a direct link between education and health or wellbeing. Raising the level of literacy is essential in helping people to control many aspects of their lives, including:

- contraception and birth control
- basic health precautions
- access to public health and social services
- access to job opportunities.

In a country like the UK where the level of education is fairly high, the link between education and health may not be so direct. But it is still there, mixed in with other socioeconomic factors. People with better education tend to have better jobs, live in better housing and have healthier lifestyles than those with a poor education.

From one point of view, education can be seen as a great equaliser – through education, everyone will have an equal chance in life. Another view is that the quality of people's educational opportunities is largely determined by their social status. Children from middle-class backgrounds go to better schools, do better in exams and have a higher chance of going on to further and higher education than children from working-class backgrounds. In this way, the education system reinforces the social and class structure of the country.

Education doesn't stop at the age of 16, 18, or 21. It can also be seen as a lifelong opportunity for personal development. For example, women who did not achieve their educational aims in their youth go back to it when their children are old enough. The number of women returners entering college courses at all levels is increasing.

Relative wealth

Wealth is shared very unevenly in this country. A Mintel report on UK lifestyles (1994) suggests that the wealth gap between the rich and poor will go on widening for the next five years.

ACTIVITY

Two of the most influential reports into health and socioeconomic factors are *The Black Report* (1980) by Townsend and Davidson, and *The Health Divide* (1987), by Margaret Whitehead. Look at these reports in a reference library. Identify the major links between wealth, poverty and health and social wellbeing.

The work environment is controlled through legislation and regulations, including:

- The Health and Safety at Work Act

- Control of Substances Hazardous to Health (COSHH)

- Health and safety (first aid)

- The Reporting of Injuries, Diseases and Dangerous Occurrences Regulations (RIDDOR)

- Manual Operations Handling Regulations.

ACTIVITY

There is increasing evidence that vehicle emissions are raising the levels of pollution in our towns and cities. Identify the main pollutants and list ways of managing the situation to reduce pollution. Explain how your ideas might help the health and social wellbeing of an affected community.

Both wealth and its opposite, poverty, are relative terms, defined by reference to the living standards of the majority in any given society. Subsistence poverty is when there is a lack of the basic resources needed to maintain health and effective bodily functioning.

Environment

Environmental factors which can affect lifestyle and health include:

- geographical location
- pollution levels
- air quality
- proximity to specific hazardous areas.

There is a link between people's level of income and the impact of the environment on health. For example, car accidents account for almost half of all child injury deaths. Cheap cars without modern safety features increase the chances of traffic death, so inequalities of income are directly related to the likelihood of being killed or injured in car accidents. Between 1981 and 1991, child deaths from traffic accidents dropped by over 30% in social classes I and II and by one per cent in social class V. During this period, the proportion of children with unemployed parents rose from six to seventeen per cent.

At home, people can to some extent control the environment. For example, they can decide whether they want the windows open or shut, but may not be able to have the heating on as much as they would like, because of cost. Services to the home or substances such as food brought into the home are often subjected to quality control, through legislation concerning the quality and safety of food and electrical appliances.

In the community, records are kept of notifiable diseases so that:

- there is a current picture of the number and types of infection in the community
- preventative measures can be quickly implemented
- doctors can be informed of the situation and have up-to-date information
- adequate provision of hospital and community services is maintained
- appropriate research can be carried out.

Relevant ONS publications include:

- *Occupational Health* – gives a picture of changing patterns of health in different occupations and provides figures for sickness absence from work

- *Communicable Diseases* – information on infectious diseases is analysed by age, sex and health authority regions.

DISCUSSION POINT

The Registrar General in the UK divides people into five occupational classes, shown below. To what extent do you think occupational class is the same as social class? Is there likely to be much mobility between occupational classes:

■ in one person's life?

■ from one generation to another?

Occupational class

Class I	professionals
Class II	intermediate occupations, e.g. teachers, nurses and managers
Class III	skilled workers
Class IV	semi-skilled workers
Class V	unskilled workers

Social class

Class refers to the distinctions between individuals and different groups in society, such as occupational classes or social classes.

In the UK, which class people belong to stems from economic factors affecting the material circumstances of their lives and the circumstances of their birth. Although there is some social mobility – movement of people from one class to another – family and cultural background still create powerful social and cultural barriers to mobility.

The two important reports mentioned on page 235 both identified differences in the health of the various social classes. Recent research has found that poor housing increases the chance of death and injury by fire. From 1981 to 1991, deaths from fires dropped by 28% in social class I but increased by 39% in social class V.

DISCUSSION POINT

Why do you think there are still differences in the health of the different social classes in the UK, in spite of the welfare state?

Age profile

An accurately forecasted age profile of a population is important for planning. In the case of health and social care services, which are particularly expensive, this profile is essential. Health authorities are responsible for planning to meet the health needs of the population and local authorities are responsible for planning to meet social care needs.

The age profile may make the balance of needs different. For example, in the UK, people are surviving to a greater age. This has implications for:

■ the type of services required – residential care places, geriatric wards

■ the amount of services.

ACTIVITY

Using ONS publications such as *Population Trends* and *Population Density, Change and Concentration in Great Britain*, research the vital statistics of the country's demographic picture. Identify how the country is beginning to change its social services and benefit system to deal with the developing scenario. Write a brief paper explaining the figures you looked at and over what period. Summarise the changes and your opinion of them.

Socioeconomic factors and lifestyle choices

Lifestyle is a pattern of behaviours that are linked to the type of job an individual has, the culture they feel part of and the people they live with.

Lifestyles are often referred to as 'risk factors' by health and social care practitioners. When people's social circumstances change their lifestyles may also change. Some lifestyle choices are particularly significant because they have positive or negative influences on the health and social wellbeing of an individual. They are:

- exercise
- diet
- balance between work and leisure
- sleep and rest
- use of substances.

ACTIVITY

Mildred Blaxter's 1990 study *Health and Lifestyles* discusses the issues between health and lifestyle factors such as class, diet and exercise. Investigate her main findings and present them in a short summary.

Exercise

Health education messages encourage people to take more exercise. Although more people are taking some form of exercise, there are many who do not. Combined with other lifestyle choices such as diet, the result is a deterioration in health, even in people under the age of 30.

ACTIVITY

The physical effects of exercise and the ability of exercise to reduce stress levels are well documented. So why do so many people take inadequate amounts of exercise?

Use the chart to list reasons why people do not take exercise. Then list some ideas that might be used to encourage people to take more exercise. An example has been done for you.

	physical	social	intellectual	cultural	emotional	financial
Why people don't take exercise		all my mates play football, but I'm better at basketball		I don't like to exercise when there are men around		
What might be done to encourage them				put on an exercise class just for women		

Diet

Choice of diet is often determined by social factors such as:

- income
- ability to get to suitable shops
- knowledge about a balanced diet
- knowledge about and facilities for preparing food
- desire to eat an appropriate diet
- time for and the costs of preparing food
- cultural beliefs
- regional habits.

All these affect whether or not someone eats a balanced diet.

One factor that affects some people's eating habits is the image of a perfect body. This image can vary from culture to culture, as well as by fashion. Images like this have little to do with health: being too thin is unhealthy, as well as being too fat. There are often psychological as well as social reasons for over- and under-eating.

Balance between work and leisure

The balance of hours spent in paid employment and leisure is gradually changing. There are more people without jobs and many of those in jobs are working longer hours. This is as true in the care sector as in other types of job, as a social worker in a children and families team explains:

66 Although my contract says 35 hours each week, it is expected that I will write up my notes and records as well. Indeed when I don't I am likely to get into trouble. We estimate that we work around 55 hours each week regularly. The problem is that if I am doing all this I find it difficult to be available to my children. Last week I forgot a parents' evening at the school. I find it very stressful and tend to take it out on the family. It's rather ironic when you think my job is to support other children and families. 99

DISCUSSION POINT

If people are technically unemployed, is all their time leisure time? Do you think it is the same for men and women?

66 I have seen the effects at both ends of the spectrum. Some years ago I worked with ten men who worked on a waste disposal site: they were working up to a hundred hours a week to earn enough to live on. Nine of them had major undiagnosed health problems. At the other end of the spectrum are the business people who, either because of the culture, or because they are setting up their own business, are so busy working that they do not know what relaxation is. They drink to relax – they 'pickle' themselves. Some people I see work seven days a week and go for years without a proper holiday. Even when they go away for half a day they take their phone and fax with them. Both of these sorts of situations lead to extreme stress. 99

doctor in charge of health screening, private hospital

Sleep and rest

Enough sleep and rest are essential to health. Researchers have demonstrated a link between sleep deprivation and an increase in the number of errors people make. They also show that people deprived of sleep take longer to carry out tasks. Many people often complain that they 'didn't get any sleep last night'. Sometimes this is true, but usually they have woken several times and slept for the rest of the time.

Employment legislation in the UK states the minimum number and length of breaks from continuous work, and says that facilities must be made available for pregnant workers to rest.

Use of substances

Some substances are taken for beneficial reasons, for example pain control, or for religious reasons. Substances which may be used appropriately or abused include:

- alcohol
- tobacco
- solvents
- drugs.

Abuse causes damage not only to individuals but also to their families and communities. Unit 7 suggests ways of informing people about the dangers of substance abuse.

DISCUSSION POINT

Some employers do not recognise the benefits of adequate breaks. What arguments would you use to convince them that in the long term they would get an increase in productivity by ensuring adequate rest periods?

DISCUSSION POINT

Why do you think people abuse substances? Why do you think they choose particular substances?

Some medical practitioners and health and social care professionals tackle substance abuse in the same way as they would a disease. Others think that habitual abuse of substances is triggered by social cues. Many community-based project workers who support substance abusers base their approach on this view. They suggest that addictive behaviour has six characteristics, shown on the left.

Addictive characteristics

- the behaviours associated with an addiction become important to the individual
- they want to repeat the experience of euphoria
- they need increasing amounts of the substance to achieve the same effect
- they suffer unpleasant psychological and physical effects when the addictive behaviour is discontinued
- there is often conflict with the people around them, and also with themselves
- there is always a danger of relapse, even a considerable time after giving up.

ACTIVITY

Research the cases of two people addicted to different substances. Describe their backgrounds, how their addiction developed and the way it altered their life.

Include a description of the substance. If appropriate, explain positive, and negative uses. Draw conclusions about what started the abuse and what might have prevented it from starting,

Impact of social policies

Social policy refers to the whole range of ways in which government affects the lives of individuals. It includes, but is not restricted to, welfare policies.

Over the last 50 years there have been radical changes in the organisation, structure and delivery of health and social care. The way services have been developed has reflected the social policies of government.

❝ *My doctor is a fundholder so she was able to allow me to go the neighbouring hospital for my hip replacement. They had a much shorter waiting list. Our local hospital said I would have to wait nine months.* ❞

retired postal worker

❝ *My mother wanted to go into the same home as Dad and the only way we could afford this was to sell her flat. The money won't last long and she had wanted to leave it to us so we could support the children through college. This is not what we expected, I always thought that the state would pay for care. We are still trying to decide what to do, and Mum doesn't understand why all her savings are being used up this way.* ❞

daughter of person in need of residential care

Currently, health and social care provision in the UK is based largely on a mixed economy (see unit 5). Delivery to most NHS users is essentially collectivist and paid for through National Insurance. Most agencies are either a purchaser of services or a provider of services, or a joint purchaser-provider.

Individual decisions

Over the last 20 years, a lot of social policy has been directed towards encouraging a greater degree of individual decision-making. This has taken two main forms:

- reduced dependence on the state, e.g. personal pension schemes, nursery vouchers
- more involvement in decision-making, and increased empowerment, e.g. through the Patient's Charter.

The amount of help that can be given to an individual is limited by the physical and financial resources available. Unit 5 looks at resourcing in more detail. The NHS and Community Care Act (1989) encourages the care of people within the community.

Several criticisms have been made of 'care in the community', all which have a bearing on individual decision-making:

- Inadequate funding – care in the home is at least as expensive as residential care, and the resources, facilities and infrastructure to cope with the new system are inadequate.
- Changes in family structure and attitude – the number of family carers may not increase at the same rate as the number of dependants. Many carers in their 70s are caring for a relative in their 90s. Increasing divorce rates mean that there may be fewer relatives available to look after older people who can't look after themselves.
- Abandonment – stressed relatives, unable to cope with a relative, may want to leave them at a day centre or hospital.

DISCUSSION POINT

When people with mental health problems are living in a hostel within the community what factors may limit their choices of activity and lifestyle?

ACTIVITY

Arrange to talk to a care manager. Find out how they support service users in individual decision-making. Are there any limits to the support that they can give?

- NHS bed-blocking – hospitals are sometimes unable to discharge patients because of delays in assessing their need and the difficulties of transferring them to a venue where a financial contribution is required from either the patient or their family.
- Viability of low-priority services – units unpopular in the community such as hostels for homeless or mentally ill people may become a low priority for the social services and so close down.

Community responsibility

Part of the philosophy of 'care in the community' is that responsibility for the care of members of the community should be based within that community. There are formal ways of encouraging this, such as:

- Community Health Councils
- representation on social services committees
- voluntary organisations.

Social and community workers work with groups of people to set up self-help or community projects. These may concern young or unemployed people.

Voluntary agencies are playing an increasingly important role in the care being undertaken by the community (see unit 5).

Competition and the open market

Most areas operate within a mixed economy of care. This means that the major agencies work together to satisfy needs. Major agencies include the health authorities, social services departments and family health authorities. These three agencies work together to produce a plan for the district they cover. The voluntary agencies and the private sector are considered at all stages of planning.

The Government encourages the private sector to play a greater role in the provision of care. Private businesses take note of the yearly plan to ensure that they are offering the right sort of service at a competitive price.

Care managers have budgets for their service-user groups. While they are not allowed to advertise a service they consider carefully the value for money it represents. They might make up a package of care for an individual from a variety of agencies.

66 *When it was first announced that all social service residential units should be inspected alongside private-sector homes there was panic. We knew that some of our facilities were not up to scratch. This change of policy can only be good for the residents.* 99

care worker in a social services residential home for the elderly

In the past, there has been criticism of the standards of care by some units, in the private sector and those run by social services departments. Recent trends have shown that with increased choice people are demanding better standards.

ACTIVITY

Arrange to talk to someone involved in a community project. Find out how and why they are involved in the project, what they are trying to achieve and why the project seemed an effective way of tackling the issues. With their permission, write up the interview and add an analysis on how the project fits in with the needs of the community and current social policy.

DISCUSSION POINT

Would care in the community collapse now or in the future if voluntary care was not available?

DISCUSSION POINT

Do you think competition between similar agencies benefits service users? Discuss a range of facilities and different users. Is your conclusion similar in every case?

Key questions

1 Which demographic characteristics are most significant for people working in health and social care?
2 What does the standard mortality rate show?
3 What is the difference between mortality and morbidity?
4 What do current demographic figures show about the number of people over the age of 65 in our society?
5 What implications do the figures have for the provision of care?
6 What are the implications of figures on suicide, crime and divorce for health and social care?
7 What are the different social classes?
8 What effect does being in one class or another have on health and wellbeing?
9 What other socioeconomic factors are associated with class?
10 What effect do lifestyle choices have on health and wellbeing?
11 How have recent social policies changed the map of care provision in the UK?
12 How do the policies specifically about health and social care relate to the wider social policies promoted in the last 20 years?

Assignment

What are the issues for health and social care planners when planning to meet the needs of the community over the next ten years? Carry out an analysis of the needs of a population, which could be:

- the whole of the country
- a region of the country
- a health authority area.

Make sure you have access to up-to-date figures on the demographic characteristics for the population you choose. Select three demographic characteristics to highlight in your report. Analyse the needs of the population in relation to these three characteristics. In your analysis:

- explain how socioeconomic factors affect health and wellbeing
- identify one social policy approach which affects the three characteristics you are looking at
- make two or three recommendations for practical actions which could improve the health and wellbeing of the population, and explain why they are relevant.

Present your responses as a strategic plan. If possible draw diagrams to illustrate your ideas.

UNIT **5**

Element 5.1
Providing health and social care

Element 5.2
Change in health and social care provision

Element 5.3
Care planning and provision

Health and social care services

This unit is about development of the health and social care sector, its structure, organisation and funding, and the services offered. The legal and economic policies guiding the service and the needs of the population are also explained. It complements unit 6 and links to units 3 and 4 on different aspects of health and social wellbeing, and to unit 2 on interpersonal interactions. It may also suggest ideas for one of your research topics for unit 8.

ELEMENT **5.1**

Providing health and social care

This element aims to give you a clear view of the health and social care services which are provided at a local level. It looks at which organisations are the providers, the legal basis for them, the ways in which they are classified, how they are paid for, and the different ways in which people can have access to them.

66 *You have the right to:*

- *receive health care on the basis of your clinical need, not on your ability to pay, your lifestyle or any other factor;*
- *be registered with a GP and be able to change your GP easily and quickly if you want to;*
- *get emergency medical treatment at any time through your GP, the emergency ambulance service and hospital accident and emergency departments;*
- *be referred to a consultant acceptable to you, when your GP thinks it is necessary, and to be referred for a second opinion if you and your GP agree this is desirable.* 99

The Patient's Charter and You, *NHS 1996*

66 *Local authorities are now the minority providers of adult residential care, and the independent sector is making a growing contribution in domiciliary as well as residential care.* 99

Progress through Change, *Summary of the Annual Report of the Chief Inspector of the Social Services Inspectorate 1996*

66 *We are funded by the city council's community development department and by community education at the county council, and through the health authority. We have an on-going grant from social services. We also got funding to cover three years of a group counsellor's post from Children in Need.* 99

senior worker (counselling), young people's counselling and information service

66 *We are part of a health authority and so are funded through the NHS, which is resourced by central government. All health authorities have to work under stringent budgets. Management costs are kept small. But as a health promotion unit we are accounted for differently: the health promotion services are not part of the management costs and as such do not affect the national league tables. Budgets for the heath promotion unit are set locally by the health authority Board.* 99

assistant director (health promotion), local health authority

Services and facilities

Statutory entitlement means a legal right to a service.

This section is about the health and social care services in your area in terms of statutory entitlement. That is, whether it is available by right or at the discretion of the organisation concerned.

For users and potential users of services some services are available in every geographical area. Who the provider is – NHS or local authority, voluntary or private – may differ locally. However, it is usual for the NHS or local authority to have responsibility for ensuring that the service is there and for monitoring its quality.

Examples of statutory entitlement for patients or clients are:

■ being on a GP's list

■ attending hospital for a diagnostic check-up and follow up treatment

■ having an eye test

■ being assessed for a home help

■ having a statement of special educational needs.

Public services are those provided by organisations such as the NHS, local councils or criminal justice services. The NHS and local councils are also known as **statutory authorities**.

Statutory entitlements

Statutory entitlement describes public services, provided through legislation, to which everyone has a right of access. This will have been established through Acts of Parliament, which set out duties and powers, later reinforced and clarified as shown in the table.

Precedence	Means	Does
First	*Act of Parliament* (primary legislation)	Places duties or powers
Second	*Statutory instrument* (secondary or delegated legislation)	Regulations which can place duties or powers
	Directions under an Act of Parliament	Delegated legislation Places duties
	Approvals made under an Act of Parliament	Places duties
	Guidance and *Codes of Practice*	Some guidances explicit under legislation whereas others issued by government departments to guide authorities
Third	*Circular Guidance*	A statement of government policy to guide authorities

Acts of Parliament and statutory instruments

Acts of Parliament define what must or may be done, or what must not be done. They do not usually set out details of how the service or facility will be

245

Health and social care services result from national and local decisions about what services should be provided. These decisions are both political and administrative. This means that the range of services, who can use them and how they are paid for are subject to change over time as government, the NHS and local authorities develop social policies and implement them. You will find that the range of services, the criteria for receiving them and how much users of services have to pay for them will differ from area to area.

DISCUSSION POINT

Think about some health and social services which you or your family have used over the last year. Were any of these services unusual or not generally available?

Membership of an NHS trust board

Members of a trust include:

- a chair appointed by the Secretary of State for Health

- up to five non-executive members, of which one comes from the medical school linked with the trust. All are appointed by the Secretary of State and should represent the local community

- up to five executive members (employed managers).

provided. This is given in the statutory instrument, directions or approvals where government ministers are able to specify matters such as:

- criteria for who will receive the service
- how the service will be paid for
- how much the user will pay
- which organisation may or may not provide the service.

Guidance and codes of practice

Guidance and codes of practice, issued by the Department of Health, explain, clarify and amplify what government expects from the NHS and local authorities.

Circulars and executive letters

These are the means by which the Department of Health informs the NHS and local authorities about its policy for health and social care. They may set out the details of national funding available for services or how changes in legislation are to be implemented. They are useful to authorities when planning, developing and defending their policies against any challenge.

Although guidance and circulars do not have the same legal force as Acts of Parliament, failure to implement them can be used by the courts or health service and local government commissioners to criticise the Government, the NHS or local councils for not providing services as 'intended by Parliament'.

Duties define the services and facilities the NHS and local authorities must provide. Usually the duty is directed towards the local population in general, for example, 'the duty of local authorities to provide home-help service for the area'. Other duties may be towards an individual, such as social services departments' duty to carry out assessment of people who might need community care services under the NHS and Community Care Act 1990.

Even where there are duties, they are usually qualified by phases such as 'where reasonable' or 'within resources'.

More often legislation gives public services the powers to provide certain services if they want to, but does not compel them to do so. For example, local authorities can issue concessionary travel passes for elderly people or make provision to help them to continue to live at home. These services are discretionary.

The way in which public services carry out their duties and powers are decided by each health authority, NHS trust or local authority. It is the task of the appointed members of the health authority or NHS trusts or the elected members of the local authority to interpret legislation.

The members of the trust or the local authority must ensure that matters prescribed by the Government are implemented. Their other decisions about services and facilities must fall within their legal powers. Where possible, their decisions reflect the approaches set out in guidance and codes of practice.

Membership of a local authority

The members of a local authority are the elected councillors. When elected, they usually stand on a political ticket. The majority political party make the decisions about the policy and direction of the council. Where the council is hung – that is, there is no clear majority party – these decisions are made by coalitions of councillors.

The business of the council is overseen by committees, of which social services is one. Detailed decisions are made by this committee.

A **judicial review** is where an individual or group go to court to claim a minister or local authority has acted outside legal parameters, has failed to act or has misinterpreted their power to act. Applicants must be people who have been affected by the decision which is being challenged.

ACTIVITY

The NSPCC is a unique voluntary organisation in that it has a statutory role laid down by Act of Parliament. Find out what this is and write a short report. List any other activities it undertakes.

Health authorities, NHS trusts and local councils are often faced with difficult decisions because the members' wish to offer a service or facility is restricted by other directions from the Government. For example, all expenditure on services is subject to government expenditure limits and requirements to demonstrate value for money.

When the father of Child B, who suffered from leukaemia, was told that Anglia Health Authority would not pay for a second transplant or expensive alternative treatment, he went to court. The case focused around the AHA decision which was based on both clinical judgement about the benefits of further treatment and its cost as compared with Child B's right to her choice of treatment. The court found in favour of the AHA.

Challenging local decision about powers

Because the details of the service result from decisions by individual health authorities, health trusts or local authorities, it is possible for decisions about how they do or do not provide a service or a facility to be challenged through the courts by judicial review.

Judges may intervene and reinterpret the legislation. The limits to a public service's discretion are that it must act reasonably, in good faith and legally. The courts may define the definitions of terms used in legislation in situations where they feel that local authorities or the NHS cannot make their own definitions or are making them inappropriately.

ACTIVITY

Each local authority has interpreted the guidance on community care in the light of their own priorities and resources. There have been challenges by users seeking to improve the service they are receiving. Find an example of a judicial review in the national or local press. Write a brief explanation of the user's case and how the authority responded. What was the outcome of the challenge?

As explained on page 245, statutory services and facilities can be provided by a wide range of organisations including the voluntary sector and private sector. In the latter case the service or facility is funded or partly funded by the NHS or local authorities. Users are not expected to pay the full cost of the service.

There is a range of practitioners who provide health care and receive funding for specific services from the health authority. They operate as independent businesses and include dentists, optometrists and pharmacists. The private

ACTIVITY

Ask your family members to tell you about the health and social care services they have received over the last year. List the different services and explain which ones the NHS or the local authority has a duty to provide.

Examples of non-statutory services are:

- counselling services at GP's surgeries
- bathing services for elderly people
- home chiropody
- drop-in centres for mothers and toddlers.

ARTHRITIS CARE

Action for people with Arthritis.

sector also includes private hospitals and an independent group of nursing and residential homes who receive no funding from the NHS.

Non-statutory services and facilities

There is considerable variation in how services are provided and who may be able to use them. Some are provided directly by the NHS or the local council, but others may be provided by a voluntary organisation or private company.

There are also local variations in criteria for receiving the service. For example, referrals to the services and facilities may be restricted or subject to the practitioner's judgement of the user's needs. There are local differences in how much the user may be expected to pay for services.

Local councils also publish details of their services.

These services can also be provided by other agencies from the independent sector, either voluntary or private.

Voluntary organisations

Voluntary organisations are involved in all aspects of a community life:

- environmental
- recreational
- educational
- health and social care.

Some voluntary organisations are national, many more are local. They work towards improvements to their communities or their quality of life.

You may already know about voluntary organisations directly involved in health and social services. They are likely to employ staff in the same way as the NHS and social services departments. Many will be professionally qualified, such as:

- social workers
- nurses
- physiotherapists.

Others may specialise in working in the voluntary sector. For example:

- community workers
- pre-school playgroup workers
- advice workers.

ACTIVITY

Investigate a local charity working in the social services sector. Find out:

■ whether it is wholly independent or part of a national charity

■ its charitable aims and activities

■ its target groups

■ facts and figures (staff, volunteers, length of time operating)

■ its principal sources of funding.

Write up your findings in a report.

Voluntary organisations support the involvement of volunteers and also encourage people to use their services:

❝ *I came to work in a voluntary organisation because I wanted to work in partnership with the users. The salary level has been lower and I've had less chance of promotion but I have felt less restricted than social workers in social services.* ❞

social worker in a charity working with the single homeless

There are other voluntary organisations which provide emotional and social support to individuals and their families. For example:

■ self-help groups

■ tenants' associations

■ youth organisations

■ religious organisations centred around a religious meeting place.

These have been set up for a different purpose from health or social care organisations but do much to improve the quality of life for their members. The activities of these organisations are more likely to be undertaken by volunteers, with perhaps one or two paid workers to administrate them.

ACTIVITY

Through a local directory of services, find out if there are any tenants associations in your area. List the activities they offer which would offer social support to elderly people or young people.

A **volunteer** is 'someone, who through their own free will, spends time, unpaid, in doing something that aims to benefit someone other than the volunteers and their immediate family.'

Volunteer Centre UK

Volunteers make an important contribution to health and social care services. They are usually associated with the voluntary sector but the NHS and local authorities also have volunteers involved in their services where this is agreed with paid staff. In these services their activities are coordinated by a volunteer organiser or coordinator.

Private independent organisations

The extent to which the private sector provides health and social care is growing, and being encouraged by government policy. The private sector comprises:

■ health professionals, such as GPs who are contracted to provide services for the NHS but may see patients outside the health service

■ health professionals, such as hospital consultants, who continue to have private patients

■ individual or groups of health and care practitioners who have contracts with the NHS but whose patients are primarily not funded through the NHS, such as dentists, opticians, osteopaths, counsellors, psychotherapists and complementary medical practitioners

■ small businesses which offer NHS services but are primarily retailers, such as chemists or opticians

DISCUSSION POINT

The extent to which the private sector is involved in providing health care is the subject of debate. Discussion usually focuses around the issue of private beds within NHS hospitals or the growth of treatment of NHS patients in private hospitals. Discuss why you think this may be contentious.

- private companies – small and large – which provide health and social care services through a contract with the NHS or the local authority, such as private hospitals or residential care homes
- insurance companies and others which provide a range of healthcare services for anyone who is insured or able to pay for the service
- national and international companies which provide goods and services to the NHS or local authorities, such as major drug companies medical suppliers or manufacturers of special equipment for disabled people.

Informal provision

Informal care is the care given by family, friends and neighbours.

66 *Most people had never heard of carers (before the 1990s) . . . We now know that there are eight million people who meet the census definition of a carer, and . . . that they save the nation £34 billion – more than the combined budgets of the NHS and local authority social services departments. Most carers want to provide the care themselves and it is help with domestic chores that they most need.* 99

Jill Pitkeathley, Director of Carers' National Association

Informal care is primarily provided by immediate family but also by:

- friends
- neighbours
- churches and other religious organisations
- leisure groups
- cultural groups
- employment or education organisations.

Who are the carers?

How much do you know about carers?

- There are approximately six million unpaid carers of adults in Britain.
- One in seven adults has a caring responsibility.
- 1.4 million carers devote over 20 hours per week to caring.
- One in five households contains a carer.
- Carers tend to be middle-aged women.
- One in five carers look after someone who is not related to them.
- Most carers look after someone who is elderly.
- Many carers look after more than one person.
- A quarter of carers receive no help from anyone inside or outside the family.
- Fifty per cent of those caring for a spouse do so unaided.

Source: Carers' National Association and Smale, Tuson, Biehal and Marsh

ACTIVITY

Talk to a member of your family, a friend or a neighbour who is elderly or disabled and ask them about their life. Make notes about who helps them with everyday activities, such as cleaning, cooking meals, gardening or shopping. List their social activities and who supports them with their hobbies or going to the cinema. Record how the helpers come to be involved in helping.

Variations in health and social care services

To provide health and social care services, organisations and practitioners have to take into account a number of variables, grouped into classifications.

These variables enable health and social care organisations to plan which services provide for their communities and how to share out resources. The classifications are used in legislation, Department of Health guidance, and circulars and information published by health authorities, health trusts and local authorities. At national level, the Government uses the classifications to decide how it will allocate funding to the NHS and local authorities.

Each social services department or health authority builds these classifications into their Community or Health Plans. The classifications influence the level of provision – the number of places available and the geographical location – and the criteria for receiving the service. They are also the basis on which voluntary and private agencies agree the services they will offer and to whom.

For practitioners in health and social care services the classifications assist them to:
- assess the needs of service users
- make decisions about the care required
- arrange for services to be provided
- monitor services and the progress of service users.

Age

Health and social care services may be classified by the age of the user. This recognises that individuals live in different social situations and have different needs according to their age. The factors related to age are:
- whether living with family, peers or alone
- employment, income and levels of poverty
- state of health
- physical ability, emotional stability, maturity and social support.

Age classifications are also reflected by legislation. Children's services and services for adults are covered by separate Acts.

The variables are:
- under-eights – day nurseries, playgroups, child-minding
- other children – foster care, family centres
- teenagers – court diversion projects, youth projects
- adults between 18 and 60 – people with physical disabilities or mental illness or learning difficulties through day centres, family support groups, bereavement counselling
- elderly – similar services to adult but with a number of services provided for those over retirement age, some designed to promote active retirement, others for people who are frail or dependent.

Types of classification

Classification is made according to the characteristics of:
- the user and their needs
- the nature of the service being provided.

Meals in the Home

This is what we promise for quality Meals in the Home

ISLINGTON COUNCIL

ACTIVITY

Select one of the age groups and find out about the services available for this group in your area. List those services specifically provided for the age group selected.

The needs of the user

Another variable defines needs which result from an individual's condition. For this to be useful for planning the services, the conditions are grouped as:

- mental health – those diagnosed as depressive, schizophrenic or psychotic but can also include those who are showing emotional or mental stress
- learning disability – those whose intellectual abilities are below average or have problems with adapting to situations
- physical disability – those with a wide range of conditions which affect their mobility, senses and stamina.

Care type

Classification for care type enables organisations to match care to needs, although some individuals may fall into more than one category. The care type can be defined by whether it is health or social care.

Health care

Health care means the care which is provided to meet medical or health needs arising from illness or accident where practitioner interventions will be required. This can be both short-term or continuous. It is usually provided through the NHS service.

Social care

Social care is provided to meet an individual's non-medical physical, emotional and social needs. It usually means providing care to individuals in their own home or through residential care. It is likely to be provided through social services departments or the voluntary and private sectors.

Another classification of care need type is:

- acute
- rehabilitation
- continuous long-term.

Acute describes immediate and short-term care. Most of the services within the hospital are acute, while joint health and social services can run 24-hour emergency services to support people with mental health problems or operate a duty service through the night to cover 'life and limb' situations.

Rehabilitation is provided to individuals who need supportive assistance to overcome illness or disability, or to develop new skills for living independently in the community. This includes physiotherapy and occupational therapy and social care activities which prepare individuals who may be leaving care or hospital for their own home in the community. It includes work with young people in care to improve the quality of lives of their family, prepare them for changes in the care provided, or to leave care.

Continuous or chronic health care is provided for individuals with long-term health or social needs requiring continuous medical or nursing care or social

> ### DISCUSSION POINT
>
> The NHS and local authorities can provide aids to mobility or similar services, for example the services of occupational therapists. Think about some of the physical and emotional needs of an elderly person. How would you distinguish between health care and social care?

> **Life and limb** describes situations where there is danger of death or physical harm

support. This category includes people with chronic illness, such as bronchitis or Parkinson's disease.

Other care types of a more specialist nature are palliative and respite care. Palliative care is provided for people who are terminally ill, in hospital, a hospice or at home. Respite care offers the carer an opportunity to have a break from their caring or provides the person being cared for with a break from their carer.

Respite care

Shared Care UK, an umbrella group for family-based short-term services, offers short breaks which give both relief to carers and a positive experience to the disabled person using the service. It supports both adults and children through making lasting links between users, their carers and the families providing respite. For example, Jessica, ten years old, who has cerebral palsy, spends a weekend every five to six weeks with her support family. There are two children in the support family and they play and share family outings.

"The reason I go to [my respite carers] is for me to have a change and for mum and dad to have a change."

Community Care 30 August 1995

Ring-fenced means identified funds from a general budget which can only be spent on a specific purpose.

From time to time the Government specifies particular services which it wants prioritised. Recently it ring-fenced funds for two priority services: mental health and people with learning difficulties.

Level of care

The levels of care are categorised as:

- primary
- secondary
- tertiary.

This hierarchy of services is defined in terms of closeness to the user and usually refers to the health services.

Primary care is available to individuals in their own homes through:

- district nurses
- health visitors
- community psychiatric nurses
- GPs' surgeries
- health clinics
- shops in the high street.

Secondary care is usually accessed through referral from the primary care practitioners, such as the GP or the health visitor and includes general hospital services, such as out-patient or in-patient care and hospital psychiatric services.

Tertiary level is the specialist services which may be provided at a regional level rather than in the local hospital. Examples are renal units or regional secure facilities for severely mentally disturbed people.

Care setting

This describes the setting in which care is delivered, such as:

- domiciliary services (delivered within the user's own home), such as nursing care, home help, meals on wheels
- day care, such as health centres, out-patient clinics, luncheon clubs and activity centres
- foster care, where an individual or family provide a home for a child or an adult needing support
- sheltered or warden-controlled housing providing accommodation which offers additional care and support to its residents
- residential care provided for a group in a special home which may have 24-hour care – for example, for elderly people, children or people with disabilities
- hospital, where medical and nursing care is provided through the NHS for out-patients or in-patients.

Service being supplied

Another way of classifying services is by listing those available from independent professionals or organisations. This is particularly helpful for users and carers looking for assistance.

Examples include:

- complementary medicine, such as osteopathy, acupuncture and homeopathy
- alternative medicine, such as aromatherapy or reflexology
- home help
- transport for people with disabilities
- counselling for people with drug or alcohol problems
- telephone helpline for children.

Some organisations, such as dentists or opticians, only offer one type of service or care setting; others, such as a voluntary organisation working with drug abusers, offer a range.

Churches also offer support both in hospital or the community.

DISCUSSION POINT

Discuss the advantages and disadvantages of varying the classifications used to plan and deliver services.

ACTIVITY

Using a directory of local services, identify three examples of care setting. Contact the services and ask for information about their activities. Summarise what each care setting offers, which practitioners work within the setting and who the client group is.

Why have variations arisen?

At some point in your life you will use a health or social care service. The reason for this may be temporary, perhaps as a result of an illness, loss of job or marriage breakdown, or longer-term if an accident, a disabling illness or growing old mean that you need regular contact with the services.

The services you use will be selected by you or a practitioner on the basis of your age and your needs.

MICHAEL

Michael is a young man with learning difficulties. He still lives at home. Since leaving school, he has attended a day centre run by MENCAP. Here he has learnt to shop, cook and clean and been encouraged to train for office work in MENCAP's employment training project. Now he feels he wants to be more independent. His social worker talks this through with Michael and his parents, and everyone agrees to make an application to a housing association for Michael to move into its group house. While he waits for a place, he has a part-time job with a local builder in the stores and is beginning to budget his money. Although his parents are uneasy about Michael leaving home, they know he will be supported by his employer, the housing association, the day centre – and he will only be living a few blocks away from them.

MRS BROWN

Mrs Brown had a very busy life – she regularly looked after her grandchildren, cooked lunch for her frail neighbour and tended her garden. Then one day she broke her hip in a fall. After a hip replacement operation and three months in hospital, she returned home to a very different routine. She was supported by nurses, physiotherapists, home helps, volunteers from a school project, her neighbours and family, and meals on wheels. Aids and adaptations were made to her house. As time went on, she decided that she could no longer manage at home and chose to move into a sheltered housing scheme where a resident warden was on call 24 hours a day. When she became too ill to be supported in this way, her GP and the social services agreed with her that she would move into a nursing home for nursing care. Two months later, Mrs Brown died in the nursing home.

As a user's circumstances change, the services they need will also change. Services can be provided to help the user:

- maintain their independence or current situation
- cope with changes in their health or social circumstances to maintain a good quality of life
- regain their health or improve skills so they no longer need services.

ACTIVITY

Look at the two case studies and list how Mrs Brown and Michael fit into the categories. Explain how and why you think Mrs Brown and Michael's classification changed over time. Explain the purpose of variations in classifications. Draw conclusions about whether the six classifications take account of all foreseeable health and social care needs.

Resources for statutory services

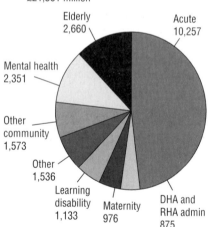

NHS expenditure 1995/96
£33.4 billion

Hospital and Community Health Services capital 2.1

Central Health and Misc Services 0.5

Departmental Administration 0.3

Family Health Service 7.8

Hospital and Community Health Services current 22.7

Hospital and Community Health Care Services
Gross expenditure by sector 1993/94
£21,361 million

Elderly 2,660

Acute 10,257

Mental health 2,351

Other community 1,573

Other 1,536

Learning disability 1,133

Maternity 976

DHA and RHA admin 875

Although much of the debate about resourcing concerns funding, resources also include:

■ buildings

■ land

■ equipment

■ personnel

■ expertise.

This section is about the resources which are necessary to provide health and social care services. It looks at where these resources come from and how they are managed.

The funding of health and social services is complex. Money comes from a number of sources:

■ central government

■ local government

■ charities

■ individuals.

The balance between sources differs according to:

■ the organisation or agency concerned

■ the service being provided

■ the ability of the user to pay.

The impact of government policy on the organisation of health and social services is covered in elements 5.2 and 5.3.

Forms of resources

The major focus of discussion about resourcing health and social services is funding. The cost of health and social services is a large percentage of the gross national product. It is also a budget which has a built-in growth factor because:

■ the number of people over the age of 65 is increasing

■ advances in medical and technological treatment are made

■ users' expectations become greater

■ services are labour-intensive.

Capital resources

Capital resources include buildings, land and equipment. If the NHS plans to build new hospitals it must borrow money. Current government policy for borrowing favours the Private Finance Initiative (PFI) which gives the NHS access to private-sector skills and expertise as well as money to fund capital projects.

The NHS is required to be cost-effective and one way to achieve this is by rationalising buildings within the district. In most areas there are examples of small hospitals closing or services being brought together onto one site. The vacant sites can then be sold.

ACTIVITY

Find out if there are any proposals to close or merge health services in your area. Write a report explaining the proposals and what the main aims are.

Human resources

These are the people who work within health and social care services. Those involved in providing health and social care include:

- managers
- qualified professionals
- paramedics
- support and ancillary staff
- volunteers
- carers.

The list includes people who are not paid. The contribution of volunteers and informal carers is significant and is taken into account when managers plan and deliver services.

Health and social care services employ a large number of staff. For example, the NHS has a workforce of nearly 1 million, of which nearly 66% provide direct care (1992 figures). In 1995/6 staff costs accounted for two-thirds of NHS expenditure. The report of the Social Services Inspectorate for the same period estimated the staff in social services as being 1 million, of whom two-thirds were in the independent sector. A substantial number of these work part-time. It is impossible to estimate the numbers of people who work as volunteers.

Expertise

Professional expertise and skills are needed to provide the services. This mainly comes from qualified and trained employees but also from volunteers, service users and their carers.

Providers of resources

The principles of funding for health and social services are laid down by legislation and directed by government policy. The Government sets limits to public expenditure through the Budget each autumn. It allocates money from taxation to the NHS and regulates the level of local authority expenditure in a settlement negotiated annually.

Central government

Central government funds health and social care services by:

- taxation – this pays for the NHS through direct payment, supports local authority social services through revenue support and other special grants, and supports individuals through the social security system
- borrowing permission – from the City and financial institutions for buildings and other capital expenditure
- private investment and charitable donations – this is encouraged by government to support new buildings and special services
- transfer of funds from one sector to another – e.g. from the social security budget to local authorities, to enable them to implement community care arrangements

ACTIVITY

Select a provider organisation. Write a paragraph describing its services and list the sources of its funding. Estimate the proportions of funding coming from central government, local sources, social security and service users.

- direction to local authorities about allocation of funding, such as the percentage of funding for community care to the independent sector
- regulations setting out how much individuals must pay for health and social care.

The NHS

Although the NHS is funded by taxation, private investment and charges from patients, it can fund other agencies participating in health care.

The NHS itself is split between health authorities which purchase health care from providers. By using surveys and analysing data, health authorities can estimate the future needs of communities within their areas. Most services are provided by other NHS organisations, such as NHS trusts. This creates a financial arrangement between the two sides called the internal market. Unit 6 explains this in more detail. Whether the health authority is prepared to pay for a service is a key factor for a provider when deciding to offer to a locality:

66 *I work for an NHS trust. The trust is the provider of the services, the health authority the purchaser. Basically they hold the purse strings. If they decide not to buy a service, the trust cannot run it. So the purchasers are very powerful and their decisions can and often do result in alterations and reductions to services.* 99

child protection adviser

Local government

Local government services are funded through:
- central government revenue grants to local government and special grants to encourage activities such as joint funding
- special central government grants for specific services or groups, such as funding for services and facilities for people from ethnic minority communities
- locally raised taxes, such as the Council Tax and Business Tax
- charges for services and facilities
- partnership with the private sector
- loans from the City and financial institutions, particularly for capital expenditure.

Local government has powers to fund other organisations offering social care through:
- contracts with independent providers of services
- grants to voluntary and charitable organisations to provide services and facilities
- payment to individuals to enable them to pay for services, such as independent living schemes or money to prevent children from coming into care.

Other ways in which the health service funds organisations are by:

- contracts with supplies and drug companies
- contracts with independent practitioners such as dentists, opticians and private health and nursing care
- joint funding for projects for community-based services
- grants to voluntary organisations.

Joint funding is money made available from health authority budgets to fund joint projects or services with the local authority. The aim is for NHS contributions to taper off after a number of years, after which the local authority meets the full costs.

In 1948, following the creation of the NHS, the trustees (all local professionals and business people) of a local dispensary – a base for doctors, a dentist, nurses and a pharmacy – sold the building. The money was invested to provide income for grants to assist the sick poor in the seven church parishes of Brixton, London. In 1996, this charity stills makes about 15 small grants to individuals for recuperative holidays, special items to help with illness, mobility or stress relief. Its trustees are clergy and nominees from local churches and the council.

A **quango** is a quasi-autonomous non-governmental organisation. The commonly accepted definition is that they are unelected agencies responsible for spending public money. This definition excludes corporations which deliver a service or run an industry. There are three types of quango:

■ executive which regulate an area of law or disseminate information or monies

■ advisory which examine specific problems and make recommendations

■ tribunals which arbitrate between government officials and people who feel aggrieved.

Charity

A charitable organisation, can be a source of funding. Some national charitable trusts have access to large sums of money used to promote research, disseminate good practice or give grants to organisations to set up initiatives.

Examples are:

■ Joseph Rowntree Foundation – funds research into housing and social conditions

■ Kings Fund – has promoted training for professionals in the health service and promoted good practice

■ Family Welfare Association – funds are distributed as grants to families in poverty and distress.

Many localities have small charitable trusts founded for the benefit of people in their area. Over the years, they have been rationalised to provide money rather than goods and target their work to supplement national and local funding. They can be tapped by organisations providing services or individuals in need.

However, many charities are involved in providing care services and must look more widely than charitable trusts and fundraising to pay for their services. Under the changed arrangements they have increasingly entered into contracts with the NHS or local authorities for those services. Funding from the contract is usually supplemented by:

■ existing charitably raised funds

■ new money collected through donations and covenants

■ charges from service users

■ special grants from central government

■ interest from investment.

National Lottery

The National Lottery, which started in 1995, distributes money through a number of quangos dealing with national heritage, arts, sports and charities. These boards set their criteria for eligibility for grants. Recipients must have arranged equivalent funding from other sources. The Charities Board is able to distribute finance for staffing and running costs. Although its first round of grants excluded medical activities, subsequent programmes cover both health and social care activities.

ACTIVITY

Find out more about the National Lottery Charities Board's criteria for giving grants. Match these criteria with a local voluntary organisation to assess what benefits and disadvantages there would be to receiving funding from the Charities Board.

DISCUSSION POINT

Public opinion varies on the issue of private insurance. Many people have made insurance contributions since 1948 in the belief that this would entitle them to care when they were ill or old and unable to look after themselves. Some people in employment question why they should be expected to pay, through taxation, for services which will also be used by people who do not contribute. Do you think the state should pay for people who are able to make their own provision through private insurance? What might be the consequences of this for those who cannot take out insurance?

ACTIVITY

Assume you are 25, single and self-employed. Get some information from two insurance companies providing healthcare cover. List what is covered and what is not. Explain when the insurance company will pay healthcare costs and how much. Estimate the monthly payments required for the options being offered. Write a summary of the provisions of both companies, draw conclusions and decide which company you would buy insurance from.

Private insurance schemes

As government has shifted away from comprehensive provision by the state, it has encouraged private insurance to extend its involvement. This is a growing area for political debate as political parties consider whether the state should provide a universal system, or a safety net for those who are unable to provide for themselves.

Forms of insurances available to support health and social care are:

- retirement pensions through an employer's scheme or private insurance

- insurance to replace income when permanent or long-term ill-health or disability strikes

- health insurance which pays for a variety of healthcare costs such as dental or hospital care

- insurance to meet the costs of community care, particularly residential care, for retired people.

Expanding the latter type of insurance is the subject of government consultation. It is suggested that individuals taking out such insurance will be able to have it off-set against the costs of residential care.

Not everyone is able to get insurance cover. This may be because of insufficient income, but could be because of ineligibility. Some groups are penalised because they already have long-term or terminal illness or disability. Other disclaimers in policies may mean certain types of treatment or illness will not be covered:

66 *The policy will be cancelled if a claimant is found to be infected by HIV, AIDS or similar or related condition or syndrome. No benefit will be paid under the policy if the disability is self-inflicted or caused by the taking of alcohol or drugs other than under the direction of a legally qualified medical practitioner.* 99

exclusions from an insurance policy protecting income
in the event of long-term ill health

Direct payment by the individual

Users have always been expected to make some contribution to their health and social care services but the extent has increased since the NHS and Community Care Act.

Some charges are required by the Government, which sets exact amounts, such as for prescription charges or dental charges. Exemptions are allowed for people who live on income support, low incomes or in other specific circumstances. You will find details of how these apply to NHS services in section 5.2.2.

Other charges are decided by the organisation providing the services. For example, local authorities now make charges for home helps, meals-on-wheels, or day centres. The amount charged and criteria for eligibility are decided by each local authority. The extent to which local authorities charge is explained in section 5.2.2.

Paying for care in residential homes for elderly people

For residents who are unable to meet the weekly charge for their residential place, the local authority must be approached. If they agree to pay, the local authority collects a contribution back from the resident. If the cost of the residential home is greater than the council can pay, then a relative, friend or charity can pay the balance.

The resident's contribution is calculated using rules laid down by the government, as follows:

- income, including state pension, social security benefits and any occupational pension
- the first £10,000 capital or savings is ignored, a percentage taken up to £16,000, and the resident asked to pay the full cost of their care until capital is reduced to £10,000.

If the resident owns a home, its value will be taken into account when calculating their capital. This usually means the resident will be expected to sell the house unless another way is found to meet the charges. Until the property is sold, a 'charge' will be put on the property to be claimed later. If occupied by a partner, relative over 60 or someone who is ill or disabled, the property is not included in the capital.

DISCUSSION POINT

People are living longer, and older people and their families resent putting their savings into paying for residential and community care. The political parties are concerned at the growing cost of community care for older people and are looking at ways to meet it. Discuss what options there might be to meet these costs. Do you feel that older people and their relatives should be expected to pay? What other ways are there of funding this?

Access to services

What is access?

This section explains how patients and clients make contact with services and facilities so that they may receive help and support from those services and facilities. This contact is known as access.

There are a number of routes by which users gain access to the services they seek or need:
- an 'open door'
- recall, referral or recommendation
- compulsion through the courts or through child or mental health legislation.

Open door services

These are where an individual may walk in or telephone for an appointment. Sometimes the service is free or available on payment of a fee. Many primary healthcare services, such as GPs' surgeries, child welfare clinics or family planning services are offered in this way.

A growing range of telephone helplines are intended to provide information, advice or counselling to assist callers with problems with addictive, family, relationship or income problems. The helplines can be organised by health services, local authorities or voluntary organisations. Examples of national voluntary organisations include the Samaritans and Childline.

Sometimes organisations involved in education may offer telephone assistance. The BBC provides a telephone line for people affected by a documentary or a drama.

Referral and recommendation

Many open door services can be the gateway to other services. The enquirer may be referred on to other services. GPs' surgeries are the major route to specialist hospital and nursing services. Social service area or district offices can assess clients for other care services. Community advice centres can provide information and support.

Some services can only be obtained as a result of referral or recommendation. These are usually at secondary or tertiary level.

Compulsion

People may be 'compelled' to receive services because of the risk they may be exposed to themselves or the risk they present to others. This is covered in more detail in unit 6.

Methods of access

All statutory services are required to publicise their services as part of their quality assurance mechanisms and measures of their performance. Other organisations and professionals also publicise their services.

DISCUSSION POINT

Talk about your experiences of using health or social care services. How did you find out about them? Was it easy to find out about them?

262

General publicity

The list of sources of general publicity is long:

- local telephone directories have pages which list health or local authority services

- local newspapers frequently have information about services – such as pharmacy opening hours at bank holiday times

- directories of charity and voluntary services are available in libraries and information centres

- articles in the press or radio and television programmes give contact addresses and telephone numbers.

Self-referral

Users may refer themselves, for example when someone makes an appointment to see the doctor or dentist. A mother can visit a playgroup or mother and toddler club to see whether she can join. A child can telephone Childline to discuss their problems.

Recall

Other services operate a recall system, for example, screening programmes. Cervical smears are offered to women over 40 years of age every three years and reminder letters are sent out by the GP or the health service. Dentists and opticians also remind their users when it is time for a check-up.

Referral

A significant route to a service is referral by one practitioner or organisation to another. The most obvious example is the GP referring patients to specialist hospital services for diagnosis and treatment. Unit 6 explains how many community care services are made available as a result of a social worker or care manager assessing the user's needs and organising a package of services to support that user.

Sometimes referrals may be made by concerned neighbours or family. These must be handled with sensitivity by the practitioner to ensure that the potential users' wishes and rights are respected. In some areas of care the referral may be made anonymously by members of the public.

66 *Anonymous referrals, for example when a neighbour rings up a health visitor about a child, are never very helpful. The health visitor would explain that the caller has to take on the responsibility of talking to social services and will need to give their name. This is because we cannot action unsubstantiated cases.* 99

child protection adviser

Recommendations

Practitioners or organisations recommend services to users so that they can refer themselves. For example, parents seeking a childminder may approach the social services department who will offer a list of registered child minders, for the parents to make their own contact.

Some recommendations may come from other users. This route is often used where the individual pays for the service, for example choosing a chiropractor, dentist or an alternative therapy practitioner on the recommendation of a friend already using the service.

ACTIVITY

Collect various publicity material, analyse it in terms of who it is aimed at, how it is disseminated, how effective it is likely to be and why you think this is. Write a page comparing the likely effectiveness of two examples of the material you have collected.

Key questions

1 Explain the meaning of 'statutory entitlement'.
2 Name three services to which people are statutorily entitled.
3 What is the independent sector?
4 List five types of private-sector health and social care services.
5 Give two examples of informal care.
6 List the three main age classifications.
7 What is health care?
8 List four care settings.
9 Name the four forms of resources.
10 Give two ways in which central government funds local government social care.
11 How does local government fund voluntary organisations?
12 List five ways a user gains access to services.
13 In health and social care terms, what is meant by recall?

Assignment

Choose five local health and social care services or facilities including at least one of each of:

■ statutory
■ non-statutory
■ informal.

Write to each of these services and ask if it would be possible to talk with a manager or organiser about the service they provide and how it is funded. Ask for information about eligibility for the services, who the service users are and how they are referred to the services.

You may find it helpful to prepare an open-ended questionnaire so that you can keep the format of your investigation consistent.

From the material gathered prepare a report which:

■ describes the extent to which there is a statutory entitlement to the services and facilities visited
■ describes how the services fit into the variations in classification and explains why any difficulties occurred
■ describes the way the services are funded and relates this to the classifications
■ explains how users accessed the services.

> 66 Community care means providing the right level of intervention and support to enable people to achieve maximum independence and control over their own lives. 99
>
> Caring for People, *Department of Health White Paper 1989*

> 66 We see more young people at the severe end of the mentally ill spectrum now because of the reduction in provision of services and trend towards care in the community. The pressure is on all organisations who can help: housing, social services, the health service. This depletion of services impacts directly on young people and their parents. There is a lot more pressure on parents at work and their relationships with their children become more stressed as a result. 99
>
> *senior worker (counselling), young people's counselling and information service*

> 66 In Britain we have caring on the cheap – in countries such as Norway they do great things with their welfare system, which is mainly possible because the people understand the need for adequate revenue from taxation. 99
>
> *doctor working in NHS hospital trust*

> 66 The changes which have affected our work recently are a combination of demographic and government policy. The number of elderly people coming in to acute care keeps going up. And with the Community Care Act we are asked increasingly to do pre-discharge assessments (what type of full-time care someone might need after they leave hospital). It is difficult with the trend towards people not being in care. 99
>
> *occupational therapy services manager, NHS hospital trust*

> 66 Changes in technology are changing the face of optics dramatically. Visual fields screening used to be quite laborious – now it's all automated. And now we have auto-refractors which can help estimate the prescription. 99
>
> *optometrist*

Change in health and social care provision

The whole of your life, and that of your parents, will have been spent under the welfare state – a comprehensive package of health and social care 'from the cradle to the grave'. The last ten years have brought major changes and an increasing challenge to the assumption that the state can and should cover all eventualities at no direct cost to the user. This element provides an overview of these developments and changes.

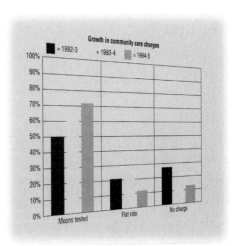

The origins and development of care services

Universalism versus selectivity

A key debate since 1942 has been whether services and benefits should be universal (available to all equally) or selective (directed to those in most need). Beveridge favoured universalism. He believed universal benefit would reach those in need since it was automatic and bore no stigma. The quality of service would remain high since all had an interest in it.

Those in favour of a selective system argue that:

- It is wasteful and bureaucratic to pay benefits to those not in need.

- Spreading resources too thinly fails to benefit those in real need.

- It is better to make adequate payment to those in need and reduce overall cost while allowing tax-payers to spend more of their own money.

- The duty of government is to maximise freedom by guaranteeing everyone a minimum income and allowing individual spending decisions.

DISCUSSION POINT

There continues to be wide public support for child benefit, which is universal. What do you think? Should there be universal benefits and services, and if so, which ones?

After the Second World War major social changes were necessary to meet new hopes and expectations, in particular, a wish to avoid a return to the poverty and large-scale unemployment of the late twenties and thirties. Together, the Beveridge Report and six Acts of Parliament laid the foundation of the welfare state:

- Beveridge Report 1942
- Education Act 1944
- Family Allowance Act 1945
- NHS Act 1946
- National Insurance Act 1946
- Children Act 1947
- National Assistance Act 1948.

Influence of Beveridge

In 1941 all political parties were agreed that the inadequacies of the general population's health, revealed through mass conscription and studies of the depression in the thirties, should be remedied.

Sir William Beveridge was asked to look at how health and welfare services should be provided in the future. Reporting in 1942, he made far-reaching recommendations that formed the foundation of the post-war social welfare services.

Underpinning the report was an assumption, which lasted until the mid-1970s, that government intervention in economic and social policy was in both the national and individual interest. This assumption had its roots in popular memory of the socially and individually corrosive effects of mass unemployment and poverty in the 1930s.

The report had three central recommendations for social provision:
- family allowances and national insurance
- full employment
- a comprehensive NHS.

By 'comprehensive' it meant a universal service, free at point of delivery, available to all when needed, at home and in hospital. This was to include equipment and rehabilitation services and to be provided by:
- GPs
- specialists
- dentists
- opticians
- nurses
- midwives.

Universalism was not new as a concept; it had long been established for education and, during the war, school meals and milk had been available for every child.

The National Health Service, established in 1948, was the nearest to Beveridge's original vision. The National Insurance Act was seen as the means of funding the NHS, sickness and unemployment benefit and pensions. Sold as an insurance scheme, it was, in fact, a form of taxation with the income used to pay for current benefit rather than the future. The fundamental purpose was to ensure that no one's income fell below a stated minimum level.

The National Assistance Act, although providing a range of means-tested benefits for those remaining uninsured, also provided the means of funding a range of services which still underpin our health and social service welfare system today. Community care is based firmly upon the services introduced by this Act.

The Children Act 1947 insisted that the care of children should be based upon the proper development of each child's 'character and abilities'.

Although there have been many changes in detail and structure, the skeleton of Beveridge's proposal still stands. Opinion polls have consistently indicated the broad popularity of the National Health Service and strong opposition to attempts to 'privatise' it.

Population characteristics

When proposing a national health service, Beveridge (in common with many others) believed that with proper income support there would be a rapidly rising level of health amongst the population as a whole. This would then lead to a reduction in demand for health services. In practice this has not been the case. Several reasons can be given to account for this.

Demand

The system which existed before 1946 had mainly restricted health services to those who could pay, had health insurance through their employment or were eligible for charitable support. Beveridge had no means of judging the real extent of demand for services. Once services became freely available they were eagerly taken up. For instance, the introduction of free eye tests and NHS spectacles led to a considerable growth in the numbers in the population wearing glasses. The extent of need was also enhanced by rising expectations.

Health of the population

With continued improvements in environmental health and wider availability of medicines, the overall health of the population has improved but:

- as life expectancy improved so the proportion of elderly in the population increased, with a consequent increased demand
- many conditions which 50 years ago were life-threatening can now be managed over a long period of time but at a financial cost
- in 1946 the health services primarily dealt with illnesses linked with poverty and malnutrition – in 1996 many diseases are linked to affluence, such as coronary heart disease.

DISCUSSION POINT

It is possible that the diseases which worry us most now will not be the ones which will concern us in the future. What do you think will be the issues in 10, 20 and 30 years' time?

Employment characteristics

The employment profile of Britain has changed greatly since Beveridge's time in a way that has had positive and negative effects:

- the decline of heavy and extractive industries (along with the related diseases and accidents)
- shorter hours and a greater amount of leisure time
- the raising of the school leaving age from 14 to 16, with a large number of 16- to 18-year-olds in education or employment training
- many people are less secure in their jobs since the 1970s
- Britain is no longer a full employment economy. As a consequence there has been an increase in the demand for benefits.

Demographic profile

The population's employment profile has also changed. Although the Second World War, like the First, saw a major expansion in the employment of women in industry, freeing men to join the armed forces, those women were later encouraged to return to the home in order to maintain full employment. Full employment meant, largely, male employment. Since then, women have moved back into the workforce. There has also been a later age of marriage and childbearing, social acceptance of divorce, and unmarried and single women bringing up their own children. This has resulted in a number of measures designed to support the changed position of women:

- a greater provision of childcare through childminding and workplace nurseries
- maternity leave and benefits
- child benefit.

Social policies

Expansion of services

The Beveridge Report, and the measures which stemmed from it, is based on assumptions about universality of service. The modern welfare state still deals with many problems with which Beveridge would have been familiar (illness, accident or unemployment), some which he would have expected to be no longer with us (homelessness), and others which might have struck him as strange (the changing nature of the family, the Child Support Agency, concepts of comparative deprivation).

The development of social policy during the succeeding half century has largely depended on three factors:

- experience of existing systems and their faults
- changing social and economic circumstances
- the balance between state and individual responsibility (collectivism versus individualism).

There have been other changes in the demographic profile which Beveridge could not have foreseen:

- large scale immigration from the 'new' Commonwealth bringing with it new conditions requiring a medical response, such as sickle-cell anaemia, and a need for cultural sensitivity in the way in which services are advertised and delivered

- a movement of populations from the city centres to the suburbs.

Field social work means social work for children, adults and elderly which is offered to people in the community. After 1970 it was usually offered through an area office which offered a 'single door' for social work services.

Following the establishment of the welfare state, there were 30 years of expansion of local government services, including major house-building and renovation schemes, leisure and recreation facilities and an expansion of secondary and further education. Health and welfare services were expanded by local authorities, using their discretionary powers. Children's services also expanded though were still largely dependent on residential services rather than foster care.

This expansion continued until the late 1970s, when successive governments, concerned at what they saw as the uncontrolled expansion of costs, began to put financial constraints on local authorities.

Fragmentation of services

One consequence was that services were fragmented. Qualified social workers were likely to be found in children's departments, working with those with mental health problems and in hospitals, while those who worked in health and welfare were either specialists for specific groups or unqualified. In 1968 the Government set up a committee under Lord Seebohm to advise on the future organisation of local government social care. This resulted in the Local Authority Social Services Act 1970 which introduced a new local authority department to manage the whole range of social services. This department used field social work teams to deal with the whole range of social work interventions for all service users, separated from the residential and day care services.

Subsequent legislative changes – the Mental Health Act and the NHS and Community Care Act – have seen the end of these generic teams and the establishment of separate teams for adult services, children and mental health with closer links to residential and day care services. However, the central planning and resourcing of the services remains under a single social services department.

At the same time the NHS was also reorganised to bring together several different services. The area health authority became responsible for primary health services, including mother and child clinics, hospitals and the health functions of the local authority medical officer of health. This left local authorities with the responsibility for environmental health and consumer protection.

It was clear that health authorities and social services departments needed to work together. Joint planning committees were created at district and service-planning levels. Joint funding was introduced to encourage projects which brought together the two services to start services which would bridge health and social care.

The move away from residential care has not been supported by everyone. Some organisations have worked for many years to provide stimulating and safe communities for people with learning difficulties and remain committed to this approach. Parents are often anxious about their children's ability to survive on their own. Recent concerns about the failure of social services to provide community care services for people with learning difficulties has strengthened the arguments of some parents and organisations to press the Government for funding so that the village communities can be retained and numbers expanded.

Care in the community instead of hospital care

As both health authorities and social services departments developed their community-based services, there was a growing recognition that the best way to meet the needs of the mentally ill and people with learning difficulties was with a social care model rather than a medical one.

For example, the changes in attitude toward people with learning difficulties included:

- dropping the term 'mental handicap' for learning difficulties
- moving people from hospitals or residential communities into small hostels and then to shared houses
- recognising that people with learning difficulties were not 'patients'
- recognising the right to greater self-determination and advocacy.

Housing

As social care supported more people in their own homes, working with housing authorities and housing associations became very important. For much of the early post-war period, local authority housing departments provided necessary housing support. Because of housing scandals and concern for the homeless, a series of Housing Acts were passed to improve the status of tenants, including provisions to assist the homeless. From 1985 local authorities were required to provide permanent accommodation for homeless people falling into three categories of priority need:

- families with dependent children
- pregnant women
- people judged vulnerable due to age or mental or physical illness.

DISCUSSION POINT

Do you think there is still a place for village communities or are services designed to provide a normal life the best option?

Special needs housing is housing which has been specifically provided to meet the needs of groups such as the elderly, or physically disabled or mentally ill. It enables the housing department, or housing association to provide care and social support as well as housing.

More recent changes have restricted the definition of homelessness and have limited choice because of the cost of housing the homeless.

Housing associations are increasingly important providers of social housing. Many started as charities to provide housing for working people or in a specific locality. The Housing Corporation, which is funded by the Government, has promoted a growth in the number of housing associations, including the provision of special needs housing.

Because of this, housing authorities are required to be involved in care planning. Many housing associations have contracts with health and social services to offer the housing component of a community care package.

Supported accommodation for people with mental health problems

A local housing association worked with health and social services to provide housing in the community. Taking over a small block of flats which were being used by the hospital it moved in twelve tenants. With finance from social services, it employed a support worker with the task of being both a housing manager and a care worker.

On the social care side, the workers ensure that each tenant has the support they need including registration with a GP, linking with daytime activities or being visited by a befriender. It is important that the tenants receive any benefit they are entitled to and they are encouraged to pay their rent and other bills. If a tenant must return to hospital the association tries to keep their flat available.

In order to manage this type of project, the association works with a number of other organisations – the hospital and community psychiatric services and housing department and voluntary organisations providing employment.

ACTIVITY

Contact a local housing association and ask whether it provides special needs housing. Describe the user group served and what social care support they provide for their tenants. Explain how they work with health and social services to promote access to their services for tenants.

The growing role of managers

In the early years of the NHS health professionals (especially consultants) held most of the power in planning. That role has gradually been ceded to managers who have a responsibility to control expenditure. Many are people who have worked as practitioners before taking on a managerial role. Hospital doctors still retain freedom of clinical judgement but are constrained by the availability of funds. GPs, particularly fundholders, have extended their decision-making for services for their patients, though many now employ practice managers.

Community involvement

The 1960s were characterised by a challenge to existing social, cultural and political norms as the first generation to have benefited from the reforms of the 1940s moved into adulthood. By the 1970s this challenge began to translate into an increasing degree of activism at various levels:

- a pursuit of improvements in services
- seeking to improve the quality of life in their communities.

Where groups represented service users or their carers, they began to achieve consultative status in planning services. By 1988 such consultation was the norm.

At the same time, practitioners in health and local government began to promote the idea of volunteers working with patients and clients. Local authorities increasingly made grants to voluntary groups offering this approach. Government also funded voluntary organisations in central government funding initiatives.

Changes in government policy

Until the mid-1970s the welfare state remained remarkably unchanged. The main reason was that a commitment to full employment had remained the centre of all government policy. As unemployment increased, it became clear that the previous ideals of the welfare state could not be upheld to the same extent. Increasing challenge to the values of the welfare state came about because of:

- an increasing government emphasis on individual responsibility and choice
- the rising cost of health care and social security
- a series of well-publicised reports into abuses and scandals
- a concern that services were being delivered wastefully and that the fault might lie in the welfare model itself
- an increasing demand for the right to complain and have access to previous confidential details
- the increasing retreat from deference to authority.

In the late 1970s successive governments began to face up to the growing costs of the public sector, including the NHS and local government. After 1983 this became a more radical shift from the Beveridge arrangements with a new framework for health and social care.

Government has increasingly operated on key principles:

- a drive to reduce public expenditure through cutting the size of public services
- a demand for value for money, reinforced by inspection and auditing of public services
- a desire to move away from comprehensive to targeted provision
- a belief that individuals could, and should, pay for their services, and an encouragement of private insurance to cover the expensive or longer-term needs
- a desire for a mixed economy with greater involvement of the private and voluntary sectors
- a belief that competition would result in efficiencies and savings
- deregulation as a means of promoting competition and efficiency.

The way these principles have been implemented in health and social care services is explored in element 5.3 and in unit 6. They include:

- the purchaser/provider split and the internal market within the health service
- the development of GP fundholding
- the encouragement of multiskilled jobs and multidisciplinary practice of practitioners
- the mixed economy of community care which encourages the provision of services and facilities by the independent sector
- compulsory competitive tendering for local services with resulting contracts with the independent sector
- the reduction of social security contribution to health and social care services
- an increase in charges for services.

Resource issues

Beveridge saw his system as being largely self-financing. The figures in the table show how much, in fact, the cost of the system has increased as a proportion of total expenditure, and how the elements have changed in relation to each other.

What do these figures tell you about the changing demands of the welfare state? Write a short report highlighting the major changes and what you think are the reasons for them.

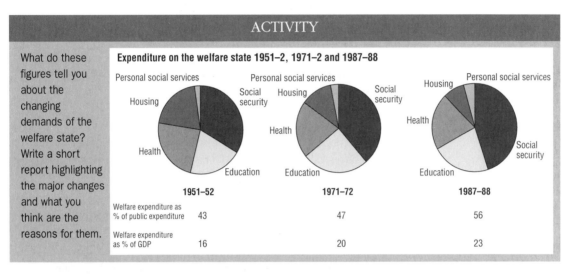

Expenditure on the welfare state 1951–2, 1971–2 and 1987–88

	1951–52	1971–72	1987–88
Welfare expenditure as % of public expenditure	43	47	56
Welfare expenditure as % of GDP	16	20	23

Because the amount of money available, and the ability of health and social care authorities to raise other finance, is directed by government, funding is very sensitive to political direction. Each political party has its own policy for the principles which will underpin the allocation of funds. This has a direct impact on the delivery of services. What do you think is the most likely effect political differences will have on your local services?

One result of the end of full employment has been that the ratio of people in work to those likely to depend on services – people under 16 and over 65 – has fallen. Consequently the amount of taxation required to fund the services has grown and governments have looked for ways to reduce public expenditure.

The social security budget has been the largest spender of funds generated by taxation but health and social services have also taken up a considerable amount.

Changes in technology

New technology has had a profound affect on all areas of the health service. Examples are:

- frozen and chilled food allowing a greater range of meals-on-wheels to be provided
- intensive support care enabling hospitals to save and keep alive acutely ill or injured people
- scanning and diagnostic equipment to detect cancers and other conditions
- improved prostheses using computerised components enabling people to communicate or have near normal mobility
- new drugs to moderate or cure illness or prevent rejection of transplanted organs
- air ambulance service
- transplant surgery
- keyhole surgery.

Our understanding of how the human body works has also advanced, allowing better diagnosis of genetic diseases and improved recovery techniques. Some of this knowledge has saved money (keyhole surgery, improved recovery techniques), but some has added to the cost of medicine. Overall the cost of medical care has grown. New technologies have had consequences for the services:

- The cost means the NHS must make decisions about whether to fund some treatments.
- Although the cost of equipment (e.g. scanners) may be met through fund-raising, the NHS is not always able to meet staff costs.
- A shortage of staff has lead to a lack of beds.
- Keyhole surgery has reduced the cost of some surgery and the length of time required in hospital.
- Savings in time and staff (e.g. new ways of bulk-cooking food).
- Independence and freedom for patients who are able to lead normal lives.

Keyhole revolution in coronary surgery
New techniques could get bypass patients
back to work in a week, not three months

How to mend a broken heart
A tiny tube has revolutionised heart surgery and
is saving thousands of lives. By Glenda Cooper

Health and social care staff have always been faced with issues of privatisation and allocation of scarce resources but these issues are becoming more complex. One of the reasons for this is the high cost of new treatments.

66 *I've worked all my life, always paid my National Insurance and never been ill until this. Now I do call on the NHS they won't pay for the treatment I need. It doesn't seem fair.* **99**

*patient with motor-neurone disease, having been told that his health authority
are not prepared to pay for a new drug treatment*

One ten-year-old boy, who was suffering from a brain clot, was unable to receive a brain scan because the scanner (paid for by £1 million raised by public subscription) only operated between 9 a.m. and 5 p.m., rather than at night when he needed the scan. The hospital was unable to afford the running costs of keeping this high technology machinery available around the clock.

DISCUSSION POINT

Should the NHS be dependent upon public subscription for new technology or is it a demonstration of popular commitment to the NHS? If the public are prepared to make this gift should a condition be that public funds are made available to ensure that it is used to maximum effect?

ACTIVITY

Invite a manager from an NHS trust to talk to your group about how their hospital offers a high-technology area such as keyhole surgery, transplants, kidney dialysis or intensive care. Ask the manager to explain what impact this technology has had on their services. Write a brief report describing the technology concerned and summarise the benefits and the problems which this change has caused for the hospital.

The effect of government policy

Government policy is a broad term and has two facets:

1 Strategic: the overall philosophies which the Government holds and seeks to implement (for example, the value of the market and competition)

2 Tactical: the practical ways in which those broader philosophies are implemented (the structure of the services and the arrangements made for their working).

The key proposals in *Working for Patients* were:

- GPs' practice budgets for large practices who could purchase a range of health care for their patients

- controls on the drugs which doctors could prescribe

- an independent audit of accounts by the Audit Commission

- separation of purchase and provider functions of the NHS, and an internal market relationship between the two sides of the split

- creation of NHS trusts as the providers, with greater freedom to set local pay levels and borrow for capital projects

- changes in the composition of health authorities and NHS trusts with members nominated by the Secretary of State

- consultants' contracts to be more detailed

- tax relief on private medical insurance for elderly people.

This section looks at how government policy affects the structure and funding of health and social care. It first considers the theoretical models from which government policy is derived and the way in which the services are funded through taxation, then explains how policy affects the way in which services are delivered and funded.

Approaches to care

The reforms of the late 1980s and 1990s radically changed the way in which the Government, and the general public, approached the provision of care services.

Central supply

Prior to the introduction of the internal market system the NHS operated a system of central supply, where all purchases were made centrally. Although this gave the NHS considerable power as a purchaser it meant that patients and practitioners were restricted as to choice. The inflexibility involved also meant that specific local needs could not be met quickly.

The market

The NHS

The current structure of the NHS, introduced by the NHS and Community Care Act, was first proposed in a 1989 White Paper called *Working for Patients*. This laid out the Government's intentions for the NHS and, as such, is a clear statement of government policy.

This White Paper introduced the idea of the internal market to the NHS. It is not a pure internal market because competition is encouraged both between NHS providers and the public and private care sectors.

An **internal market** is a competitive system between different parts of the same organisation. It is not open to competition from outside organisations.

The descriptions used for the different players in the market are 'purchasers' and 'providers'. You will find an explanation of the purchaser/provider split in element 5.3.

Social services departments

The proposals for community care in local authority social services departments are contained within another White Paper, *Caring for People*. This proposed that social service departments would introduce the purchaser/provider split to encourage a mixed economy of care. It was introduced into the NHS and Community Care Act.

Mixed economy of care describes an approach to providing social services through public, voluntary and private agencies rather than just through social services departments

Social services departments were required to separate those responsible for assessing and purchasing social care from those providing the services. They were also encouraged to purchase services from the voluntary and private sectors. This fitted very well with compulsory competitive tendering which local authorities were having to adopt in other departments.

This system is not an internal market as it was assumed that, over a period of time, social service departments would divest themselves of all direct services. Section 5.3.2 has examples of how this split is working.

Resourcing through taxation system

❝ *A national insurance scheme means that people in work now pay for people requiring care in the hope that when they need help it will be there.* **❞**

adviser to the Select Committee looking at the funding of residential care, 1996

The NHS

The NHS is funded primarily through general taxation, with contributions from national insurance and charges making up the rest.

The amount of money to be allocated each year is decided by the Treasury, in consultation with the Department of Health, and agreed by the Cabinet. This process is both administrative – the NHS needs to know how much it can spend and how – and political.

Once the annual budget is agreed, it is distributed through the regions to health authorities using a formula based on agreed population criteria and reflecting their budget projections for the next year. Ministers are able to make variations in order to favour particular service areas or redistribution of resources. One example is the way resources have been redirected away from London and the South East.

Controlling expenditure

Each level monitors the planned and actual spending of the level below – the Department of Health monitors the NHS Executive, which monitors the regional offices, which monitor the health authorities, who control their providers by the terms of the contracts.

Value for money

As well as ensuring that accounts are correct, each level is responsible for seeing that money is well used. The Department of Health seeks statistical evidence on how the NHS achieves value for money by:

- performance indicators collated into league tables
- publication of providers' prices
- monitoring doctors' prescribing habits and introducing practice drug budgets.

Redistribution of NHS funds away from London and South East

Historically, the Thames regions covering London have received a greater share of funds. It is argued that London is over-provided with hospital services. In 1991 the Tomlinson Review of London's health services recommended:

- increased expenditure on primary care and community health services
- rationalisation of specialist provision to fewer hospitals
- a reduction of between 2,000 and 7,000 hospital beds by the year 2000.

This would be achieved by the merger or redeployment of three pairs of teaching hospitals and the rationalisation of services in West London. These proposals are opposed by hospital staff, patients and local MPs.

ACTIVITY

Find out the details of your local health authority's annual budget. What are the main budget headings? How much is spent directly on the running costs of the authority, how much is used to purchase services from NHS and how much on independent providers?

Controlling the expenditure

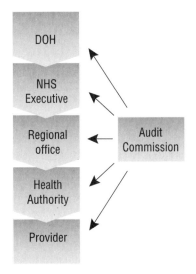

Social services departments

The level of social services expenditure is agreed by elected councillors as part of their function of planning and agreeing the budget for all their services. The amount of money available locally for social care and children's services is directly affected by how local government is funded.

General taxation goes into funding local authorities through the revenue support grant and represents 80% of local authority income. The Government has powers to vary the way that it distributes the revenue support grant, which is a source of disagreement between central and local government.

Also, there are special grants available to local authorities to:
- take on new responsibilities, such as community care arrangements in 1993
- change direction in services, such as the introduction of locally managed schools
- meet the costs of disasters.

Unlike the NHS, local councils have independent sources of income – the council tax – which is set annually and is paid by each household based on banding valuation. Councils cannot charge as much local tax as they might like because they are restricted by:
- government-set limits to the level of council tax
- public opinion expressed through the ballot box at local elections.

In addition to the council tax, paid by residents in an area, commerce and business pay a business rate, the level of which is set by the Government and distributed according to population.

Councils are able to charge for their services. government policy is to encourage local authorities to seek new ways of generating income and this now represents a growing part of local authority income.

ACTIVITY

Local authorities are required to publish information about their annual spending. Obtain from your local council a copy of its information for the last financial year. Identify the different services funded and the breakdown of expenditure across these services. What does this information tell you about the priority it gives to social services and how the budget has been allocated across the children's and social care services?

Joint funding between the NHS and social services

The different funding arrangements between health and social care has always been a problem. Arrangements for joint funding tried to overcome this where both the NHS and social services had a responsibility to provide services. It was usually targeted at services:
- where the patient moved home after hospital discharge
- where long-stay patients were relocated into the community
- where users were no longer seen as needing special healthcare provision.

With the NHS and Community Care Act, social services became the lead authority for people requiring community care, taking over some of the responsibilities of the NHS. Since 1993 health authorities have redrawn their priorities, moving towards a narrower definition of their responsibilities, and services are now more focused on meeting acute needs. Local authorities have taken on the support of people with significant health problems being cared for in their own homes or in residential care.

As a result the Department of Health issued guidance to try to remove discrepancies. Local authorities and health authorities must now collaborate on plans to meet the health and social care needs of their communities with final responsibility for defining criteria for access to health services being the health authority's. The responsibility and funding for everything else is the local authority's.

NHS responsibilities for meeting continuing health needs

This made four key points:

- Under the community care arrangements the majority of people requiring continuous care in a nursing home setting are likely to have these met through social services.
- The NHS has responsibility for patients with complex or multiple health needs who require continuing and specialist medical and nursing provision.
- The remainder may be cared for in a nursing or residential home arranged by themselves or the local authority.
- Where either the health or local authority proposes to change the pattern of service, there must be consultation.

Department of Health Guidance, February 1995

The consequence of this arrangement is that local authorities, who must decide funding for social care in competition with education or housing, must meet a greater responsibility for supporting people in their communities although required to reduce their overall expenditure.

Services available on the NHS

There are details of health services covered by the NHS in section 5.1.1. The main intention of the original NHS – a service universally available and free at the point of delivery – is still largely intact, although there are an increasing number of exceptions.

Most primary health care, delivered through a GP or a health clinic, is free at the point of delivery. There are exceptions to this, such as medicals conducted for insurance purposes. There is a basic charge for each item on a prescription but also a range of exemptions based on age, income or medical condition. Opticians charge for eye tests with exemptions similar to those for prescriptions. Glasses and contact lenses are now available at a widening range of retailers with patients, or customers, being encouraged to shop around.

There are fees for dental treatment – an examination fee plus scaled charges for a range of treatments such as fillings or extractions. Again, there are exemptions on the same basis as prescription charges. For some work the dentist may have to get permission from the health authority, for example, for cosmetic surgery, and other treatments may not be able on the NHS.

66 Having paid into the system for so long, I now can't find an NHS dentist anywhere. It's not a choice of dentist but a choice between private dental care or no dental care. 99

man talking about his search for an NHS dentist after his dentist retired

Dental treatment on the NHS

Most dental treatment is provided by dentists in general practice. Since the foundation of the NHS dentists have had contracts with the NHS to treat NHS patients. They have also had private patients. The contract was based on fees for each item of service. A new contract was introduced in 1991 in which dentists received a capitation fee per patient on their list. As dentists considered that this reduced the amount they received, many have reduced or stopped their NHS work and concentrated on private practice. Consequently, private insurance companies have expanded their involvement in this area.

The new NHS dentists' contract and arrangements with private insurance companies have promoted preventive work rather than the more costly payment for restorative work.

Most hospital treatment is free, although patients may opt to be a consultant's private patient or to pay for a private room. There are some charges, however, such as a basic fee charged to the driver in traffic accidents.

DISCUSSION POINT

Some economists argue that people requiring treatment as a result of smoking or drinking should contribute towards the cost. Given the need for rationing within the health service and the high cost of treatment, what do you think?

Mobility and other aids are also free, provided the patient is prepared to choose from the range available. Payment must be made for additional or specialist equipment. Health authorities have a degree of discretion in some matters. For example, fertility treatment may be free in some areas but only available through private healthcare schemes in others.

Social services

66 We are faced with a stark choice – we either reduce services or impose charges. [We know] charges alienate service users and threaten the existence of social services by replacing state provision with the economics of the market place. They create poverty traps and are costly to administer. 99

director of social services

66 The introduction of means-testing for community care is so shocking and dismaying to elderly clients that many are walking away from care. 99

senior officer with Age Concern England

There are details of local government services in section 5.1.1. A wide range is provided free, such as information and advice, assessment and care planning. For services provided with a degree of compulsion, such as mental health interventions or child protection work, it would be counter-productive to charge.

For example, for some children's services, such as voluntary care, the general practice is not to make charges because the cost of collection is greater than the income generated. Some authorities also argue that charging discourages parents from requesting care for their children.

Local authorities are increasingly introducing changes for all or parts of the community care packages being devised. With the exception of residential care, local authorities have discretion to agree both the criteria for who pays and how much is paid as either a flat-rate or a means-tested charge.

ACTIVITY

Investigate and list five different services provided by the NHS and the local authority. Indicate whether users are required to pay for the services and if so, explain how the level of payment is calculated.

Commons Health Committee report on long-term care

The main findings were:

■ Britain does not face an elderly care crisis

■ long-term care funding is perceived as unfair

■ government plans for partnership insurance are not the answer

■ the private insurance market must be regulated

■ NHS payment of the nursing element of nursing home fees should be considered.

Growth in community care charges

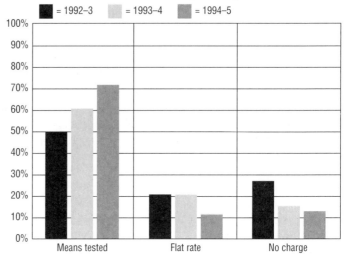

Source: Community Care, 6–12 October 1996, from a survey by the Local Government Anti-poverty Unit

Local authorities are required to ensure that residents pay a contribution towards the cost of residential care. The rules for working out the user's contribution is set out in section 5.1.4.

Payment for residential and nursing care highlights a contrast between the NHS and social care. The Government has suggested that private insurance might be the preferred option for assisting people to pay for residential care. This has been considered by the Commons Health Committee in July 1996, which said that:

❝ *People should receive free nursing care in their old age, whether in an NHS hospital or a private nursing home.* ❞

Private services

Private medicine has continued to exist alongside the NHS. For example BUPA, one of the largest medical insurance companies, was formed in 1947. In social care there has been a strong private residential care sector for many years. What has changed since 1990 has been a government drive to ensure that private health and social care has a larger slice of the market and that new companies can join the sector.

Private healthcare is paid by a combination of the individual's own income and private insurance. The way in which private insurance works can be found in section 5.1.4.

Focus of intervention

Prevention or cure

The assumption behind the Welfare State was that it would both cure and prevent illness and social distress. The NHS would make the population healthy by treating a range of illness and disabilities and, if it did not do so, social care would provide support. In the early days many of the financial mechanisms supported cure rather than prevention.

For example, earlier legislation and approaches focused on treatments or interventions which:

- removed children or mentally ill people from the family or community
- treated rather than prevented dental decay
- concentrated health promotion on mass programmes such as TB or cervical scans rather than general wellbeing
- imprisoned offenders rather than using community-based alternatives.

Technological changes also tended to be focused on diagnosis and cure.

We are now more concerned with the prevention of illness and disability, recognising that a higher cost for health and social care services is paid if measures to prevent illness and accidents are not taken. An early example of a comprehensive health service which focused on prevention is mother and baby clinics, set up in the 1930s for all mothers. The purpose was to ensure the health of future generations.

More recently the Government has sought to encourage prevention through:
- *The Health of the Nation* (see section 6.2.1)
- encouraging GPs' practices to offer a range of preventive services
- emphasising prevention in the Children Act 1989
- community care packages aimed at keeping people in their own homes
- recognising the role of carers.

Focus of responsibility

Individual versus collective
Since the mid-1980s the aim of the Government has been to limit comprehensivness, arguing that it creates a 'nanny state' which stifles individual responsibility and delivers services inefficiently. Therefore it acted to shift the balance of responsibility to individuals rather than the state.

The Children Act 1989

With its emphasis on the need for children to be looked after in their homes wherever possible, the Children Act encourages interventions to prevent family breakdown. Section 17 in particular focuses on strategies for 'children in need', giving social services departments the power to spend money in this way. Unfortunately, growing pressure on local authority finances has meant that most work deals with crisis intervention – child protection investigations, removing children from their families – rather than intervening at an early stage.

Individualism versus collectivism

At the heart of the evolving debate about the future of the welfare state is a conflict between collectivist and individualist values. Taken at their extremes, they mean:

- collectivism – all provision is made by the state with all contributing according to ability and receiving according to need
- individualism – it is no business of the state to interfere in individual choice – people must be free to make their own choices and arrangements.

The NHS is essentially a collectivist model, the state makes arrangements for services and, either by the health district or a fundholding general practice, decisions are made for the patient. By going to private medicine, an individualistic model, the patient makes their own decision about the services to purchase.

The collectivist believes that as well as rights we have obligations to each other and that the rights of the individual must, to a greater or lesser extent, be submerged for the greater good. The individualist regards this as patronising and that allowing individual choice encourages enterprise and freedom.

The argument is essentially about where the balance should be drawn. Feelings about the balance have shifted over time and have been affected by many factors, including government policy, satisfaction with the degree of service being delivered and overall levels of affluence.

DISCUSSION POINT

Where do you think the balance should be drawn? Are there some choices which should always be the province of the individual? Are there matters on which the collective good must always be more important than individual choice?

This shift in the balance of responsibility showed itself through financial aspects such as:

■ introduction of a charge for eye tests and dental check-ups
■ encouragement of private insurance.

The move from the collective to the individual was also reflected in an increased focus on the needs of the service user rather than the services available. *Caring for People* spelt out how the arrangements for providing community care would have the user at their heart.

Another way that the Government encouraged health and social services authorities to focus on the individual was to introduce statements of what a patient or a client could expect, together with performance measurements. The Government requires public authorities to:

■ publish information about their services and what users can expect
■ publish how they meet performance measurements set out by the Government.

The Government has set an example by producing the Patient's Charter. It also publishes league figures showing how health trusts have met certain targets during the year.

DISCUSSION POINT

The Patient's Charter has been distributed widely to encourage people to have higher expectations of their health services. However, some practitioners argue that it has made their jobs harder because patients have begun to make unrealistic demands. For example, GPs say that they now have more night call-outs. The emphasis of the Patients Charter is upon the duties that the service has to its users. Should it also state the limits of those duties and recognise that users may also have obligations?

Category	Guy's and Thomas'	King's College	St George's	National average
Outpatient appointments; seen within 30 mins.	83%	86%	82%	90%
A&E; patients assessed within 5 mins. of arrival	100%	88%	100%	94%
Operations cancelled; parients not admitted within a month of cancellation	16%	80%	88%	8%
Outpatient waiting times; seen within 13 weeks	80%	88%	86%	83%
seen withing 26 weeks	97%	98%	98%	97%
Inpatient waiting times; admitted within 3 months	75%	77%	78%	71%

Everyone is able to call upon the health services when they are ill and many still have full access to social services. What has changed is that after an initial contact, the service user may find that they have to pay for some or all of the service.

How demographic characteristics affect priorities

Section 5.2.1 outlined the demographic aspects of the development of the NHS and community care. This section looks at the way that the NHS and local authorities take this into account when planning health and social care services. Central government bears in mind these characteristics of the population and health when it allocates resources.

At a local level, health authority and social services interpret population characteristics when commissioning and purchasing the care for their communities.

ACTIVITY

Get hold of a copy of the Community Care Plan or the Health Authority's annual plan for your area. List the information it has about the population it services. Summarise what this information tells you about:

■ the age profile

■ the incidence of disease or disability

■ how and why the local position differs from the national position.

Age profile

The largest single category of service users are the elderly. In the case of the NHS over half the beds at any one time are occupied by people over 65, and around 45% of expenditure goes on services for the care and treatment of this age group. A similar proportion of social services expenditure goes on care services for elderly people.

Services for children feature very heavily in the preventive aspects of health and social care. (Element 6.2 looks at health promotion and prevention in more detail.) Maternal health and services are also important. Health authorities use statistical data to plan their services and develop health promotion programmes to improve the health of mothers. Children's services have a high priority with social services under the Children Act.

Incidence of disability

The number of people with a disability or who are likely to become disabled is important for purchasers to know. Apart from degenerative disabilities, most support is likely to be by social care, so social services departments look very carefully at these statistics.

Information comes from a number of sources:
■ surveys under the Chronically Sick and Disabled Persons Act
■ the Census
■ individual care assessment.

The birth notification system

In the UK there is a statutory responsibility for the person (usually the midwife) who delivers a baby to give information about the birth to the Director of Public Health of the district in which the baby resides. This is done to alert the community health services and to provide demographic information which can be used to improve maternity and child health services. The basic information sought is about birth weight and gestation period but districts can ask for additional information, for example, about the ethnic origin of the mother or whether the mother smoked during pregnancy.

ACTIVITY

Obtain either the Community Care plan for your social services department or the annual plan from your health authority. Identify how the statistics about disability and disease are presented in these plans and summarise how these statistics are used to reach decisions about future services.

Incidence of disease

As *The Health of the Nation* makes clear, it is essential to plot diseases such as TB, HIV/AIDS, meningitis and leukaemia in order to plan future health needs. Planning on the basis of past health trends means that new developments, such as an unexpected epidemic, can severely strain resources.

Geographical location

Geographical location is significant. Inner-city areas have a higher incidence of mental illness, accidents and environmental illness such as asthma. At the other extreme, services in rural areas tend to be inadequate.

66 *Finding ways to get services to people in rural areas is a major challenge: scattered populations, poor public transport and a high proportion of people on low incomes mean that services are inappropriately based in one location and are inaccessible to the people they are designed for.* 99

operational manager for children's services in a Welsh authority

Services for rural communities are spread causing service users to travel to hospitals or day centres. Informal care can be stretched because there are fewer people to provide support, particularly in a commuter village or where a high proportion of residents are elderly.

DISCUSSION POINT

The balance of priority between urban and rural areas has varied over time depending on political considerations. What do you think are the factors which governments should take into account when seeking to meet the needs of rural communities?

The influence of the independent sector

The independent sector

The independent sector's involvement in the health and wellbeing of individuals and communities predates state health and social care services. The concept that the state would take responsibility for services implied that voluntary and private organisations would have a reduced role in providing services. In practice this did not happen. The voluntary sector diversified its activities to find new activities to complement and supplement the state services while the private sector worked alongside Government to offer health care.

By the time the current structure was established, the independent sector was in a strong position to be an integral part of its arrangements.

Voluntary organisations

Voluntary organisations are a collective response to meeting needs. They do not make profits, but put surplus funds back into the activities of the group.

The majority of voluntary organisations providing local health and social care services are registered charities having legal security to fundraise, employ staff and buy property, with some tax benefits. Their charitable status allows them to receive money from statutory authorities and make contracts for services or facilities. There is information about how they are involved in providing services in section 5.1.1

The private sector

The private sector includes professionals in private practice, sole owner companies, and large national and multinational organisations. Owners and shareholders take profits from the activities of the company. Private insurance companies increasingly contribute to funding healthcare costs.

Element 5.1 looks at their involvement in providing health and social care services. Section 5.1.4 covers their role in the funding of the health service.

Pressure groups

Both the private and voluntary sectors seek to influence government and potential government policies. In health and social care the focus of this lobbying is as likely to be about better services for a specific patient or client group as for the organisation's own health and financial benefit.

Private-sector pressure groups

Private-sector pressure group activity is usually through:

- interest groups such as the Independent Hospital Association or the United Kingdom Home Care Association, which seek to represent the views of their membership
- lobby groups representing a single large company or group of commercial companies such as drug manufacturers

> ### DISCUSSION POINT
>
> The Government, keen to remove anti-competitive restrictions and to encourage new providers, has suggested lifting some of the regulations for registering residential homes. Most organisations involved in residential care are unhappy at this, believing regulation protects their residents. How important do you think it is that health and social care organisations compete with each other? Or is service users' protection more important?

- professional associations which register their members to practice, e.g. the British Medical Association and the Royal College of Nursing.

Voluntary organisations

There is a long tradition within the voluntary sector of campaigning for improvements to services. Dr Barnardo was not the only Victorian who used his good work with children to press Parliament to pass laws to protect children.

Voluntary organisations continue to campaign for many causes, both nationally and locally. The role of some is to bring voluntary organisations together to promote and represent the sector. The National Council for Voluntary Organisations does this at a national level. In many districts, councils for voluntary service fulfil a similar function.

Examples are:
- self-help groups where the members are seeking a change in legislation or resources to meet their needs
- promoting changes in attitudes on how best to provide services
- promoting the interests of the Third World.

If the voluntary organisation is a registered charity, the extent to which they can campaign is carefully monitored by the Charity Commission which ensures that any campaign falls within the charity's main purpose and does not occupy too high a percentage of its activities.

The Commission on the Future of the Voluntary Sector

The report of this enquiry, published in 1996, is a robust defence of the independence and diversity of the UK voluntary sector. It emphasises that voluntary organisations should continue to have a campaigning role even when providing services through contracts with statutory services. It encourages charities to form partnerships with statutory agencies but not to forget that users should be part of the partnership. It also offers a new definition of charity – benefit to the community – which would widen eligibility.

Charitable donations

Section 5.1.4 explains that voluntary and charitable organisations involved in providing health and social care services rely heavily on funding from the statutory sector. However, they do have access to other funding.

Older charities have been founded by endowments and legacies or the sale of land. New charities have recently been established specifically to raise monies for particular causes. Examples are:
- Comic Relief, which makes grants to organisations working in the third world and young people and people with disabilities in the UK

DR BARNARDO

In 1995 Barnardos, a leading charity working with children founded in 1866, mounted an exhibition of photographs of orphan children taken into their homes. They were intended by Dr Barnardo to shock middle-class Victorians into making donations to the charity and press government to improve conditions for children of the poor.

Barnardos still provides care and support for children, but no longer just offer residential care. They:

- support families to stay together
- provide safe houses for children who have run away from home
- support young people caring for their parents
- work with children with HIV.

■ hospital leagues of friends, whose purpose is to fund extras for patients or residents.

DISCUSSION POINT

Should charitable fundraising be used to raise money for statutory services? What might be the effect of this on other charities?

Charitable money is raised through the following means:
■ legacies and endowments
■ covenants (which have tax relief)
■ schemes for regular payment from salary (which also have tax relief)
■ local lotteries, raffles or street collections
■ radio and television appeals
■ advertising in the press.

Fundraising through lotteries, raffles and street collections must be licensed by the local authority. The Charity Commission also monitors fundraising activity and investigates any complaints.

Voluntary organisations can also raise money through trading activities. Many of those working overseas have charity shops or mail order trading. In many cases this activity promotes fair trade in crafts and goods. This trading activity is excluded from charitable relief of tax and is usually undertaken by a separate company.

Key questions

1 List the six Acts which founded the welfare state.
2 What is a universal service?
3 List three major changes in the health of the population since 1946?.
4 In which year was the Local Authority Social Services Act passed?
5 List the three categories of priority need for housing.
6 Give three ways in which the NHS and Community Care Act 1990 changed health and social care.
7 Give four examples of technological change in health care.
8 Explain the purchaser-provider split.
9 What is meant by the internal market?
10 Name three NHS services for which the patient pays a fee.
11 Give three ways in which users pay for residential care.
12 How does the Children Act 1989 encourage prevention?
13 What is meant by individualism?
14 Which age group occupies more than half NHS beds?
15 Describe five ways in which charities raise their money.

Assignment

Collect information about the structure of health and social care in your country since 1946. Write a report which:

■ gives a brief account of the structure of health and social care set-up following Beveridge
■ explains how these services changed from 1990
■ identifies and describes in detail three effects of recent government policy on the structure and funding
■ gives three examples of how demographic characteristics of your area have effected health and social care policies
■ explains the role of the independent sector and how it has influenced the provision of health and social care through pressure group and fundraising.

> **66** *The purchaser/provider relationship cannot simply be restricted to formal negotiations . . . It has to be constant and ongoing. Both must realise that it is not a contest about who wins or loses in the contracting negotiation process. A dialogue needs to be developed in which purchasers and providers jointly work to achieve their objectives.* **99**
>
> Dr Brian Mawhinney, then Minister of Health, to Royal College of Physicians in 1993

> **66** *[We] recognise many people's concern about the introduction of apparently alien commercial concepts into services whose prime function is to care for people.* **99**
>
> The Audit Commission's report, Community Care: Managing the Cascade of Change

> **66** *I think contracts for services will give users more choice as we build up a more varied network of providers from the voluntary and private sector.* **99**
>
> head of contracting in a social services department

> **66** *Contracts sound like a very powerful, definite tool for ensuring certain work is delivered. In reality it is a complex negotiation which requires health authorities to listen to service providers, and vice versa. Often, for one service to be added, something else has to be sacrificed due to the lack of significant amounts of new money.* **99**
>
> assistant director (health promotion), local health authority

> **66** *We don't have much muscle at the moment where getting support for the psychological services is concerned. We are doing research and building networks to improve this. I am working with various agencies to get recognition of the need for a professional body and for adequate skills and training. If you don't have much training, how do you deal with a situation where someone asks the question: 'How do I tell my five year old that I'm dying?'* **99**
>
> head of medical counselling and family services

> **66** *The health authority decides what services it is going to buy. If they decide not to buy a service, the trust can't run it. So the purchasers are very powerful and their decisions can and often do result in alterations and reductions to services.* **99**
>
> child protection adviser

ELEMENT **5.3**

Care planning and provision

This element looks at the split between the commissioning and purchasing of services and facilities and their delivery in health and social care. This division is described and the relationship between the two sides explained, followed by a closer look at how it works across the planning and delivery of services. The final section looks at the impact of the split on health and social care agencies.

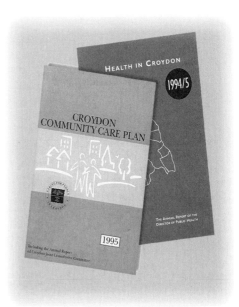

The structure of health and social care

New structure of the NHS (England)
From April 1 1996

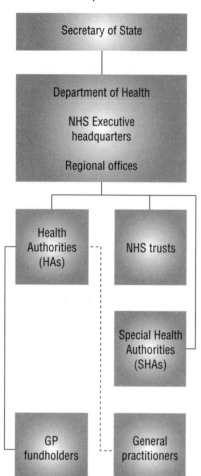

The structure of the NHS (England)

The NHS and Community Care Act 1990 introduced a new structure which changed the nature of the relationship between the centre and delivery at a local level:

- The NHS from the Department of Health downwards was restructured.
- The NHS Executive was set up to manage the NHS.
- A new relationship between different parts of the NHS was established – the purchaser/provider split.
- The role of general managers was enhanced.
- Performance measurements were introduced.

The National Health Service Executive was established to:

- ensure good management throughout the NHS
- monitor performance of the health authorities
- oversee the implementation of the NHS and Community Care Act.

Its membership comprises a chief executive and six directors responsible for different aspects of the work.

Other goals include:

- promoting integration across primary and secondary care
- identifying services which the NHS needs to provide
- managing the human resources
- undertaking research.

DISCUSSION POINT

The supporters of decentralisation argue that it enables the NHS to be more responsive to local conditions. Its opponents argue that centralisation is the best way to ensure that there is an equality of service throughout the country. What do you think?

Scotland

Although the NHS and Community Care Act applied to the whole of the United Kingdom, Part II refers particularly to Scotland.

The Secretary of State for Scotland is accountable to Parliament for the Scottish Health Service, the service being overseen by the Scottish Home and Health Department based within the Scottish Office. The SHHD also has responsibility for police services, criminal justice and other protection services.

Wales

As the laws of Wales are almost the same as England's the arrangements for health and social care are very similar. The provisions of the NHS and Community Care apply to Wales with responsibility for the health services resting with the Welsh Office.

Northern Ireland

In Northern Ireland health and social services are integrated and the responsibility of four Health and Social Services Boards which are nominated by, and accountable to, the Secretary of State for Northern Ireland. This arrangement has reduced the need for joint planning and joint financing arrangements as these already exist internally in the organisation.

Neither the NHS and Community Care Act nor the Children Act yet apply to Northern Ireland, although consultations have taken place with the intention of it applying within the province's particular local requirements.

Social services departments

English local authorities are responsible for social care services, and decisions about which services will be provided are the responsibility of elected councillors under powers from Parliament. This is described in section 5.1.1. Central government direction of local government social care services comes through the Department of the Environment, but with professional advice from the Department of Health. The means of ensuring local authorities keep in line with government policies are:

- legislation over their duties and powers and how they must use them
- funding from taxation with restrictions on how local authorities can raise local taxes
- guidance and circulars.

With these restrictions many local councils are finding it difficult to afford the quality of services promoted by the spirit of the children and community care legislation.

Scotland and Wales

The arrangements for social services in Scotland and Wales are very similar to England and are overseen by the Scottish and Welsh Offices respectively. The legislation for the services in Scotland is separate because of the different legal system there. Social work departments (the Scottish equivalent of social services departments) include probation and aftercare services. Both Scottish and Welsh unitary councils, created in 1995, will provide social services and housing when they are fully implemented.

Northern Ireland

As already explained above, health and social services are integrated into a Board in Northern Ireland. Housing is provided centrally in Northern Ireland.

The purchaser/provider split

Element 5.2 explains how *Working with Patients* and *Caring for People* outlined a major change in the way that statutory authorities provide health and social services, as set out in the NHS and Community Care Act 1990.

ACTIVITY

If you live in Scotland, Wales or Northern Ireland investigate how the NHS is organised in your country and write a brief account.

ACTIVITY

If you live in a reorganised local authority area, collect information about the new council and the services it will be offering. Write a brief description of the changes and explain how these changes might affect those who use the services.

A **free market** is one in which there are no restrictions on who may purchase or supply. Government intervention is limited to defining the parameters of the market place rather than who can be a player.

The philosophy behind the purchaser/provider split is that it:

- enables services to be focused on the needs of service users
- frees resources from being service-led to being driven by, and therefore responsive to, people's needs
- promotes the values of care (you will find these in Unit 1)
- devolves responsibility to managers or practitioners who are closer to the user.

Particularly significant is the separation of those who buy services (purchasers) from those who sell (providers).

This is not a free market because health and social care cannot be treated as a commodity, such as food or insurance, where the purchaser is free to choose a supplier without constraint. On the contrary, the Secretary of State has powers to create and dissolve trusts and GP fundholders, set healthcare priorities and limit financial boundaries. In addition, consumer protection laws and other legal restrictions apply. For health services, the Department of Health controls the prices which can be set by providers, while health purchasers have clear cost efficiency targets.

The impact of restructuring on the health side has been a devolution of financial responsibility to health authorities and GP fundholders, with the management of services going to trusts. Alongside has been a tightening of control by the National Health Service Executive and the Department of Health.

The main effect for local authorities has been the growth of partnerships with both existing voluntary and private organisations and new providers moving into the services.

The roles

The changes have created three new roles:

- commissioning
- purchasing
- providing.

The commissioning role

A commissioning organisation has the role of defining what services are required for their geographical or service area and then authorises itself, or another organisation, to provide these services, facilities or goods. The commissioning role is usually undertaken alongside that of purchasing.

Health authorities, social services departments, housing authorities and other agencies have a responsibility to:

- assess needs
- determine a strategy to meet those needs
- arrange for services to be purchased to meet them.

There are a few health authorities who have special responsibilities, such as secure hospitals for the criminally mentally disordered or the blood transfusion service.

ACTIVITY

Contact your local health authority and ask for information about their role in commissioning health services for your area. Ask specifically for information about what they have identified as the health needs of your community. Summarise the services that they have agreed need to be purchased.

The purchasing role

Purchasing organisations are those which have a responsibility to buy, through contracts and other formal arrangements, the services, facilities and goods which are required for patients and other service users.

The responsibility for purchasing can be undertaken by a separate organisation or through a separate unit within an organisation also providing care. Increasingly, two or more authorities work together to jointly purchase a service, thus sharing the administrative costs of purchasing.

Purchasing applies to contracts for a whole service or number of places or beds (blocks of care), or to an arrangement for an individual health or social care user (spot contract). Organisations which purchase are:

■ health authorities
■ GP fundholding practices
■ social services departments.

The way that services and facilities are purchased is firmly regulated by the Department of Health and the Department of the Environment. The process for doing so is explained in section 5.3.2.

GP fundholding

The NHS and Community Care Act set up opportunities for GP practices to become purchasers through the GP fundholding scheme. The government sought through this to make health authorities and trusts more responsive to local needs. The scheme was also intended to enable GPs to refer patients to the hospital of their choice.

> **GP fundholding**
>
> Larger GP practices are able to hold and manage a budget so that they can buy:
>
> ■ hospital in-patient, day care, out-patient and diagnostic services for their patients.
> ■ community services, health visiting and counselling
>
> Their budget covers the costs of prescriptions and employment of staff. There is a limit of £5,000 on the total a practice can spend on any one episode of care for a particular patient.
>
> The scheme began in 1991 with about seven per cent of the population covered by fundholding practices. By 1993 they covered over 25% of the population.

The provider role

The individuals, groups or organisations supplying health and social services to service users and patients are called providers. The majority of these services are supplied through a contract or formal agreement with a purchasing organisation but also includes various services provided by community groups or informal care. Element 5.1 looks at the providing organisations.

So far as social care and child care services are concerned, the social services department is both a purchaser and a provider but there must be a clear separation of the two roles in the way that the department and budget is organised.

How these roles have been implemented in statutory health and social care organisations

The NHS

As explained in element 5.2, the 1990 reforms introduced a new economic environment to the NHS by making more explicit the ideas of the internal market and managed competition. It did so by a deliberate separation between different health service organisations.

By 1993 when the purchaser/provider split came into effect, there were 54 hospital and community service organisations ready to be awarded NHS trust status. By 1994, virtually all district health-managed services had become trusts, separated from health authorities.

Initially, the separation was less clear when related to the primary health care overseen by the Family Health Services Authorities. The FHSAs' work included:

- regulating the agency contracts with doctors
- regulating the agency contracts with dentists
- regulating the agency contracts with opticians
- purchasing other primary health services.

From April 1995, the FHSAs have been merged with the district health authorities to become health authorities, which now have this dual role.

GPs not within fundholding practices have the task of identifying the services required by their patients and sending them to one of the providers contracted by their health authority.

NHS hospital and community services trusts have negotiated contracts with health authorities and with GP fundholders for some primary and all secondary and tertiary health services.

Local government

The purchaser/provider split has been introduced into social services in a different way. The new arrangements brought together a number of strands:

- the introduction of compulsory competitive tendering for a wide range of local government services under the direction of the Department of the Environment

- a direction that local authorities should ensure that the purchase of social care is separated from the provision of care within their own organisations
- the promotion of the private and voluntary sectors through a mixed economy of care
- inspection which is separate from the management of the purchasing or delivery of services.

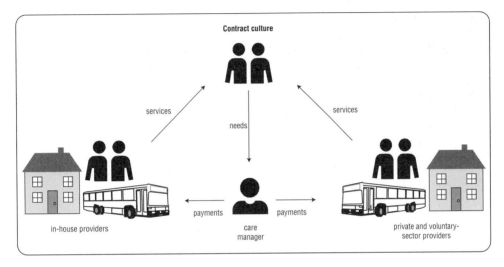

The split between purchasing and providing in local government takes two forms:

- an organisational arrangement which divides the staff within the department into those who buy services and those who deliver in-house services
- an individual arrangement, which enables a care manager or social worker to purchase a package of care for a service user.

As well as making sure that the purchasing side of the department is separated from the in-house services, the department has an inspection unit which is responsible for ensuring that providers comply with all statutory registration and inspection requirements additional to any contract specifications.

ACTIVITY

Write to your local social services department and ask for information about how it has organised the purchaser-provider split and inspection. This will be described in a Social Services Committee report or in the local Community Care Plan. The department may have an organisation chart which sets out its structure. Write a brief report on how it has made the split for both its community care services and its childcare. Explain how the inspection unit fits into this.

Section 5.3.2

The role of purchasers in meeting the needs of the population

Stages in the commissioning cycle

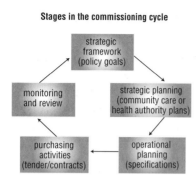

This section examines in greater detail the process for purchasing services. It introduces the Community Care Plan or Health Authority Plan which describes the needs of the area served and explains how the commissioning organisation proposes to meet those needs. It explains about the tendering system through which services are offered out to contract. It looks at service specifications, the types of contracts which can be agreed, and how they are monitored and evaluated.

The purchasing process

Section 5.3.1 describes the roles of commissioning and purchasing. It explains that some health and social care authorities have the responsibility of defining the needs of their communities, planning to meet those needs and then purchasing from a wide range of providers.

The principal organisations undertaking purchasing are health authorities, GP fundholders and local social services departments. To 'buy' the best services for their communities or individual patients and clients, they are expected to use a clear process which is designed to:

- identify and assess the health and social care needs of the population
- plan how to meet these needs
- encourage and stimulate a range of providers
- assess the ability of providers to deliver
- draw up and negotiate contracts for services
- monitor and evaluate those services against contracts.

Purchasers are expected to work throughout with other organisations, such as:

- users, carers and organisations which represent them
- other health and social care commissioners and providers
- other central and local government agencies, such as social security, housing authorities or environmental, health and safety organisations
- actual and potential providers.

The diagram shows the stages in the process and the involvement of users, carers and providers.

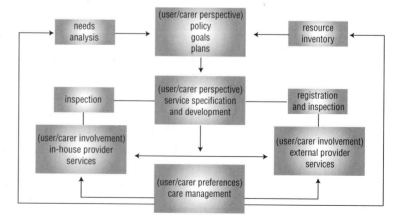

Assessing the health and social care needs of the population

The starting point for the new market approach in health and social care is the assessment of the needs of the community. This determines the decisions the health authority or social services makes about purchasing. In the case of health districts, need is defined by the NHS Executive as 'the ability to benefit from health care'. Social services are expected to define need in terms of their population and socioeconomic conditions.

Each health authority has a duty to collect data about the health of the area's population and to put together an assessment of the health needs of its population. The health authority relates the data to the priority areas in *The Health of the Nation*, and to services existing within the community and then makes recommendations on how those needs can be met. There is more about *The Health of the Nation* in element 6.2.

Although the commissioning authority is responsible for assessing needs, other organisations have a role in providing the information which goes into that assessment. For example, GPs' practices are responsible for providing information on the needs of their patients and their communities. Users and carers can help build up a picture of local needs and the options for choices which they would like to have. Community health councils and voluntary groups make an important contribution by providing information about the adequacy of existing services and the effectiveness of the delivery systems.

Community health councils were set up after the reorganisation of the NHS in 1974. Their broad task is to represent the views of local health service users.

Section 46 of the NHS and Community Care Act requires local authorities to prepare and publish plans for the provision of community care services. They are expected to consult with:
- district health authorities
- housing authorities
- voluntary housing associations
- voluntary organisations representing service users
- provider organisations
- others as directed by the Secretary of State.

Guidance from the DoH sets out the scope and content of the Community Plans as:
- the local authority's strategic objectives for meeting the needs of their population and the time frame
- targets for expected changes in the level and patterns of service
- desired outcomes for service users and carers
- assessment of care needs of the community
- the client groups and types of services which they intend to arrange
- the steps being taken to ensure quality.

An example of a community care plan, and a public health report on the assessment of health needs produced by a health authority

Local authorities have a duty to collect data about their area. The data include:
- age distribution
- numbers of people with disabilities and mental health problems
- the social and environmental make-up of the area
- minority ethnic groups
- numbers of homeless or transient people.

297

Local authorities are also expected to:

- show in their plan how they will increase user choice and how they intend to consult with other interested organisations
- consider the resource implications, both financial and human, and how they will improve cost effectiveness
- plan their personnel and training strategy for meeting both short- and long-term developments.

Planning how to meet health and social care needs

The purpose of the Community Care Plan and the annual health service plan is to enable the health and social care purchasers to plan the details of services required and identify the funding for required services.

NHS organisations have devised and updated plans for their patients since 1948. The 1990 Act strengthened the need for a strategic direction to planning, requiring authorities to set out the desired goals and how to meet them. It is the responsibility of the health authorities to prepare this.

NHS trusts, as providers, will be making their plans for how they will respond to the demands identified by the health authorities.

In the same way, the local authority's Community Care Plan sets out the plans for the year. These have several features:

- proposals about changes to levels of service
- proposals for changing existing services or introducing new ones
- funding available for the services.

The Community Care Plan is then used by service planners and managers for more detailed planning of the services and for contracts.

Stimulating service provision where it is missing

66 *In areas where there is little existing choice in service provision, or where a need has been identified . . . SSDs should consider ways of encouraging them. They should develop strategies which will enable them to provide appropriate information and a supportive climate in order to encourage and facilitate the creation of new services by private and voluntary providers.* 99

Department of Health, Community care in the next decade and beyond

66 *We have kept an eye on the market place and tried to identify providers able to meet unmet needs. An example is the opening of a Gujarati vegetarian restaurant in the borough with whom we have negotiated to provide mobile meals for Asian elders.* 99

director of social services

The concept of the enabling authority or enabling role is central to the reform of the NHS and community care. It is particularly relevant at this point, as purchasers seek to identify providers for their services. A governmental policy

---

ACTIVITY

Contact your local health authority and ask for a copy of its annual service plan. List details of where they are proposing to change or initiate a new service. Briefly describe the new services and the steps they have said that they intend to take to implement them.

direction in favour of involving the independent sector means that purchasers are expected to take steps to find providers outside their own organisation.

The process of putting specific pieces of work or services out to tender is also being used by voluntary agencies.

Included in local authorities' strategy to encourage the mixed economy of care are:
- using relevant information about the range of providers which could supply services to their area
- advertising for providers for specific or all services.

Authorities have procedures for how they will select potential providers. Depending on the services required, or existing working arrangements, selection is done by:
- open tendering
- putting together a list of potential providers from which to select
- direct negotiation with an existing provider
- setting up new organisations.

Where services have been put out to tender, council staff in the service concerned are themselves able to tender. In this case there are clear procedures for ensuring that the staff drawing up the specifications and selecting the provider are separated from those delivering the service. The council service staff have to meet the same criteria as external organisations.

Whichever method is used, it is important that the authority demonstrates that they are not closing the door to competition, that choice is being offered to users and they are receiving value for money.

Assessing service providers' ability to deliver services

66 *Tendering for meals-on-wheels is not the same as collecting rubbish from the front door; staff hold keys to some of these front doors. It means that we have to make sure that the provider organisation does not go bust or is unsatisfactory. Elderly people will have to be able to trust the private contractor with their front door keys.* 99

social services contact manager

It is very important in health and social care that the provider is able to deliver the services in a manner which satisfies the user, the purchaser and the tax-payer.

The primary way that purchasers ensure the provider will supply what is required is through:
- clear descriptions of the service required – the specifications
- proper procedures for vetting potential providers
- performance measurements, quality standards and feedback for users
- proper arrangements for working with the provider, including financial audit
- independent inspection.

DISCUSSION POINT

It is claimed that the mixed economy system gives an advantage to larger organisations which are better able to meet the specifications. What procedures do you think are more likely to favour small local organisations?

Contracting out through competitive tendering

A local authority took a decision in 1993 to contract out a number of its social services including meals-on-wheels, day centres and residential homes for elderly people.

The process began with a review of services by an external consultant. The department then drafted specifications for each service which outlined:

- the care practice required
- the legal requirements
- staffing levels
- quality standards
- monitoring.

More detailed service specifications were agreed by the social services committee in July 1993 when it was agreed that the contracts would run for three years. The department then:

- asked private and voluntary organisations if they were interested in running any of the services
- placed advertisements for potential contractors with a date for bids to be received
- made decisions on the basis of the tenders received
- allocated a contracts manager to each service provider to monitor the service.

Having received an application to tender, a purchaser examines it to ensure that it matches with the detailed specifications. Before a provider is awarded a contract, the purchaser needs to check the professional, technical and financial standing of the provider.

In doing this they will be able to draw on:

- their existing knowledge of the provider, including evaluation of any previous work with the purchaser
- references from other purchasers
- advice from specialists within their own organisation.

Contracting with service providers

Agreements reached between the purchaser and the provider are called contracts and are based around the specifications already described.

Within the NHS, a contract is not seen as a legal document but as 'an opportunity to discuss and agree how improvements to patient care can be secured and over what time'. This means that any disputes are dealt with internally and are not subject to court intervention in the event of disagreements.

The key purpose of NHS contracts is to manage the cost, quantity and quality of services. As such they could more accurately be described as service agreements.

Social services contracts cover a full range of agreements from:

- simple written agreements with carers, neighbours or local shops to provide services
- agreements with voluntary groups to provide community support
- partnership arrangements with independent organisations
- tightly specified contracts as a result of tendering.

The new community care arrangements have introduced a more formal approach to many partnership arrangements at group or service level. The examples show agreements with external organisations. Similar written agreements are used to define the relationship within the social services department between the purchaser and the service provider. This is likely to be recorded through a service level agreement.

Service level agreements are written expressions setting out who does what and how. The agreement can be reached between the purchaser or funder and the provider, perhaps a voluntary organisation. They can also be the written agreement between one section of an organisation and another. SLAs, unlike a contract, are not legally binding.

Monitoring and evaluating services against contract

Once the provider has been awarded the contract, the purchaser is responsible for monitoring how it delivers the service.

> **Evaluation** involves measurement of quantities, assessment of qualities, and judgement on performance standards.

During the period of the contract, the purchaser works with the provider and others to collect information about the quality of the service, whether it has met the objectives of the contract and whether it has been value for money. This evaluation contributes to the planning of future developments and is also used when making decisions about who will provide the service in the next contract.

In addition to monitoring and evaluating specific contracts, health authorities and social services departments are responsible for regulating and inspecting health and social care services in order to ensure that they meet legal and quality standards. This activity fits into a quality assurance system.

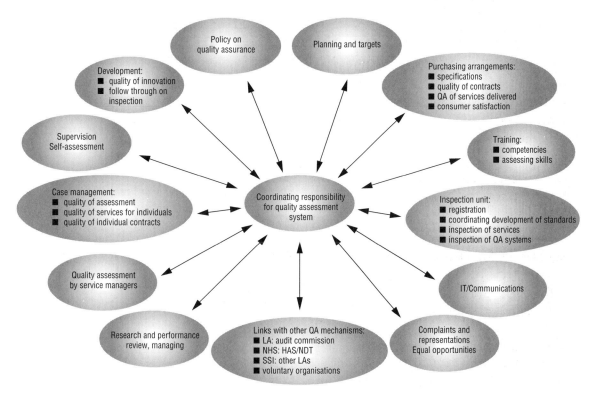

The NHS and Community Care Act required social services departments to put in place inspection units to:
- evaluate the quality of care provided and the quality of life experienced by users
- ensure that a consistent approach is taken to the inspection of public, private and voluntary provision
- respond to demands and opportunities for quality control created by the growth in contracted out services
- undertake their duties even-handedly, efficiently and cost-effectively.

Single and multi-agency purchasers

Most of the agencies which purchase services or packages of care work on their own.

But there are occasions when there is joint purchasing of services. For example, social services departments and health authorities work together to purchase services where the user's needs are for both health and social care. This is often the case for mental health teams or centres.

Joint commissioning offers social services, health and other authorities, such as housing, the opportunity to come together to achieve more effective service delivery. The benefits of joint commissioning are that it:

- can deliver services in a seamless manner from the user or carer perspective
- ensures that the response is based on the needs of the individual not the service of the particular organisation contacted by the user or their carer
- avoids arguments about who is responsible for meeting needs
- enables purchasers to plan and purchase services for their communities unhindered by different boundaries
- enables all the authorities to plan more effectively to meet future needs
- maximises value for money by coordinating purchasing power and securing services which complement each other.

Purchasers for individuals

66 The separation of the purchaser and provider roles is shorthand for the distinction between two aspects of work: the assessment of the individual's need together with the arrangement and purchase of services to meet them. A major advantage of this separation is that it clarifies expectations, gives the assessor the opportunity to consider what the service user really needs, and enables selection to be made from a range of resources whether in-house, voluntary or private. This in turn extends the choice of service. 99

senior officer in a social services department

Most purchasing work is aimed at groups specified by age, group or type of service but it is possible for purchasing organisations to use a contract to meet a specific individual's need.

The thinking behind the new community care arrangements was for care managers to match a package of care to the client's assessed needs. Section 6.1.1 outlines the process for producing these packages.

Purchasers for communities

The community plan gives the blueprint for services for communities. Both health and social services authorities purchase to meet the community needs.

The changes caused by purchasing and providing

This section looks at some of the changes which health and social care agencies have had to make to respond to restructuring and the market approach. Implementation has brought about other changes – some foreseen but others unexpected.

The impact has been felt by practitioners who have become purchasers and by those who are directly involved in providing services. It has also had consequences for the voluntary and private organisations who have more formal contact and relationships with the statutory authority.

The reforms remain controversial but it is already possible to see some balancing consequences. For example, they have:

- enabled more effective control of allocation and management of budgets, although the market has meant new managerial and administrative expenditure in order to keep the purchaser and the provider separate
- devolved responsibility to practitioners directly working with the user, though transferring decision-making about resources from practitioners to managers
- offered stability and opportunities through contacts to organisations, though bringing uncertainty to those employed in services put out to tender
- increased the participation of independent organisations, but has not promoted smaller or less formal community groups
- improved systems for monitoring and evaluating quality, but, where the specifications are poorly drawn, has decreased flexibility
- focused services on the needs of the user, but, through concentrating on block contracts, has not offered as tailored a service as hoped.

Structures

Section 5.3.1 describes the structure of the NHS. This is still evolving as the Government seeks to simplify the structures.

Local government has changed its structures to introduce competitive tendering, which, in social services departments, focuses round the purchaser-provider split. Further changes are being made to slim down local authorities to reflect changed powers, priorities and services moving to outside contractors. These changes have been accelerated where councils have been reorganised to become unitary authorities. These new structures can:

- bring social services and another service, such as housing, together
- reorganise services for a clearer focus on a user group or type of service
- reduce the levels of management and devolve decision-making closer to the client
- reduce central functions such as policy development or training.

Independent organisations have also been reorganised to respond to the new opportunities. Some national voluntary organisations have contacted social services departments to negotiate contacts for blocks of service. They have been able to offer specialist knowledge and expertise with working with particular user groups. Taking on contracts in a number of districts has created structures which are similar to those of the statutory authorities.

Accountability

Organisations and individuals are accountable for their decisions and actions. Section 5.2.2 looks at how each level of the NHS is responsible to the next level and accountable to Parliament. The Audit Commission and the Health Advisory Service are the other national mechanisms for checking on the respective standards of financial management and quality of care being provided by individual hospital services.

Another aspect of accountability within the health service has been the changed balance of responsibility between the practitioner and the manager. Consultants, in particular, retain clinical responsibility for their patients in ensuring that their health needs are being met. However, decisions about which services will be available and the criteria for offering those services, are increasingly the responsibility of trust or unit managers.

Accountability has a personal dimension. Practitioners are responsible for their decisions about their patients and clients. The purchaser/provider split has strengthened the personal accountability of managers and responsibility of practitioners.

Contracts

66 *Cost is not about accountants running the health service but making sure the service is being run well for the users. It must be possible to develop contracts which take into account softer areas in both health and social care. We have a responsibility to work within the system and turn it to the user's benefit. We have to be pragmatic and realistic about what we can achieve.* 99

general manager for an NHS trust

66 *Before the Community Care Act, we worked to local authority standards of registration. If one council accepted our fees that price became the norm. Now every single local authority wants to negotiate their own price. If we have service users from Scotland to Cornwall, every authority would like to use their own contract. We are certainly looking at a large number of separate contracts and they bear little resemblance to each other.* 99

director of care for a national voluntary organisation providing residential and domiciliary care services for people with disabilities

66 *We have no vested interest in who provides the services. Voluntary organisations have an important role to play in care but they have to manage properly.* 99

senior quality manager in a health authority

Contract terms

In section 5.3.2 there is a description of contracts and what is included in them. Although there had been formal agreements between local authorities

Changed relationship with the voluntary sector

Contracts or service level agreements can give a provider security for three or more years. Some voluntary organisations are looking carefully at the consequences of entering into such a contract or agreement:

- Will it restrict their freedom to do other work or challenge the health or social care purchaser in other areas?

- Does the agreement fit in with the aims and objectives of the organisation?

- What happens if the relationship between the funder and provider sours?

and voluntary and private organisations before the NHS and Community Care Act, these were not as formal and specific as they are now. Local authorities have therefore developed their own contracts, which in some cases has caused problems for providers.

The first contracts tended to be inflexible but, with experience, authorities and their providers have moved towards contracts based on negotiation. Apart from providers working with a different contract for a number of authorities, other problems have been that the contracts have been inappropriate, such as:

- similar contracts to those for road cleaning or repairs – leaving out specific care aspects

- expecting the provider to disclose commercial matters unrelated to the service being provided

- allowing the purchaser to unilaterally terminate the contract at any time

- giving no room to negotiate details of the service or the terms

- measuring value through price rather than quality.

In-house providers

The discussion about stimulating providers in section 5.3.2 concentrates on external providers. Purchasers also look within their own organisation. Independent organisations tend to feel that in-house providers have advantages, but the in-house providers view the purchaser/provider split with apprehension. The Government expects authorities to view their own services as being in competition with current and potential providers.

In some ways in-house providers do not have many advantages over external providers because they:

- have to depend on the council's annual budget cycle for their funding base

- cannot borrow capital from financial institutions

- are locked into national pay and conditions of service, so they can be undercut by the external provider

- have to carry overhead costs resulting from council central services.

User and carer involvement

The NHS and local authorities are continuing to develop their mechanisms for consulting and involving users and carers. Some of the ways in which this is being done include:

- representatives of users and carers are serving on planning groups

- the setting up of user and carer forums

- the surveying of users and carers

- monitoring and evaluating the outcomes of the care planning cycle.

Unit 6 looks at how practitioners can involve service users in planning and delivering care, and how action by individual and groups of service users can give them more control over care arrangements.

Key questions

1 Explain the commissioning role.
2 List the three types of organisations which purchase health and social care.
3 How are purchasers split from providers in the NHS?
4 Which Act of Parliament introduced the purchaser/provider split?
5 What is the mixed economy of care?
6 List three types of organisations which local authorities should consult when drafting the Community Care Plan.
7 Why is it important for local authorities to advertise for new providers?
8 How do purchasers ensure that providers supply what is required?
9 What is a service level agreement?
10 What is the role of the social services inspection unit?
11 Give three benefits of joint commissioning.
12 Describe the line of accountability in the NHS.
13 What is meant by an in-house provider?
14 List four ways in which users and carers are involved in the purchaser/ provider split.

Assignment

Write to a health or social care purchaser and ask if it would be possible to arrange to talk with a manager about the role of purchaser. Find out how they plan services, encourage providers, and contract services. What do they require from their providers and how do they monitor quality of service?

Choose three local providers – one each from public, voluntary and private organisations – and find how have they have had to change the way they work in order to become providers.

Write a report which:
■ describes the role of your purchaser
■ explains the changes required of your three providers to meet the needs of your purchaser
■ sets this into the context of the overall structure of health and social care.

UNIT **6**

Element 6.1
Planning care and interventions

Element 6.2
Promoting health and social wellbeing

Element 6.3
Service users and care provision

Health and social care practice

This unit focuses on the care planning cycle for individual service users and explains the services working with the wider community such as public health and community work. It also explores users' experiences of health and social care provision. It links closely to unit 5 as well as units 3 and 4 on various aspects of health and social wellbeing, and units 1 and 2 on individual rights and interpersonal interaction.

ELEMENT **6.1**

Planning care and interventions

This element considers care planning as it is put into practice for individuals and their carers and explains what is meant by needs. It looks at the kinds of practitioners who are involved, what kinds of actions (interventions) can be taken to improve a user's situation and how users and carers are encouraged to take part in planning and interventions. It also explains some recent developments which have changed the way that care planning is undertaken.

It has links with element 5.1, which explores the new arrangements for organising care, and also with element 5.3, which looks at the responsibilities of health authorities and social services.

66 *The HEA has been much more clearly centred in recent years on how people have the power to change their lifestyle. Five or six years ago we might have thought more generally, in terms of only providing information, but now we emphasise the message that people can make certain choices about their health and wellbeing. This is certainly the approach the DoH wants health education to take.* **99**

physical activity manager, Health Education Authority

66 *We put together lifestyle plans with clients. I would start by spelling out the dangers of certain types of behaviour on their health and then look at their most hazardous habits and work out how they might limit these. For example, in the case of a woman who is two stones overweight and smokes 40 cigarettes a day, I would much rather she gave up cigarettes than got rid of the two stones.* **99**

doctor in charge of health screening, private hospital

66 *Sometimes we contribute to discussions with other health professionals about a young person, but only if the young person wants this. And we support the young person's interests in gaining referral to appropriate facilities, for example those provided by the Health Authority, or work as an advocate with them and Social Services to gain accommodation.* **99**

senior worker (counselling), young people's counselling and information centre

66 *We do our own care plans, which cover the next three or four months. They're action plans which look at all the care and help needed. These are used in conjunction with and inform the health service care plans which are reviewed annually. They are a way of monitoring to see how residents are getting on and any changes which need to be made.* **99**

project manager, supported housing scheme

The care planning cycle

Working out a care plan is done through a process of consultation, weighing up of choices and allocation of resources. Through this process, users, carers, practitioners and other professionals develop plans that aim to put in place the most appropriate and effective support systems for service users.

A care plan is a statement of the service being provided and its goals.

What is the care planning cycle?

The care planning cycle is the process by which individual needs are matched to available services. It can be expressed as a cycle with nine stages.

Information about services

Prospective users and carers need information about the services which are available and whether they are eligible to receive them.

Lily Moore was recently admitted to hospital because she had suffered a stroke. She had been living in a ground-floor flat near her daughter Polly and her family. Polly helped with shopping and heavy cleaning which she fitted into her part-time job. The time has come for Mrs Moore to be discharged from hospital. She has lost most of the functioning in her right arm and leg which means she will need support if she is to continue to live in her flat.

The ward sister talks to Mrs Moore and Polly about her illness and gives them an information booklet on rehabilitation services for stroke victims. She tells them about a voluntary group which supports stroke victims. They also discuss the difficulties Mrs Moore is likely to experience when she returns home.

DISCUSSION POINT
Think about the services Lily Moore might need to allow her to continue to live in her own home.

Before a full assessment of needs can be made and care planned, two things need to happen:
- potential service users and carers need to get information
- practitioners needs to decide whether the enquirer should be assessed.

Referral for assessment

Not everyone asking for information will be eligible for an assessment. Healthcare organisations have procedures for responding to requests for advice, assistance and services. Questions at this stage are limited to what is thought essential:
- finding out what the enquirer wants to know
- the name, address and telephone number of the potential user
- whether there has been any previous contact with the organisation
- the urgency of the assistance being sought
- a convenient time for follow-up
- any other information which would help further contact, such as whether there are any language or other communication difficulties.

ACTIVITY
One device which helps staff to respond quickly is a referral form. Design a form which could be used to pass on information to practitioners so they can think about what action to take.

When the doctors feel Mrs Moore is nearly ready for discharge the ward sister refers her to Miss Sharpe, a hospital social worker, for an assessment of her immediate needs and longer-term care. Miss Sharpe attends a ward round, talks with Mrs Moore and Polly, and asks other practitioners to report on Mrs Moore's needs.

Miss Sharpe draws together the information from other practitioners to get an accurate picture of Mrs Moore's ability to look after herself. For example, the occupational therapist advises that she will have problems with bathing, dressing and cooking for herself initially. Miss Sharpe asks Mrs Moore what she feels she can do for herself. She also asks Mrs Moore about her financial circumstances and explains that there may be a means-tested payment for some services. Following this consultation, Miss Sharpe's assessment suggests that:

■ Mrs Moore can return home as soon as support services can be organised

■ the goals of these services should be to re-establish as much independence as possible

■ there should be a review in three months.

It is now her task to plan the details of the support services.

People may be distressed, hostile or anxious when asking for assistance. Reception staff or those answering the telephone can help by making allowances for this.

Assessment of needs

The practitioner talks with potential service users and with their carer or advocate so that they can:

■ understand the user's needs
■ relate them to the organisation's policies
■ agree what can be done to help.

The assessment should be as simple, quick and informal as possible at this stage and focus on the user. The practitioner listens, observes and clarifies what they are being told or shown and then records any agreements made about the assessment of needs.

The result of the assessment of need is an agreement of the goals and objectives for the care plan. The user's needs are prioritised so that urgent or key services are arranged while others are still being organised. Unless there are grounds for compulsory intervention, practitioners must respect the rights of individuals to decline the services offered.

ACTIVITY

Most social services departments use a standard assessment form. Ask the social services department in your area if you can have a copy of theirs. List the types of information being collected. Does all the information relate to the assessment? Is any other information being collected?

Identifying what services are already being provided

A good point at which to start planning is immediately after the assessment because the practitioner then knows:

■ which services and practitioners are already providing support and care
■ whether there is a carer involved and level of care they are already giving
■ what social or peer groups are supporting the user.

If there is already a carer it is very important that they feel able to continue. Carers can have their needs assessed separately as part of a care plan.

Mrs Moore wants her daughter to continue to support her but knows that this is difficult because Polly has children and a job. The ward sister has spoken with Polly, who thinks she will be able to spend some time with her mother every day. After talking with Mrs Moore, Miss Sharpe telephones Polly for an appointment.

The care plan – the health and care services to be provided

The care plan sets out the most appropriate ways to achieve the goals identified in the assessment. If the user's need is for a single service the arrangement is simple, but, when the care plan indicates the continuation of services from a number of organisations it can be complex.

When appropriate services are identified the practitioner discusses them with the user and the carer and visits are arranged. The user must have the opportunity to weigh up the options.

If the service being offered is one for which the user has to make a financial contribution, this is agreed before the arrangements in the care plan are finalised.

DISCUSSION POINT

The social worker is aware that building Mrs Moore's care around Polly's support would not make any demands on the department's budget. But Polly may not want or be able to provide more care than she did before the stroke. What do you think the social worker should do at this stage in the care plan? List your ideas and draw conclusions.

A written care plan is agreed with all the parties concerned when:
■ the services have been arranged
■ the social services department and other funders can meet the cost.

A care plan should contain:
■ the overall objectives
■ the specific objectives of the user, the carer and the service providers
■ the criteria for measuring the achievement of the objectives
■ the services to be provided and by whom
■ the cost to the user and the contributing agencies
■ the other options considered
■ any point of difference between the user, carer, care planning practitioner or other agency
■ details of any unmet needs with reasons
■ the named personnel responsible for implementing, monitoring and reviewing the care plan
■ the date of the first review.

Department of Health: *Care management and assessment – practitioners' guide*

The consultant proposes a date for discharge. After discussion with Mrs Moore, Polly and the relevant providers, the care plan is agreed, to include:

- support from the social services hospital discharge team for the first six weeks

- meals-on-wheels for five days a week with Polly cooking at weekends

- a physiotherapy appointment at the local hospital once a week, transport to be provided

- a reassessment by an occupational therapist after one week in Mrs Moore's home, then appropriate equipment to be ordered

- visits from the community nurse and social worker to check on progress

- Polly to visit at the same time as the community nurse and to accompany Mrs Moore to her physiotherapy appointment.

Mrs Moore agrees to pay for the services of the discharge team and meals-on-wheels. All the visitors agree to complete a diary sheet which Mrs Moore will keep. These arrangements are to be reviewed after five weeks, before the discharge team has completed its contracted six weeks.

The ward sister confirms the date of discharge so that Miss Sharpe can alert everyone. She ensures the budget is allocated and the manager of the discharge team has home carers ready. Polly takes some time off work so that she will be available to settle her mother back into her home. Mrs Moore is greeted at home by her daughter and her key home carer. Mrs Moore's first meal-on-wheels arrives on time on her second day at home.

Everyone visiting Mrs Moore had agreed to complete the diary sheet. After a week, Miss Sharpe calls to check how things are going and finds it has not always been done. She reminds the community nursing service and the manager of the discharge team when she telephones for their view of progress. Mrs Moore asks to be put in touch with the stroke support group.

Implementing the care

When the care plan has been agreed, the practitioner ensures that the user and the carer receive the services.

The practitioner's tasks include:

- ensuring user and carer participation
- agreeing the timing and pace of the delivery of services
- confirming the budget
- following up any breakdowns in service delivery
- establishing arrangements for monitoring.

Monitoring progress

The arrangements for care plan delivery include an agreement on how it is to be monitored. Monitoring covers the:

- care plan objectives
- services being provided
- contract specifications
- budget
- feelings of the users and carers
- information required for the evaluation of the service.

Monitoring is carried out by:

- visiting users and carers
- telephone calls
- letters
- questionnaires

> In the sixth week, Miss Sharpe visits Mrs Moore and Polly for the first review. A week before the visit she asks each of the services working with Mrs Moore to provide a progress report. This is important at this stage, as the discharge team is due to withdraw shortly.
>
> Mrs Moore is a little down-hearted: she thought she would progress more quickly. She has been to a stroke victims' support group meeting but there was a problem with transport. As a result, it is agreed to extend the care from the discharge team by four weeks. By that time, Mrs Moore feels that she could cope with getting herself to bed but not with getting up. The only other issue to sort out is to ensure that the community nurse visits when Polly can be there. This will be discussed with the health clinic. The review is re-corded and passed to all the organisations.

- meetings with the users, carers and providers
- inter-agency consultations.

Reviewing and evaluating the care plan

The review of a care plan is user-focused, that is, concerned with ensuring that the user's needs, views and preferences have been met. The frequency of reviews depends on the complexity of the user's needs and their care plan.

A record of a review of a care plan includes:

- an evaluation of the achievement of objectives in the care plan
- an evaluation of the quality and cost of the services provided
- a reassessment of the user's needs
- a reappraisal of eligibility for the services
- a revision of the care plan
- any changes to services required
- any points of difference between the parties to the review
- the identification of any needs which cannot be met
- the date of the next review.

Department of Health: *Care management and assessment – practitioner's guide*

Making modifications to the care plan

Although modifications are most likely to result from changes in the user's needs, there are other reasons they might be necessary, including:

- The provider organisation may no longer be able to offer the services because they have ceased to have a contract with the social services department, changed their staff or changed their services.
- The user may no longer be able to afford the charges or may not wish to attend the facility .
- The carer may no longer be able to cope with the level of care needed .
- The social services department may have changed its criteria for eligibility.

Following the review meeting Miss Sharpe telephones the agencies. She arranges for the discharge team to continue for another four weeks and constructs a revised care plan which includes:

- arranging for Crossroads Care to replace the discharge team
- renegotiating the community nurse's visits to coincide with times when Polly is not at work
- finding a driver from the volunteers' bureau to take Mrs Moore to the stroke victims support group.

Finally, as Mrs Moore is no longer in the process of discharge, responsibility for managing her future package of care is transferred to another worker. Miss Sharpe refers her case to the elderly people's services manager to be reallocated.

ACTIVITY

Write a revised care plan to take account of Mrs Moore's changed care needs should Polly become ill and no longer able to take part in her mother's care plan.

What are the client's needs?

The assessment of the user's needs is the key event in the cycle. It is the starting point for defining the services.

Definition of Need: a comparison between the NHS and social services departments

NHS Executive Guidance definition 1991	Community Care – DOH definition 1991
The ability to benefit from healthcare.	The requirements of individuals to enable them to achieve, maintain or restore an acceptable level of social independence or quality of life, as defined by the care agency concerned.

Practitioners in care planning

This section looks at the practitioners involved in care planning and how they work together.

Mrs Moore's care plan enabled her to return home from hospital after a stroke. Some of the practitioners involved in her care plan and their functions were:

Practitioner	What they did
■ hospital social worker	coordinated the care plan
■ hospital consultant	agreed date for discharge and recommended follow-up treatment
■ ward sister	provided information about services; made referral to hospital
■ social worker	confirmed date of discharge
■ physiotherapist	confirmed physical abilities; provided once-a-week session after discharge
■ occupational therapist	confirmed ability to cope; visited after discharge to see how coping; provided equipment
■ home carer	provided personal care and support
■ community nurse	visited to check on health progress

A **key worker** is a person primarily accountable for one particular service user. In a field-work setting this is usually the person responsible for coordinatiing care services. In a residential setting it is the person who has responsibility for maintaining a special interest and undertaking specific work with the user.

ACTIVITY

In the case of Mrs Moore, other practitioners would probably be involved in addition to those mentioned. List these and write a short account of the role each might play.

Individual practitioners

Even when the user's needs are complex and several different services are involved, one practitioner is responsible for coordinating the main stages in the care plan. This is usually a:

- GP (particularly for the health care of people over 75 years of age)
- community nurse (where healthcare needs predominate)
- hospital social worker (where the care plan results from hospital discharge)
- field social worker or care manager (in adult or elderly service)
- field social worker (acting as key worker in children and family services for children and young people)
- probation officer (where there is an alternative to prison, parole, aftercare, or bail conditions).

The table on the next page shows practitioners employed in the statutory, voluntary and private sectors. The coordinator of the care plan cycle is normally employed within the statutory sector. Depending upon local arrangements and the user's needs, the practitioners who provide care may come from all three sectors.

Health and social care practitioners who may be involved in the care plan

Health care		Social care	
Doctors	GPs hospital-based	Social workers	field social workers approved social workers care managers
Nurses	hospital-based community nurses health visitors community phsychiatry nurses	Residential and day care	day centre workers residential social workers care assistants childminders foster carers
Support workers	healthcare assistants nursing auxiliaries radiographers paramedics ambulance workers	Domiciliary support	community support workers home carers family aids
Professionals in both health and social care	physiotherapists occupational therapists speech therapists counsellors		
Voluntary and community groups	befrienders advocates advice workers community workers		

The table of practitioners shows those whose main roles are to provide health and social care. Other people also contribute to the care plan, including:

■ reception and administration staff

■ managers who are responsible for ensuring that resources and personnel are available for the care plan (see also element 5.3).

Mrs Moore might not have been able to return to her home if her disability had been greater or her flat unsuitable for her level of mobility. She might have decided that she needed more support and applied to a housing association for warden-supported accommodation.

Workers in other organisations

Assessment often identifies needs which cannot be met by health or social care. Other professionals who may be involved include:

■ housing managers, who arrange alternative accommodation or modifications to existing accommodation

■ housing support workers and wardens, who support users in special needs housing

■ social security officers who reconsider pensions or benefits

■ vocational and employment workers who can help people with disabilities, learning difficulties or mental health problems join an employment training scheme

■ recreational workers who can put users in touch with a wide range of educational, leisure and recreational activities.

ACTIVITY

If possible, ask the manager of a multi-disciplinary group at primary care level to come and talk about their service. Write an account of how the team works, how it has developed processes for the coordination of different professionals and the methods of liaison with the relevant health and social care organisations.

Multi-professional teams

The care planning process requires a number of practitioners and agencies to work together:

66 *The closer relationship between health and social services has saved time, money and hassle and has improved service quality. Previously, details of a case had to go through three or four different people before meals-on-wheels could happen. Now it takes a day or two. Clients used to get confused by all the separate visits, and we used to waste so much time trying to get hold of each other.* 99

social services officer whose post is jointly funded by an NHS trust and a social services department

Client and carer working alongside practitioners

66 *[users and carers should be enabled] to exercise genuine choice and participation in the assessment of their care needs. Assessment procedures must be readily accessible by all potential services users and their carers. Authorities will need to take positive steps so that people with communication difficulties arising from sensory impairment, mental incapacity or other disabilities can participate fully in the assessment process and in the determination of service provision.* 99

Department of Health Policy Guidance 1990

Legislation now draws a distinction between the user and the carer. Practitioners may need to act as brokers between the two or reach a decision on how best to meet the interests of both.

DISCUSSION POINT

What do you think the hospital social worker should do in this case to work through the different feelings and expectations?

When Dora and John bought their house 15 years ago there was a 70-year-old sitting tenant, George. Over the years George minded the children, carried out minor repairs and worked in the garden. In return Dora and John helped with his shopping and laundry. Reaching his 85th year, he had a full social life which included a daily lunch at the local church and evenings spent with friends from a political group. When he became ill and was taken to hospital for tests and treatment it was clear that his problem was not illness but old age. He needed domiciliary support, not acute care. He was keen to be discharged and assured the consultant and the hospital social worker that Dora would be happy to support him. When she visited Dora was horrified to learn that she had been volunteered by George. She didn't know what to do: hurt the feelings of her friend, who treated her as a daughter, or take on the burden of caring.

Common interventions

Types of intervention fit into one or more of these categories:

- enabling
- caring
- treatment.

In the context of health and social care, intervention means taking action to maintain or improve the quality of someone's life. This section explores the range of interventions offered through the care plan.

Enabling

Health and social care practitioners describe the way they encourage users to build up their personal strengths and overcome difficulties as 'enabling'.

Enabling interventions help users to live as independently as possible by:

- caring for themselves
- moving into their own accommodation
- gaining or keeping employment
- speaking up for themselves
- supporting others through user groups, advocacy or volunteering.

ACTIVITY

Michael has a learning difficulty. He hopes to move into a room in a house where he will share the kitchen and a sitting room. He attends a living skills programme at his day centre. Draw up a checklist of skills that he will need to learn in his living skills programme.

66 *We take it in turns to do the cooking. One person cooks for everybody and we do the shopping for what we want at the supermarket. We also help with cleaning our rooms and the living room. I like living at the bungalow more than at the [residential home]. Here I can do what I like.* 99

ex-resident of a residential home talking about his new living arrangements in a shared house

Physiotherapists teach people new physical skills or restore old ones. Occupational therapists are concerned with equipment and adaptations, and also focus on enabling people to manage their disabilities. Social workers may use enabling interventions for the rehabilitation of families, teaching parents new parenting skills and encouraging them to have the confidence to bring up and care for their children without support.

Enabling interventions provided through primary health and social care include day centres or employment training schemes.

DEVELOPING CONFIDENCE

Audrey, the mother of three children under five, lived for six years with her violent husband. The children were placed on the child protection register. Her husband reacted violently, but with the support of her social worker Audrey was finally able to leave him and seek shelter in a refuge. The staff reported that, because of her long experience of being dominated, Audrey had little confidence in her ability to parent unaided. After careful discussion with Audrey and the refuge staff the social worker obtained resources to pay for a six-month placement in a family unit where Audrey was taught new parenting skills and gained the confidence to trust some of her old skills. She was also encouraged to seek legal help and by the end of the six months had started divorce proceedings and gained legal possession of the family home.

Coping

An extension of enabling interventions is helping users to cope by understanding themselves and their situation or condition to:

■ overcome loss
■ move to a new situation
■ deal with substance abuse or mental stress.

Services which help people to cope include:

■ counselling
■ befriending
■ information and advice
■ encouragement to join social groups.

Caring

Caring describes interventions which assist users to maintain their level of functioning. It can range from 24-hour nursing to support for just one or two activities, and includes:

■ personal care, e.g. bathing, dressing, mobility
■ befriending or good neighbour support
■ foster care, supported lodgings or shared housing.

Caring includes work with those who are terminally ill, offered through a hospice or to patients in their own home. A principal aim of this kind of intervention is to enable people to die with dignity and the minimum of pain.

THE MARIE CURIE FOUNDATION

Founded in 1948 to investigate and allay cancer, promote the welfare of cancer patients and their families, and contribute to the training of professional and lay people, the Foundation runs nursing homes or hospices for those suffering from cancer as well as community day and night care in the patients' own home. Healthcare practitioners are employed and support is offered by nursing auxiliaries and healthcare professionals. Patients are supported to die in dignity with their families and friends around them.

Treatment

This describes any procedure, medication, clinical interventions or therapy designed to cure or moderate a condition or behaviour.

Therapies or procedures are:

■ short-term or immediate
■ aimed to cure or change a condition or behaviour
■ controlled and standardised.

Treatment in health care includes:

■ surgery
■ medication
■ manipulation and exercise
■ specialist services offering assessment and treatment, e.g. occupational and speech therapy
■ physiological measurements.

ACTIVITY

Many GP surgeries offer more than just a consultation. Find out what other services are provided at a local GP's practice. List all the different treatments which can be given there. Are there any major treatments for which the GP will refer their patients to a hospital?

Needs and interventions

This section looks at the needs people have and some of the interventions which are available to meet these needs.

Social needs

Most of us need contact with others – with friends, relatives or family pets. For those confined to their own homes, social contact can be a window on the world.

Meeting social needs can be an effective way of enabling users and carers to take control because it can give people greater confidence.

66 *Having regular meetings with other foster carers really does help me do my job. Often, when I'm having difficulties with my foster son, other foster carers give me really useful ideas from their own experience. But sometimes everybody says 'we've had that problem and couldn't find an answer either.' That's reassuring because it says that it's not me being useless.* 99

foster carer

Volunteers

Volunteers work on their own or as part of a group within voluntary, statutory or private organisations. They can act as a bridge between services and users. Their involvement can encourage users to make use of services. Some volunteers and users become friends.

Support groups

User groups which offer mutual support can also be an effective treatment intervention in some areas of mental illness. Users can gain confidence in their ability to manage by sharing experiences with friends.

Physical needs

The most direct way of meeting physical needs is by providing equipment and making adaptations to the physical environment. For example, someone may be physically able to cook but not have sufficient mobility to enable them to go out shopping. Providing a volunteer or a shopping service will allow them to continue to remain independent in the areas where they can.

Other treatment strategies are medical, for example, operations for joint replacements.

Intellectual needs

Without appropriate stimulation, children become developmentally impaired and adults become lethargic.

ACTIVITY

Talk with someone about the treatment they received for traumatic injury or illness. Write down the interventions which dealt with their physical needs. What other interventions did practitioners use to help their recovery?

MUSIC THERAPY WITH ELDERLY PEOPLE WITH DEMENTIA

. . . in two residential homes in Cambridge . . . a local musician [worked] with groups of eight to ten residents with Alzheimer's disease and their carers. Using a portable keyboard, violin and harp, she encouraged elderly clients to touch them before she played. The residents played percussion instruments.

The therapy sessions were used to:

■ build on remaining memories

■ encourage communication

■ provide stimulation.

❝ *There were people who sang all the words of the hymns, yet they were the same people who five minutes earlier couldn't remember the name of their spouses.* **❞**

As well as being therapeutic for the residents, the personal histories that emerge through linking the music with family and community memories has benefited the staff. They are better able to respond to the residents' need for care and social contact.

Community Care 26 October 1995

DISCUSSION POINT

This is a good example of where three types of intervention work together. Explore which needs are met by this kind of work.

ACTIVITY

Try to get an idea of what it is like to experience sensory loss, by using a blindfold, ear plugs, or communicating without using speech. Make absolutely sure that this experiment is carried out in safe, controlled conditions. Then discuss your experience with your group. Write down what it felt like. What were the impairments to communication? What strategies did you use to overcome the sensory loss? How dependent were you on the help of others?

Communication needs

The need to communicate is a fundamental one. Methods of communication need to be appropriate to be successful. Suitable language should be used. Face-to-face speech, sign language, telephone, letters, tapes or Braille, can be chosen depending upon need. For example, not everyone speaks English, and even those who do may feel more comfortable communicating in their first language.

For someone suffering sensory loss or impairment the ability to communicate can be seriously affected and new skills may have to be learned.

Caring interventions, in terms of regular contact and news of the outside world, are also an important means of communication.

Mrs Frost had helped at an afternoon club for blind people for over a year when she was asked whether she would be interested in visiting Miss Pink, a resident in a local retirement home. Miss Pink was deaf and blind and rather depressed because, apart from the deputy manager, no one could use deaf-blind signs. Mrs Frost was apprehensive about her ability to help but social services offered to teach her some deaf-blind signs. She visited Miss Pink for two years, and during that time, Miss Pink helped her to become quite skilled in the signs.

There are many treatment interventions which aid communication, for example:

- teaching a stroke victim to speak again
- operating to remove a hearing, speech or visual impairment
- helping children who are speech delayed, or having difficulty, to form sounds distinctly
- enabling people with impaired hearing to make best use of residual hearing.

Emotional needs

Our emotional needs are for:

- love
- understanding
- sympathy
- empathy
- acceptance
- security
- choice.

We all experience crises in our lives and, at some time, suffer the death of someone we care about. Bereavement counselling is available through a range of sources – statutory, voluntary and private. Groups such as Cruse deal with bereavement in a group or social setting, sharing with others who have suffered loss and developed strategies for coping. For many people groups like these provide a social focus which enables them to move on to a new life.

Self-help groups also play a major role for people with a history of addiction or substance abuse. There are also mutual help groups for families who suffer from living with an addicted member.

HIV/AIDS has presented a particular challenge as it has certain features which together distinguish it from other illnesses:

- it is a terminal illness
- its course can be lengthy and unpredictable – there is a range of different symptoms
- sufferers are mainly relatively young
- it has a high level of social stigma.

One response to the challenge of supporting people with HIV/AIDS has been the 'buddy' schemes. Volunteers are specially trained to work with AIDS sufferers throughout their illness. This is a particularly important intervention for people who may find themselves socially isolated because of the nature of their illness.

ACTIVITY

Find out the names of organisations which offer bereavement support from your local library, or a directory of local services. Describe how they provide support and counselling (e.g. through telephone support, visiting, counselling or group activity).

Encouraging users and carers to have a say in care arrangements

The Department of Health offers the following statement of shared values in its guidance document on care management:

■ A commitment to ensure that all users and carers enjoy the same rights of citizenship as everyone else in the community, offering an equal access to service provision, irrespective of sex, race or disability.

■ A respect for the independence of individuals and their right to self-determination and to take risks, minimising any restraint upon that freedom of action.

■ A regard for the privacy of the individual, intruding no more than necessary to achieve the agreed purpose and guaranteeing confidentiality.

■ An understanding of the dignity and individuality of every user and carer.

■ A quest, within available resources, to maximise individual choice in the type of services on offer and the way in which those services are delivered.

■ A responsibility to provide services in a way that promotes the realisation of an individual's aspirations and abilities in all aspects of daily life.

Department of Health, Care management and assessment – practitioners' guide

66 *The HEA has been much more clearly centred in recent years on how people have the power to change their lifestyle. Five or six years ago we might have thought more generally, in terms of providing information, but now we emphasise the message, that people can make certain choices about their health and wellbeing. This is certainly the approach the DoH want health education to take.* 99

physical activity manager, Health Education Authority

Shared values

Values can operate as a kind of language, a platform from which we can launch a common understanding. With shared values, as with shared language, no interpreter is needed and better communication occurs.

How do practitioners involve users and carers?

The user's perspectives

Within the care planning cycle the practitioner should encourage the user's participation by:

■ providing information about the services available and offering choices and options

■ giving an opportunity to feed their feelings, views and preferences into the assessment

■ enabling them to comment on the services being proposed

■ encouraging them to take an active part in their care

■ ensuring they comment on the service provided and take an active part in monitoring

■ involving them in the review of the plan.

The carer's perspective

Carers now have a right to be assessed separately from users. The actions outlined above are relevant to carers as well as to users.

It is important that practitioners take consultations with carers seriously, check understanding and keep any promises made.

MOVING INTO A
CARE HOME

THINGS YOU NEED TO KNOW

Caring for People

Providing information

Users and carers need to have information about:

- the purpose of the care being provided
- the standard of service they can expect
- their rights to a service and what they are expected to do when they receive the service
- how decisions are reached and who takes the decisions
- how they can complain.

To be useful, information should be:
- given at right time
- advertised and available as widely as possible
- presented in simple language (and offered in other languages if appropriate)
- offered with help if people need clarification.

Providing advice

Advice and support is particularly important at these points in the care planning cycle:
- while assessing needs
- when talking through the service options
- when being told about decisions
- when commenting on the services provided
- when the care plan is being evaluated and modified.

A relaxed atmosphere is necessary to allow the user or carer to express their views clearly.

Practitioners need to help users and carers by making sure that:
- the procedure and nature of the review is explained
- reports are available before the meeting and the user and carer given an opportunity to talk them through
- the user and carer are offered a representative or advocate
- the meeting is structured and well-chaired
- the user and carer are welcomed to the meeting and their contribution to the discussion supported
- the agreements and decisions are summarised and the next step explained.

Development of skills

Even with support and access, an individual may not be able to gain maximum benefit because they lack confidence in their own abilities and expertise. Without the practitioners' understanding of what is needed to build confidence and skill at taking part, the care planning process is likely to reinforce existing feelings of inadequacy.

> ### DISCUSSION POINT
>
> It can be argued that empowerment in the decision-making process is time-consuming and expensive and makes no different to the final decision. Why not just leave things to the experts? What do you think?

Responsibility for deciding how resources should be used

In most circumstances practitioners and their managers are the people who can release resources and therefore the final decision about the package of services is made by them and their organisations. Users and carers do not usually have an equal say in how resources should be used.

The most effective way to enable users and carers to be actively involved is to share information openly and honestly.

Questions and answers

Which skills are needed when resources are scarce?

- advocacy: speaking up on behalf of service users and carers
- the ability to prioritise appropriately and decisively
- negotiation skills
- the ability to make alliances with others in the struggle for resources
- imagination in making the most of scarce resources and seeking resources
- the ability to develop trust and invest in relationships

What are the key communication skills?

- skills in listening, responding and action – not one or two of them, but all three
- being able to communicate information reliably and accurately, particularly in relation to the availability and nature of resources
- skills in checking understanding, to ensure that communication has been effective – what you have said has been understood
- avoiding ambiguity, so that there can be agreement about what is meant

What are the key skills required for collaboration?

- handling yourself and other people in such a way as to demonstrate respect
- the ability to ensure that collaboration is based on agreed purposes, aims and goals
- the ability to understand conflict and maintain respect even when there are honest differences of opinion
- awareness of the potential for exploitation of carers and service users and the skill to avoid this

Source: Beresford and Trevillion, 1995

Responsibility for deciding how care should be delivered

Care managers are 'gate-keepers' between the user and carers and the services available. They have listened to and taken into account the views and needs of the user and carer, and they have access to a range of services and facilities which can meet those needs.

Angela is 25 and has learning difficulties. Although she stills lives at home, she has successfully been through a training scheme with an employment training project. She works in a local bakery and would like to move into her own home but her recently widowed mother is opposed to this.

Angela's mother has arthritis and finds her mobility is becoming restricted. The GP refers her to social services because he feels she needs more support with Angela's care. An adult services care manager visits and talks to Angela's mother, Angela, and staff at the employment training project who have known both women a long time. After assessing the needs of both, the practitioner suggests that the best care solution is for Angela to move into a nearby group home and for her mother to have some adaptations to the home, together with practical help with shopping from a local volunteers group.

To implement this plan, the care manager has to help Angela's mother accept that Angela is ready and able to live more independently. This means helping Angela and her mother to change their assumptions about the support someone with learning difficulties needs. If the care manager achieves some of these changes, then Angela and her mother will feel that they have been involved in the care decisions.

ACTIVITY

In this case study, Angela and her mother could be described as either user or carer. If you were asked to contribute to the care decision, how would you define both women? Give your reasons.

**Support for Families
who Care for Children
with Disabilities and
Special Needs**

**Information for Parents and
Professional Workers**

User and carer networks and forums

Users and carers can be helped to play a greater part in their care through user and carer networks. These networks:

■ provide mutual support to members who share an illness, disability or situation

■ provide information, advice and representation for individual members

■ contribute to the planning and monitoring of services

■ comment on the quality of services and campaign for better and different services.

There is more about this in section 6.3.5.

User and carer networks

National

Contact A Family is a national organisation which brings together families with children with special needs to provide mutual support and joint representation to health and social services. It also offers national networks, through meetings, telephone contact and information, for families of children with rare illnesses or disabilities.

Local

A mental health project is set up by mental health workers, local community groups and residents to meet concerns about the high level of compulsory admissions to hospital and the lack of community services which meet the needs of young clients. The project has a number of aims including:

■ establishing a dialogue between young people and mental health services

■ promoting and establishing self-help groups within the community for young users of mental health services

■ encouraging the existing health and social care services to be more sensitive to issues involving youth and mental health.

ACTIVITY

Using a directory of local services, list some of the organisations which support user or carer networks. Contact five of them and find out how they are involved in assessment and care planning. Write up your findings in a report.

One result of the NHS and Community Care Act has been that local authorities have set up formal consultative groups to enable users and carers to contribute to the overall planning of services. There is more about this in element 5.3.

Service users managing their own care

There is no reason why users should not be managers of their own care. Many people who require care run their homes, bring up children or go to work.

327

Changes in practice in care planning and interventions

> 66 *We would like to think that we were achieving something better than before. The procedures, with our specialised reception and referral teams, should mean that we are less likely to make inappropriate assessments, or to fail to provide essential services. Also, the inclusion of occupational therapists in our team does help to ensure that assessments are comprehensive and speedy.* 99
>
> team manager, social services adult services

> 66 *The new system is supposed to mean that professionals work together so that people get the service they need. This does seem to fall down when individual professions don't seem to want to cooperate. The division between health care and social care can still mean that each service says that it's the other's responsibility. For instance – when is a bath a health bath or a social bath?* 99
>
> community worker with Age Concern

Practitioners in health and social care have expressed concerns about how the recent changes might affect their work. In particular, concerns have been raised about:

- how practitioners' roles might change
- how they would acquire the new skills and knowledge needed to carry out their new responsibilities.

Empowerment of users

At the heart of care planning are users and their needs. A number of changes have been necessary for this to happen, including:

- better information and access to services
- systems which encourage users to take part in their own care planning
- opportunities for practitioners to learn new skills.

The care planning process

Traditionally, the practitioner's approach to care planning was based on the services being offered by their organisation. They are now moving to a more participatory system for care planning. An assessment checklist is still a part of the assessment process, but now users can be asked to complete a lot of it for themselves.

Models of assessment

Procedural:	assumes that the managers who devised the procedure know best
Questioning:	the practitioner asks questions and forms the assessment on the information provided – the practitioner is assumed to be the expert
Exchange:	the practitioner gathers the user's, the carer's and other practitioners' perceptions of the problems and their views on possible solutions

Developing new skills

The introduction of care planning has meant that practitioners are now required to:

- encourage users and carers to communicate their own needs and preferences
- be sensitive to language, cultural, racial, sex and age differences
- be able to help people through transitions, such as loss, distress or major changes
- negotiate and conciliate between people with different status and power, and different perceptions, values, attitudes, expectations, wants and needs.

Spectrum of care

In recent years there has been a growing interest in forms of treatment, some of which are found alongside conventional medicine and some of which are considered alternative.

You may have come across the terms complementary and alternative medicine used as synonyms, but they do have separate, if overlapping, definitions. They tend to have in common a holistic approach, seeing the user as a whole person rather than a set of symptoms. This approach means that the practitioner spends more time talking to users than most doctors of conventional medicine are able to offer.

Complementary medicine

Complementary therapies are those which are often practised alongside conventional medicine. Practitioners may be conventionally trained practitioners who have added to their skills, or they may have trained in their chosen complementary field. The training tends to be rigorous and long. Examples are:

- homeopathy
- osteopathy
- chiropractic
- acupuncture
- herbalism.

Alternative medicines

Alternative medicine is generally further from the mainstream and as yet is less organised in terms of professional training and regulation than complementary medicine. Examples include:

- aromatherapy
- reflexology
- hypnotherapy
- iridology.

Alternative therapies may also include activities which are considered to be self-care or relaxation techniques, for example yoga or t'ai chi.

ACTIVITY

Investigate and prepare a report on the complementary and alternative medicines available in your area. Which are available within the NHS and which only through private practice?

Multi-skilling of professionals

Many health and social services authorities have joint community mental health teams which bring together psychiatrists, clinical psychologists, community psychiatric nurses, social workers, occupational therapists and community support workers. They provide individual therapy and counselling, support people with long-term mental health problems in the community and make formal assessments under the Mental Health Act. Where there are social workers, the team is likely to be involved in the community care planning process.

Greater use of support staff

Whereas professionals are very much concerned with diagnosis, assessment and prescription, actions designed to enable, support and care are more likely to be the domain of support staff. The numbers of support staff have grown as health and social care needs have grown.

In some services, their role has moved from being an assistant to having defined responsibility for caring or enabling interventions. For example, the Sainsbury Centre for Mental Health survey (1995) found that support staff were more likely to be working with long-term users with severe problems than the professionally qualified.

DISCUSSION POINT

There is a growing number of support workers who can do valuable work but have no professional qualifications. Health and social care practitioners are divided about how far support workers are used as substitutes for professionals. Some support this development because they say it enables qualified workers to use their skills appropriately and effectively and enhances the enabling and caring roles of the support workers. Others believe that it is a way to provide care more cheaply and to undermine the power of the professional. User and carer groups also feel concerned about the increased role of support workers. What do you think?

Key questions

1 List the nine elements of the care planning cycle.
2 List five things a care plan should contain.
3 Give three reasons why the care plan might need to be changed after it has been reviewed.
4 Why is it important for the service user to be involved in the care plan cycle?
5 What does a care manager do?
6 Explain the roles of three practitioners who might be responsible for the care plan.
7 Why is it important for different practitioners and organisations to work together?
8 List the three types of intervention.
9 Explain the main purpose of caring interventions.
10 List the five main categories of user needs.
11 Give two examples of physical needs.
12 Describe two examples of enabling interventions which are used to meet social needs.
13 List five things users need to have information about.
14 Why is advocacy important?
15 List five practitioners who might be part of multi-professional teams.

Assignment

Arrange to interview a care manager, or a practitioner who coordinates a care plan for service users and ask them to explain how they undertake care planning. The interview should include questions about the formal process their organisation has set up for care planning, and the forms which are used for assessing needs, recording the care plan and reviewing it.

Ask the care manager to take you through the case of a real or a model user. (The care plan selected should involve at least five different practitioners from a range of organisations and services, and at least two different interventions.)

Write a report which:
■ describes the care planning cycle and how it was used for your client
■ identifies which practitioners were involved and explains whether they worked alone or with others, including the user and their carer
■ describes at least two interventions used and how they met the user's needs
■ identifies what steps were involved in the care planning cycle to involve the user and their carer
■ evaluates how effective this was and makes suggestions about how this involvement could be improved.

Describe two recent changes that have affected the care manager's care planning and the interventions that they can provide to meet users' and carers' needs.

ELEMENT **6.2**

Promoting health and social wellbeing

This element looks at those aspects of care service provision which are most closely connected to promoting the health and wellbeing of groups and communities, including health education, environmental protection, and immunisation and screening programmes. It considers areas of legislation which allow the liberty of others to be restricted for their own or others' health and social wellbeing and some of the ethical dilemmas which may arise.

66 There are loads of people who can promote health and social wellbeing. They complement the HEA's work. Almost everyone has a role to play. A few examples might be: a nurse advising a client on prevention; a fitness adviser from a leisure centre talking informally to people they meet to encourage new people to take more exercise, rather than just providing facilities for the people who already do; a teacher can encourage students by getting them keen on sport; friends, colleagues, children, employers – it could be anyone who may influence someone's thinking on keeping themselves healthy. 99

physical activity manager, Health Education Authority

66 The work of the department includes accident prevention, community development, physical activity promotion and library services. So we work with a number of different health professionals, and other professionals, for example youth workers and teachers. We also work with the general public direct, and with local authorities, environmental health, housing, transport, community development and leisure people, and with journalists. 99

assistant director, health promotion, local health authority

66 We work with the statutory community psychiatric team, Social Services, doctors and so on. If we have a problem they can help us with, they come out. For example, because of the move towards care in the community, sometimes people who are unable to cope come here. Some are able to stay in the community less than 24 hours before reverting to their usual state, normally because they haven't been taking their drugs. In cases like this we would have to inform the community psychiatric team and we have unfortunately had to section people back to psychiatric hospital. They can sometimes come back on the condition that they stay on their drugs and/or have a continuing psychiatric assessment of their care. 99

community coordinator, community for homeless people

66 Our outreach worker is responsible for promoting the work of the centre. She goes to schools and colleges and to a young people's venue on Friday nights. She also invites young people in to show them the inside of the Centre. They see it is comfortable and has an easy atmosphere. She mails to secondary schools and gets posters placed. We have to be 'visible' to young people. Our aim is that every person aged 12–25 in the area knows that we are here and what we provide, if ever they should need us. 99

senior worker (counselling), young people's counselling and information centre

Practitioners involved in health promotion

In this section you will explore the range of people who are involved in promoting the health and social wellbeing of the population. Some practitioners are just involved with the promotion of health and social wellbeing, others have a number of different roles within their jobs of which health promotion is just one.

We each carry responsibility for the health and social wellbeing of ourselves and, to varying degrees, for that of others. For example, parents have a responsibility for the health and safety of their children and for teaching them the benefits of safety, cleanliness and good health.

It is the task of a range of practitioners to promote good health practice. This section considers:

- who the practitioners are
- how they carry out their task
- how the task fits in with other aspects of their daily work.

Strategies for health promotion

Five broad approaches can be identified:

- interventionist – direct intervention to prevent or ameliorate conditions which are damaging to health or social wellbeing

- behavioural change – seeking to change people's individual behaviour and attitudes

- educational – giving information and knowledge so that well-informed decisions may be made

- user-centred – working with individuals to help them to identify what they want to change and then assist them in taking action

- societal change – effecting changes on the physical, social and economic environment in order to make it more conducive to good health and social wellbeing.

The promotion of health and social wellbeing is a combination of activities designed to deal with the direct personal effects of, for example, illness and those designed to encourage healthier practices.

Practitioners for whom promotion is their main job

66 *The work of the department includes accident prevention, community development, physical activity promotion and library services. So we work with a number of different health professionals, and with other professionals, for example youth workers and teachers. We also work with the general public direct and with local authorities, environmental health, housing, transport, community development and leisure people and with journalists.* 99

a health promotion worker

The Health Education Authority is a key player in the promotion and attainment of the Government's health targets presented in *The Health of the Nation*. See element 7.1 for more about the HEA and these targets.

Many practitioners' jobs have promoting health and social wellbeing as their primary function. Some work in a particular geographical area or organisation; others work at a national or regional level to promote good practice in a particular area of concern. Many work in ways which combine these aspects.

Health promotion

Most health authorities and trusts have specific departments whose function is health promotion. They mirror at a local level the work of the Health Education Authority and are staffed by people who offer direct health advice and information.

Occupational health

Many working days are lost through industrial injury or work-related disease. The Health and Safety at Work Act aims to make working conditions safe. The Health and Safety Executive employs inspectors, engineers and doctors to enforce the Act.

Some larger organisations employ their own staff to ensure the health and safety of staff.

Those concerned with specific areas of work

Increasingly, health and social care practitioners may specialise in one area of work, for example in the areas of substance abuse or HIV/AIDS. They work in a number of different settings:

■ health
■ social services
■ joint health and social services projects
■ voluntary organisations.

Their tasks are varied and can include:

■ working with a target group to encourage good practice
■ advising on and developing policy for an organisation
■ preparing publicity material

ACTIVITY

Collect some recruitment advertisements for people to work in the promotion of health or social wellbeing. Summarise what these advertisements tell you about the jobs. Who will the worker be working with? What sort of qualifications are required?

- informing the general public, including seeking to change public attitudes
- advising staff who work directly with particular user groups on best practice.

Crime prevention officers

All police stations have crime prevention officers whose task is to work with the local community to prevent opportunities for crime. Their work involves:

- visiting business people and householders to advise on the measures to protect their property
- meeting with community groups to discuss the role that the general public can play
- promoting Neighbourhood Watch groups.

Fire safety officers

Prevention is an important part of the work of the fire service. Fire prevention officers are mainly involved with checking on the safety measures of workplaces and other public buildings to ensure that the fire risk to the public is minimised, but also advise employers and managers on best practice.

Practitioners for whom promotion is one aspect of their job

66 *In the last year or so the issue of public information has come very much to the fore. We were getting lots of cases where babies had been severely damaged or even killed by the parents shaking them. We see it as mainly an education issue. Some people don't know that shaking a baby is extremely dangerous. The NSPCC produced a brochure called Handle with Care which gives very clear information about this in a non-threatening and non-judgemental style. In this authority the parents of every new baby receive a parent-held record. This is a small file which holds all the information about the baby. Healthcare professionals that the parents come into contact with, for example the health visitor, put information leaflets into the parent-held record. Everyone receives a copy of the Handle with Care leaflet, so parents don't feel they're being singled out and there is no stigma attached.* 99

child protection adviser

All health and social care practitioners are concerned with promotion as a central part of the preventive aspects of their work. But this varies considerably according to the work they do.

For example, child protection social workers are concerned with the prevention of abuse, but the main focus of this aspect of their work will be with families where there are already concerns. Most of them are not normally involved in promotion to the general public.

The practitioners discussed here are by no means a comprehensive list – they are examples to give you an idea of the range of settings where practitioners undertake the promotion as a part of their work.

Community police officers

These officers need to enlist the support of their community to achieve effective crime prevention. They are central to the strategy called 'policing by consent', where policing is seen as being with and for the community. Their many promotional tasks include:

- promoting a positive image of the police in their local area
- building relationships
- encouraging safe practices on the part of children and parents.

Environmental health officers

Environmental health officers investigate and prosecute on breaches of the environmental health laws, such as air pollution or food hygiene. They also advise on good practice. Some may do this as part of their investigative function, others as part of promoting good public health and safety.

Health practitioners

All practitioners have the promotion of good health as a central part of their work through the interventionist approach. They also seek to promote good health practice. Some of the key practitioners in health promotion are:

- doctors
- dentists
- dental hygienists
- nurses
- health visitors
- community midwives
- dieticians
- community psychiatric nurses
- chiropodists
- alternative health practitioners.

Community work

This is undertaken by a variety of practitioners and involves:

- setting up community facilities
- assisting with the organisation and support of community or user-based groups
- organising and campaigning for social change.

Health and social care practitioners use community networks to reach members of their user groups who might not otherwise be contactable, for example, community nursing or health promotion to single homeless people.

Youth workers

Youth workers operate in similar ways to community workers. They provide appropriate promotional and educational input themselves or put young people in touch with people who can advise them.

Advice givers

These operate in many settings, such as libraries, reception areas of hospitals or town halls or within agencies such as Citizens Advice Bureaux. They have a major role to play in ensuring that information and advice is available to the general public.

Education

A wide variety of people in education are concerned in the promotion of health and social wellbeing in other ways than through teaching. Health and welfare staff on university campuses have a specific role for the wellbeing of students who may be away from home for the first time. They provide advice and counselling services.

People in contact with the public

People whose work brings them into contact with the public can also promote good practice, for example housing officers and people working in recreation and leisure.

For some people, particularly those who are confined to home, their minister of religion can be the most familiar face from outside. Ministers are able to support people through major life changes such as bereavement. They can put people in contact with appropriate help, or encourage them to seek it.

People working within closed environments

People working within closed environments, for example in prisons, have a major responsibility for the health and wellbeing of their residents, who may have no other source of information. Some people in prison may indulge in unsafe sexual practices or substance abuse. Prison staff and others may need to be involved in specific health promotion projects on drugs or HIV/AIDS awareness.

They also encourage prisoners to prepare for life outside prison – encouraging them to take up adult education opportunities, for example. Staff within the prison who are likely to be involved in promotional activities are:
- prison officers
- probation officers
- education officers.

> **ACTIVITY**
>
> Make a list of all the health and social care practitioners you have come into contact with. Describe what you have learned from them that has helped or improved your personal health or social wellbeing.

> **ACTIVITY**
>
> If possible, arrange to talk to someone who works in a residential home for elderly people. Who might be involved in promoting health and social wellbeing in this setting? Describe how each of these people might do this. Write up the results of your investigation.

Section 6.2.2 — Practitioners involved in creating healthy environments

We exist in a range of environments, some of them related to our physical world, some with social conditions, some to do with lifestyle and life choices. Those environments include:

- natural environments
- socioeconomic conditions
- housing
- social welfare
- social conditions
- working environments.

The significance of some of aspects of our environment is clear, such as water, air or housing. There is more about socioeconomic conditions in section 4.3.2.

There are many people and organisations who are involved in creating and maintaining healthy environments. Some of them, such as environmental health officers, may operate across many environments: others, such as occupational health nurses or OFWAT, in only one.

This matrix shows the spread of functions of a number of practitioners and organisations.

	Amenity group	Community health	Communit psychiatric nurse	Community worker	Environmental health officer	General practitioner	Health and Safety Executive	Health visitor	Housing officer	National Rivers Authority	OFWAT	Occupatinal health nurse	Occupational therapist	Police officer	Social worker	Solicitor	Spech therapist	Teacher	Welfare rights worker	Wildlife Trusts
Natural environments	√			√	√					√						√				√
Water	√	√			√	√	√	√		√	√					√				
Air		√			√	√	√	√								√				
Socioeconomic conditions		√	√	√	√	√			√	√			√	√	√			√	√	
Housing	√	√	√	√	√	√			√				√		√	√			√	
Social welfare		√	√	√		√		√					√		√	√	√	√	√	
Social conditions		√	√	√		√		√					√	√	√	√		√		
Working environments			√	√		√						√				√				

ACTIVITY

Think of five more health or social care practitioners, draw up a similar table and locate them on it.

Practitioners involved in protecting the public

Immunisation programmes

Three important factors which have led to longer, healthier lives for many Europeans in the twentieth century are:

- improvements in public health (better drains etc.)
- improved diet
- large-scale immunisation programmes.

There are five categories of immunisation:

- against disease – such as poliomyelitis, diphtheria, pertussis, measles, TB and mumps
- following specific exposure to a danger of infection – such as tetanus or rabies
- protection against the risk of fetal infection and damage – the most common being rubella
- against epidemic (particularly for high-risk groups such as children or the elderly) – such as influenza or meningitis
- against diseases occurring in other climates – such as typhoid or yellow fever.

Immunisation has protected millions of people through national and international immunisation programmes, but not all diseases can be dealt with in this way. Viruses such as influenza and HIV are able to change their form quickly, thus negating any protection provided by immunisation.

Screening and contact tracing programmes

A key element in treating many diseases is early detection and intervention. In some cases the patient's awareness of their ill health may be too late and can affect the chances of successful treatment.

Screening

These programmes have been set up to increase early detection. Examples include:

- cervical and breast cancer screening
- eye tests which also look for disease while checking vision
- tuberculosis and other lung disease chest X-rays which can identify other problems
- developmental checks for under-fives
- occupational diseases, such as emphysema amongst miners
- a range of screening tests for pregnant mothers to ensure that the mother and the baby are well.

GPs' surgeries and health clinics also offer regular checks for blood pressure or blood tests, as well as more thorough check-ups through Well Woman and, less frequently, Well Man clinics.

Contact tracing

With some diseases it is necessary to try to trace anyone who might be at risk of infection. For example, staff in genito-urinary and HIV/AIDS clinics ask

UNIT

6

ELEMENT **6.2**

A range of practitioners are involved in immunisation programmes, including:

- general practitioners
- school nurses
- hospital medical staff
- community health workers
- health visitors
- immigration services.

Examples of practitioners who carry out screening are:

- doctors
- community nurses
- health visitors
- radiographers
- midwives.

As well as doctors and nurses, environmental health officers and epidemiologists work towards tracing the origins of the illness or infection.

patients their sexual contacts so staff can try to trace them to invite them to be checked for the infection.

Tracing will also be carried out when there is:

- an epidemic, for example of meningitis
- a potentially contagious disease that has been brought into the country
- an outbreak of food poisoning, such as salmonella
- an illness within an environmental source, such as legionnaire's disease
- an infectious disease, such as TB.

Child protection

We are unique among animals in the length of time that we take to grow to adulthood. There is more about this in section 4.1.1. There are many dangers from which it is necessary to protect children, including:

- physical accident (as a result of being unaware of potential dangers)
- physical abuse by family or strangers
- sexual abuse by family or strangers
- neglect because of parental incompetence.

The principal role of protection rests with parents, who are expected to be aware of potential dangers and of the daily needs of food, love and security. This role is supported and monitored by the state through a range of practitioners.

This support and monitoring is mostly done through education, health monitoring, nursery provision. The state supplies information and advice to parents and a degree of financial support, some universal, some means-tested.

However, sometimes it will be necessary for the state to intervene to protect children. Under Section 47 of the Children Act (see section 6.2.4 of this unit) local authorities have a duty to investigate where there are concerns for the welfare of a child. Agencies such as the police, health services, education and housing have a legal obligation to assist in this process. Investigations may be triggered in a variety of ways:

- a parent may report a concern
- a practitioner such as a teacher, a health visitor or a doctor may express concern
- a social worker already working with the family may think an investigation is necessary
- someone may make an anonymous report
- a report may be made by the police.

During an investigation a social worker must give priority to:

- the safety and welfare of the child
- working in partnership with families wherever possible

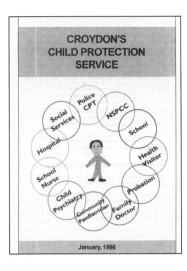

CROYDON'S
CHILD PROTECTION
SERVICE

January, 1996

- inter-agency cooperation
- keeping detailed and careful recordings of all details.

Sometimes the indications are that a crime has been committed which could result in a criminal prosecution. In these cases social workers must ensure that they do not act in such a way as to prejudice any possible prosecution. The key document for all of those involved is a government guidance document called *Working Together*.

❝ *The role which social workers have means that they must sometimes take very difficult decisions on behalf of children, decisions which can effect those children for the rest of their lives. Being involved in some cases really brings home the power you have over people's lives, and that's sometimes difficult to live with.* **❞**

social worker

If at the end of an investigation it is clear that there are grounds for concern then a child protection conference is called. They invite all those practitioners with a concern for the protection of the child (such as social workers, police, teachers, doctors, health visitors, nursery staff), as well as the child's parents. They meet to evaluate all the evidence and plan any action which may be necessary.

The conference will also decide whether or not to enter the child's name on the child protection register. There are four main reasons for registration:
- physical abuse
- sexual abuse
- emotional abuse
- neglect.

Under the Children Act several people have key roles to play in the protection of children.

Parents

Parents are responsible for the protection of their children, defined in the Children Act by the concept of parental responsibility. Failure to fulfil duties and responsibilities as a parent can result in criminal proceedings. The Children Act places on local authorities a duty to work in partnership with parents in the interests of their children.

Social workers

Social workers have specific legal responsibilities to investigate when they have suspicions that a child may be suffering, or is likely to suffer from, significant harm. If a child is found to be at risk and their name is placed on the child protection register the social worker has responsibility for monitoring the child's protection and for implementing a protection plan. This plan is designed to help the family change the pattern of their parenting.

The **child protection register** is a central record of all children in a local authority area about whose welfare there are concerns and for whom support is being provided through inter-agency planning. This register is usually held by social services who will share responsibility with the police and the health service. Each case is reviewed every six months and a decision is taken about whether a child should remain on the register.

Parental responsibility

❝ *All the rights, duties, powers, responsibilities and authority which by law a parent has in relation to the child and its property.* **❞**

This responsibility is held automatically by the mother, by the father if he is married to the mother, and by any others who have acquired it by agreement or court order.

Police officers

In the UK the police have the principal role for the protection of all citizens from harm. With children they have specific duties under the Children Act and duties under criminal law where children are victims of crime, such as physical and sexual abuse or neglect. Most police forces now have specialist teams called child protection teams who work closely with social workers in the investigation of child abuse.

Doctors

Doctors may have contact with children who have unexplained injuries or illnesses which cause suspicion. Hospital doctors in casualty departments may have suspicions about a series of similar injuries occurring to a child. In cases like these, doctors make reports to the social services department.

Health visitors

Health visitors have statutory responsibilities for all children under five, many of whom may not be seen by any other agency. As such they are likely to be the first to become concerned about neglect, injuries or failure to keep appointments for medical check-ups.

Teachers

Teachers and nursery personnel have regular contact with children and so are in a position to observe any physical or behavioural indications of abuse. They are able to observe younger children with their parents or hear of concerns from other parents. This role is of particular importance if a child's name is already on the child protection register.

Guardian ad litem

When court proceedings are started on a child the court appoints a qualified and experienced social worker called a guardian ad litem (literally, a guardian in law) to investigate the child's circumstances and report back to the court. Although the guardian works closely with both the social worker and the solicitor appointed for the child, their principle responsibility is to ensure that the child's welfare is the court's paramount consideration. They have an important role in ensuring that the rights of the child are not abused.

Mental health services

Many people suffering from a mental illness are treated in the community with medication, counselling or a mixture of both. For others a period in a mental hospital is necessary, either as a voluntary patient or through compulsory admission.

Patients who are being treated voluntarily can refuse treatment or discharge themselves. This right can be overruled by doctors and nurses who have short-term holding powers if they consider that treatment is necessary.

ACTIVITY

These people may also be involved in making decisions about the welfare of children:

- school nurses
- foster carers
- day nursery staff
- probation officers
- solicitors
- magistrates
- judges.

Investigate what the main tasks of each of these people would be in relation to the protection of children and write down your findings. Then examine more fully the role of one of the key people given in the main text.

Approved social worker

Under the Mental Health Act 1983 only a social worker who has received specified post-qualifying training is authorised to exercise the extensive powers which are given. This worker is called an 'approved social worker'.

ACTIVITY

List the various medical practitioners involved in psychiatric work. Find out what specific tasks each has and the various settings in which they might carry out those roles. Are there are any other people working in the field of mental health who are not listed above?

The approved social worker plays the principal part in protecting the rights of mental health patients. When considering compulsory admission to hospital, they must investigate all other treatment and care opportunities.

The approved social worker's role is social rather than medical. The decisions about medical judgements, treatment and nursing support are made by a range of health practitioners:

- general practitioners
- psychiatrists
- mental health nurses
- community psychiatric nurses.

These practitioners have a role to play in:

- assessment and diagnosis
- treatment
- prevention
- after-care.

They undertake these roles in a range of settings:

- the patient's home
- day centres and hospitals
- residential care
- hospital care.

Criminal justice services

You might think only of police officers, judges and lawyers when considering who works within the criminal justice system, but there are many other people involved. They carry out a range of functions, some of them preventive, some of them curative and some promotional.

ACTIVITY

Choose one of the jobs which a police officer may undertake and find out what is involved in carrying it out. Write down your findings and explain how you think the community is protected by this work.

Police

Although a police officer's principal task is the detection of crime and apprehension of suspected criminals they have many other roles. Some of the many responsibilities of the police force are:

- crime prevention
- traffic management
- child protection
- community policing
- school liaison.

Probation

Probation officers have to apply many of the same skills as social workers. Their work includes:

- preparation of social reports prior to sentencing
- alternatives to imprisonment (such as probation, community service, etc.)
- monitoring paroled prisoners
- prison after-care
- work with people in prison (this can include both rehabilitative work and helping to maintain links with home and family).

Youth justice workers

These work in a similar way to probation officers, but with people under 17 years of age.

Crown Prosecution Service

In England and Wales the Crown Prosecution Service (CPS) is responsible for bringing criminal prosecutions to court. The CPS operates within general guidelines by which it assesses the probability of a successful prosecution. If it feels that the evidence available is insufficient it may either encourage the police to strengthen their case or decide not to prosecute. In this sense it could be said to operate as a court of first jurisdiction.

Victim support

For the victims of crime, particularly the victims of violent or sexual crime, the trauma does not end with the crime itself, nor with the punishment of the offender, if that occurs. The fears and feelings of insecurity that result can last for months or years. In most cases, the trauma extends to the victim's family.

Victim support schemes using trained volunteers work directly with victims and their families, in particular during the period immediately following the crime. Victim support schemes work closely with the police, from whom they usually receive their referrals.

ACTIVITY

Find out about the roles of all of the people mentioned in the text who are involved in the criminal justices services. Write up your findings in a short report. You will find the information about the courts in section 6.2.4 helpful.

Section 6.2.4

Legislation to protect health and wellbeing

Our daily lives are regulated by the law in many ways. There are laws governing:

- the quality of food that we eat
- how we drive our cars and their roadworthiness
- the payment of taxes
- the health and safety of our workplaces.

In these circumstances the law acts as the oil of society, ensuring its smooth functioning and enabling the parts to work in harmony with each other. Imagine what would happen if there were no traffic laws telling us which side of the road to drive on! We all must surrender a degree of freedom to help us negotiate safely through our daily lives.

For health and social care practitioners there are a number of important laws which are concerned with protecting people by restricting freedom. They cover three broad categories:

- people who put others at risk
- people who put themselves at risk
- people who are put at risk by others.

> Joan and Arthur Green are the parents of two children, Wayne and Samantha, aged eight and three. Arthur is a heavy drinker. When he is drunk he often beats his wife, occasionally to the point of unconsciousness. The children are frequent witnesses of the violence. Wayne has begun to bully his sister. Joan has become increasingly depressed and has stopped feeding herself and the children. Alerted by neighbours, social workers and police enter the house. They find that Joan and the children are severely malnourished. Also, Samantha has extensive bruising caused by Wayne hitting her.

The Green family illustrate not just the three categories of risk but also three important areas of legislation which may be used to offer protection against those risks.

Mental Health Act 1983

When people are confused, depressed or psychotic they are unable to consider their own or others' best interests. The Mental Health Act lays down procedures designed to draw a balance between the needs of society for protection and the needs of the patient to be protected from abuse of their rights. The Act:

- specifies procedures for the compulsory admission of patients to hospital
- defines their rights while in hospital
- defines the circumstances of their treatment
- lays down procedures for their continued detention
- lays down procedures for their discharge
- defines who may exercise powers of detention and, in some cases, the training that they must have.

345

Christopher was a diagnosed schizophrenic who had been discharged to care in the community. During a severely psychotic episode he stabbed and killed a complete stranger. This case led to public demand for a review of the circumstances in which potentially dangerous patients are readmitted to the community.

ACTIVITY

Find out what type of support voluntary organisations working with people with mental health problems (such as MIND) offer to patients or ex-patients. Write a short report on how they help people to protect their rights to consultation about their treatment or their care.

The view that children are best looked after in their families is not confined to the Children Act. The Code of Practice for the Mental Health Act says that, where considering the compulsory admission of a young person:

any intervention in the life of a young person . . . should . . . result in the least possible segregation from family, friends, community and school.

A patient may be compulsorily detained if it is judged to be necessary for their health and safety or for the protection of others. In the case study of the Green family there might be consideration of the compulsory admission of Joan if she were to refuse voluntary treatment. However, the Act contains a central assumption that compulsory admission to hospital is very much a last resort.

The Act covers people who have a 'mental disorder'. This is defined in terms of four categories:
- mental illness
- severe mental impairment
- mental impairment
- psychopathic disorder.

The Act contains a series of safeguards of patients' rights where compulsory treatment is concerned. The more serious the level of medical intervention (e.g. psychosurgery or electro-convulsive therapy) the stricter the safeguards. Other safeguards of patients' rights are embodied in the Mental Health Review Tribunals (which consider applications for discharge) and the Mental Health Commission which has a general power to review the exercise of the Act's powers.

Children Act 1989

The Children Act brought together in a single piece of legislation the law relating to children. It covers:
- private childcare law (e.g. custody in divorce proceedings)
- public childcare law (e.g. the means by which children are looked after by local authorities)
- the duties of local authorities to children in care
- the powers and duties of local authorities to protect children from abuse.

The basic principles which underlie the Act are that:
- '. . . children are generally best looked after within the family with both parents playing a full part and without resort to legal proceedings'
- the interests of the child are paramount
- parents have parental responsibility which is only given up in the event of the child being adopted.

DISCUSSION POINT

The Children Act says that local authorities must:
- safeguard the welfare of children
- so far as is consistent with that duty, promote children's upbringing by their families.

Might there be any dilemmas caused for social workers working towards the fulfilment of these two principles?

What means of meeting both of the above do you think that social workers would use?

Although the Children Act takes the view that children are best raised in their own families it also recognises that this may not always be possible. The Act provides means by which a child may be removed from its parents:

- police protection
- emergency protection order
- care order
- residence order.

The first two powers are for limited periods, but the third and fourth may continue until the child becomes an adult.

When applying for a care order social workers must prepare a care plan outlining what their intentions are. The principal aim should always be for rehabilitation, but, where this is not possible, the plan may be for adoption with the parents losing all rights as parents.

Again, the underlying assumption is that children will continue to have contact with their parents as often as is reasonable. The Act also allows contact to be restricted, supervised, or non-existent, where this is felt to be in the best interests of the child. Where it is necessary to restrict or prevent contact social workers have only emergency powers and must get agreement from the court if the restrictions are to continue.

Criminal Justice Act 1991

The criminal justice system is concerned with the detection, trial and sentencing of crime. Although the rehabilitation of offenders should generally play some part, the concept of punishment for wrongdoers is inherent in the system. There is a tension between these two concepts which often leads to intense political debate.

Most criminal cases are heard in magistrates' courts. In some cases the accused may elect to be heard at this level or to be tried at Crown Court before a judge and jury. More serious cases may only be tried at Crown Court. In these cases the magistrates' court hears the case for committal, where the only decision to be made is whether there is a case to be answered.

Beyond the Crown Court there is an appeal structure on both sentencing and points of law which can go all the way to the House of Lords, which is the country's supreme court.

The diagram describes the court structure of England and Wales. Different systems apply in Scotland and Northern Ireland.

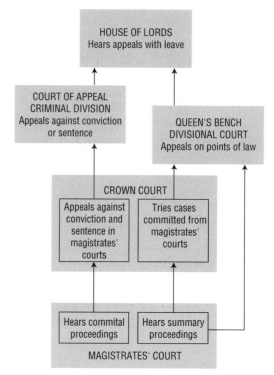

ACTIVITY

Find out about the other legal systems of the UK. How do they differ from the system in England and Wales? What are their court structures? Write a brief description of the system in either Scotland or Northern Ireland.

The main aim of the Criminal Justice Act 1991 was to try to reduce the number of people being sent to prison. It introduced four categories of sentences:

- discharges (absolute and conditional)
- fines
- community sentences
- custody (i.e. imprisonment).

Other than the first category, all of these involve some loss on the part of the accused. Fines are calculated according to a formula which takes into account both the seriousness of the offence and the means of the accused person. Community sentences involve a range of alternatives to imprisonment – probation, community service, attendance centre orders or curfew orders – all of which involve either a surrender of time or a restriction on freedom of action.

There are a number of questions raised about imprisonment for certain crimes, including:

- If it prison is intended as a deterrent, why do many people risk imprisonment?
- Will people learn not to reoffend when in prison in the company of other criminals?
- Is it right to punish their families as well as the offenders?

Ethical dilemmas and the liberty of individuals

Section 6.2.4 explains that many laws exist to help society function more easily. This works well when there is agreement, such as driving on the left-hand side of the road. There are other issues where opinion is more divided and where it is difficult, if not impossible, to achieve a consensus.

Individual or collective

An individual's right to opt out can have an effect on others. A parent's decision not to immunise their child could result in the child catching an infection. It also increases the risk of spreading the infection.

In some cases the state can intervene directly in order to remove an individual's right to make a personal decision. For example, Jehovah's Witnesses believe that the use of blood transfusions is wrong but local authority social services departments have taken care proceedings on the children of Jehovah's Witnesses where their lives have been in danger if they did not receive transfusions.

Similar dilemmas arise for health and social care practitioners when making decisions about their patients and service users.

What are the best interests of the service user?

There are many ways of defining a service user's best interests. The following people have a particular perspective and certain powers to make decisions based upon that perspective:

- the service user
- a close relative
- doctors
- psychiatrists
- care managers
- educational psychologists
- social workers
- residential care staff
- police officers
- magistrates.

Perspectives vary widely. For the service user the perspective could be: 'I want to be free to make my own choices', 'I want to feel safe' or even, in some cases, 'I'm frightened of what I might do if not placed in a secure environment'.

The practitioner's perspective, although it can be affected by a particular ideological standpoint, primarily depends upon the type of service user, the role the practitioner has in relation to them, the policies and practices of the organisation, and, for some, their legal responsibilities.

Perspectives often change over time. For example, the views of society can change radically. Former prevailing attitudes sometimes seem completely wrong to people today.

DISCUSSION POINT

The rights of individuals to 'opt out' are important, but so are the rights of others not to be placed at risk by that right. Do you think that there should be compulsory immunisation, either as a matter of course or during an epidemic, or do you think the rights of the individual are more important?

ACTIVITY

List all the people you think might be involved in making decisions about the freedom of another. Find out and write down what their powers are, when they might be able to use them, and what perspectives you think they might use.

Risk and learning difficulties: a historical perspective

In historical terms, people with learning difficulties were mistakenly perceived as a risk or danger to society. They were seen variously as antisocial (potential or actual criminals), dangerously immoral and promiscuous. The Mental Deficiency Act 1913 created special institutions to contain such alleged risks.

Policies emphasising civil rights and the principles of ordinary living have challenged these ideas. The philosophy of normalisation has been central in arguing that people with learning difficulties have a right to have everyday experiences, make choices and to take risks.

Adapted from *Community Care*, 19 October 1995

ACTIVITY

Think of someone you know about (a neighbour, relative or person whose case has been well publicised) whose freedom has had to be restricted at some time. List the factors, for and against, that would have to be considered in making that decision.

The practitioner's range of perspectives include:

- the best interests of the service user
- the best interests of society
- the safety of others
- the requirements of the law
- individual rights
- the fear of damaging publicity
- the fear of being sued for having taken the wrong decision.

The concept of risk is central to the practitioner's decision-making when considering restricting the freedom of others. These decisions depend on the balance of risk involved and should start from assessing what is in the best interest of the service user. The factors which must be considered are:

- the understanding and wishes of the service user
- personal security
- the right to take risks consistent with the safety of others
- the service user's personal happiness.

Joe is a person with moderate learning difficulties and some mental problems, which result in a tendency for him to be aggressive under pressure. He has lived for several years in a residential unit and now wishes to move into his own flat. In deciding whether he could do so, his social worker has to weigh up the risks:

For	**Against**
■ Joe's desire for independence	■ poor daily living skills
■ aggression controlled by medication	■ risk of neglecting diet
■ distress at remaining in the residential unit	■ might stop taking medication
■ would be supported by an integrated team	■ an unconventional lifestyle might make monitoring difficult

The social worker also balances Joe's wishes against the risk he might be to others.

Who is at risk?

Legislation which restricts personal liberty sets out three categories of individuals:

- those who put others at risk
- those who put themselves at risk
- those who are put at risk by others.

These categories are not mutually exclusive and some people may fall into two or all three categories. For example, Joe, who has moderate learning difficulties and mental health problems, might fall into all three:

- Because of his difficulties in providing himself with an adequate diet he might place himself at risk of neglect.

- If he becomes aggressive because he fails to take his medication he might place others at risk.
- His poor living skills might place him at risk of being exploited by others.

Practitioners who take decisions about the freedom of others have many issues to consider. They may be subject to pressures from external factors such as:

- political pressures
- resource pressures, such as the ability to pay for alternatives to incarceration
- public opinion and whether their organisation is willing to accept the outcry if a wrong decision is made.

Jamie Bulger was a small boy who was snatched from his mother in a Liverpool shopping centre, tortured, and then murdered by two eleven-year-old boys. Young people who commit murder are subject to the jurisdiction of Section 53 of the Children and Young Persons Act 1933 which allows them to be detained 'at her Majesty's pleasure'. The Court advises on the length of detainment but the final decision is taken by politicians at a later date.

The two boys in this case were sentenced by the judge to eight years imprisonment, which was later increased to ten. There was widespread condemnation (including from the parents of Jamie Bulger) of this sentence as too lenient. The Home Secretary intervened and increased the sentence to 15 years. This was later overturned by the European Court which found that the Home Secretary had acted unreasonably.

The boys' sentences will at first be spent in a secure unit for young people, where the emphasis will be upon treatment and change rather than punishment. When they are older they will be transferred to a prison.

What is the potential risk?

If good social work practice is really about user advocacy and empowerment it will inevitably involve risk factors. The legislation is normally referred to when the risks seem too great, but where the best long-term outcome must be rehabilitation the law does not necessarily help. There is never any right or wrong answer – just varying levels of risk: risk to the social services department if anything goes wrong; risk to the professional credibility of the professionals involved; and risk to the clients.

social worker, mental health team

Some risks may be immediately obvious, such as a child with severe physical injuries. It may be possible to quantify the degree of risk, for example, if a child is not immunised against whooping cough and catches it. For many risks there is no statistical evidence available. The practitioner must use their knowledge, skills and experience.

The more known risk factors that occur in a case, the higher the risk. For example, the risk factors for suicide are:

- elderly
- male
- divorced, widowed or single
- social isolation or living alone
- terminal illness
- other major physical illness
- history of self-harm
- family history of suicide
- family history of alcoholism or mood disorder
- childhood bereavement
- social class I or V
- psychiatric illness and personality disorder
- access to the means of suicide such as firearms or medication.

Of course, someone with a high number of these factors may not become a suicide and people in other circumstances may also take their own lives. The list is a tool for identifying those most likely to be at risk.

What damage will be done to the individual or others if liberty is restricted?

When considering restricting someone's liberty the risks that must be considered are not just those which may stem from taking no action, but also the risks there may be in taking action.

This dilemma is seen with young people in the youth justice system. The risks of disturbed young offenders who are placed in detention, indulging in degrees of self-harm (including suicide) are known to be high. The decision whether or not to detain these young people lies not with social workers, probation officers or psychologists, but with judges and magistrates, who may be advised but not directed. Many judges will make their decisions with care and sensitivity but the variation in sentencing decisions between judges suggests that some are more concerned with issues of public policy and presentation than with issues of risk to the young person.

If the wrong decision is taken, the results can lead to death or damage.

DISCUSSION POINT

Does society need to be specially protected against schizophrenics? Or is the loss of liberty implied for the massive majority of schizophrenics too high a price to pay for the extra protection and sense of security offered to society? What do you think?

DISCUSSION POINT

Which do you think is more important:

- The right to a secure and loving environment or the right to a physically safe environment?
- The right of the foster carers to make their own decisions whether or not to smoke or the right of their foster daughter to a healthy future?

In a recent well-publicised case foster carers of an eleven-year-old girl with cerebral palsy were told that if they did not give up smoking the girl would be removed from them, even though this might mean that she would be placed in a residential unit.

The foster carers were described as being distraught. They are reported to have told a journalist:

❝ *How are we going to explain to her that she will not see us again? She won't understand.* **❞**

The local authority's case was that the girl was severely asthmatic and that living in a home in which people smoked could have been life-threatening.

Key questions

1 List three practitioners for whom the promotion of health and social wellbeing is their main job.
2 What are the five target areas named in *The Health of the Nation*?
3 Describe three ways in which health services protect the public.
4 What are the four categories of registration in child protection?
5 List five people who might attend a child protection conference.
6. Explain the main task of an approved social worker.
7 What are the three main Acts of Parliament concerned with limiting freedom?
8 What are the three basic values of the Children Act 1989?
9 Name two courts in which people may be sentenced to imprisonment.
10 What are the four categories of sentencing
11 Describe three categories of risk which social workers might have to deal with.
12 Give two sources of pressure which might be placed on a social worker when considering restricting someone's liberty.

Assignment

Survey health and social care journals and national newspapers over a period of two months to find examples of dilemmas practitioners may face when balancing the liberty of service users against the concerns of the community or society in general.

Organise this material according to which areas of the legislation are involved. Select two different dilemmas which you will analyse further. Identify which parts of the legislation are most important for your selected dilemmas.

Write a report which:

■ describes the dilemmas and the actions being taken by the practitioner
■ explains any differences that there may be between different practitioners in terms of their responsibilities and their perceptions
■ compares the different balance of risks involved in the two dilemmas and how it differs for each person involved
■ describe and explain the different ways in which the dilemmas and risks were perceived in the popular press as compared with the specialist journals.

ELEMENT **6.3**

Service users and care provision

This element looks at how users and carers experience health and social care provision from four broad perspectives: their experience of receiving services, how they can influence those services, how their views can be taken into account by those planning the services and what can be done to encourage greater involvement.

66 My experience in care was a sense of not really belonging. You lived in a home and had what was then called aunts and uncles but I was aware of my ethnicity and that having white people looking after me was an anomaly, but having said that, it was my home. 99

Kriss Akabusi speaking about his experience of being brought up in care, Community Care October 1994

66 I've always been made to feel at my ease, apart from one experience. It was distressing because the gentleman was very abrupt in his manner and I would have to say he was cold, really. When we were discussing my case he said something about some cancer on my lungs, which I had known nothing about. He seemed as surprised as I was that I hadn't been told about it. It wasn't his fault I hadn't been told, but he could see I was worried and he didn't try to change his manner towards me. That would have helped to cushion the shock, I think. I came out feeling he was keeping something from me. This turned out not to be the case, but because he didn't come across in a caring way I didn't quite trust him.

I felt all the other staff were willing and supportive. Where I felt upset was not to do with the people caring for me, it was with the arrangements and lack of facilities and funding. For example, when it came to the operation I was admitted but then I had to get dressed and go home again because there was an emergency and they needed the bed. I had to wait two more weeks before another bed was available. The staff were very sympathetic and I can see it is worrying for them too.

Someone from the regional health service came out to interview me about the care I had received. The interview lasted about an hour, so it was quite in-depth. It was part of a countrywide evaluation of cancer care. I received a report on the care in the region. It did say that things could be improved and suggested more communication between doctors and patients.

One administrative difficulty was the letter with a form asking me to ring after 9.00 a.m. to see if there was a bed available, when I'd received a letter asking me to be there at 9.30 – I live more than an hour away so it was impossible to comply with the instructions. That happened three times. When you're worried about your state of health you can do without that sort of thing. In the end I wrote to the chairman of the hospital and after that the form was changed. So in my experience it is possible to get your voice heard. I felt I had helped to bring about a change for the better. 99

Lilian, who is undergoing treatment for cancer of the thyroid

Users' perceptions of health and social care services

Two important government White Papers, Working for Patients and Caring for People, have promoted the principle that service users and carers, the consumers of the services and facilities, should be involved in their planning and delivery.

This may seem an obvious point, but practitioners can become preoccupied with the challenge of organisational arrangements and the frustration of funding restrictions and because of this may not involve service users enough.

The starting point is for organisations and practitioners to listen to what users say about their experiences of care. There is more about this in section 6.3.5.

Control of the process

Some of the reasons cited by practitioners for maintaining control of the process include:

- Involving clients would breach confidentiality.
- Users would not be able to understand all the issues.
- It might undermine relationships with users and carers if the answers are not what they wanted to hear.

Respect as an individual

We all like to feel appreciated. You can probably think of many examples from your own experience.

66 *What was appreciated most was honesty, naturalness and reliability, along with an ability to listen. Clients appreciated being kept informed, having their feelings understood, having the stress of parenthood accepted and getting practical help as well as moral support. The social workers whose assistance was valued had a capacity to help parents retain their role as responsible authority figures in relation to their children.* 99

Social Work Decisions in Childcare: Recent Research Findings and their Implications,
HMSO, 1985

Being respected as an individual means being seen as a whole person rather than a set of labels. For example, a person with disabilities, learning difficulties or mental health problems should be seen as a person not as a condition. If the condition is long-standing or permanent it becomes a part of who that person is, but it is not the whole person.

Trust can be established by:

- acknowledging the validity of an individual's own experience
- meeting people on their own terms and in a setting where they feel comfortable.

The sociologist Irving Goffman investigated life in psychiatric hospitals in the USA, including why patients remained the whole day in their bedclothes, even when they spent most of the day out of bed. Having expected to find that there were medical reasons for this, his conclusion was that it was merely for the convenience of the staff who did not need to supervise patients while they were changing or look after two sets of clothing. Nobody had asked the patients whether it was comfortable for them and they did not question the practice because that was the way things were always done.

At the beginning of 1996 the London Borough of Islington carried out a random survey of 80 service users. They asked about users' degree of satisfaction with their home care, day centre or respite care:

- What services do you receive?
- Are people who come to help you (home carer, support worker) reliable?
- Do they arrive on time?
- Are they thoughtful?
- Are they caring?
- Are they able to do what you ask them?
- Do you have a good personal relationship with them?
- Is there continuity?

The results showed that users and carers expected from home care workers:

- reliability
- flexibility
- continuity
- friendliness
- a caring relationship
- keeping to standards.

Source: Islington's Community Care Plan, 1996–99

ACTIVITY

Look at national and local newspapers over three or four weeks and collect items which feature health and social care service users or carers. Record the service and what the user or the carer has said about it. Write a report on what you have learnt about how users and carers feel about services.

Care received

Users or carers may view the care being received very differently from how the practitioner or their organisations see it. For instance, is the care what the user really wants or is it what those making the assessment think they need?

Problems may occur if the nature of the care does not match the user's own wishes. This may be because of financial constraints or because an appropriate service is not available. The user's disappointment will be worse if the reasons for the mismatch are inadequately explained.

The way care is delivered affects how the user feels about it. A friendly home carer who uses appropriate language, who listens and is able to be flexible is more appreciated than one who is surly and rigid.

Information given

When making a choice, you will want to have information which allows you to weigh up the pros and cons, before you decide. Users and carers deserve:

- clarity
- honesty
- a reliable process
- rights
- choices.

DISCUSSION POINT

Collect information in the form of leaflets and brochures from your local authority or health services. Look at them as if you were a potential service user. Would you know how to contact the service or what rights you have?

Services and facilities

Matching the service to the user – and not the other way round – is the key requirement of the care package. For example, an elderly person would not expect to find themselves booked into the local youth club for day care. Other important factors include culture and class.

Practical support services, such as respite care, are useless unless they are able to maintain the cultural traditions of people's lives. Mr and Mrs Khan, the parents of two severely disabled young women, were unable to make use of the monthly respite care they were offered because the residential home did not provide for the language, religious or dietary needs of their daughters . . . but the local authority is satisfied that respite care has been offered to the family.

Comment from the Black Community Care Group on behalf of service users

Seamless services for users

Health and social services use various terms to describe how they seek to deliver care, such as:

- seamless service
- continuous provision of care.

There are key points in the user's relationship with health and care services:

- admission to care
- transition from one care setting to another
- transfer from one worker to another
- leaving care services.

Element 6.1 describes the ways organisations plan and deliver services.

Seamlessness of service

The definition of seamless is 'without a seam or seams; unbroken; flowing' (*Chambers Dictionary*). In the context of care planning, a seamless service is one which attempts to coordinate all the different services a user receives.

Natasha, a single mother of two boys, Mark and Peter, aged eight and five, broke her back in a serious car accident. She is now tetraplegic, unable to walk, with only limited use of her arms, and dependent on others for even basic bodily functions.

While their mother was in hospital, where she had a full assessment of her post-hospital needs, Mark and Peter were looked after by foster carers. The plan was for the family to live together in the community and a housing association offered a purpose-designed house. Visits were made to the hospital by Natasha's care manager, the boys' social worker and a representative of the housing association, to discuss the care plan with Natasha and hospital staff.

The final care plan involved several elements with money coming from more than one source:

- Natasha was given a purpose-built house.
- She received day care 24 hours a day, funded by community care, but paid so that she was able to employ the carer herself.
- A monthly sum was paid to her from the 'children in need' budget to employ a nanny.
- The children in care budget was used to pay for a respite foster care placement on alternate weekends.
- Natasha received regular input from the district nurse and physiotherapist.

Natasha and the various workers met together every six months for a 'network' meeting to ensure that the various contributions remained coordinated.

Continuity of provision

In Natasha's case the practitioners worked together to produce a care plan and tried to ensure that the various parts worked together harmoniously. They involved her fully in the planning and review of the service.

Few people have a care structure as complex as Natasha's, but many have more than one practitioner involved. It is important that practitioners do not take actions or give advice that is in conflict with that of other practitioners, particularly where there is more than one worker providing the same service (e.g. part-time home carers) or where there is a change of worker. Most users and carers are willing to accept different styles of working, but would not be happy if changes are made to the structure of care without consulting them.

Smooth transition from one care setting to another

Changes are a normal part of life, but people prefer them to occur in a way that gives continuity. When moving house, people often maintain contact with former neighbours. This continuity is important in giving a sense of who we are and where we come from. It is important to maintain a sense of smooth transition, from the time an individual enters a service to when they leave.

Admission to the services

First contact or admission can be through:
- a response to a letter requesting help
- a telephone call
- an office visit
- admission to a hospital or residential unit
- a home visit by a practitioner.

Moving from one care setting to another

Plans can change for many reasons, including:
- the changed circumstances of the user
- the user moving from assessment to long-term provision
- the original care plan proving unworkable
- the changed circumstances of the carer
- a change in the pattern of local provision
- a change in the focus of the agency providing the service
- the agency being no longer contracted by the social services department to supply the service
- new technology or medical or social practice
- new legislation affecting what may be provided
- altered financial circumstances.

Change can be threatening, but can be easier to accept when we have been prepared and involved in planning it.

One group particularly subject to changes are young people in care. In the past it was not unusual for young people to be moved suddenly and without

> ### ACTIVITY
>
> Choose two of the situations in the list and write down how you would like to be treated if this were your first contact. What are the things which could go wrong and what would be your impression of the service if they were to go wrong?

> ### ACTIVITY
>
> Think of a time when you had a major change in your life, such as moving to a new school, and write down what you can remember of it. What was good about it? What could have been better about it? Did you feel well prepared for the change?

any knowledge of where they were going. The Children Act now places much emphasis on the need for continuity.

There may be occasions when children or young people must move from:

- an assessment unit to longer-term provision
- a foster home to an adoptive home
- a care setting back to their own family.

In all of these cases there should be careful preparation with prior visits and time spent explaining the need for moves. In the case of children or young people moving to adoptive homes their social worker will spend a lot of time with them building a life story book, an account of who they are, where they have come from, who they have lived with and what has happened to them. Without this, they may well feel when they are older that a part of their life has 'gone missing'.

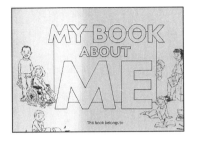

Smooth transition from one care worker to another

If a user is supported for any length of time, changes in practitioners are inevitable. If it is someone such as the care manager where the relationship is not close, it may not be too important. But the loss of a long-standing and reliable home carer can be the loss of a friend. The change can be made to feel an easier process by:

- giving notice of the change
- giving an explanation of the reason for the change
- involving the person who is leaving
- arranging an introduction or formal 'handing over' by one practitioner to another.

The candle ceremony

For children who are in care and moving from one care setting to another the change may be painful as they will have taken time to trust their carers. If they are moving to an adoptive family or long-term foster carer rather than to their birth parents this may be particularly difficult.

One way of helping is to hold a ceremony using candles. There will be a candle for each carer the child has had in their life. The first candle will be lit and the child told that the flame represents their parent's love for them. Each candle will be lit in turn from the previous one to represent the love which is passed on, but the candles will be left burning to show that love does not die. If the old and new carers are part of the ceremony, showing how they both carry the duty of trust that goes with love, then the ceremony can have a powerful impact upon all those involved.

Leaving care services

Many practitioners provide a service for a limited period of time. Following an accident there is intensive health and social care support with many services being involved until recovery. The goal of this treatment and care is to work for independence.

When Patrice, an interior designer, moved into her first flat after being in care for 16 years she had so little furniture she painted a TV, chairs and a table on the wall. 'I was pregnant when I was 15, had a baby when I was 16, and was put into a flat when I was 16. All I had was a bed and a cot'. She recalls that she had no help or support. 'The attitude was "Just get on with it".'

Community Care, October 1994

ACTIVITY

List the things you think you would need to know about if about to live on your own for the first time. Also think of the things you would need, such as furniture, utensils and equipment and estimate how much they would cost.

ACTIVITY

Using the information collected earlier for section 6.3.1, carry out a content analysis. Is the information clear? What does it tell you about the service? Is the information available in other languages? What would you feel about the service if you were a potential user?

Young people moving from care to independent living can find the experience very difficult. Many young people leaving home for the first time are able to choose the moment of departure and have the reassurance of knowing that they can return home if things do not work out. Young people leaving care have little choice about when they leave. It must happen by the time they are 18 (unless they are in full-time education) and they cannot go back if things do not work out. Research shows that many young people slide into debt and homelessness.

The Children Act places a responsibility on local authorities to continue to help young people who have been in care but it does not specify the type and extent of 'help' they are required to provide.

Smooth flow of information

We all have files kept on us by many agencies, for example:

- doctors
- schools or employers
- banks.

These files are continually being added to. Only authorised people are allowed access to them, in order to maintain confidentiality. We have certain rights of access to some, but not all, of this information. When we do, it is important that the information is understandable. A number of factors help understanding and trust:

- clarity

  Is the information expressed clearly? Is there someone available who can explain things? Is the information in a form which meets the needs of all users, for example on audio tape or in Braille or in other languages?

- honesty

  Is the truth being told or is there dishonesty by omission? Few things are more irritating than being given promises that are not kept. If the person making those promises knows that they cannot keep them the effect is more damaging.

- who does what

  Who are the practitioners who will be involved, why do they need to be there and what can they do and not do? If there are things that they cannot do, why can't they?

- service availability

  What services are available? Who provides them? Where can they be found? Who will pay? How easy will access be?

- process

  Are users kept informed of the process?

- rights

  Are users clear about their own rights and the limits to choices available?

Support for people receiving care

> 66 *I am a single parent living in a middle-class suburb with my son who has visual and hearing impairment and a form of autism. In 1993 a social worker and I drew up a care plan which included respite care, home support and day care. A year later I had still not received any of the services promised in the care plan. In the end I went to my MP for help. Two years on, I have only had occasional respite care.* 99
>
> mother describing her experience of care planning in a survey of users

Section 5.1.2 looks at the ways in which services are classified.

A user's definition of needs is more likely to focus on:

- physical support
- financial support
- emotional support
- knowledge of what is available
- understanding from practitioners
- social support from family, peer group and the community.

For the practitioner other criteria apply:

- what can be afforded
- what is available
- the limitations on availability
- if choices are necessary, which of the user's needs is to be given the highest priority?

Physical support

We all have certain basic physical needs:

- somewhere to live
- reasonable health
- food, water and breathable air.

How these physical needs are met vary according to the needs of the individual. For example, a user with severe respiratory illness (either permanent or intermittent) obviously needs access to breathing apparatus.

Housing support

Suitable housing, adaptations and equipment are important for meeting the physical needs of users. A survey by RADAR of 700 complaints from people with disabilities found that the largest number were about housing, adaptations and equipment.

Equipment or adaptations encourage independence. Physiotherapists or occupational therapists are responsible for identifying the most appropriate adaptation to meet the user's physical needs.

Mobility

There is a lot of equipment which aims to give improved mobility, for example, walking frames, wheelchairs and specially adapted cars. Transport is

ACTIVITY

Choose a case about someone
with restricted mobility.
Investigate ways in which their
mobility could be improved. What
mobility support might be suitable
and how might it be supplied?

often necessary to enable users to get to services or for the services to get to
them.

Sometimes a user's mobility needs can be inappropriately met. For example, it
would be inappropriate to offer meals-on-wheels to someone who does not
cook if the real problem is their inability to get to the shops.

Home care

It cannot be assumed that everyone is able to feed themselves adequately. For
some users, who can do no more than simple cooking, meals-on-wheels
guarantees the provision of at least one hot meal a day.

Safety and hygiene

A clean and safe environment is another physical need. The user's home
needs to be made as safe as possible – free of germs or hazards to mobility –
without affecting their rights and choices. The home care service plays a key
role in ensuring the maintenance of a reasonable level of safety and
independence.

Financial support

An income gives people choices, independence and flexibility. Great tact is
needed when investigating peoples' financial means. Many people are
secretive or evasive about their financial situation because of:

■ the shame of being financially dependent
■ the fear of losing possessions or capital
■ their age or their cultural expectations.

The national service with responsibility for providing financial support for
those who are not working or on low pay is the Department of Social Security,
through the Benefits Agency.

Health authorities and social services departments have limited powers directly
to provide financial aid, for example:

■ social services departments may provide money for children in need often
in the form of cash or kind (such as food or nappies)
■ support for young people leaving care
■ contributions to a disabled person under 65 so that they can manage their
own care package.

Practitioners can take a number of actions to assist users with financial matters:

■ ensure that users are receiving full social security entitlement, especially
where one benefit allows access to others
■ ensure they receive housing or council tax benefit
■ give emotional support to users and carers if there are problems or delays
in payments
■ help users and carers manage their weekly budgets.

Emotional support

Vulnerability creates a need for emotional support but can inhibit willingness to accept it. For example, experiences with family and friends may have caused the unhappiness or a sense of betrayal. Users may distrust anyone offering support.

KIM

Kim, who is twelve, came into care four months ago on a voluntary basis. Her parents had separated when she was six and she initially went to live with her mother and her mother's new partner. After a year her mother had a new baby and, feeling that she could not cope, asked Kim's father to take her. Two years later Kim's father remarried and her new stepmother brought her own two children into the home. Kim found the newcomers difficult to adjust to and began to steal money. After another year her father asked his own mother to look after her, but after 18 relatively stable months, her grandmother became ill and could no longer care for Kim. Kim went back to her own mother but after only three months, back to her father again. Three months later, he asked the social services department to take Kim into care because he had been provoked into hitting her and was fearful of doing more damage.

After two months in an emergency foster home, Kim was moved to a longer-term foster placement. She has begun to steal, stay out late and damage property. She has told the foster carer 'I hate you because you are only doing it for the money.'

Emotional support can be provided to deal with situations such as:

- isolation
- bereavement (of a loved one, limb, job, home or community)
- adjustment to changes in lifestyle.

66 *Everyone grieves in a different way – people probably see me in the street laughing . . . nobody knows what goes on inside. The only person I have really cried in front of is Barbara. I know she's there for me. If I need to talk I can pick up the telephone. If it wasn't for her, I couldn't have come through this.* 99

user of a bereavement scheme run by casualty nurses

Support may be offered one-to-one, in a group, or even by regular telephone contact. A specific crisis telephone number can be an important way of offering support at times of emotional crisis. An example is the telephone contact provided by the Samaritans, an organisation of volunteers who talk to people who feel suicidal.

People can also take emotional comfort from familiar objects, such as photographs, letters, ornaments or clothing. For this reason, users entering into residential care are encouraged to bring their own belongings, including furniture, with them.

Knowledge

If users and carers are to have power within the system they must have access to information. Section 6.2.4 explains how practitioners can enable users and carers to participate in care planning; section 5.3.3 looks at the requirement for health and social care organisations to keep people informed.

The user, or their carer, requires more than a description of the service or the procedure. For instance, they need to know:

- information relevant to their situation
- how to gain access to resources and services
- the processes through which resources are allocated
- how to make best use of the services provided
- how to present themselves in a way which puts them at their best advantage.

To take advantage of the information, users and carers need to understand the jargon practitioners use and to have the confidence to deal with the system.

Advocacy

Advocates can provide representation and information to people in many settings on behalf of the user. Where the user is unable to handle knowledge themselves an advocate can become the holder and user of knowledge for them.

> An **advocate** is someone who speaks on behalf of another and has the faith, confidence, and trust of the person they are representing.

❝ *It's the first time anyone asked me what I want . . . the advocacy service has a totally different attitude. The people there are on the side of reason rather than just trying to get away with things or pass the buck. I'm often treated as a 'disabled person' but the advocacy service treats you as a 'person with a disability'.* **❞**

user of an advocacy service

By using their knowledge of the system advocates can represent users at case conferences, assessment meetings or in care plan reviews. They have only one interest to represent and argue for – that of the user.

Practitioners encourage some users to attend a training programme or college course as part of their route to becoming independent. Training can offer opportunities to learn new skills, acquire information and knowledge and, for young people or adults of working age, a chance to become qualified.

ACTIVITY

Imagine that you are an advocate for an elderly person or someone with mental health problems. Write down what kinds of information they would need to have in order to meet with the social worker who is coming to talk about changing their existing services. What help would you be able to give? Where might you speak on their behalf?

Understanding

❝ *. . . a pattern of one-to-one communication had to be resurrected as elderly people had often been 'talked over' on the assumption that they were unable to understand.* **❞**

research report on a community care project in Gateshead, 1990

DISCUSSION POINT

Look at the prospectus of any further education college (or community school, if appropriate). What does it offer which could be tapped by users and carers to meet their knowledge needs? Think about how accessible the college is for health and social care users.

To communicate their needs effectively, users need to understand what their needs are and be able to express them. Practitioners are unlikely to have had the same experiences as their users but they can share them through discussion and empathy.

The crux of empathy is communication. It means offering support and care in a way which is acceptable to the user.

> 66 *When I went to the doctor's one time, the receptionist gave me the prescription. Well she gave it me and it went through my hand on to the floor. She went straight and reported to the doctor that I had thrown it on the floor.* 99
>
> patient with arthritis

Practitioners can show empathy by:

■ not jumping to conclusions
■ not assuming that what they see is the real picture
■ not taking a fellow practitioner's view as the only one
■ not being misled by appearances.

Social support

> 66 *I'd like to be able to get out. I don't like being caged in. Now as the weather gets warmer and brighter I get sadder. My husband takes me out at weekends but I'm back indoors from Mondays.* 99
>
> disabled women who is active in her community but can only get out when transport is available

> 66 *June [the respite carer] and I do a lot together. We go to the cinema and the theatre. Sometimes June comes round to my flat or we go to her country cottage. I really look forward to seeing June as we have some really good times together. Respite is all about making friends and having fun.* 99
>
> young disabled woman talking about her experience of respite care

Family, interest or peer groups, and the community we live in are also important in helping to ensure that we have a good quality of life. People who have disabilities or who are ill, elderly or vulnerable can be restricted in their participation in a social life.

Think what it would feel like if you suddenly found yourself surrounded by strangers who dealt with you brusquely and impersonally. People in hospital or other residential provision may experience care like this. Routines may be organised so they benefit the organisation or the staff, rather than the patients. Shift patterns or rigid meal times can make visiting difficult.

Visits from friends and relatives or friendships with other patients or residents are an essential link with normality. For this reason many hospitals have adopted flexible visiting hours and, in the case of children or patients in intensive care or people who are dying, facilities are provided for parents, carers and immediate family to stay with them.

Appropriate care takes a more dynamic and proactive view of encouraging social contact. Practitioners need to ask themselves a series of questions:

■ Do they know who the user's friends and relatives are?
■ Are the user's family members or friends accessible?
■ Will the local community be supportive?
■ Are there facilities to encourage social interaction?

| Section 6.3.4 |

Ways in which users and carers can take control of care

This section gives examples of how health and social services have encouraged user and carer involvement. It links with element 6.1.4.

Practitioners need to ask two major questions when planning or providing a service:
- What are the needs?
- Do we have the resources to meet them?

The similar questions of the client are likely to be:
- What do I need?
- How can I can get my needs met?

66 When it comes to looking after my daughter I am the expert. The practitioners are not the experts in her but they are there to advise me in the particular aspects of her care in which they are expert. I want to be advised by them, not told what to do. 99

parent of a cerebrally palsied child

Taking control

A sense of control can come from contributing to decisions. Factors that help give users a sense of control include:
- access to information
- a feeling that their opinions and experiences are valued
- recognition of their knowledge, abilities and skills
- knowledge of the choices
- a clear understanding about which choices are theirs to make and which are not.

Obtaining information

Access to information is the key to empowering users and carers. A lot of information about services is provided by health and social care agencies and voluntary and community groups. Commercial organisations or private care organisations also provide information.

Obtaining advice

For people to feel valued and empowered information must be:
- honest and clear
- easily available
- freely volunteered.

Silence can breed suspicion. If a practitioner has to wait for information to pass on to a user or carer, they should contact them to explain what is happening. This way the user or carer will feel that they have not been forgotten.

A skill that can make a great deal of difference to a feeling of control is the ability to keep records, however simple.

Development of skills

People needing health and social care support have the same need to develop skills as people who are not users. For this reason enabling interventions are frequently chosen by care managers. For young people, or those with disabilities, learning difficulties or mental health problems, access to education and leisure facilities can be an important factor in them going or returning to work or developing the skills needed to live independently.

For users who may be older or more limited in their mobility, retaining or learning new movements can ensure that they maintain their quality of life or independence.

UNIT

6

ELEMENT **6.3**

ACTIVITY

Select a user group. Write a case study about their skills development. What are they learning and why and how are they learning it?

Deciding how resources should be used

It is unusual for users to have direct control of all financial resources needed to pay for their care. The care manager normally does this. However, users and carers should be involved in discussions about resources. Where some needs cannot be met, the priorities chosen should be discussed with users and carers and reflect their preferences.

Deciding how care should be planned and delivered

The extent to which users and carers are involved in planning and delivery varies according to where they live. User groups are keen to encourage their members to take an active part in planning their own care. They provide information, advice and support to users so that they can have more say in this.

User and carer networks and forums

User and carer networks and forums are important in providing a voice for their members. They support individual users by providing information, advice and advocacy. Some provide services through self-help initiatives such as outings, clubs, befriending or relief care. Many contribute to the community care planning process and raise broader issues relating to health and social care.

User and carer groups have been founded by:
- practitioners, voluntary groups and residents
- voluntary groups (as an extension of their services or community activities)
- practitioners (as an extension of their activities)
- the health or social services department as a means of formally listening to users and carer's views
- users and carers.

Many such groups operate on a local basis, although they are part of a national network, because this is the best way of encouraging participation. The aims of such groups vary, but include:

- a mutual exchange of knowledge and experience
- a social setting for people facing similar difficulties
- a campaign for better resources
- the encouragement of better public understanding
- an opportunity to research local facilities and needs.

Consultation with carers

Birmingham City Council pioneered consultation with carers in 1987 through its Community Care Special Action Project. The project sought the views of over 300 carers about what it was like to be a carer in Birmingham and what kinds of support services they found useful. While practitioners were invited to the meetings, they could only listen, not speak. In this project, and other consultations with carers, carers gave this advice to practitioners about how to address their needs:

- Recognise carers' contribution and needs.
- Tailor services to individual circumstances, needs and views, through consultation.
- Ensure services reflect an awareness of differing racial, cultural and religious backgrounds.
- Give opportunities for short and longer breaks.
- Give practical support.
- Provide opportunities for talking about feelings.

ACTIVITY

Investigate local organisations which represent service users and list them. Write down their views on user participation. Do they produce information for their members designed to help them to participate? Do they provide an advocacy or befriending service for those who are less able to represent themselves? If so, how do they provide this service?

Users managing their own care

One of the problems faced by people receiving care is that they do not generally have control over financial resources. One exception is where the user has received compensation as a result of an insurance or court settlement.

However, legislation in 1996 has extended users' rights to be given funding by local authorities to pay for their own care. Also, the number of independent living schemes has increased as local authorities begin to see the benefits of user management.

DISCUSSION POINT

If users are to be given public money to make their own choices over care, to what extent should those choices be advised or guided by practitioners?

368

Involving users in improving services

How I was affected by moving into the community

An elderly service user who is resident at an Anchor Housing Association flat at Northbourne, Gateshead, reflects on life in the community.

■ What would have made your transition into the community better?

I came out of a nursing home and I needed help in getting beds and furniture, and putting up the curtain rails.

■ Do you work in partnership with the people providing the service?

We do work in partnership at Northbourne. Our agreement and our choices are also incorporated within care plans and reviews.

■ Did you have some say in the way your room was decorated?

I decorated my own room and chose the wallpaper.

■ Do you get the chance to learn new skills, cooking for example?

If I want to cook, the facilities are provided and there is assistance available from staff if required.

■ Do you get to see your family as often as you like?

I cannot visit my family as most of them live in upstairs flats, but they visit me at Northbourne.

■ Do you feel you are treated as an adult?

Yes I am.

Community Care, 24 August 1995

The former approach of welfare services of 'doing things for people' has slowly changed over many years to 'doing things with people'. This has had a number of causes:

■ an increasing emphasis on people having a right to express their views

■ a popular feeling that 'experts' do not have all the right answers

■ the spread of equal opportunities practice and legislation

■ a greater emphasis on consultation and rights through legislation and government charters

■ a greater emphasis on empowerment for service users

■ a market-based model of provision which has encouraged providers to see service users as 'customers'.

The concept of partnership, with user and carer empowerment, is fundamental to health and social care practice.

Listening to users and carers

❝ *I was always pleased that my mother was supported by so many people, such as the district nurse, a home help and physiotherapist. But it would have been nice if they had just stopped to ask me how I was feeling. Perhaps they were worried I might grumble. The GP did ask me, but then I was his patient too.* **❞**

former carer

66 *They need good listening skills, and I mean really good listening skills, because we don't always say to other people what we want to say . . . It takes a lot of trust to be able to tell someone the truth about how you feel.* **99**

disabled man talking about social workers

> **66** *They need good listening skills, and I mean really good listening skills, because we don't always say to other people what we want to say . . . It takes a lot of trust to be able to tell someone the truth about how you feel.* **99**
>
> *disabled man talking about social workers*

DISCUSSION POINT

One of the problems of a provider organisation asking for comments from their service users is that respondents are unable to be honest in their response because they feel 'grateful' or are anxious that they will lose the help that they get. What do you think organisations could do to overcome this?

Where can we hear the voices of users and carers telling us what they want, how they feel and what it feels like to receive care? Some ways of collecting views include:

- talking with service users and their carers – for many users the most important thing is to be listened to
- listening to the views of user and carer support groups
- through complaints procedures
- articles in newspapers and magazines
- getting feedback through response questionnaires
- undertaking surveys of users
- reading independent surveys and research.

Unit 8 looks at the topic of research in more detail.

Information exchange

The past 20 years have seen an increasing emphasis by government on providing formal processes by which the user's views can be heard as part of a dialogue, an exchange of information.

The oldest of these is the Community Health Councils, which were established to represent the patient's voice in a formal way. They have open meetings and rights of access to those in power in the NHS. They often conduct their role in a dynamic way, seeking out the views of users and researching their experiences of the process of health care.

More recently, charters of service such as the Patient's Charter have sought to lay down benchmarks by which people may judge the standard of service they are receiving. Organisations which fail to deliver can be made to change their procedures.

The various channels by which complaints may be made give feedback to providers and a means by which complainants may obtain an explanation of their treatment. Those channels are:

- local councillors
- MPs
- MEPs
- ombudsmen.

Section 1.1.4 looks at the variety of routes for seeking redress.

Improving care services

The emphasis of this section is on testing your understanding of what you have learnt in this unit about services – how they are planned and delivered and how practitioners involve the user and their carer in the planning and delivery of services matched to their needs.

The case study about Jackie illustrates the stress that caring for an elderly and difficult relative can have on families and the limitations of the help that is available to them.

UNIT

6

ELEMENT **6.3**

For 20 years Jackie and her husband Clive looked after her mother Edith, who had Alzheimer's disease. They also had the responsibility of bringing up their two daughters. As Edith's condition worsened and she needed closer attention the demands on the family increased. The family bought an off-licence with accommodation attached in the hope that Jackie and eventually Clive could work from home. But Edith's condition deteriorated and they had to employ assistants in the shop to free Jackie to care for Edith. Clive worked very long hours to make enough to live on.

The family had four hours help a week from care attendants, and social services supplied night sitters for Edith for two nights a week. For the remaining five nights the family had to manage. For a short time a district nurse came to put Edith to bed but it was decided that this was not a medical need and this source of support was withdrawn.

The family could not have outings together and were able to have only two short holidays in the previous ten years.

Eventually the business collapsed under the financial strain and Clive and Jackie were declared bankrupt. They were successful in suing the government in the European Court to extend the right to Invalid Care Allowance to married women caring for disabled relatives.

Edith died in 1994 and the family's finances became stable again, but the emotional stress of the death was a problem. 'When you're dealing with a situation 24 hours a day and it just stops, it is a big shock,' said Jackie in an interview. In 1995 Clive moved out.

Jackie now believes that her determination to keep Edith out of residential care led to her family being bankrupted, deprived their daughters of the childhood they deserved and eventually cost them their marriage.

DISCUSSION POINT

The case of Jackie and her family is an extreme one but it demonstrates the pressures of caring and how families must often deal with conflicting needs, even when the caring stops.

What could have been done for Jackie to enable her to care with less stress on her whole family? How could her needs and views have been assessed in a way that involved her fully in the process? What support do you think she needed after Edith's death and who might best have supplied this?

ACTIVITY

You are a new care manager who finds that community care in your area tends to be delivered to a formula, very much geared to what is available rather than what is needed. As a result there have been complaints, not just from users but also from other practitioners, in particular the local GPs. Your managers have given you a brief to suggest improvements to the service. Write a report to your manager outlining how you would set about doing this.

The report should cover a number of aspects, including:

■ broadening the services available

■ involving potential providers

■ encouraging flexibility

■ consulting service users and carers about their view of the current service

■ involving users in planning, improving and monitoring services.

You will find it helpful to speak with a care manager on how they maintain the responsiveness of their services.

Key questions

1 What do you understand by respect?
2 List five things a service user might want to find in information given to them about a service.
3 List the five categories of users' perceptions of care.
4 What does seamlessness of care mean?
5 Explain five reasons why users might change their care setting.
6 List the six areas of support a service user might require.
7 List five possible sources of emotional support.
8 What do you understand by empathy?
9 Explain four ways in which a practitioner can enable a user to take control.
10 Give two examples of how a user or carer network can promote a user's involvement.
11 Give four reasons for a greater emphasis on user involvement.

Assignment

Approach a local community health council or similar body for users or carers and ask them for information or reports which comment on services that they have provided to the health authority or social services departments. Analyse the reports and list the main criticisms of services and comments about ways in which they could be improved.

Contact a health or social care service and negotiate with the manager to interview at least two service users to seek their views about the services. Before the interview, draw up a set of questions to find out their views on the services they have been provided with and how much they have been consulted about their care. Collate the responses and compare them with the reports from the community health council or user network.

Write a report which includes details of:
■ the services the users have received
■ the choices they were given
■ their involvement in planning and reviewing their care
■ the information they have been given
■ what differences they would like to see in their care.

The report should include your own recommendations on how services could be improved, reflecting the comments of the people you interviewed.

UNIT **7**

Element 7.1
Health education campaigns

Element 7.2
Reasons, sources and methods

Element 7.3
Evaluating a health education campaign

Educating for health and social wellbeing

This unit identifies a range of health education campaigns, the organisations responsible for them and the reasons for their interest. Unit 3 about the physical aspects of health and social wellbeing and unit 4 on the psychosocial aspects are also relevant.

ELEMENT **7.1**

Health education campaigns

In this element you will look at a range of health education needs and examine how health education campaigns formulate objectives for reaching target audiences.

Introducing the National Food Guide

The Balance of
Good Health

Information for educators and communicators

The new National Food Guide, *The Balance of Good Health*, aims to help people understand and enjoy healthy eating. It shows that people don't have to give up the foods they most enjoy for the sake of their health. But variety and a change towards more vegetables, fruit, bread, breakfast cereals, potatoes, rice and pasta is what matters. Snacks as well as meals count towards the healthy balance.

Fruit and vegetables
Choose a wide variety

Bread, other cereals and p...
Eat all types and choose high... kinds whenever you can

Meat, fish and alternatives
Choose lower fat alternatives whenever you can

Fatty and sugary foods
Try not to eat these too often, and when you do, have small amounts

Milk and dairy foods
Choose lower fat alternati... whenever you can

66 *The Active for Life campaign focuses on encouraging people to take part in physical activity. The campaign was launched at a PR event attended by the junior Health Minister in March 1996. This launch was planned to coincide with the first day of the TV advertising. The advertisements appeared on national TV (ITV and Channel 4). The advertising was linked to the broader campaign, involving lots of health and leisure professionals (about 4,000) in local promotion. Their activities vary from launch events – for example, coverage in the local media – to promotion 'on the ground' – for example a charity walk, fun run or exhibition. We provide support to local professionals for these local events. There has been no paid press advertising – but a lot of unpaid press editorials in newspapers and magazines. In this first year of the campaign there has been no radio advertising either, though we are considering this for the second phase. We have produced tons of promotional leaflets and we have campaign packs to promote the aims of the campaign.*

The message of the campaign is aimed at as wide a target group as possible – the general population. In the first year we aim to establish the credibility of the campaign. However, there are three particular groups we will be focusing on as the campaign progresses through its second and third years, because research has shown these groups are most in need of the encouragement and information we can provide. These are middle-aged men, older people (50+) and 16- to 24-year-old women.

The campaign has been targeted quite broadly so far, but there have been some aimed at specific groups, for example, features in women's magazines. The results of our qualitative research suggested that different messages would be needed to encourage increased levels of physical activity in different target groups. The men rated enjoyment and sociability highly, women tended to put store by keeping weight down and enhancing physical appearance, and older people thought the important benefits of exercise were to do with maintaining physical and mental agility, thereby helping themselves to stay independent. 99

physical activity manager, Health Education Authority

Health and social wellbeing and health education campaigns

In the UK today, everyone is the target of health education campaigns. Cartoon characters encourage children to brush their teeth and follow the Green Cross Code. Music stars and magazines give young people messages about the dangers of solvent and drug abuse. And the adult population is constantly fed information on health issues through newspapers, leaflets, advertisements, TV and radio.

The goal of health education campaigns is to improve the population's mental, physical and social health and wellbeing. They aim to do this by providing advice and information to help people make informed choices about their own and others' health and wellbeing.

Campaigns can be divided into three categories:

	Aims	Examples
Primary health education campaign	To prevent health problems arising	Discouraging children from starting smoking Advice on healthy eating Advice on safe sex Immunisation programmes
Secondary health education campaign	To identify and tackle health problems people already have To change people's bad health habits	Screening programmes to identify disease Advice for smokers to help them give up Information aimed at overweight people on how and why to lose weight
Tertiary health education campaign	To help people cope with chronic or serious health problems	Advice for people with cancer about the different treatments available Information on services for people with disabilities Advice on rehabilitation after serious illness

ACTIVITY

As a group, brainstorm a list of different health education campaigns you have experienced, dividing them into primary, secondary and tertiary campaigns. Which type of campaign is most commonly targeted at your age group?

Whether they're primary, secondary or tertiary, health education campaigns may use any of these information channels:

- national media (newspapers, television, magazines, advertising)
- local media (local radio, local newspapers)
- health education leaflets
- promotional events (such as workshops on giving up smoking).

The manager in charge of a health authority's health promotion unit explains how these different information channels interact:

" Our health promotion calendar involves a mixture of local, national and even international events. For example, in April we focused on four main highlights: World Health Day, Eye Safety Week, Cystic Fibrosis Week and Arthritis Care Week. These involved a combination of reports in national newspapers, magazines and on TV, local promotional events (such as competitions, workshops and debates), and coverage of the events and issues in local newspapers and radio programmes. In every case, health promotion leaflets produced by national organisations and by our own education unit played an important part, giving people some information they could take away. "

All health education campaigns focus on one or more of four main aspects of health and social wellbeing:

- reducing the likelihood of disease – for example, heart disease, cancer, HIV
- promoting healthy living practices – for example, improving diet, taking more exercise
- minimising the risk of potentially harmful living practices – for example, cutting down on smoking and alcohol consumption
- promoting personal safety and security – for example, household security, road safety, gas and electrical safety.

As the diagram below shows, some of these aspects are interlinked, and are often tackled together in health education campaigns.

> **DISCUSSION POINT**
>
> Look back at the list of health education campaigns you brainstormed, and decide which aspect of health and social wellbeing is covered by each campaign. Do some cover more than one aspect?

The chain of health education

PROMOTING HEALTHY LIVING PRACTICES | Lack of exercise and poor diet can cause disease | REDUCING LIKELIHOOD OF DISEASE | Smoking, alcohol, drugs and unsafe sex can cause disease | REDUCING HARMFUL LIVING PRACTICES | Smoking, alcohol and drugs can cause accidents | PROMOTING PERSONAL SAFETY AND SECURITY

Reducing likelihood of disease

Disease – from influenza and mumps to heart disease and cancer – is obviously one of the major threats to people's health and wellbeing. Health education campaigns aim to reduce the likelihood of disease in two key ways:

- preventing disease (primary health education) by
  - promoting the benefits of immunisation programmes
  - promoting the benefits of healthy living practices throughout life, such as exercise and a balanced diet
  - encouraging people not to adopt harmful living practices, such as smoking and excessive alcohol consumption.

- curing disease or preventing it getting any worse (secondary health education) by
  - encouraging people with health problems to adopt healthy living practices
  - encouraging people to cut back and stop harmful living practices.

Immunisation programmes

Immunisation against infectious disease has been one of the most successful breakthroughs in medicine, responsible for eliminating or drastically reducing the incidence of potentially fatal diseases such as poliomyelitis and diphtheria.

Immunisation – also known as inoculation or vaccination – involves giving people a vaccine orally or by injection. The vaccine is made up of parts of the organism which cause the disease, related organisms which cause a similar but milder disease, or dead organisms. These provoke an immune response in the body without actually causing the disease. The body produces antibodies, and is able to fight much more effectively if it encounters the disease again.

Most people in the UK believe that all children should be immunised against diphtheria, whooping cough, tetanus, polio, measles and tuberculosis. All girls should also be vaccinated against rubella between the ages of ten and fourteen, to prevent damage to the fetus if they catch the disease when pregnant. At the start of the winter, people at risk of lung infections (such as elderly people and asthmatics) are advised to be inoculated against influenza.

Doctors are given money to promote immunisation, and regular health education campaigns are run to:

- inform individuals of immunisations they may need, for example telling travellers what they should be immunised against when visiting different countries, advertising flu jabs in the winter
- inform parents about immunisation, so they know when their children should be immunised against different diseases
- emphasise the benefits of immunisation
- allay people's fears of immunisation.

DISCUSSION POINT

As this graph shows, immunising children against measles has resulted in an enormous drop in the number of cases of measles in the last 50 years. Yet some parents are still unwilling to let their children be vaccinated because they are worried about side effects. What type of health education campaign do you think would combat their fears most effectively?

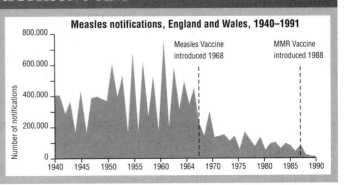

Measles notifications, England and Wales, 1940–1991

Measles Vaccine introduced 1968

MMR Vaccine introduced 1988

It is not possible to immunise against all diseases. In these cases, health education focuses on promoting lifestyles and behaviour which reduce the likelihood of the disease. In particular, campaigns focus on:

■ heart disease

■ cancer

■ HIV

■ sexually transmitted diseases.

Heart disease

Heart disease is the most common cause of death in the UK, and as such is the target for many health education campaigns. It is usually caused by atherosclerosis – the build up of fatty patches in the arteries which affect the flow of blood. This may result in either:

■ coronary heart disease – angina and heart attacks (which caused more than one in four deaths in the UK in 1990)

■ strokes – also known as cerebral thrombosis, when the brain is affected by poor circulation (more than one in ten deaths in the UK in 1990 were caused by strokes).

The Health of the Nation, a plan to improve health in the UK produced by the Government in the early 1990s, focused on coronary heart disease and strokes as one of five key areas for improvement. It recognised that many of the causes of heart disease – such as smoking, raised blood pressure, raised blood cholesterol levels, obesity and lack of exercise – are within people's control. In line with this, it set these targets:

■ by the year 2000

  – reduce heart disease death rates in people under 65 by at least 40%, and among people between 65 and 74 by at least 30%

  – reduce the death rate from strokes among people under 75 by at least 40%

  – reduce the number of people smoking by about a third

■ by 2005

  – reduce the number of people aged 16 to 64 who are obese by at least a quarter for men and at least a third for women

  – reduce average intake of fat by 12%, and saturated fats by 35%

  – reduce the number of men drinking more than 21 units of alcohol per week and women drinking more than 14 units per week by a third.

As these targets suggest, health education campaigns tend to focus on the risk factors which increase the likelihood of heart disease.

ACTIVITY

Collect leaflets, booklets and videos on preventing heart disease from your doctor's surgery, local library or health education centre. List the points they focus on. Can you identify which group of the population each leaflet is aimed at?

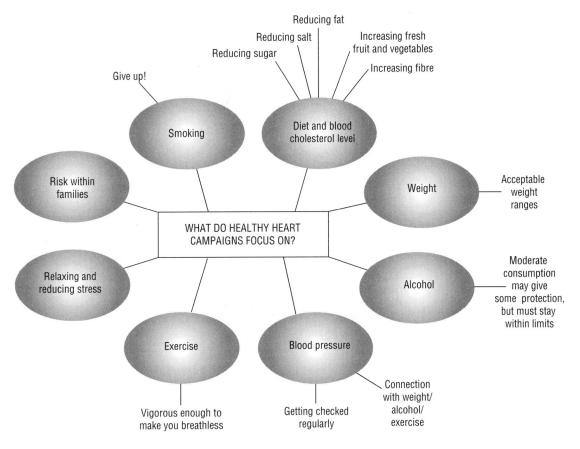

Cancer

Cancers are the second most common cause of death in the UK – in 1990 about a quarter of all deaths were as a result of cancer. The Government's *Health of the Nation* plan identifies cancer as another key area for improvement, setting these targets:

- by the year 2000
  - reduce the number of people smoking by about a third
  - reduce the rate of breast cancer deaths among women invited for screening by at least 25%
  - reduce the incidence of invasive cervical cancer by approximately 20%
- by 2005
  - halt the increase in the incidence of skin cancer.
- by 2010
  - reduce the rate of lung cancer deaths by at least 30% in men and 15% in women under the age of 75.

To achieve these targets, campaigns focus on discouraging potentially harmful living practices and the early identification of cancers.

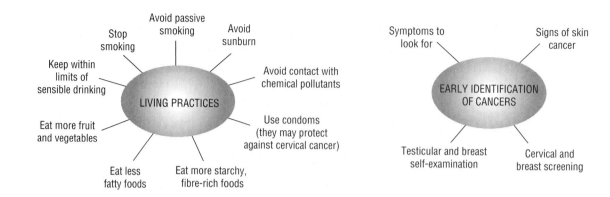

On the whole, cancer has the image of being a mysterious, unavoidable disease. Yet in the UK:

■ 30% of cancer deaths are caused by smoking

■ 30,000 people die of lung cancer

■ 8 out of 10 lung cancers are caused by smoking.

How do you think people could be educated to understand that, in some cases, the risk of lung cancer can be avoided by a change of lifestyle?

Sexually transmitted diseases and HIV infection

People having unprotected sex run the risk of catching a sexually transmitted disease.

Sexually transmitted diseases (STDs) – such as gonorrhea, genital herpes and hepatitis B – are usually caused by bacteria or viruses. Health education campaigns aim to prevent the spread of STDs by:

■ advising people to use a barrier method of contraception

■ advising people to reduce their number of partners

■ helping people to recognise the symptoms of STDs, so they can get treatment and avoid spreading the disease to others.

Since the 1980s, the risks of unprotected sex have become greater still, with the threat of HIV infection which causes AIDS. HIV is spread in three main ways:

■ by unprotected sex, as the virus is carried in semen and vaginal fluid

■ from mother to baby

■ among drug abusers, by sharing needles, syringes and other injecting equipment.

ACTIVITY

From your own knowledge, and from looking at leaflets, draw charts like the others in this section to show the main areas you think an HIV/AIDS education campaign for adolescents should focus on.

Early AIDS education campaigns have been criticised for scaring people without giving them enough information. Since then, HIV and AIDS education aiming to reduce the likelihood of the disease has focused on:

- providing information to students in schools and colleges (sex education, including information on HIV/AIDS, has been compulsory since 1993)
- offering guidelines on safe sex
- offering advice for people particularly at risk, for example, those travelling abroad
- providing information and support for intravenous drug users, including addresses of needle exchanges
- providing guidelines for carers and medical staff who come into contact with body fluids.

Promoting healthy living practices

Many health education campaigns focus directly on living practices, rather than on the diseases they may cause. They do this in one of two ways:

- by promoting healthy living practices, such as a balanced diet and physical exercise
- by encouraging people to minimise potentially harmful living practices, such as smoking, alcohol consumption and unsafe sex.

ACTIVITY

Do you think these guidelines are helpful? Collect leaflets on healthy eating from your health promotion unit, and make notes on what each point means in practical terms. Are health education campaigns providing clear enough advice on diet? Write your recommendations on how the messages could be improved.

Promoting healthy eating

Recent healthy eating campaigns have highlighted the importance of eating more vegetables, fruit, bread, cereals, pasta, rice and potatoes, and less fatty, sugary and salty foods. The emphasis has been on enjoying a varied, balanced diet rather than eating less and counting every calorie.

The Government's *Health of the Nation* plan gives eight simple guidelines for a healthy diet:

- enjoy your food
- eat a variety of different foods
- eat the right amount to be a healthy weight
- eat plenty of foods rich in starch and fibre
- don't eat too much fat
- don't eat sugary foods too often
- think about the vitamins and minerals in your food
- if you drink, keep within sensible limits.

DISCUSSION POINT

Do you think food companies are making a useful contribution to health education by labelling their products as 'healthy' and 'low-fat', or is it simply a marketing ploy?

Information and advice on healthy eating is probably more widely available than any other health education material. This is partly because food manufacturing and retail companies have recognised consumers' growing concern about the food they eat, and have started displaying leaflets in supermarkets, publishing advertising features on healthy eating in magazines, and promoting their own low-fat recipes.

Promoting exercise

The following chart summarises the main points which exercise campaigns focus on.

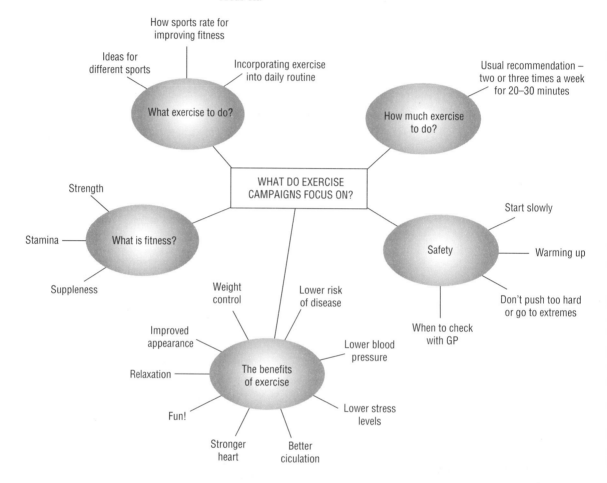

How sports rate for
improving fitness

Ideas for
different sports

Incorporating exercise
into daily routine

What exercise to do?

Usual recommendation –
two or three times a week
for 20–30 minutes

How much exercise
to do?

WHAT DO EXERCISE
CAMPAIGNS FOCUS ON?

Strength

Stamina

What is fitness?

Suppleness

Start slowly

Warming up

Safety

Don't push too hard
or go to extremes

When to check
with GP

Weight
control

Lower risk
of disease

Improved
appearance

Lower blood
pressure

Relaxation

The benefits
of exercise

Fun!

Lower stress
levels

Stronger
heart

Better
ciculation

DISCUSSION POINT

Ron, a 60-year-old who has always been keen on sports, has strong views on fitness education.

66 *Exercise isn't a natural part of children's lives any more. They sit in front of TVs and computers instead of playing outside with a football. Teachers are scared to push competitive sport because it's not fashionable. So children get bored, exercise less, get unfit, put on weight, and don't learn to enjoy sport.* 99

Do you agree? How do you think young people should be educated about the benefits of exercise?

Minimising the risk of potentially harmful living practices

Four harmful living practices are the main focus of health education campaigns:

- smoking
- alcohol consumption
- drug abuse and misuse
- solvent abuse.

All can be grouped together under the general heading of substance abuse – using substances in a damaging way.

Health education to minimise the risk of potentially harmful living practices has two main aims:

- raising awareness of the risk of harmful practices to discourage people from starting
- persuading people to change the harmful habits they already practise.

Minimising the risk of smoking

Smoking is legal, widely accepted and practised yet it is known to cause more preventable disease and death than any other harmful living practice:

- one in five fatal heart attacks
- about 30% of cancer deaths (smoking can contribute to cancer of the lung, pancreas, cervix, bladder, lip, mouth, larynx, oesophagus and to leukaemia)
- 30,000 deaths from lung cancer a year (in the UK alone)
- many other diseases and health problems, including strokes, stomach ulcers, emphysema, bronchitis and fertility problems
- damage to unborn babies, if pregnant women smoke
- damage to non-smokers through passive smoking.

Despite these facts, young people are still starting to smoke for social reasons or because of peer pressure. The Government's plan, *Health of the Nation*, recognises this, and one of its targets is to reduce the number of people smoking by a third by the year 2000.

However, the social acceptability of smoking has decreased dramatically over the last 20 years or so. Many public places are now smoke-free zones, so non-smokers can avoid passive smoking.

UNIT

7

ELEMENT **7.1**

ACTIVITY

Collect a range of:

- health education materials on smoking (including some aiming to prevent people starting smoking, and some aiming to help people stop smoking)
- advertisements and sponsorship pictures promoting cigarettes.

List the main points made by each, and analyse the impact you think the different materials would have. Do you think allowing tobacco companies to advertise detracts from health education against smoking? Tobacco companies spend millions of pounds sponsoring sport – do you think they should be allowed to do this? Keep a record of your views.

DISCUSSION POINT

Why do you think smoking has become less legal? How has health education played a part? Despite the general trends, why do you think there has been an increase in the number of teenage girls who smoke?`

As with other campaigns to minimise the risk of harmful living practices, health education on smoking focuses on preventing people from starting, and helping people to stop.

Minimising the risk of alcohol

Alcohol is the most legal, and commonly abused, drug in the UK. Yet too much alcohol can cause a wide range of serious short-term and long-term health problems.

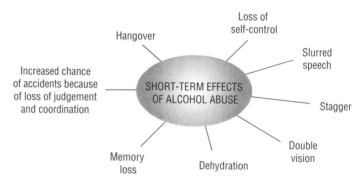

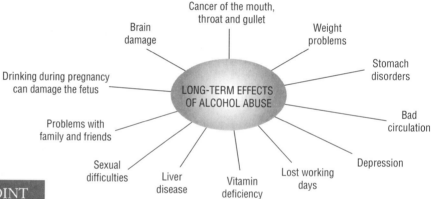

Health education campaigns aiming to minimise the risks of alcohol focus on:

- making people more aware of the dangers of too much alcohol
- encouraging people to drink sensibly, within recommended limits (21 units per week for men, and 14 units per week for women)
- helping people with alcohol problems to cut down the amount they drink.

As a small amount of alcohol does you no harm, and can be enjoyable, campaigns emphasise the importance of drinking sensibly, rather than giving up completely (unlike smoking campaigns).

Minimising the risk of drug abuse

Drugs are chemicals which affect the way the body works – anything from aspirin and caffeine to ecstasy and heroin. Problems with drugs can be divided into:

- drug abuse – using illegal drugs such as cocaine and ecstasy

- drug misuse – misusing a legal drug so the effects are harmful, which is possible with drugs such as painkillers or tranquilisers
- drug dependence – being dependent on a drug for its effects or to avoid withdrawal symptoms.

Health education campaigns focus on the problems caused by four main groups of drugs:

- stimulants – such as amphetamines, cocaine and crack
- depressants – such as tranquilisers, sleeping tablets and alcohol
- hallucinogens – such as LSD, cannabis, magic mushrooms and ecstasy
- narcotics – analgesic drugs (painkillers) such as heroin, opium, codeine and morphine.

Most campaigns aim to:

- persuade people not to start abusing drugs by
  - explaining why people take drugs and how to avoid it
  - emphasising the dangers of drug-taking
  - increasing awareness of different types of drugs and how to recognise them
  - explaining the legal repercussions
- help people who are abusing drugs by
  - giving information on specialist support services
  - giving information on needle exchange schemes, to reduce the risk of HIV
  - providing advice on how to stop
- help people recognise when someone is abusing drugs by
  - helping people to recognise the signs of drug abuse
  - providing information on what different drugs look like and how they are taken
  - providing advice on what to do if you suspect someone of taking drugs.

DISCUSSION POINT

In a group, talk about the different drugs health education you have encountered since childhood. Think of as many examples as you can of drugs education which appear in:

- the national media (newspapers, TV, magazines, advertising)
- the local media (local radio, local newspapers)
- health education leaflets
- promotional events.

What approach do you think works best? Why?

Minimising the risk of solvent abuse

Solvents are liquids – such as glue, petrol, lighter fluid, paint thinner and correction fluid – which give off intoxicating fumes. Solvent abuse is easy to hide and cheap so is popular among young people. Every year over 100 people, mostly teenagers, die as a result of solvent abuse.

Solvent abuse is dangerous because it causes:

- similar effects to drunkenness
- headache
- hallucinations
- vomiting
- confusion

and can lead to coma and death.

ACTIVITY

Some of the most widely available health education materials on drugs and solvents is aimed at alerting parents to the signs and dangers. Do you think this is a good idea?

Carry out research into solvent abuse, then draw a chart to show the different types of information you think should be included in a parent's guide to solvents.

Promoting personal safety and security

Although most people think it will never happen to them, accidents are the most common cause of death among people under 30. Very few accidents happen by chance, and many could be avoided if safety advice was followed.

Health education campaigns focus on two main places in which accidents often happen:

- in the home
- on the road.

Safety and security in the home

Although people tend to relax and feel safe in their own homes, the home can be a dangerous place, particularly for children and elderly people. Over 4,000 people in the UK die each year as a result of accidents in the home, and millions more need medical attention.

Health education campaigns focus on the following areas of home safety and security.

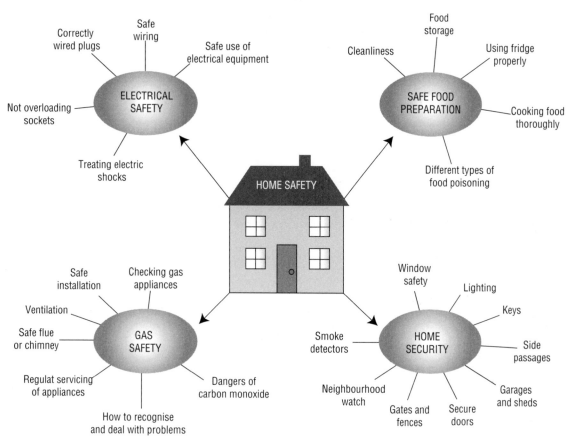

Safety on the road

Half of all accidental deaths happen on the roads – about 16 people are killed on roads in the UK every day. Children and elderly people are particularly at risk.

Educating children about road safety begins early with projects such as the Green Cross Code and the Tufty Club. For adults road safety campaigns focus on the dangers of speeding and, in particular, drink-driving, which causes a third of all deaths on the roads.

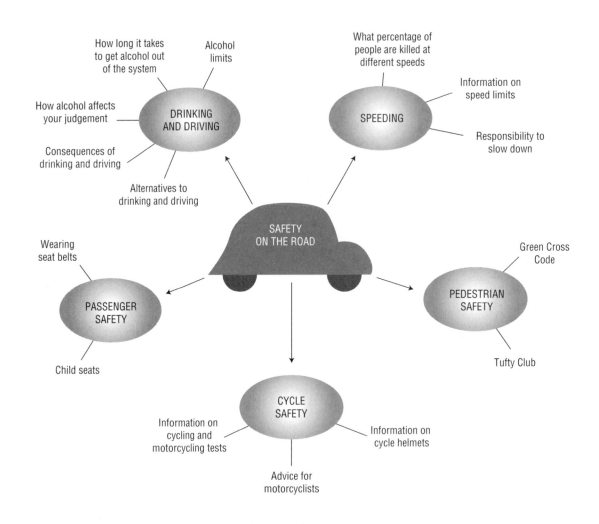

How long it takes
to get alcohol out
of the system

Alcohol
limits

How alcohol affects
your judgement

**DRINKING
AND DRIVING**

Consequences of
drinking and driving

Alternatives to
drinking and driving

What percentage of
people are killed at
different speeds

Information on
speed limits

SPEEDING

Responsibility to
slow down

**SAFETY
ON THE ROAD**

Wearing
seat belts

**PASSENGER
SAFETY**

Child seats

Green Cross
Code

**PEDESTRIAN
SAFETY**

Tufty Club

**CYCLE
SAFETY**

Information on
cycling and
motorcycling tests

Information on
cycle helmets

Advice for
motorcyclists

ACTIVITY

Choose either to focus on:

- home safety and security, or
- road safety.

Over a week or so, collect as much information as you can on your chosen
topic. Look at:

- national media (newspapers, TV, magazines, advertising)
- local media (local radio, local newspapers)
- doctors' surgeries, health centres, hospitals (health education leaflets
  advertising national or local promotional events).

Use the information you collect to put together a display on the aspect of
health and social wellbeing you have chosen, and how it is tackled in
health education campaigns.

Health campaigns and target populations

People involved in planning and developing health education campaigns need to know who their audience is before they can decide how, where and when to target their campaign. The target group for a campaign will affect the language used, the way information is presented, the content, and the message given.

A health promotion officer who specialises in smoking prevention explains how campaigns differ depending on the target audience.

66 *Take just two groups – teenagers who are starting to experiment with cigarettes, and adults who have been smoking for some time. My aim with teenagers is to discourage them from starting smoking. I explain the drawbacks of smoking in language they will relate to, using messages from pop stars and sportspeople who are against smoking. I emphasise the antisocial aspects of smoking at a time when they are keen to form new relationships and friendships – bad breath, passive smoking, waste of money.*

With the second group, the emphasis is more on how to give up smoking. I begin by reinforcing the negative effects of smoking – health problems, expense, deaths caused by smoking. I then go on to offer advice on how to stop smoking and where to get help. You can't just give the same messages across the board. Everyone has different needs, and you have to make sure you work out what these are, and then give them the right information and advice. 99

The target audiences for health education campaigns are usually distinguished by:

- age (for example, teenagers, mid-life adults, elderly people)
- activity (for example, smokers, substance users)
- sex
- specific needs (for example, people with learning difficulties).

Age-related target groups

Health education materials are often targeted at specific age ranges, for example:

- young children (3–8)
- children (8–12)
- adolescents (13–17)
- young people (17–30)
- mid-life adults (30–60)
- older people (over 60s).

Although not all the people within each of these categories will be the same, it is likely that many of them will share common interests, concerns and needs. As a result:

- the content of a campaign can be targeted to suit their level of understanding and to meet their needs
- the emphasis of a campaign – the messages it conveys – can be adapted to meet their concerns and needs
- messages can be presented in an appropriate format, using language which the target group will understand and relate to.

DISCUSSION POINT

How many different target groups can you think of for health education campaigns about road safety? What type of messages would you give to each group?

ACTIVITY

Look at a range of leaflets and advertisements on aspects of health and wellbeing, and divide them into groups according to the age range you think they are targeted at. What clues are there? Make a list of how you can tell the age of the target audience (for example, content, language level, presentation, format).

Activity-related target groups

As section 7.1.1 showed, many health education campaigns focus on persuading people to change habits which put their health and wellbeing at risk. These campaigns are activity-related – targeted at groups of people who carry out activities such as smoking or substance abuse.

A health practitioner specialising in drugs explains how the campaigns she organises are related to target groups involved in particular activities:

66 *About half the campaigns I'm involved in are targeted at activity-related groups, intravenous drug users, nightclubbers who take ecstasy, sportspeople who abuse anabolic steroids and so on. The other half of my work focuses on persuading people not to start taking drugs, and informing parents and teachers of the signs and dangers of drug abuse.* 99

The type of messages conveyed by activity-related health campaigns, and the way in which these messages are presented, varies from activity to activity. In the case of a legal, socially acceptable activity like drinking alcohol, campaigns are often quite light-hearted, using cartoon characters and catchy slogans. In the case of drug abuse, the approach tends to be more serious.

Sex-related target groups

The physical differences between women and men mean that they have different medical needs and problems. As a result, many health campaigns are targeted by sex.

Helping women to understand and care for their bodies has been an important issue for several decades now, and well woman clinics are well established across the UK. Pregnancy, menopause and breast cancer are just some of the issues which have been the focus of high-profile health campaigns.

In recent years, awareness has grown of a similar need to educate and help men with their particular concerns, and clinics, events and literature targeted at men are now on the increase.

DISCUSSION POINT

Over 90% of all drink-drivers are male. Do you think it is justifiable to target drinking and driving campaigns directly at men as a result?

Target groups identified by specific needs

Some health education campaigns are aimed at meeting the specific needs of a particular target group. These needs fall into two main categories:

- special needs which mean information has to be presented in a certain way (for example a workshop may be run to help adolescents with learning difficulties understand the dangers of drug abuse, or leaflets may be translated into other languages for people whose first language is not English)
- circumstances which mean that people need a particular type of help and advice (for example an education campaign may be targeted to answer the questions of women with HIV who want to have children, or a healthy eating drive may aim to show families on a low income how they can eat healthily on a tight budget).

The content and objectives of campaigns

When planning a health education campaign, organisers need to decide its objectives, or goals, from the outset. These can then be used to:

- determine the content and approach of the campaign
- make sure the campaign keeps on track
- evaluate the success of the campaign after it has finished.

Evaluating a campaign is particularly important, as it gives health promotion officers guidelines on how to run future initiatives, and enables them to see what areas still need to be covered. Objectives should be SMART:

- Specific
- Measurable
- Agreed
- Realistic
- Timebound.

All health education campaigns have the underlying objective of changing behaviour. Their more specific objectives can often be determined by looking at their content.

To meet health targets

The majority of campaigns are either organised by:

- national organisations or government departments, in response to nationally identified health priorities
- local health authorities or organisations, in response to locally identified priorities.

National targets

The most influential health education initiative of recent years has been *The Health of the Nation*, a plan to improve health in the UK produced by the Government in the early 1990s. This:

- sets out key areas for immediate action, and sets targets for the year 2000 and beyond
- highlights areas where considerable progress has already been made, and proposes new targets for the future.

It focuses on five key areas:

- coronary heart disease and strokes
- cancers
- mental illness
- accidents
- HIV/AIDS and sexual health.

In some cases, the national objectives of a health education campaign are explicitly stated – as in the guide to healthy eating on the next page.

ACTIVITY

Get hold of a copy of *The Health of the Nation* or *Healthy Wales*, and make notes on the target areas for improvement. Collect health education literature related to each of these areas, and produce a chart identifying how their content relates to national health targets.

A new environmental health target was announced in July 1996, relating to noise, radon and lead in water. Carry out research into this target, and add the information to your poster or wallchart.

Introducing the National Food Guide

The Balance of Good Health

Information for educators and communicators

The new National Food Guide, *The Balance of Good Health*, aims to help people understand and enjoy healthy eating. It shows that people don't have to give up the foods they most enjoy for the sake of their health. But variety and a change towards more vegetables, fruit, bread, breakfast cereals, potatoes, rice and pasta is what matters. Snacks as well as meals count towards the healthy balance.

Fruit and vegetables
Choose a wide variety

Bread, other cereals and potatoes
Eat all types and choose high fibre kinds whenever you can

Meat, fish and alternatives
Choose lower fat alternatives whenever you can

Fatty and sugary foods
Try not to eat these too often, and when you do, have small amounts

Milk and dairy foods
Choose lower fat alternatives whenever you can

The Balance of Good Health

In other cases, the national objectives of a campaign can be deduced from clues in its content. For example, the drink-driving leaflet shown on the left was produced by the Department of Transport and refers throughout to national statistics.

Local targets

At a local level, local health authorities and health promotion units work towards both national targets and local projects. This involves:

- identifying particular health problems in the area
- setting targets for improvement
- organising campaigns with the aim of achieving these targets
- evaluating the campaigns, and organising initiatives for the future.

"Don't forget, some one night stands last forever"

BE A CLEVER DICK. USE A CONDOM.

Northumberland Health Authority

To promote the interests of particular groups

Health education campaigns always try to reflect the beliefs and values of the group behind them – whether this is the Government trying to improve health nationally, or a slimming product manufacturer trying to convince consumers of the benefits of weight loss.

In some cases, campaigns are coordinated by organisations with a particular viewpoint on, or interest in, a health-related issue. For example:

■ a charity that provides respite for carers might publish a leaflet to explain the stresses on carers, inform people about the service it offers, and try to gain financial support for its cause

- a women's group might distribute a poster emphasising a woman's right to choose, with the aim of educating women in the options available in the case of an unwanted pregnancy
- a carers' group might distribute leaflets about the support and benefits for which they may qualify.

To promote a hidden message

As already mentioned, commercial companies also coordinate health education campaigns on relevant topics. For example:

- a high-street chemist producing leaflets on why it is important to lose weight, and giving information on different types of slimming products stocked in the store
- company which makes nicotine substitutes advertising its products through a campaign emphasising the dangers of smoking.

Companies may have several objectives in running health education campaigns:

- to improve people's health
- to promote their products
- to gain a competitive advantage over other companies
- to create a good image and enhance their public relations.

Key questions

1 What is the difference between a primary health education campaign, a secondary campaign, and a tertiary campaign? Give an example of each.
2 What four aspects of health and social wellbeing do health education campaigns focus on?
3 Give three examples of diseases which health campaigns aim to reduce.
4 Why do health campaigns place so much emphasis on diet and exercise?
5 Name four potentially harmful living practices which are the focus for health education campaigns.
6 Describe four main issues covered by campaigns on safety in the home.
7 Why might the content of a health campaign vary depending on the age of the target audience?
8 What is an activity-related target group? Give three examples.
9 Why are some health education campaigns targeted just at women, and others just at men?
10 What are the five key areas for improvement highlighted in the Government's *Health of the Nation* plan?
11 Why do some commercial organisations run health education campaigns?

Assignment

Over a fortnight, collect as much health education material as you can (you may already have collected some recently as you worked through the elements). This may include:

■ articles in national newspapers and magazines
■ advertisements
■ features in local newspapers
■ health education leaflets
■ information about promotional events.

Sort the information you have collected into groups according to the aspect of health and social wellbeing on which the campaign focuses. Then choose three campaigns to look at in more detail, each of which should focus on a different topic for a different target group.

Write a report on the campaigns you have chosen, describing in each case:
■ the main aspects of health and social wellbeing on which each campaign focuses, and how you identified this
■ what the objectives of the campaign are, how you identified them, and how they relate to national or local targets
■ how the campaigns convey their messages for different target groups
■ how effective you think the health education material is.

ELEMENT **7.2**

Reasons, sources and methods

In this element you will explore why and how health education messages are promoted, who promotes them and how effective their methods are for particular target groups.

66 *The dentist and I visit playgroups to give talks about teeth. We ask the children what they know about teeth and how they think they can look after them. We give out stickers, which they really like at that age, and we leave posters for teachers to put up – about what food is best and how to look after teeth and gums. We give them all a free toothbrush and toothpaste. We're trying to get them to see the importance of looking after their teeth properly and to get them into good habits which will make a big difference to their future dental health. They might listen to us even if they try to resist their parents telling them the same things!* 99

dental assistant

66 *After the report on vitamin E as a factor in preventing heart disease the whole stock of the store's leaflets on vitamin E disappeared within a couple of days.* 99

pharmacist

66 *The Active for Life campaign grew as a response to the findings of the Allied Dunbar National Fitness Survey, which we commissioned jointly with the DoH, the Sports Council and Allied Dunbar Assurance. It showed that more than 70% men and 80% of women were not exercising enough. There was a general tendency for people to overestimate their level of fitness. We are promoting the message to encourage people to exercise in order to stay healthier – one of the major reasons is to reduce the risk of heart disease. There are no national targets to increase the amount of physical activity people take, but there are targets relating to decreasing coronary heart disease, so there is a strong link with what this campaign aims to achieve.* 99

physical activity manager, Health Education Authority

66 *The national campaign run by the Health Education Authority on increasing physical activity, Active for Life, is an example of how we supported and developed work which was initiated centrally. We launched the campaign locally with newspaper articles and on local TV. We instigated a weekly column in the local weekly newspaper which both built on the work of the national campaign and incorporated our own activity.* 99

assistant director (health promotion), local health authority

Sources of health education campaigns

A wide range of people help to communicate health education messages:

- Community workers
- Doctors
- Employers
- Environmental health wokers
- Health and safety officers
- Health practitioners
- Health visitors
- Journalists
- Leisure and recreation managers
- Nurses
- Nutritionists
- Occupational health nurses
- Parents
- Police
- Social workers
- Students
- Teachers
- Voluntary workers
- Youth leaders

ACTIVITY

Look at the chart above and identify at least one situation in which the individuals listed might provide health education.

What messages do these people communicate? Where do they get their health education information from? For most purposes, there are three sources of health education campaigns:

- public service (both national and local)
- private companies
- the voluntary sector.

Public service

Public-service organisations include:

- government-funded bodies such as the Health Education Authority and the police
- government departments such as the Department of Health
- local government and health authorities.

Between them, these organise health education campaigns on both a national and local basis.

National bodies

The main public organisation which promotes health in England, Wales and Northern Ireland is the Health Education Authority. Originally set up in 1968 as the Health Education Council, this government-funded body is responsible for:

- organising national and regional campaigns, including training and education events
- providing information and resources (in particular leaflets and posters) for health promotion officers
- funding research.

In Scotland, a similar role is performed by the Scottish Health Education Group.

Many of the leaflets you see in doctors' surgeries and health promotion units are clearly stamped with the Health Education Authority's logo.

Government departments – such as the Department of Health, the Department of the Environment and the Department of Agriculture – also organise campaigns and provide information for the general public on health education issues.

Local bodies

Locally, the Department of Health provides budgets for health authorities to spend on health education. Most areas have their own health promotion unit, which plays an important role in:

■ working towards national health targets

■ identifying and meeting local health targets

■ organising health education campaigns

■ providing information and support for other organisations' health education campaigns in the area

■ organising preventive programmes, such as immunisation and screening.

Find out more about the work of your local health promotion unit and, if possible, ask a representative from the unit to talk to your group about the different sources of local health education campaigns. Write up your research as a short report (one side of A4).

Collect a range of health education materials produced by private companies (for example, leaflets on display in supermarkets, advertisements in magazines). In each case, read the information and list the reasons you think the company has for investing in the campaign. Do you think the materials play a useful role in health education? Or do you think the company's commercial aims undermine the objectivity and value of the information? Write down your evaluation.

People often volunteer to support a campaign or organisation when they feel strongly about an issue, perhaps because of personal experience. Do you think this forms a good basis for involvement in health education?

Local government departments – such as social services and education – often support health education campaigns in the area. Collaboration between a range of local bodies can:

■ help to ensure information is accurate and comprehensive
■ spread the burden of costs and resources
■ strengthen the impact of a campaign.

Police forces are also involved in local health and social education campaigns, focusing in particular on road safety, home safety, substance abuse, and the victims of violence. They organise displays and activities at local events, publish newsletters on safety issues in the area, and produce leaflets on issues of local concern.

Private companies

Many private companies – in particular, manufacturers and retailers of 'healthy' products – play an active role in health education campaigns. A campaign like this might have a number of aims:

■ to encourage a healthy lifestyle and improve people's quality of life
■ to associate products with good health
■ to improve the company's image, increasing sales and profit margin.

Private companies often issue leaflets which provide general information on a health-related issue, linked to details of products they manufacture or sell. Campaigns that are sponsored or coordinated by private companies usually feature the company's name and logo prominently, so that the general public is aware of the source of the campaign. This helps to ensure that the campaign achieves its commercial aims as well as health education goals.

Voluntary sector

Many groups which depend on the work of volunteers play an important part in health education in the UK. Voluntary-sector organisations involved in health education campaigns include:

■ national charities – for example, Help the Aged produces leaflets and advertisements to inform older people on their rights and advise them on their wellbeing
■ pressure groups – for example, LIFE lobbies Parliament and organises campaigns aimed at the general public advocating the rights of the unborn child
■ local organisations – for example, most areas have a community centre staffed mainly by volunteers, which provides information and advice on health and social care issues.

Why are sources promoting their message?

CASE STUDY: NORTHUMBERLAND HEALTH PROMOTION UNIT

Northumberland Health Promotion Unit aims to enhance the quality of life of the people who live and work in Northumberland by helping them to be more knowledgeable, better motivated and more able to acquire and maintain good health.

The unit is part of Northumberland Community Health Trust. It provides a range of health promotion services throughout the county to any individual or organisation carrying out health education and promotion activities. Programmes of work are designed to address five key areas, all of which are identified in *The Health of the Nation* and *Northumberland Health Promotion Strategy*: cardiovascular disease and strokes; mental health; accidents; cancers; sexual health, including HIV and AIDS.

The unit also determines health education and promotion priorities for the district, carries out research into health education and promotion issues, and monitors and evaluates health education programmes.

A wide range of organisations invest a large amount of money, time and effort in promoting health messages. Their obvious aim is to inform and educate, but what other factors motivate them?

To meet health targets

Both national and local public service organisations run health education campaigns with the aim of meeting health targets.

National health targets

National health targets are set by the Government, which constantly monitors statistics on health and social wellbeing in order to identify areas needing special attention. Medical experts advise MPs, who then set targets and launch campaigns.

Documents such as *Health of the Nation* and *Healthy Wales* highlight these areas and targets, and national and local public-service organisations tailor their health education programmes in response. For example, *Health of the Nation* identified five key areas where particular improvement was needed:

- coronary heart disease and strokes
- cancers
- mental illness
- accidents
- HIV/AIDS and sexual health.

Since the document was issued, public-service organisations have launched many health education campaigns aiming to raise people's awareness of the issues so that national targets can be achieved.

Local health targets

As well as responding to national health targets, local public-service organisations – such as health authorities, health promotion units, and local government departments – identify and aim to meet specific local targets.

The case study on the left, which is adapted from a leaflet issued by the Northumberland Health Promotion Unit, explains how health targets influence the campaigns run in the region.

To promote the interests of particular groups

Health education from the voluntary sector usually aims to promote the interests of a particular group. For example:

- children's charities provide information and advice on children's issues
- anti-smoking groups raise awareness of the dangers of smoking and passive smoking.

Voluntary organisations may wish to promote the interests of their group for a number of reasons:

- to raise money (leaflets often include a contribution slip)
- to achieve change (e.g. a pressure group or charity lobbying Parliament on a health issue)
- to raise awareness of a problem or cause among the general public
- to give people information and advice.

To take preventive action

In *The Health of the Nation*, the Government emphasised that:

“ Promoting good health and preventing ill health are . . . as important as treating illness and making sure that those who suffer a serious disease or illness can lead as full a life as possible. **”**

As a result, both national and local public-service organisations are involved in promoting preventive action, in particular:

- immunisation programmes
- screening programmes.

Immunisation programmes

As *The Health of the Nation* suggests, the Government has given a high priority to promoting immunisation programmes at a national level. In 1994 it spent £20 million on a measles vaccination campaign alone, in response to the threat of a measles epidemic.

At a local level, doctors are funded to promote immunisation. They run regular health education campaigns which inform individuals of immunisations they may need and inform parents about immunisation and counter any fears they may have for their children's wellbeing.

Screening programmes

Screening programmes for breast cancer and cervical cancer are also given high priority by the Government (targets to reduce the incidence of breast cancer and cervical cancer are included in *The Health of the Nation*).

There is a national screening programme for breast cancer, and it is thought that if all women between 50 and 64 took up invitations for breast screening checks, as many as 1,250 lives could be saved each year. Similarly, more than 1,500 women die of cervical cancer every year, and most of these cases could be prevented if the cancer was detected before it developed. Women are sent letters telling them when they are due for screening, and doctors remind their patients to make appointments.

Organisational targets

Private companies may promote health messages in order to meet organisational targets. The marketing manager of a large company which manufactures cycle safety helmets explains:

66 *People buy our product for safety reasons, not because it's particularly trendy or a fashion accessory. In line with this, our company name has to be synonymous with safety and reliability. One way we achieve this reputation is by sponsoring and organising road safety education campaigns. Last year we ran a high-profile advertising campaign on the benefits of wearing cycle helmets, and this year we produced a series of leaflets on different aspects of cycle safety. We employ a marketing research company to find out how these campaigns affect the general public's perceptions of us and our products. Their findings show that our involvement in health education campaigns helps us to achieve several key organisational targets: raising our profile; reinforcing our reputation as experts in cycle safety; and ultimately increasing our market share. People recognise our name, remember our good reputation for safety, and choose one of our cycle helmets over our competitors.* 99

DISCUSSION POINT

Look back at the leaflets or advertisements produced by private companies that you collected earlier. Choose one company's material to focus on. Do you think the material would help the company to meet any of its organisational targets? What might these targets be?

Promotional methods

The promotional methods used in health education campaigns differ in three main ways:

- the mode used to communicate the message (for example, television, radio, leaflets, workshops)
- the way the information is designed (for example, how colour and graphics are used)
- the content of the message (for example, the use of factual information or shock stories).

So what factors do organisations need to take into account when deciding what promotional methods to use?

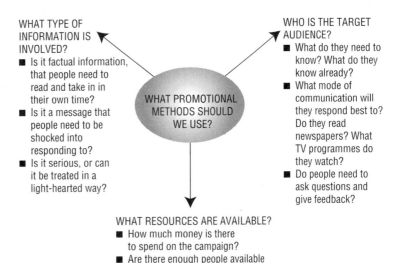

WHAT TYPE OF INFORMATION IS INVOLVED?
- Is it factual information, that people need to read and take in in their own time?
- Is it a message that people need to be shocked into responding to?
- Is it serious, or can it be treated in a light-hearted way?

WHO IS THE TARGET AUDIENCE?
- What do they need to know? What do they know already?
- What mode of communication will they respond best to? Do they read newspapers? What TV programmes do they watch?
- Do people need to ask questions and give feedback?

WHAT PROMOTIONAL METHODS SHOULD WE USE?

WHAT RESOURCES ARE AVAILABLE?
- How much money is there to spend on the campaign?
- Are there enough people available to communicate face to face?

Mode

When launching a campaign, organisations need to decide what promotional mode to use to communicate their message:

PROMOTIONAL MODES USED IN HEALTH EDUCATION CAMPAIGNS

Leaflets · Advertisements · Posters · Newspaper features · Workshops · Videos · Books · Art · Magazine articles · Films and plays · TV news and documentary programmes · Exhibitions · Radio news and documentary programmes · TV drama · Talks · Radio drama

These different modes can be divided into two key categories:

- Communication without personal interaction – through radio or TV programmes, advertisements, newspapers and magazines, or leaflets and other printed materials. This is a good way to reach a large audience, but doesn't allow for personal feedback or for messages to be tailored to meet particular people's needs.
- Face-to-face communication – through workshops, presentations and roleplay. This is a good way to communicate with a small audience, as people can ask questions and give feedback. However, its success depends on the knowledge and skill of the person running the session.

Television and radio

There are significant advantages to using television and radio to communicate health education messages:

- They can reach large numbers of people (almost every home in the UK has a television or radio).
- Messages carry added weight if they are included in a television or radio programme (though people are less credulous when the message comes in the form of television or radio advertising – see later in this section).
- They can have a powerful instant impact – particularly in the case of television because it combines pictures and sound.

The disadvantages include:

- There is no chance to repeat or explain information, or for people to ask questions.
- With such a wide audience it's impossible to pitch the information at the right level for everyone.
- Buying time on TV or radio is expensive (especially TV).
- People can switch off or stop paying attention if they don't like what they're seeing or hearing – they're not a captive audience.

Health issues are covered in many different types of TV and radio programmes:

- documentaries often focus on health topics
- programmes specialising in health, safety and lifestyle – such as *999* and *The Good Food Show*
- shows that involve the general public in debate – such as *The Oprah Winfrey Show*
- consumer programmes – which highlight issues of concern to the general public
- drama programmes (such as *Eastenders* and *The Archers*) – which incorporate health and social care issues into the lives of their characters
- news programmes.

Public-service organisations and voluntary bodies often contribute to these programmes by providing:

- information and advice to journalists and producers
- experts who can discuss an issue on air.

Magazines and newspapers

The main advantages of using magazines and newspapers to communicate health education messages are:

- They can reach large numbers of people.
- Specialist magazines can be a good way to target information at a particular audience.
- People can reread the information as often as they need to.

The disadvantages include:

- There is no chance for people to ask questions or give feedback.
- Newspapers have a wide audience, and it's hard to target information.
- Buying space in national newspapers and magazines is expensive.
- People can turn the page if they're not interested or want to avoid thinking about an issue.

Articles in newspapers and magazines often provide information, advice and opinions on health issues. Most newspapers have a regular health column, written by medical experts or journalists specialising in health stories. Press officers from public service organisations (like the Health Education Authority) and voluntary bodies (like Age Concern) send information to journalists in the hope that issues they are concerned about will gain coverage.

Newspaper articles can publicise the work of charities indirectly by covering related stories with a human interest. It can be difficult to target particular groups of the population through newspapers but it is easier to do so through magazines, which are often designed for a specific readership. Teen magazines can have a particularly powerful influence over their target audience.

DISCUSSION POINT

How important a role do you think teen magazines play in health education? Do you think this is a good way for young people to find out about health issues? How can magazines fulfil their responsibility to provide good advice?

Leaflets and posters

The advantages include:

- They can reach large numbers of people.
- People can reread the information as often as they need to.
- They are easy and cheap to produce.
- They can be distributed in large numbers, for example through clinics, health education units.
- Posters can be a good way to attract attention if they're displayed in a good place.

The disadvantages are:

■ There is no chance for people to ask questions or give feedback.

■ It's hard to target information.

■ People don't have to read the information if they're not interested or want to avoid an issue.

■ Posters are often glanced at, rather than read carefully.

Leaflets and posters are widely used by all sources of health education campaigns – public-service organisations, private companies and voluntary bodies. Their main advantage over television and radio is that they are relatively cheap and easy to produce so they can be used on a small scale by local groups, and in large quantities by national campaigns. The coordinator of a community drug centre explains why leaflets and posters are so useful:

66 *Our main aims are to help drug users; offer support to relatives; and provide information and workshops for the community to promote a better understanding of drug use and people who use drugs. We have three sets of leaflets – one for each of these different target audiences. As our budget is limited we keep them simple – usually just in black and white with our logo and phone numbers on the front, information and advice inside, and a map of where to find us on the back. They're an excellent way of getting our message across. They're also easy to distribute – we display them in stands at doctors' surgeries, the community centre, local hostels, the library, etc. Once or twice a year we also organise a poster campaign to try to attract the attention of a wider audience.* 99

Advertisements

The advantages include:

■ They can reach large numbers of people

■ The message can be repeated over and over again.

■ They can be printed or broadcast, combining the advantages of both media.

The disadvantages are:

■ There is no chance for people to ask questions or give feedback.

■ It's hard to target information.

■ People often ignore advertising, flipping past it in magazines and newspapers, or switching over the television during commercial breaks.

■ People don't always believe advertising, dismissing it as propaganda.

Interesting, well-targeted advertising campaigns can be an effective way to communicate a health education message. Deciding where to advertise is an important starting point. Advertisements can be:

■ on national or local television

■ on national or local radio

■ in national or local newspapers

■ in magazines

■ screened in cinemas

■ displayed on billboards or on public transport.

Choose two health education leaflets – one produced by a large public service organisation, such as the Health Education Authority, and one by a local voluntary group. Compare the way the two leaflets have been written and produced. How can you account for the similarities and differences between the two? Do you think they are an effective method of communicating in each case?

Advertising in the national media is expensive. Private companies that manufacture health- or safety-related products sometimes tie in health education messages with advertisements. Government departments, such as the Department of Health and the Department of the Environment, often run high-profile advertising campaigns. For example, every Christmas the Government coordinates a campaign against drink-driving, which includes regular television advertising slots.

Who do you think is the source of this advertisement? Note the two organisations which it mentions.

ACTIVITY

Advertorials – pages in a newspaper or magazine that look like news articles but are in fact advertising features – are becoming increasingly common. Collect examples of advertorials from magazines and papers. What do you think would be the advantage of promoting health education information in this way? What type of organisations do you think would be likely to use advertorials? Write down what you think about this.

Face-to-face contact (presentations, workshops, etc.)

The advantages include:

- Information can be tailored to the understanding and needs of the audience.
- People have a chance to ask questions and give feedback.
- The audience is captive – it can't just switch off or turn the page.

The disadvantages are:

- The person running the session must be well-informed and interesting, or the audience will soon stop paying attention.
- People may be too intimidated to participate fully in workshops, especially activities such as roleplay.

Face-to-face contact – through presentations, workshops and discussion groups – is the best way to communicate a health education message to a small group of people. Unlike forms of communication where there is no personal contact, the person running the session can respond directly to the needs of the audience, and expand and clarify information as necessary.

Most face-to-face health education is organised by public-service organisations, which have the resources to coordinate both national and local campaigns at community level. Workshops and activities are a particularly good way to communicate messages to young children, who don't have the skills or inclination to read information. Schools have an important role to play in health education. For example, they must provide sex education and information on AIDS.

HACKNEY DRUG EDUCATION TEAM

East London and City Health Promotion has a team which focuses on drug education in schools. Run in conjunction with the North-East London Drugs Prevention Team, the Metropolitan Police, the youth service and drugs agencies, the team delivers programmes in primary and secondary schools in the London boroughs of Tower Hamlets and Hackney.

At primary level, the drug education team's work focuses on giving children the information and skills they need to decide for themselves what to do about drugs. Hour-long sessions are designed to be lively, informative and participative. The children carry out a range of exercises, including:

- looking at two drugs scenarios and writing and drawing what they would do

- having discussions in small groups and reporting back to the large group

- word-searches

- a worksheet on moral dilemmas

- body maps to find out the children's knowledge of how drugs affect the body.

DISCUSSION POINT

From your own experience, what modes of communicating health education messages are most effective? Have you been influenced by a workshop on a health education topic? Or do you pay more attention to what you read in magazines? How have school lessons influenced you?

ACTIVITY

Videos, OHP slides and roleplay are often used during face-to-face sessions on health education. Make a copy of the following table and write in what you think would be the advantages and disadvantages of each. Which would you choose to use with a group of young children? With an audience of bored 14-year-olds?

	Advantages	Disadvantages
Video		
OHP slides		
Roleplay		

Design

Good design can make or break a health education campaign. If something is well designed it will:

- grab the audience's attention
- be easy to read and understand
- hold the audience's attention
- be memorable, with a lasting impact.

Printed materials for national health education campaigns are designed to a brief by graphic designers, who specialise in bringing together words and

This leaflet, published by the Royal Pharmaceutical Society, uses bright colours and simple illustrations to reflect the content – child safety. Its front cover is bold and would stand out amongst a rack of materials.

ACTIVITY

Look through health education materials for examples of:

■ factual information

■ analogies

■ shock or scare stories

■ appealing to ideal models.

Write a short report on the different ways of communicating messages, with examples of each. Which methods do you think are most effective for your age group? And for younger people?

pictures to communicate messages clearly. With the spread of desktop publishing, many small, local organisations now design their own health education materials. However, if there is any money to spare, it is well worth investing in employing the skills of a graphic designer and printing in colour, rather than in black and white.

ACTIVITY

Look at a selection of health education materials – including leaflets, advertisements and posters. Which attract and keep your attention? Why? How has the designer used colour, graphics and aesthetic appeal to convey the health education message?

Choose three which you think work well and list the things that make them effective

Content of message

Depending on the subject matter and its source, the content of health education campaigns may be presented in a range of different ways:

■ as **factual information** – some campaigns focus completely on facts and figures, aiming to give people the information they need to make choices about their health and lifestyle

■ using **analogies** – for example, 'The liver is like a car with one gear – it can only work at one rate. The liver can only burn up one unit of alcohol in an hour.'

■ using **shock or scare stories** – for example, telling the story of someone who is dying of a smoking-related disease, to try to persuade smokers to give up the habit

■ **appealing to ideal models** – using famous people that the target audience looks up to, such as sports personalities or pop stars, to endorse messages about healthy lifestyles.

DISCUSSION POINT

What promotional methods would you use if you were:

■ a GP with a small budget who wanted to promote the benefits of flu injections to elderly people?

■ coordinating a national children's road safety week and had been given a large budget?

Talk about:

■ the promotional mode you would use (for example, TV, radio, advertisements, leaflets and posters)

■ how you would attract and keep people's attention through design

■ how you would present the content of your message (for example, through factual information, analogy, shock or scare stories, or appealing to ideal models).

Shortfalls in campaigns

Once a health education campaign is under way, it is important to evaluate whether it is achieving its aims so that shortfalls can be identified, corrected and avoided in the future. Common shortfalls are:

- a campaign not reaching its target group
- information being misinterpreted by the target group
- the target group not identifying with the message.

If any of these is the case there is unlikely to be an alteration in behaviour or improvement in health.

Unlikely to be accessed by target group

Unless a campaign is promoted in the right place at the right time, the target audience may never see it or hear it. For example, there would be little point in screening TV advertisements about drink-driving during children's programmes, or putting a leaflet about exercise during pregnancy in sheltered accommodation for elderly people.

Organisations planning national advertising campaigns spend large amounts of money researching what type of people read particular magazines and watch certain TV programmes. Placing an advertisement in the wrong magazine, or screening it at the wrong time, can be a costly mistake.

Open to misinterpretation by target group

Health education campaigns must be easy to understand and pitched at the right level, or they may be open to misinterpretation by the target group. A sexual health coordinator who organises campaigns to inform teenagers about safe sex explains:

66 *We run regular workshops and discussion sessions in secondary schools, to encourage young people to talk openly about sex. To support this work we produce a range of leaflets and hand-outs, answering common questions about contraception, sexually transmitted diseases and so on. After the first couple of sessions, it became clear that we had overestimated the knowledge of the younger pupils. They didn't understand all the terminology we had used, and the materials we gave them were actually confusing them, rather than answering their questions. As soon as we realised this we produced new leaflets for the younger age range, having learnt the danger of making assumptions about what people know and understand.* 99

Target group doesn't identify with message

One of the most common shortfalls of health education campaigns is that the target audience simply doesn't identify with the information provided. They either feel that 'this doesn't apply to me', and ignore the message completely, or are annoyed by the approach taken, and refuse to pay attention.

This is particularly common in the areas of diet and exercise, where the general public faces a constant stream of advice and information – much of it conflicting. People may become frustrated with the confusing messages they receive, and also feel they should be allowed to make their own choices.

ACTIVITY

By looking at the publications on sale in newsagents, and talking to family and friends, identify three magazines or newspapers in which you would place an advertisement:

- encouraging men under 21 to use condoms
- advising elderly people how to stay warm in the winter and telling them about the grants that are available.

DISCUSSION POINT

If you had to organise a campaign to promote healthy eating among people in your own age group, how would you make sure that your target audience identified with your message?

Key questions

1 Name three national public-service organisations which are the source of health education campaigns.
2 Give three examples of local public-service organisations which are the source of health education campaigns.
3 What types of voluntary-sector organisations organise health education campaigns?
4 What health targets do local campaigns aim to meet?
5 Why do private companies promote health education messages?
6 Give an example of a health education campaign run to promote the interests of a particular group.
7 Explain two types of preventive action.
8 What factors do organisations take into account when planning how to promote a health education message?
9 What are the advantages and disadvantages of promoting a message on television and radio?
10 Why are leaflets and posters so widely used in health education campaigns? What sources use them?
11 Explain different types of advertising used in health education campaigns.
12 What are the advantages and disadvantages of promoting a message using face-to-face contact?
13 Explain three ways in which design can increase the impact of a health message.
14 Give one example of each: a campaign focusing on factual information; using analogies; using shock or scare stories; appealing to ideal models.
15 What are the three most common shortfalls in health education campaigns?

Assignment

Choose two of the health education campaigns you collected information for in section 7.1 (one of the campaigns should originate from a public-service organisation, and the other from a private company or a voluntary-sector organisation). In the assignment for this section, you will analyse these sources and the methods they use in more detail.

Prepare a presentation comparing the two campaigns. Your presentation should include:

- a description of the sources of the campaigns
- an analysis of the sources, with an explanation of why they are promoting their message
- an explanation of the different promotional methods used in the campaigns
- suggestions on why the sources chose particular promotional methods
- an identification of any shortfalls in the campaigns.

Make your presentation as lively and interesting as possible (visual aids would be helpful).

ELEMENT **7.3**

Evaluating a health education campaign

In this element you will evaluate one particular health education campaign by carrying out research with the target audience.

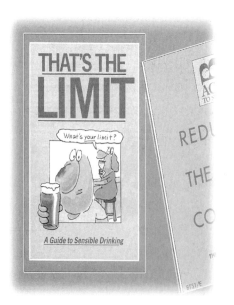

> 66 We evaluate against objectives. For example, the objectives of the No Smoking campaign included the target of briefing and resourcing 80 local centres to equip and display their own campaigns. We set up three evening briefings with 35 people at each, and kept records of how many packs were taken away for this purpose so were able to check this had happened. We also assess current performance against previous performance and check we have ensured being within budgetary limits. We measure the response from the public either to services or campaigns and these comments are reviewed and acted upon. 99
>
> *assistant director, health promotion, local health authority*

> 66 Our main evaluation tool is a big survey we do every year with the same set of about 7,500 people spread over England – a national spread, selected by random sample. This is done by face-to-face interviews using a questionnaire. It gathers information concerning physical activity, in three areas: their knowledge, attitudes and behaviour. We find out what they know by asking questions like why they think physical activity is healthy and how much is healthy. To collect data about attitudes, we ask them what they think about various things. And of course questions about their behaviour hinge on what they actually do.
>
> We also consult health and leisure professionals in a telephone survey to gather different sorts of information. We want to find out if they are taking the new message about physical activity on board and whether they are actively involved in promotional activities. We will be using these methods of evaluation throughout the three-year run of the Active for Life campaign. 99
>
> *physical activity manager, Health Education Authority*

What are the objectives?

Evaluation is an important stage of any health education campaign. During a campaign, evaluation should be carried out regularly to highlight and resolve problems. At the end of a campaign, evaluation should be carried out to assess whether the campaign has achieved its objectives and why it succeeded or failed. The lessons learnt can then be used to improve campaigns in the future.

UNIT

7

ELEMENT **7.3**

NORTHUMBERLAND HEALTH PROMOTION UNIT

For national No Smoking Day, the Northumberland Health Promotion Unit offered advice to help local people plan anti-smoking campaigns. As part of this, they emphasised the importance of carrying out an evaluation:

Please don't forget to evaluate your campaign following the big day. The following checklist could be adapted for your event. You need to consider:
- the audience you reached –
  - how many people attended your event?
  - what interest did they show in the event?
  - was the event suitable for all ages?
- the press coverage obtained –
  - keep cuttings from local newspapers.
  - analyse the coverage. was it fair, accurate or representative?
- the activities you offered –
  - were the public interested in the activities offered?
  - did they participate (where relevant)?
  - what was most/least popular?
  - what response did competitions gain?
- the cost of the event –
  - remember to include both resource materials costs and man hours.
- the benefits to you and your colleagues of the event –
  - what did you gain from the event?
  - what would you change in the future? why?
  - what recommendations would you make for others?
  - what follow-up work can be done after No Smoking Day?

This process of evaluation is an essential component of any event. Judith would welcome copies of any reports, press cuttings and photographs that you may produce about your campaign.

Overall, the main aim of evaluating a health education campaign is to see whether it has achieved its objectives. The objectives of any campaign should be SMART:

- Specific
- Measurable
- Agreed
- Realistic
- Timebound

DISCUSSION POINT

Why do you think the Northumberland Health Promotion Unit places such emphasis on the evaluation of campaigns carried out by different groups in the community? How do you think the information they receive could help them coordinate similar campaign initiatives in the future?

People involved in organising a health education campaign should know exactly what their objectives are, so that they can refer back to them throughout the campaign in order to monitor progress. In some ways this puts them in a good position to evaluate the campaign, although if they have invested a lot of time, energy and ideas they may find it hard to carry out an objective evaluation.

If you are asked to evaluate a campaign in which you haven't been directly involved, the first thing you need to do is determine its objectives. You can only start to evaluate the success of a campaign if you have a clear idea of what it was trying to achieve in the first place. Often, the best way to determine a campaign's objectives is to contact the source of the campaign and ask them. They may have copies of reports and written objectives which they might be willing to give you.

However, in some cases you may need to rely on analysing the information available to determine the objectives of a health education campaign.

As described in section 7.1.3, health education campaigns have three main objectives:

- to meet health targets (national and local)
- to promote the interests of particular groups, such as charities and lobbying organisations
- to promote a hidden message (often commercial).

The chart below lists clues you can look for in information to help you determine which of these three is the main objective of a campaign.

To meet health targets	■ Information will probably be produced by a public-service organisation (either national or local, for example the Health Education Authority, or a local health promotion unit).
	■ It will be widely available in doctors' surgeries, health promotion units, libraries and so on.
	■ The content will tie in with national or local health targets. For example, it may relate to one of the areas for concern highlighted in *The Health of the Nation*, or to a local problem.
	■ The information may refer directly to national or local statistics or targets.
To promote the interests of particular groups	■ Information will be produced by a charity (such as Age Concern) or a lobbying organisation (such as ASH).
	■ It will usually contain general information on a health issue, backed up by details of the group's work.
	■ There may be a form which readers can fill in and send off for more information, or a slip asking for donations.
To promote a hidden message	■ The information will be produced or sponsored by a commercial organisation, for example a pharmaceutical company or a food retailer. The organisation's logo will usually be shown on the front or back cover of any information.
	■ If the company has shops or offices, it will be available there. It may also be generally available in doctors' surgeries, health promotion units, and so on.
	■ The information will usually consist of general information on a health issue, followed by details of how the company's products can help. For example, a leaflet on sun safety produced by a chemist will include general advice followed by information on their relevant products.

What aspects of health and social wellbeing is it promoting?

As well as determining the objectives of a health education campaign before starting evaluation, it is useful to identify the main aspects of health and social wellbeing which it is promoting.

Many health education campaigns encourage people to change their lifestyle or attitude. To assess how far a campaign has succeeded, evaluation questions need to focus on the main aspect of health and wellbeing promoted by the campaign. This may be:

- reduction of disease
- promoting healthy living
- minimising the risk of potentially harmful living practices
- promoting personal safety and security.

ACTIVITY

Look back to section 7.1.1, which focused on the aspects of health and social wellbeing promoted by health education campaigns. Draw up a list of the areas covered by each of the four main aspects above.

Determining the main aspects of health and social wellbeing which a campaign is promoting is usually easier than identifying its objectives. Simply looking at the front cover of many leaflets gives a good indication of the main topics tackled. For example, it is clear that this leaflet *Reducing the risk of cot death* is aiming to reduce disease. While the main aim of the leaflet *That's the limit* is to minimise the risk of potentially harmful living practices.

ACTIVITY

Analyse the health education information you looked at in the activity on page 413 in order to determine the main aspects of health and social wellbeing which each campaign is promoting. If a campaign covers more than one main aspect, rank them in the order which you think is most important to the campaign.

Sometimes, health education campaigns promote several different aspects of health and social wellbeing at once. For example, the *That's the limit* leaflet aims to:

- minimise the risk of potentially harmful living practices by giving advice on safe amounts to drink
- reduce alcohol-related disease
- promote healthy living practices by suggesting alternatives to alcohol
- promote personal safety and security by reducing the risk of accidents caused by drinking and driving.

Designing an interview schedule

DISCUSSION POINT

Have you ever been interviewed by someone carrying out a structured interview? Or have you ever carried out a structured interview yourself? What do you think are the advantages and disadvantages of structured interviewing as a research technique?

All health education campaigns are aimed at a particular target group. In order to assess whether a campaign has been successful, evaluative data has to be collected from this target group.

Structured interviewing is usually the best way to collect evaluative data. A structured interview consists of a list of questions which are put to respondents face to face or over the telephone. The interviewer is told how to pose the questions and given suggestions for prompts to encourage respondents to say more. By following the same schedule with every respondent, the interviewer aims to ensure consistency between interviews and results.

One of the most important factors in carrying out successful structured interviews is to identify the right target group for the research, and to select an appropriate sample to interview.

As explained in section 7.1.2, the target groups for health education campaigns are usually:

- age-related (for example, children aged 8–12)
- activity-related (for example, people who smoke)
- sex-related (for example, information on cervical cancer)
- with specific needs (for example, pregnant women).

THE GNVQ TEAM

Two students working towards Advanced Health and Social Care GNVQ decided to evaluate the effectiveness of the following leaflet on its target audience.

They began by determining the objectives of the campaign, noticing that the leaflet is produced by Durex Information Service for Sexual Health. They then analysed the information to determine the main aspects of health and social wellbeing it promotes. They decided that its aim is to minimise the risk of potentially harmful living practices by explaining:

- why it is good to use condoms
- how to use condoms
- where to buy condoms.

The students also decided that a secondary focus of the leaflet is reducing the incidence of sexually transmitted diseases.

Keiko, one of the students, explains how they went on to evaluate the effectiveness of the campaign for its target group.

❝ Looking at the leaflet, it is pretty clear who the Wise up to condoms campaign is targeted at. It uses colloquial language rather than technical terms – words like 'wised up' and 'cool dude'. It includes quotations by 17- and 18-year-olds of both sexes about having sex and using condoms. It has sections on men and women buying and using condoms. From this, we decided that the target group is:

- young people (17- and 18-year-olds in particular)
- sexually active, or may soon start having sex
- male and female.

To evaluate the success of the campaign, we decided to carry out structured interviews with a sample of ten people. As the target group is our own age group, it was easy for us to find people to interview. We chose five girls and five boys in our year who we know have boyfriends or girlfriends. Our aim was to encourage the sample to evaluate the actual or likely effectiveness of the campaign in altering their behaviour – i.e. making them more likely to use condoms.

We decided that the best way to evaluate the campaign would be to give each respondent ten minutes to read the leaflet, and then to work through a structured interview.

```
Have you see this leaflet before today?
If yes, where?
Who do you think the leaflet is aimed at? Why?
Do you think the leaflet is written in an appropriate style for its target audience?
Do you think the information is presented in an appropriate way for its target audience?
If yes, why?
If no, why not?
Did you notice who produced the leaflet?
If yes, what do you think their aims were in producing it?
After reading the leaflet, can you give five good reasons for using a condom?
Did you find the information on how to use a condom useful?
If no, why not?
Did you find the information on sexually transmitted diseases and AIDS useful?
If no, why not?
Having read the leaflet, do you think you would be less embarrassed to buy condoms?
Would this leaflet make you more likely to buy a condom made by Durex?
Having read the leaflet, would you be more likely to use a condom?
If no, why not?
```

Lee and I each interviewed five people. Before the interviews we spent time talking about each of the questions and practising how we would ask them. We agreed to stick to the prompts written into the interview schedule, and not to ask people to expand on their answers in any other way. By being this strict, we hoped to make sure that the answers we got were as consistent as possible, without being influenced by us. 🙦

ACTIVITY

Working in pairs, choose a health education campaign you are familiar with. By looking at the information available, identify:

- the objectives of the campaign
- the main aspects of health and social wellbeing which it is promoting
- the target group.

Bearing in mind these points, draft a structured interview schedule you could use with a sample of the target group to evaluate the actual or likely effectiveness of the campaign in altering their behaviour. Test your interview schedule on one or two people, and make any changes you think are necessary.

Analysing the results of an evaluation involves:

- recording the answers given to questions
- looking at the responses to questions
- presenting the responses as tables, graphs or charts, to provide a picture of people's views and feelings.

THE GNVQ TEAM

Keiko recorded the responses of two of the people she interviewed as follows:

RESPONDENT I (MALE)

1 No.

2 Teenagers. Language, quotes by young people.

3 No, a bit patronising.

4 Yes. Easy to read, looks like a teenage magazine.

5 Yes. To encourage people to use more condoms and to sell more of their product.

6 5. Protection against STDs; reliable; no medical side effects; easy to buy; make sex less messy.

7 No. Already knew how to use one.

8 No. Not enough detail and already knew most of it anyway.

9 No. Wasn't embarrassed before.

10 No.

11 No. Already used them.

RESPONDENT 2 (FEMALE)

1 Yes. In doctor's surgery.

2 16- to 19-year-olds. Quotes are by people in that age group, uses young language.

3 Yes.

4 Yes. Illustrations of how to use a condom are helpful.

5 Yes. To give people information about condoms and make them less embarrassed about using them.

6 4. Protection against STDs; no side effects; protect against cervical cancer; make sex less messy.

7 Yes.

8 Yes. But would probably look for specific leaflets if needed information on STDs.

9 Yes.

10 Yes.

11 Yes.

ACTIVITY

Experiment with different ways Keiko could record these responses. Think about how the answers could be laid out so they are easier to compare.

ACTIVITY

Keiko and Lee recorded the following responses to question 11 of their structured interview schedule – 'Having read the leaflet, would you be more likely to use a condom? If no, why not?'

	Yes	No	
Question 11	5 (3 F, 2 M)	5 (2 F, 3 M)	F = female M = male

	Already use condoms regularly	Didn't tell me anything new	Don't like using condoms
If no, why not?	1 F, 2 M	1 F	1 M

What do you think would be the best way to present these responses? Try different formats for charts and graphs. You may find element 8.3 (page 461) helpful.

Conclusions must be:

- Consistent with data
  - tied in closely with facts and figures
- Related to purpose
  - relevant to the campaign's objectives
- Based on evidence
  - not based on assumptions

Recommendations must be:

- Based on the conclusions
  - backed up by the evidence of research
- Constructive
  - positive and practical, rather than concentrating on criticisms
- Realistic
  - capable of being put into practice, bearing in mind time, resources, etc.

Conclusions and recommendations

Once the responses to a structured interview schedule have been recorded and presented, it is possible to compare the answers to different questions in order to:

- draw conclusions
- recommend ways the health education campaign could be improved.

This usually involves writing a research report based on the findings, which people can then read and respond to.

When writing a research report, it is important to ensure that the conclusions you draw and suggestions you make for improvements are valid.

If conclusions and recommendations meet these criteria, then they can play an important part in shaping and improving health education campaigns in the future.

Key questions

1 Why is it important to evaluate health education campaigns?
2 Why do you need to know a campaign's objectives before carrying out an evaluation?
3 How might you be able to tell by analysing information that a campaign has the main objective of promoting a hidden message?
4 What are the four main aspects of health and wellbeing promoted by campaigns?
5 What is a structured interview schedule?
6 Explain how you would choose a sample group for structured interviewing.
7 What is involved in analysing the results of an evaluation?
8 How might you present people's responses to a structured interview schedule?
9 How would you check that the conclusions you drew from an evaluation were valid?
10 List three characteristics of good recommendations for future campaigns.

Assignment

Choose one health education campaign which is aiming to improve the health and wellbeing of the population. Collect information on the campaign, and analyse it to determine:

- the objectives of the campaign
- the main aspects of health and social wellbeing which it is promoting
- the target group for the campaign.

You may find it helpful to contact the organisation which produced the information. Write a description of the campaign based on your findings, explaining how its objectives and subject matter relate to its target audience.

Produce a structured interview schedule which you can use to evaluate the effectiveness of the campaign for its target group. After trialling your interview format, carry out interviews with at least six individuals in the target group and record their responses. Present your findings and use them as the basis of a research report, which should include:

- evidence obtained from the interviews
- clearly reasoned conclusions
- recommendations on how the campaign could be improved.

UNIT **8**

Element 8.1
The research process

Element 8.2
Planning research and gathering
data

Element 8.3
Presenting the findings
of research

Research in health and social care

This unit is about the research process. You will
undertake and write reports on one or more
health and social care research projects of your
own. You are encouraged to link your research
with the subjects covered in previous units.

ELEMENT **8.1**

The research process

This element is an introduction to research. People who work in health and social care jobs do research to keep up to date with developments in their profession. For example, nurses need to know about the latest methods of dressing wounds or how to produce computerised care plans. Someone working in mental health might need to know what services are available locally for people with a mental illness. Research is a very practical activity with a direct effect on the quality of care. But to be useful, it has to be done properly, which is why this element introduces the process of research.

66 *Research is incredibly important for my job. I couldn't advise people effectively if I didn't keep up to date. I look at research with a view to relating the findings to practice. I think it's equally important to update and extend one's own skills and knowledge. I'm currently doing an MA. One of the things I am looking at is 'disguised compliance' in carers – for example, turning up to the bare minimum of appointments, but not enough to move forward. Cases where this occurs have a high incidence of child abuse so it is an important area to examine.* **99**

child protection adviser

66 *Research is important to my job. Through my recent study on hormone replacement therapy (HRT) I have been able to provide more appropriate counselling. Also, I haven't needed to go away and look things up so it benefits the customer as they get the information more quickly.* **99**

pharmacist

66 *Research is very much a part of our work. Every four years we do research in schools, which we use to inform our work. The outcomes of this survey give us information on trends in young people's health and allow us to track progress.* **99**

assistant director (health promotion), local health authority

66 *The purpose of research at the Centre is to look at current practice and see how we might develop the service. The age of our client group is wide: twelve to twenty-five. We use research to help us pinpoint the different needs of the different ages. For example, we tried to find out what the word 'confidential' means to a 13-year-old. Do they realise it means the counselling they receive is private and we really won't tell anyone else about it?* **99**

senior worker (counselling), young people's counselling and information service

The structure of research questions

define what research
is needed

identify ethical issues

develop methods and
obtain the data

analyse the data and
produce results

use results to suggest
recommendations

A **hypothesis** spells out exactly
what you decide to investigate.

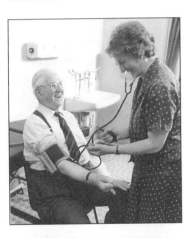

ACTIVITY

Dental care is one aspect of
personal health and neglecting
teeth can lead to a range of
health problems. Develop a
hypothesis which links brushing
teeth to the dental health of
individuals.

In the health and social care sectors, people are constantly investigating:

- how to improve the delivery of services
- causal factors – the reasons why things happen
- different types of treatment and intervention
- the occurrence of different diseases and other health-related problems.

They do this to improve the quality of care provided. There is a direct link
between research and practice. In all research, whether it is about specific
treatments or wider issues of policy, there is a discipline which will allow the
outcomes of one person's research to be used by others. The five sections of
this element look at how this discipline works in practice.

All research should be relevant and produce useful information. So the first
step in doing research is to think carefully about what it's for by defining what
research is needed. This section looks at how that is done.

Hypothesis

A good hypothesis states clearly what the investigation aims to do and sets
limits on it. A poor hypothesis doesn't narrow the investigation down enough
and doesn't provide a clear focus for the research. People who start with a
poor hypothesis may find themselves trying to investigate too many things at
the same time.

GP FUNDHOLDER: THE VALUE OF EXERCISE (1)

One job of practice managers in fundholding GP practices is to identify
new services and evaluate their success. One practice manager set up a
three-month programme of exercise classes for people suffering from high
blood pressure and wanted to evaluate the impact. Her hypothesis was
that the patients' health had improved as a result of this service.

The hypothesis stated:

- what she wanted to investigate – measurable improvements in the
  health of patients with high blood pressure

- who she wanted to investigate – patients who had high blood pressure
  and regularly attended the exercise classes

- how she could gain the information – by measuring relevant indicators
  before the classes started and when the programme had finished.

The practice manager also decided to compare patients who had done the
classes with a similar group who had not enrolled. This meant that she
could also suggest a 'null hypothesis' – the opposite of the first hypothesis.
In this case, the null hypothesis would be that the exercise classes made
no difference to the health of people with high blood pressure.

It is important to take account of other factors that may influence the research.
For example, if the practice manager's results showed that the health of
patients who did the exercise classes improved over the three-month

programme, she would also need to consider what other factors might have contributed to the improvement.

Area of study

The topic people are interested in researching may be quite broad. For example, someone involved in childcare may want to look at the way nurses and others interact with children who are afraid of injections. There are several issues which could be investigated here, such as:

- the range of strategies that nurses use for calming children and how effective these strategies are
- technical innovations that could make injections less traumatic for children
- how nurses develop the skill of calming distressed children.

Researchers have to decide where their priorities lie so the research is practical. This will also help to define its scope more clearly. The person investigating children's fear of injections might need to decide:

- the setting in which the injections are given
- whether the injections are routine inoculations or part of the treatment for a medical condition
- the age of the children.

The decision may be governed by practical considerations, such as the situation in which the person works, and the problems of getting children to be involved in research.

Selecting a sample helps to focus the area of study. Who to select depends on the hypothesis being tested and the information already available. For example, the practice manager in the case study on page 423 might select patients in a particular age range who display a specific range of symptoms.

DISCUSSION POINT

Look back at the hypothesis you developed on page 423 about the effect of brushing teeth on health. How could you clarify the area of study in your hypothesis?

A **sample** is a systematic selection of people from a given **population**. For example, one definition of the 'population' of a GP practice is all the patients listed with the practice. This population could be sampled in different ways:

- every twentieth patient
- all patients visiting in a particular week
- all patients with a particular condition.

GP FUNDHOLDER: THE VALUE OF EXERCISE (2)

Following a brief examination of patient records, the practice manager decides to limit her investigation and adapts her hypothesis.

Hypothesis

A planned exercise schedule for patients between the ages of 50 and 60 suffering from high blood pressure contributes to the improvement of both the overall health of the patient and the lowering of blood pressure when it is carried out as a supplement to other treatments.

The area of study is now very clear. The adapted hypothesis:

- limits the ages of the people being studied to those between 50 and 60
- allows other factors to be taken into account – for example, the practice manager could also compare the diets of people in her sample.

The hypothesis also now states clearly the relationship between two variables: improvements in health, such as lowering of blood pressure, and a planned exercise programme.

Previous research

How many times have you been annoyed by people asking the same questions to get the same information? It seems a waste of time and effort and you wish you could tell the questioners where to go to find out all they need to know. The same applies to research. Work is often repeated – wasting time and effort – because not enough desk research was done before the study starts.

Very few pieces of research break completely new ground. Most relate in some ways to previous research. For example, they might:
- build on research that has already been started
- use the findings from previous research as a starting point
- check that the outcomes from previous research are applicable in another situation, or geographical area – for example, a survey on the link between mental illness and unemployment might be done in several geographical areas and checked over a period of time.

Looking at the outcomes of previous research can:
- reveal similar studies and show how researchers handled the situations
- suggest a method or a technique for dealing with a problematic situation which may help solve similar difficulties
- suggest new or unfamiliar sources of data
- help to put a study in perspective and in relation to earlier investigations of the same problem
- provide new ideas and approaches.

People can find out about previous research by looking at the sources listed in the box on the next page. Or they can ask others. For example, someone interested in a particular sports injury might ask staff working in a sports injury clinic if they know of research related to the particular condition.

Whenever you search out some information, make sure you know the exact subject headings to look for. Do this by examining the hypothesis to find key words. These are words which can be used in the indexes or referencing system to narrow down the field. In the case of the practice manager investigating the effect of exercise classes, key words could include:
- blood pressure treatment
- planned exercise routines
- 50- to 60-year-olds
- in GP practices.

Sources of information about research

Sources of information relevant to research in health and social care are wide-ranging. This is just a selection:

sources	types of information
newspapers and magazines	short reports of recent research; occasional in-depth features
professional journals, e.g. *Nursing Times*	more detailed reports of research in health care; summaries of research projects
specialist journals, e.g. *Journal of Child Psychology and Psychiatry*	detailed, often technical reports of research in specific areas of health care; clinical reports into treatments and interventions
conference reports	papers and records of discussions, often in areas of topical interest
government-sponsored research	research carried out by government agencies or the voluntary sector

These and other sources are available in libraries, hospital information centres, on-line databases such as Med-Line and on the World Wide Web, via the Internet. It is often worth starting with reference books called abstracts, which contain summaries of a whole range of books and articles. An example is *Health Service Abstracts*. There is also a national register of research on health issues, coordinated by the Department of Health.

ACTIVITY

Pick out the key words in your hypothesis about brushing teeth. Try using them in a library or database to search out relevant material. Have a look at two or three of the sources you identify. If your search has come up with many sources, how could you narrow it down further so you have a manageable amount to read?

The word **data** refers to all the information collected during the course of a research project. It is a plural word, so you should use a plural verb – 'data are'. You might come across it with a singular verb as well. **Primary data** are collected during the research itself. **Secondary data** are collected by someone else, often for a different purpose.

Research methods and data sources

The four main methods for getting information from research are:

- observation
- interviews
- questionnaires
- experimental methods.

These are looked at in more detail in section 8.1.3. The research question, or hypothesis, determines the most appropriate method in each case. In some cases, more than one method is used. For example, the practice manager assessing the effect of exercise on the health of patients with high blood pressure is using experimental methods and observation. Someone finding out about the psychological impact of an unfavourable diagnosis would need to use sensitively managed interviews.

Primary data can be obtained from any of the methods listed above. There is a great deal of secondary data also available. Much of this may be valuable to a research study even if it has been collected for a different purpose. Some data sets contain large amounts of data, often drawn from representative samples across the whole country or a region, which researchers can analyse or use as comparisons with their own outcomes. For example, the population estimates produced by the Office for National Statistics contain demographic data which are used to establish funding levels for NHS regions.

Health authorities and trusts collect health-related information for their populations, including statistics on morbidity (the incidence of illnesses and disease) and mortality. Much of this information is collected routinely, which means it is done automatically as part of people's work. GP practices collect some data but most data related to health comes from hospitals. Data on epidemics are collected by the Public Health Laboratory Service, through its communicable disease surveillance centre. Social services departments and voluntary organisations also collect information (see unit 5).

HIV-1-infected persons by exposure category, UK to end of June 1996

How HIV infection was probably acquired	Male	Female
Sexual intercourse		
between men	16542	–
between men and women		
exposure to 'high risk' partners	106	496
exposure abroad	1945	1811
exposure in the UK	162	258
investigation continuing/closed	131	151
Injecting drug use (DU)	1999	904
Blood factor treatment (e.g for haemophilia)	1226	11
Blood/tissue transfer (e.g. transfusion) abroad/UK	89	94
Mother to infant	178	179
Other or investigation continuing/closed	623	128
Total	23001	4032

Adapted from a table published by the PHLS Communicable Disease Surveillance Centre

ACTIVITY

Look at a copy of the *Guide to Official Statistics*, published annually by the Office for National Statistics. This describes the various different types of data collected by the Government. Use the *Guide* to identify relevant sources of data that you might consult in your own research project (see element 8.2).

USING DATA FROM HOSPITALS: HEART SURGERY

A study was carried out in 1993 to investigate differences in access to heart surgery for men and women. The research was based on data from several districts in a health authority region collected over a period of four years. Using various categories of data collected by the hospitals, the researchers selected 24,000 patients with a primary diagnosis of heart disease and compared the management of all cases.

Statistical analysis of the results showed that women were less likely than men to receive surgery for heart disease.

Section 8.1.2   Ethical issues

Ethics is a branch of philosophy which is concerned with human morals and behaviour. In health and social care, ethics is an important practical consideration. It can't just be left to the philosophers.

All research affects somebody, somehow, even if it is only the person doing the research. When other people are involved, they must:

- know what is going on – the objectives of the research, what they will be doing, how the outcomes will be used
- agree to take part and know that they have the right to withdraw
- be given the chance to comment on the outcomes.

To some extent, ethical considerations apply to all research. They are especially important when the research involves experiments with or observations of other people.

HOW UNETHICAL IS IT?

A research student wants to find out more about how people behave at raves and similar events. She is particularly interested in what drugs people take, why they take them and where they get them from. She would like to establish whether there is a link between patterns of drug use and various social and lifestyle factors, including employment status, educational bakground and amount of available income.

She plans the research in two phases. In the first phase, she plans to go to a number of raves and get to know five or six people who take drugs. Her aim is to become known to them and accepted as one of the group. She does not intend to reveal her role as a researcher at this point.

In the second phase, she plans to visit each of the five or six people individually and ask them a series of questions about drug use and social and lifestyle factors. At this point she will tell them about her research.

Then she goes to discuss the proposed study with her supervisor.

DISCUSSION POINT

In what ways is the proposed research study described above unethical? How might it have damaged the individuals who participated without even knowing? How could similar findings have been obtained in an ethical way?

Many professions working with people have ethical standards or codes (see the box below). If researchers in a health-related area of study intend to use patients or service users as research subjects, they may need permission from the ethics committee of the trust, health authority or care organisation.

Ethical principles for conducting research with human participants apply to school and college students as well as members of professional bodies.

The British Psychological Society has published a set of ethical principles. They require researchers to:

- get the informed consent of all participants (or their parent or guardians if they are under 16 or have impairments that limit communication)
- not withhold information except where absolutely necessary for the research
- discuss with participants the purpose of the research and their experience of taking part
- make sure they know of their right to withdraw
- state that information will be treated confidentially
- protect participants from physical or mental harm during the investigation
- respect the privacy and psychological wellbeing of the individuals studied
- be cautious about giving advice.

A student who carried out research in an old people's home into an aspect of care says:

66 I wasn't sure if I should be asking questions of people much older than me. I thought I might come across as intrusive or ignorant. The manager at the home suggested I should ask the residents themselves. So I made a short list of headings that I wanted the interviews to cover and talked to three residents about them. One said she wouldn't mind being asked about all those things but two objected to one of the headings, so I took it out. Then I wrote out the questions I wanted to ask in the interviews and tried them out on the same three people to make sure they weren't upset by anything I asked. 99

Effects of research

For ethical reasons, it's important to anticipate the effects of the research – on individual participants and on all the people who will benefit – at the earliest stage. It is no use having a brilliant idea of what to study if the only way of getting the results is by breaking ethical principles or codes.

Research has risks and benefits. The main benefit is the knowledge gained from the research, which might help both the participants and everyone else in a similar situation. The risks include any physical or psychological harm to the participants that might result.

Confidentiality

In the UK, confidentiality is a duty under common law and not a statutory requirement except for information held electronically. European laws and regulations are being developed and may come into force in the future. In health-related areas, organisations like the British Medical Association, the Royal College of Nursing and associations of service users are all campaigning for a statutory framework to safeguard the confidentiality of information.

The Hippocratic oath, which guides the ethical behaviour of doctors, says that they should not reveal anything they 'see or hear, in the life of men, which ought not to be spoken of . . . '. A more recent set of guidelines, the Patient's Charter, states that service users have the right 'to know that everyone working for the NHS is under a legal duty to keep your records confidential'. The same right applies to research.

When participants give their consent to take part in research, it is usual to guarantee confidentiality. This guarantee applies to:

- how the information is kept
- how it is used in the report or other outcomes
- what other use is made of it.

Information should be kept safe and secure, whatever form it is in – e.g. hand-written notes, taped recordings of interviews, returned questionnaires or

Confidentiality means respecting the privacy of any information that is disclosed and only using it for the purposes for which it was originally intended.

entries on a computer database. In a large survey, it is normally easy to hide individual details in the overall results. But in a small sample of subjects, personal details in a report may make individuals readily identifiable. Information about them should not be changed, but it can be presented in such a way as to preserve confidentiality. This can be done by:

- changing people's names
- leaving out details which might identify them, such as any distinguishing physical features or behaviours that others might recognise.

A third aspect of confidentiality is the ethical duty only to use any information gathered during research for its original purposes. The Data Protection Act states that personal data can only be held for specified purposes and 'shall not be used or disclosed in any manner incompatible with . . . those purposes'.

DISCUSSION POINT

Look back at the case study on page 428 which describes a proposed research study designed by a student (but not carried out). What other purposes could the information gathered during this research have been put to? What risks were there for the participants if confidentiality had been broken?

The ethical duty of confidentiality may sometimes conflict with the ethical duty of care, as a child protection adviser explains:

66 *Doctors and nurses often have a problem with that. They want to make a report where they feel an incident has taken place, but they're worried about breaching confidentiality. We would advise that government guidelines state that the child's best interests must come first and disclosure is the best course of action. When they can see that they would be doing it for very sound reasons they usually feel happier about it.* 99

Participants' rights

Everyone involved in research has the right to:

- agree whether or not to take part in the research, without coercion or pressure – this is called giving 'informed consent'
- withdraw from the research if it is causing distress or inconvenience
- see the outcomes and comment on them.

In medical research, informed consent is essential. If someone is to be given an experimental drug, or have their treatment withdrawn or changed, they must be aware of the possible consequences. Any research which involves a change in treatment also poses risks and requires informed consent. As the student quoted on page 429 discovered, even talking to people about things relating to their wellbeing may be stressful for them.

There are two difficulties in getting informed consent. First, it is not always possible to describe the research process fully. For example, you might know that you want to interview the subject, but may not know how long the interview will take. Second, if the person doing the research also has a caring role, there may be conflicts between the two roles.

DISCUSSION POINT

What examples can you think of where there might be a conflict between someone's role as a researcher and their role as a carer? Look out for cases where this has happened in any reading you do around this subject.

Researchers have an ethical duty to report the findings of their research accurately and fairly. But they should also give participants an opportunity to see the outcomes and comment on them before they are made public. This can be done by:

■ discussing the outcomes with participants before writing them up
■ giving participants a draft of the report and allowing them to comment – some comments might be included in the final version of the report.

The culture of the researcher

People from different cultures have different values. One of the core values of anyone working in health and social care (examined in element 1.3) is to respect the values of others. In research, this means:

■ identifying any cultural issues in the sample – for example, does the research involve people from different ethnic backgrounds, or does it touch on sensitive issues of belief
■ ensuring that the research question will not be offensive
■ checking that the research methods chosen are free from bias.

Research is different from ordinary finding out because it is more planned and systematic. It starts with a limited hypothesis and then selects a method which is likely to get usable, reliable outcomes. The four main types of method are:

- experiments
- questionnaires
- interviews
- observation.

An **experiment** is a controlled way of looking at what happens when one or more variables are changed.

The skills needed to do research are not very different from the skills used in everyday life to find things out. Suppose you are thinking about applying to a particular university and want to find out more about it. In this situation, you might not be happy just with reading about it. You might want to:

- talk to friends who had been there
- go there yourself for a couple of days
- try finding accommodation in two or three different areas.

In other words, you would carry out interviews, do some observation and try out an experiment. The only thing you probably wouldn't do in this situation is produce questionnaires and give them to a sample of students to fill in – though you would probably be interested in reading the outcomes of such a survey.

Experiments

In medical research, different drugs are tried out on a group of volunteers. If the only variable is the kind of drug, any differences in the way the volunteers respond can be attributed to the effects of the drug. The problem is that even under laboratory conditions, it is difficult to eliminate all other variables. When researchers are studying human behaviour, rather than clinical symptoms, the difficulties get even greater.

Experiments always start with a hypothesis which suggests a link between two variables, such as the time spent talking to patients on admission to hospital and how satisfied they say they are with their treatment when they leave. There are two ways of carrying out an experiment like this:

- test the subject before and after – if everything else stays the same, any changes observed (such as greater satisfaction) have been caused by the change to one variable (talking more to patients when they arrive)
- divide a number of subjects into groups – one group is exposed to an intervention (such as a drug), other groups are exposed to no intervention at all (or a placebo), or to a different intervention.

A lot of experimental data comes from clinical practice and trials. Some data may come from measurements, like the data on blood pressure and other health indicators collected by the practice manager in the case study on page 423. Clinical trials of drugs are experiments on a much bigger scale.

Clinical measurements are vital for doctors and healthcare professionals who work directly with patients – so that they can plan an appropriate treatment. A wide range of equipment is used for collecting data: thermometers, watches and weigh-scales, used in routine situations, and highly technological equipment, such as scanners and digital imaging techniques to measure blood flows in the brain. The important thing is to choose the most appropriate equipment for the experiment. For example, a project assessing the effect of changes in diet on body weight might only need an accurate and consistent set of bathroom scales. On the other hand, research which aimed to compare the toxic side-effects of different forms of treatment for breast cancer would need to record far more complex changes in patients' conditions, including their quality of life.

Questionnaires

Questionnaires are a relatively quick way of collecting a lot of data. But they need designing carefully.

There are two types of question: 'open', where people are free to answer in any way; and 'closed', where they choose from a limited set of answers. Open questions are difficult to analyse but can provide more information. There are four different types of closed question:

- questions with only two answers, like 'yes' or 'no'
- multiple-choice questions with a range of answers, like 'excellent, good, poor, very poor'
- questions which ask people to look at a range of statements and pick the one that best fits their own views
- questions asking people to give a score to several alternatives – they are good for finding out which issues people feel most strongly about.

It may sometimes be better to ask indirect questions rather than direct ones. For example, instead of asking 'What do you feel about the new opening hours at the surgery?', you could ask 'What do you think the general feeling is about the new surgery opening hours?'. People are sometimes more comfortable expressing negative opinions if they can attribute them to others.

A questionnaire is a written set of questions which people answer either on their own or with an interviewer to guide them.

ACTIVITY

Experiment with different types of question using the situation described in the health centre case study. First, make sure you know what you are aiming to find out. Then start writing the questions. When you have written eight or ten, stop and:

- analyse what types of question they are
- try them out on someone else
- see if you need to change the type, e.g. from a question with two answers to a multiple-choice
- see if you need to make the wording clearer
- check if the order of the questions affects the answers you get.

HEALTH CENTRE APPOINTMENTS

A local health centre on a crowded, inner-city estate has just changed its appointment system to try to avoid the problem of people having to wait a long time before they can see a doctor.

The centre is open six days a week. On four days, there is a normal appointment system. On the other two days, there are open surgeries: everyone waits to be seen in turn. They might have to wait longer than normal, but patients will be seen on the same day.

Another change is to have specialist clinics on regular days so that people do not have to travel long distances to see specialists.

The health centre manager wants to find out what people think of the changes, and is writing questions for a questionnaire. He intends to try them out with a small group of patients the next day.

Interviews

Interviews are good for collecting information that is sensitive or can't be predicted in advance. Although they take a lot of time, the information can be very useful. Interviews may be the only way of getting information from

ACTIVITY

Try preparing for a semi-structured or unstructured interview. Select a topic. For example, the health centre manager in the case study above might decide to talk to three or four patients before writing his questionnaire, so he can get an idea of what they are feeling about the new appointments system.

Think about your topic for five minutes and write down things that you would like to know about it. Spend another five or ten minutes sorting the questions into themes. At the end, you should have a few themes – no more than three or four – and a few questions under each theme.

DISCUSSION POINT

When are the four methods of obtaining data – experiment, questionnaire, interview, observation – used in health and social care research? Discuss some research you know about in various contexts: medical, nursing, health education, social work etc. Which methods did they use? What made these methods particularly appropriate for the context?

groups such as visually impaired people or children, who would not be able to fill in a questionnaire themselves.

> An **interview** is a conversation between the researcher and a respondent. Interviews can be carried out face to face or by telephone. Social care often uses group interview techniques.

Interviews can be:

- structured – this is like a questionnaire, when everyone is asked the same questions in the same way
- semi-structured – where the same basic questions are asked, but the interviewer can vary the order and 'probe' for more information
- unstructured – where the interviewer just has a list of topics to cover and is free to discuss them in any way; it's like a guided conversation.

If you go through the process described in the activity above, the actual questions tend to come back to you in the interview itself. So the conversation isn't broken up by constantly looking at a list of questions.

Observation

Some research is done by watching people in a particular situation and recording what they do. There are plenty of opportunities for doing this – for example, you might sit in a cafe in a railway station and watch how people behave. But you probably wouldn't learn much unless you knew exactly what you were watching for and had a systematic way of collecting the data. There are four ways that a researcher can observe people systematically:

- by becoming a member of the group and hiding their role – this can lead to ethical problems and isn't usually justified (see section 8.1.2)
- by becoming a member of a group and telling the others about their role – this avoids some ethical problems but it may mean that others don't act normally with the researcher; it may also lead to a conflict of roles
- by watching the participants from outside, but also spending a small amount of time with them
- by becoming a 'fly on the wall' and watching entirely from the outside, with no interaction at all.

A group leader at a youth centre explains why observation is central to his job:

66 Of course I'm always watching the people in my group. It's absolutely vital that I know what's going on between them and can sense the changes of mood. We're dealing with young people who come from difficult, sometimes violent, backgrounds. They change moods very quickly. I'm involved with what they do – we agree the programme for each session together and I take part. But I'm also a bit detached. They know that and on the whole they respect my dual role. 99

Methods of analysing data

Quantitative data is data in a numerical form, which can be counted and analysed using statistical methods. **Qualitative** data is data in written or spoken form, which is analysed using other methods.

Data collected from research come in different forms:

- words – interview notes or tapes, notes of observations, comments on questionnaires
- numbers – ticks on a questionnaire, multiple-choice sheet or tally sheet, scores (e.g. 1 to 5), numerical records of observation, such as the number of people asking for a particular piece of information in a period of time.

Although many research projects use a combination of methods, there is a real difference between the two types. An occupational psychologist explains:

> 66 *Think of yourself outside a crowded, well-lit room, looking in through the window with a notebook in your hand. In quantitative research, you are looking at the world from the outside, as an observer. The aim is to be objective and collect precise, measurable data. Now think of yourself inside that room, talking to people, soaking up the atmosphere. In qualitative research, the aim is to try and get inside the world you are observing.* 99

Some research will collect both kinds of data. For example, a survey of how nurses make use of a work station on a hospital ward might collect:

- numerical data from observation – the number of times each nurse uses the work station, how long they stay for, what they do there, etc.
- verbal data from interviews – what nurses think about the layout of the work station, what improvements could be made and so on.

DISCUSSION POINT

Why is it often a good idea to collect both numerical and verbal data? What kinds of things can verbal data tell you that numerical data can't? What about the other way round?

Quantitative methods

Numerical (or quantitative) data is analysed using statistical methods. These are not especially complicated: according to one professor of mathematics, statistics requires 'nothing more that common sense and arithmetic'. Statistics have two main functions:

- to describe the data – this is called descriptive statistics
- to interpret the data in relation to a hypothesis (see page 423) – this is inferential statistics.

Describing quantitative data

The results of a quantitative survey or experiment are usually in the form of a mass of numbers. To understand what the numbers mean, you have to sort them out. One way of doing this is to work out an average. The three types of average (mean, median and mode) are described in the box on the next page.

Mean

The mean is the most common type of average. You get it by adding up all the results and dividing the total by the number of results. For example, if three nurses spent 3 minutes, 4.5 minutes and 6 minutes at their work station in one hour, you get the mean by adding up the time (3 + 4.5 + 6 = 13.5) and dividing it by the number of nurses (13.5 ÷ 3 = 4.5 minutes). The mean can give a misleading impression if it is distorted by one or two untypical results – for example, if one of the nurses spent three-quarters of an hour at the work station.

Median

In the US, the word 'median' describes the raised strip on a motorway separating traffic going in opposite directions. In maths, the median is the middle value in a set of numbers. You get it by arranging all the results in order and choosing the middle one. It is useful when there are one or two extreme results. If one nurse spent three-quarters of an hour at the work station and the other two spent 3 and 4.5 minutes, the median would be 4.5 (the middle of the three numbers). What would the mean be in this case?

Mode

The mode is the result which occurs most frequently. If someone asks a nurse how long she usually spends at her work station in an hour, she might say:

❝ *If I'm busy with patients, which I usually am, I spend about five minutes. If we are short-staffed or under pressure, I might not go there at all, whereas if I'm on nights I can sometimes spend 30 or 40 minutes there catching up. But most of the time, I'd say it's about five minutes.* ❞

Here, the nurse is giving the mode.

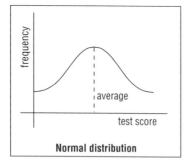

Normal distribution

To describe data, you have to know whether your results fall into a pattern. This is sometimes called the 'distribution' of results. For example, if a health visitor measured the weight of a hundred babies of the same age and drew a graph to show the results, it would probably look like the graph on the left. It is called a graph of 'normal distribution', because data normally falls into this pattern.

Many characteristics of human beings, such as height, birth weight, resting pulse rate and intelligence, follow a normal distribution curve like this. A midwife in a maternity hospital says:

❝ *We measure the weight of all babies when they are born. That means we can calculate the average birth weight of male and female babies in a year. We can also compare this average to the averages in previous years, or the averages in other parts of the country, and see how our average fits in with wider trends in childbirth.* ❞

When measuring health indicators, it is often important to know the variability of the results – how much they vary from the mean score. Two measures are useful:

- the difference between the highest and lowest score – this is called the 'range'
- how much, on average, the results vary from the mean score – this is known as the 'standard deviation' (i.e. how much the results deviate from the standard).

ACTIVITY

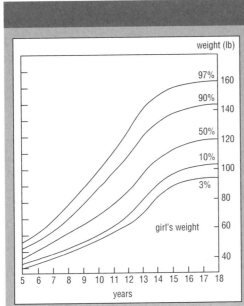

A childcare worker worker has been monitoring the weight of a girl who was born with a digestive disorder. She plots the results on a graph (shown on the left) which shows the standard weight (the mean) and two deviations from the mean. The standard weight is shown on the graph as 50%. Any weight above or below the first standard deviation, shown as 10% and 90% on the graph, indicates that there might be cause for concern.

On the right are the figures she has collected. Plot them on the graph and look at the deviation from the normal range. What conclusion can you draw from the curve?

age	weight (lbs)
5	36
6	40
7	43
8	46
9	55
10	60
11	68
12	80
13	96
14	104
15	110
16	112
17	114
18	114

Statistical significance

Results from epidemiological studies and other studies which produce large data sets need to be assessed to see if they contain any statistically significant data. For example, the normal incidence of a particular condition in new-born babies, for mothers between certain ages, might be 1 in 2,000. If the figure is 3 in every 2,000 in one area of the country, there is a difference. But it many not be significant either clinically or statistically. To assess whether it is statistically significant, other tests need to be carried out such as the t-test or the chi-squared test.

Often, the purpose of a quantitative study is to establish whether there is a relationship between two values such as a woman's age when she has her first baby and her length of stay in hospital after the birth. The relationship between two values can be expressed as a figure, known as the 'correlation coefficient'.

Interpreting quantitative data

The aim of quantitative research is to establish whether the data supports, or fails to support a research hypothesis. This is done by creating a 'null hypothesis' and testing the data against it. In the case study on page 423, the null hypothesis is that a planned exercise programme makes no difference to the blood pressure of men and women between the ages of 50 and 60 who are known to have high blood pressure. If the data supports the null hypothesis, then the research hypothesis is not supported.

The tests that are used fall into two groups:

- comparing results with the normal distribution of the population (as the health visitor did in the activity above)
- carrying out tests to find out the 'statistical significance' of the data.

Qualitative methods

Researchers collecting qualitative data decide how they are going to analyse the data while the study is still being planned. This is because – unlike numerical data – verbal data are not easy to analyse. If the research provides transcripts or notes of interviews, fieldnotes or other written materials, how are researchers going to make sense of them all? There are two main approaches, which both involve categorising the data in some way:

- look for themes and patterns
- use codes to record what you see and hear.

Themes and patterns

If the research has been designed to test a hypothesis, it is usually possible to decide on themes or patterns in advance. Researchers might look for:

- themes in what participants say – for example, a survey to find out the reasons why people fail to stop smoking might establish six themes (effect on diet, effect on mood or temper, social pressures, etc.)
- stages in a process – the same research might categorise participants by length of time between stopping smoking and starting again
- particular words or phrases – these can be indicators of themes and patterns ('I feel bad-tempered at coffee time if I can't have a cigarette')
- attitudes – for example, how smokers feel about non-smoking flights; attitudes can often be scaled, allowing some numerical analysis.

Researchers sometimes start by looking for a few broad themes and patterns. As they get deeper into the analysis and become familiar with the material, they can make more distinctions.

Codes

Another approach is to code the data. This is a particularly useful method for analysing data from observation. Remember the occupational psychologist's image of looking in through a window at a crowded, well-lit room. How can you make sense of what you see? It's a lot easier if you know exactly what you are looking for.

Codes can be developed to categorise:

- non-verbal behaviour – movements of the body, gestures
- spatial behaviour – the way in which people move towards or away from each other, or in relation to particular locations such as the nursing station
- language – particular phrases or categories of language, e.g. swearing
- verbal behaviour – how quickly people speak, interruptions, loudness.

DISCUSSION POINT

A community psychiatric nurse is helping a middle-aged man readjust to home and work life after a short period of treatment in a mental hospital. The man was admitted to hospital after he attacked a colleague at work. Over a period of several weeks, the nurse visits his patient at home and at work. What themes or patterns might the nurse look for? What sort of things might he decide to code?

<table>
</table>

Section 8.1.5

Conclusions and recommendations

When they have finished analysing data, researchers should be ready to:

- summarise the results
- provide an interpretation of what the results mean
- draw conclusions from the study
- make recommendations based upon these conclusions.

This process is the same, whatever the research aimed to do and whatever its conclusions are.

Confirm policy and practice

Some research outcomes confirm that the way things are done now is right or acceptable. Even so, beware of claiming too much for the outcomes of research. Researchers can't say that their hypothesis is 'proved' or 'disproved' by the outcomes. All they can say is that it is 'supported' or 'not supported'. If outcomes do show a correlation between the variables in a hypothesis, be careful about identifying cause and effect. The recommendations can suggest further work that could be done to investigate this relationship.

The practice manager looking at the effects of a planned exercise programme on blood pressure (see pages 423 and 424) explains:

66 The outcomes showed more or less what I expected. There does seem to be a connection between taking part in the exercise programme and maintaining reduced blood pressure levels. I am reasonably confident that these reduced levels are a result of the exercise, because the group of patients that didn't join the classes did not show a similar level of reduction. But I can't be certain about the effect of other factors, including the social benefit of coming to the classes and possible reductions in stress. 99

In this case, the practice manager is justified in continuing the classes and encouraging other patients with similar conditions to join them. She might also want to carry on the research process by changing the exercise programme and monitoring the effects on blood pressure.

Disprove propositions

Sometimes the outcomes of research do not support the hypothesis. In this case, it may be that the hypothesis was wrong. Or there might have been something wrong with the way the study was designed or carried out. If their hypothesis is not supported the first time, researchers often want to try again and check their results. They may use a different method. However, even when a hypothesis is disproved, they may still be able to draw valuable conclusions.

Extend knowledge and understanding

Research sometimes breaks new ground and adds to the 'knowledge base' of a profession. Some new knowledge is scientifically valid and significant. For example, the work done in the human genome project is building up a more complete understanding of people's genetic make-up and could provide radically new forms of treatment in the future. Some of the work done by pharmaceutical companies on drugs is also at the cutting edge of scientific discovery.

More often, knowledge gained through the research carried out by health and social care workers is related to practices and procedures. Most health and social care professions are very practical and a lot of valuable knowledge is to do with ways of caring for patients or service users or relating to other service users.

HELPING PEOPLE WITH ASTHMA

People suffering from asthma can benefit from drugs which dilate the airways. A nebuliser is sometimes used for this, particularly in patients who need high doses. A nebuliser works by converting a solution containing the drug into a fine mist so it is easier to inhale. It can be self-administered.

A clinical nurse specialist in one trust decided to carry out a survey to see how reliable its nebuliser service was. Around 50 users of the service were identified and sent a questionnaire. Three-quarters of them responded. The questionnaire asked how the patients used their nebulisers and also asked about servicing the equipment.

The study highlighted the need for more and better information about the use and care of nebuliser equipment. It also made several practical recommendations for raising the standard of care, including:

- a central register of patients who have the equipment at home
- spare equipment available 24 hours a day in case of breakdown
- a recall system to ensure equipment is serviced properly
- leaflets offering standard and consistent advice.

Improve practice

A lot of the research carried out by health and social care professionals aims to improve the quality of care. People who work in these sectors are in a good position to identify problems or incidents that they do not fully understand. These can often be the starting point for highly practical, relevant research.

IMPROVING PRACTICE

Here are three examples of research which came out of people's practice.

A practice nurse felt that she could make a special contribution in the area of health promotion. She identified that one of the most significant lifestyle changes people could make was to give up smoking. She started running anti-smoking classes, but take-up was not encouraging. She decided to carry out a research project on methods of improving attendance at classes of this kind.

A children's nurse felt strongly that many young people below the age of consent should be allowed more say in important decisions about their treatment. She decided to investigate law and practice in this area.

A researcher working for a national charity looked at the pressures on informal carers, usually family members, who cared for people with dementia. Her findings were used to:

- help doctors realise the significance of a formal diagnosis
- suggest how medical staff could provide more easily accessible information about the condition
- identify the needs of informal carers for day care and support.

DISCUSSION POINT

How might the practice nurse and the children's nurse in the case studies use the findings from their research to improve practice?

Analysing the research process

At the start of this element, the research process was broken down into five stages. These stages can be combined into three main phases, as the diagram shows.

How does the process work in practice?

Research questions

The aim of this phase is to define the problem and answer the question: What exactly will be studied? It is likely to include:

- a review of existing research findings in this area (sometimes called a 'literature review')
- a statement of purpose, giving the reasons for doing the research and indicating its exact area of study (its 'focus')
- identifying any ethical issues that affect the research
- selecting the research design – what method is appropriate (quantitative, qualitative or both) and whether the data is primary or secondary
- selecting the sample – who is going to be involved in the research?

define what research is needed

→ research questions

identify ethical issues

develop methods and obtain the data

→ forms and methods of obtaining data

analyse the data and produce results

→ nature of analysis and outcomes

use results to suggest recommendations

AFTER SURGERY: WHAT IS THE QUESTION?

Day surgery is often seen as beneficial for patients because they do not have to stay in overnight. But very little is known about the experience of patients after they have been discharged from day surgery. A researcher interested in surgical nursing decided to investigate.

First, she reviewed existing research by looking for relevant articles in professional and specialist journals, including the *Journal of One-Day Surgery*. She found that a study carried out in the US had identified both physical and social problems. This gave her ideas about what to look for in her own study. She identified five categories of data: two of them were classed as 'physical elements' and three as 'personal elements'.

Then she chose her sample and method. She decided to interview six patients, four men and two women. They had all had a general anaesthetic and the operations had gone well. She called her research a 'phenomenological' study, which means it was based on people's experiences.

DISCUSSION POINT

Was the research method chosen for this study mainly quantitative or mainly qualitative? What made the method chosen a suitable one?

Forms and methods of obtaining data

The aim of this phase is to collect accurate, relevant data in a form that is easy to analyse. It includes:

- planning how to collect the data – by questionnaire, interview, observation or experiment
- identifying limitations on the study – for example, if the study uses observation there may be limits on certain areas of the building or at certain times
- developing or obtaining the 'instruments' for collecting data – questionnaires, interview questions, tally chart, experimental equipment, etc.
- collecting the data.

AFTER SURGERY: COLLECTING THE DATA

Data on the experience of patients after being discharged from hospital was collected in a series of face-to-face interviews with six patients in their own homes, two to four days after being discharged.

Data was collected relating to two physical and three personal elements:

Physical elements

■ pain

■ movement and posture

Personal elements

■ communication and information

■ knowledge and understanding

■ the process of recovery

Nature of analysis and outcomes

The aim of this phase is to analyse and interpret the data, summarise the results and produce recommendations. It is likely to include:

■ one or more data analysis procedures – statistical procedures for quantitative data and a systematic analysis of themes, patterns, behaviours, etc. for qualitative data

■ interpretation – do the data support the hypothesis? how do the data answer the research question?

■ drawing conclusions – what are the conclusions and what do they mean?

■ communicating the outcomes, usually in a written report

■ forming recommendations – how does this research affect practice? what other questions still need to be asked?

AFTER SURGERY: ANALYSIS AND CONCLUSIONS

The researcher analysed her interviews with patients in relation to the five categories she had determined at the start of the research process. She then grouped the specific experiences of each patient into further categories.

For example, data in the category 'process of recovery' could be analysed into four types:

■ patients talked about actions over which they themselves had control

■ they also mentioned activities that measured progress to recovery, such as having a bath

■ all the patients mentioned disruptions in family life

■ they all said they had resumed normal activities too soon.

After completing this detailed level of analysis, the researcher was in a good position to form conclusions and make recommendations for practice. She formed three main conclusions. The first was expected, the other two were an unexpected result of the study:

■ patients need better methods of controlling pain

■ communication over what to do after being discharged needs to be improved

■ personal control over the process is a crucial factor for satisfactory recovery.

Her recommendations were clear:

■ doctors should prescribe adequate analgesia and inform patients how to preempt pain

■ carers should have pre-discharge discussions with patients and inform them more clearly about what to expect

■ further research should investigate how patients can resist pressures to resume tasks in the home and at work until the recovery has reached a sufficiently advanced stage.

Key questions

1 What is a hypothesis?
2 How do researchers clarify the area of study in their research?
3 What is the difference between primary and secondary sources of data?
4 What sort of guidelines should researchers follow to make sure their study is ethical?
5 What are the main issues in research relating to confidentiality and the rights of participants?
6 What are the four main research methods used by people in health and social care?
7 What are the differences between quantitative and qualitative data?
8 Which methods are appropriate for certain situations? (Give two examples of when each method would be appropriate.)
9 How do researchers analyse data and form conclusions?
10 What different types of recommendation do researchers into health and social care make?

Assignment

The aim of this assignment is to show that you understand the process of planning and carrying out research. It is in three parts.

Part 1

Produce a booklet showing the stages of research. Start by showing a flow chart of all the stages. Then at each stage:

■ describe what researchers do – where there are various options, such as choosing a research method, briefly describe each option
■ highlight any ethical issues which they may have to think about.

Part 2

Look at some research reports in nursing, medical or social care journals. The list of secondary sources on page 426 may give you more ideas of where to look. Choose one report to analyse in detail. If your own research (see Part 3) is mainly quantitative, choose a report that describes mainly qualitative research, or vice versa.

Describe what the researcher did at each stage:

■ what was the research question?
■ what methods were used to collect the data?
■ how were the data analysed?
■ what were the conclusions and recommendations?

Part 3

Describe the research you plan and carry out for the activities in elements 8.2 and 8.3 in the same way.

ELEMENT **8.2**

Planning research and gathering data

In this element, you will be planning your own research into an aspect of health and social care that interests you, and collecting the data. You can do this on your own or in a group with others. If you do it in a group, keep a record of your personal contribution to the process of planning the research and collecting data. By doing all the activities in this element, you will produce all the working papers you need for the first part of the assignment. You will be analysing the data and presenting your findings in element 8.3.

66 You need to decide before you start research how best to collect the data. You need a fully worked-out plan of what you want to achieve. It's important to get the right amount of data but limit your research to what is practical. Time is a big factor. So stick to the range you have chosen for all your variables, even if it's tempting to broaden them because of your interest. **99**

optometrist

66 We do street surveys and use the results in publicity to support our campaigns. One recent one was concerned with people's feelings about smoke-free dining areas. **99**

assistant director (health promotion), local health authority

66 I am collaborating on a programme with the local teaching hospital, looking at middle-aged women's post-menopausal health and health options. We hope to prove the validity of the role of screening in determining bone mass, to enable a woman to make decisions about looking after her bone health and avoiding a hip fracture. **99**

doctor in charge of health screening

66 In the 1960s, the Government funded a research project to study the quality of nursing care. Interest grew in nursing research in the 1970s, when a government report recommended that nursing should become 'a research-based profession', so research became part of nurse training. During the 1980s, key areas of research were identified, including standards of care, primary health care and the need to define clinical roles. By the 1990s, the idea was widely accepted that nurses and midwives, occupational therapists, physiotherapists and others should be involved in research as a normal part of their work. **99**

lecturer at a university school of health

The rationale for research

The **rationale** for research means the reasons for doing it in the first place.

Why should people who work in health and social care be interested in research?

A child protection adviser explains why it's important:

66 *I don't think you can be an effective practitioner if you're not doing research regularly. I'm not just talking about knowing the latest legal judgments and keeping an eye on the professional journals for new approaches. I'm really saying that you need to be looking at your own practice through the eyes of a researcher as well as a practitioner. Doing research makes you aware of the disciplines of analysis and evaluation. It helps you be a more responsible and reflective person in your work.* 99

Research question

When health and social care practitioners think about a topic for research, they start with their own situation. They ask themselves questions like these:

- What do I need to find out about?
- How is it relevant to my practice, and the practice of others in jobs like mine?

You should do the same when deciding on your research topic. If you have (or have had) a job in the health or social services, that should give you a lead. If not, start by identifying an area of practice that particularly interests you. Find out what the 'hot topics' of discussion are in this area. Which of them seems interesting to you? It may be easier to gain access to participants in social care than in health care: discuss this with your tutor before deciding which area of practice to research.

Target audience

Who is the research for? For health and social care practitioners, one answer is almost certainly themselves. Research results are useful for other people too:

- immediate colleagues – especially if the research looks at a local aspect of practice, such as how to make sure there is always a stock of bandages on a surgical ward
- people in similar jobs elsewhere – a good method for keeping track of supplies might be useful in other hospitals and on other wards in the same hospital
- other practitioners – if they know that the research has already been done, it means they don't have to do it again, or they can build on the results
- planners – people who plan or develop services often take research findings into account.

All research has to be done properly and follow the stages described in element 8.1, to ensure that the results are reliable. But knowing who it's for can help decisions like exactly what information they need and how to publish the results. For example, the outcomes of research into supplies of bandages could be presented in:

445

ACTIVITY

List the target audience for your research. Restrict yourself to a maximum of four groups, one of which should be yourself and another the assessor for your GNVQ. Against each group, write down:

- exactly what you think they need to know

- how they would expect the outcomes of the research to be presented.

Look at your completed list. Will your research question produce the information all these groups are looking for? Do you need to change the question in any way?

A lot of research is geared towards organisations, as well as individuals. For example, research done by the Social Services Inspectorate is designed to encourage good practice in local authority social services departments. The Children Act and community care legislation both offer opportunities to monitor and adapt ways of working.

- a memo or set of guidelines for the ward staff
- the hospital newsletter
- a training session to staff
- a professional journal like *Nursing Times*.

In the case of your research, knowing who it's for can also help you focus on exactly what information they need and how best to present it.

Links to previous research

Before finalising the research question, researchers look to see what other research has already been done into this aspect of practice. They do this by carrying out a search of books and articles in journals (sometimes called a 'literature review').

The standard method of searching the literature has five stages:
- identify texts relevant to the subject, using databases, indexes and abstracts (many are now available on CD-ROM or networked versions)
- list the details of relevant texts on cards or computer database
- get hold of the texts, read them and make notes
- identify any important references quoted in these texts and add them to the list
- select the texts which seem most important, then briefly summarise the ideas they contain.

It makes sense to start with the most convenient sources – probably the school or college library. There may be more relevant books and journals in the library of a teaching hospital or university. Libraries can borrow books and journals from other collections. There are also services that download the text of articles directly onto a computer. The amount of material available on-line is growing all the time and researchers sometimes make contact with others in their field on the Internet.

Reading about other people's research can be fascinating, but it also takes time. The box below gives hints about how to read fast.

Reading fast

You don't always have to read everything carefully, word by word. Here are two ways of reading fast:

- scanning
- skimming.

Scanning is when you let your eye run down a page until you see a significant word. You scan a telephone directory to find the name you are looking for. Scanning is useful when you are checking to see whether something is worth reading in more detail.

ACTIVITY

Carry out your own review of existing research in the area of study covered by your research question. Don't spend too long doing this, or it will turn into a research study of its own. If you are working in a group, split the task between you and then share the results.

How does your research question link to previous research? Are you going over similar ground? What differences are there in the information you hope to find out? Do you need to go back and change your question a bit?

Skimming is looking quickly through a text to pick out the main ideas. If you get a letter telling you whether or not you've succeeded in getting an interview for a job, you would probably skim it quickly to get the general meaning of what it said before reading it more slowly. Skimming is useful if you think that a text has information which you already know something about. You're just looking for the new bits.

It's useful if you can switch between reading techniques. For example, you can scan an article until you find a word which relates to whatever interests you. You can then skim the section until you find an idea you want to know about. Then it's time to slow down and read carefully.

How general is the research?

Some research is specific to a time and place. For example, a survey to find out whether staff want a change in the shift system only applies to one specific ward at a particular time. It may not be much use to anyone else.

But what if the survey also aimed to find out how staff react to the idea of change? That's a much more general question. It would need a different and more complicated research design, but the outcomes might be useful to anyone wanting to bring about change in an organisation.

A part-time tutor in psychology at a college explains the difference:

66 *There is no reason why all research should aim to produce outcomes that can be generalised across a range of situations. A lot of practice-based research may be more useful if it is designed to produce very specific information. It is usually easier to do as well. Designing a research study that can produce outcomes applicable in different situations can be quite tricky. For most students, I suggest starting with a specific situation and designing their research round that. They can always see whether the outcomes might have a general interest later.* 99

The physical activity manager at the Health Education Authority explains how the results of many years of research can be put together to form a health policy:

66 *In 1996, 45 international experts were brought together to review the evidence and arrive at a consensus view on the strategy to adopt. Their report gave the recommendation that everyone should aim to do 30 minutes of moderate intensity physical activity on at least five days per week, which should ideally be sustained through the 30 minutes. A wide range of activities are suitable for this, including swimming, brisk walking, heavy housework, gardening and climbing stairs.* 99

DISCUSSION POINT

Look at your research question again. Are the outcomes likely to be of general interest or are they specific to a particular time and place? If you wanted the outcomes to be 'generalised across a range of situations', how would you need to alter the question?

UNIT

8

ELEMENT **8.2**

The research question is a starting point for asking:

■ What data are needed to answer this question?

■ How can the data be collected?

Answers to both of these questions should be suggested by the research question itself.

STRESS SUPPORT

Healthcare organisations need to look after their staff as well as care for their service users. A counsellor for one community care trust was asked to investigate the high stress levels experienced by staff. He set up and facilitated several support groups for community nurses, district nurses and school nurses.

After the groups had been running for several months, the counsellor was asked to carry out an evaluative study. The aim of the study was 'to evaluate the perceived advantages and disadvantages of attending facilitated staff support groups.'

To answer the research question, data were needed about:

■ what expectations people had of the groups

■ whether their expectations were met

■ advantages and disadvantages of the groups

■ how group members felt about the role of the facilitator.

The counsellor decided to collect these data from primary sources by sending a questionnaire to all 34 members of the groups. A first version of the questionnaire was piloted with a small number of the population, who helped to formulate the questions for the final version. The questionnaire asked respondents to:

■ answer a set of closed questions, using a five-point rating scale to record how helpful or unhelpful they felt various aspects of the group were

■ write their own open-ended comments on these aspects.

The questionnaire would therefore provide both quantitative and qualitative data.

The counsellor also decided to look at secondary sources to see whether other people in similar situations had tackled stress in the same way, and to draw on others' experiences of facilitating support groups.

ACTIVITY

Look carefully at the final version of your research question. What data are needed to answer the question?

Draw four columns on a piece of paper, or use the table function on a wordprocessor. List the data needed in the left-hand column (see the example produced by the researcher looking at stress support). Keep the paper or save your document: you will need them for later activities in this section.

Stress support: data requirements

data needed			
expectations of groups			
whether expectations met			
advantages/disadvantages			
role of facilitator			
dealing with stress			
facilitating support groups			

Primary sources are the original sources of data. They include participants in research projects and first-hand data collected by hospitals, GPs and other organisations. Examples include morbidity and mortality statistics and hospital activity data.

Primary sources

Some research projects aim to get data directly from the participants themselves, by interviews, observation, questionnaires or experiments. These might include gathering user responses, e.g. to a new service, or conducting attitude surveys. The participants are called primary sources. Other primary sources include demographic data about service users and data about diagnoses collected by hospital and other trusts and GPs. Primary sources are valuable because they provide first-hand, up-to-date data.

Hospital activity data

Information about service users is collected at the start of their stay in hospital. Data are entered from then on at different stages and by a variety of people, including:

- demographic details – things like sex, date of birth, marital status, ethnic origin

- diagnosis – codes from an international classification of diseases (ICD codes) are used

- operative procedures – another set of codes, known as OPCS codes, are used for this.

The number of times a service user sees a consultant, and the outcomes of each 'consultant episode', are also recorded. A simple surgical case may have three consultant episodes compared to five or six for a more complex case.

ACTIVITY

What data do you need to collect from primary sources to answer your research question? Which sources do you intend to use? What practical difficulties might there be in collecting the primary data?

Look back at the list of data you made in the activity on page 448. In the second column, put a P against the data that will come from primary sources. In the third column, note down what the sources are. In the fourth column, note down any practical difficulties you might face in collecting the data.

Stress support: data requirements

data needed	P/S	sources	practical difficulties
expectations of groups	P	members of support groups	possible low response rate to questionnaire
whether expectations met	P	as above	
advantages/disadvantages	P	as above	
role of facilitator	P	as above	
dealing with stress			
facilitating support groups			

Secondary sources are data that have been collected and analysed for another purpose. They include:

- quantitative data such as statistics on mortality, morbidity and hospital activity

- qualitative data such as research reports and case studies.

Secondary sources

Most researchers look at secondary sources in the early stages, when they are defining the research question. This is because they need to relate their own idea to research already carried out in the same area. If they find that the same question has already been asked in a similar situation, there may be no need to repeat the research. Or they might decide to:

- carry out a repeat study to check the outcomes of the first study
- build on the outcomes, by looking at one or more of the questions that remained unanswered in the first study or required further investigation.

Part of the research itself may involve secondary sources. For example, the counsellor in the case study on page 448 decided to review the outcomes of previous research into dealing with stress and facilitating support groups. The findings of this review were incorporated into the results of his own research with primary sources.

ACTIVITY

What data do you need to collect from secondary sources to answer your research question? Which sources do you intend to use? What practical difficulties might there be in collecting the secondary data?

Look back at the list of data you made in the activity on page 449. In the second column, put an S against the data that will come from secondary sources. In the third column, note down what the sources are. In the fourth column, note down any practical difficulties you might face in collecting the data.

Stress support: data requirements

data needed	P/S	sources	practical difficulties
expectations of groups	P	members of support groups	possible low response rate to questionnaire
whether expectations met	P	as above	
advantages/disadvantages	P	as above	
role of facilitator	P	as above	
dealing with stress	S	personnel journals, books on stress, NHSME papers etc.	many sources: need to define search categories closely
facilitating support groups	S	personnel and psychology journals	not much relevant experience in UK

Identifying an appropriate method

Methods for collecting and analysing data are described in sections 8.1.3–4. When researchers select their methods they check:

■ that the data collection method is 'fit for purpose' – will it provide the data needed?

■ sample size – what size of sample is needed to provide meaningful data? is it practical to collect data from this sample?

■ effect on participants – how will they be affected by the process of carrying out the research and by its outcomes?

■ data analysis – what statistical methods will be used to analyse quantitative data? how will the qualitative data be analysed systematically?

Fit for purpose

Some methods are better suited than others to certain types of research with primary sources. For example, the clinical trial of a new drug requires a special form of experiment called a 'double blind' trial so that neither the researcher nor the participants know which of them is trialling the drug and which has a placebo. Research into the possible effects of a stoma on the sexual activity of patients would require a very different approach.

Experiments are at one end of a 'spectrum' of research methods. They usually produce quantitative data. Other approaches are shown on the diagram below. They may use questionnaires, interviews or observation and tend to produce qualitative data (though they may produce quantitative data as well).

experimental approaches	**ethnographic approaches**	**phenomenological approaches**	**emancipatory approaches**
■ testing the validity of a hypothesis	■ studying how people interact in particular situations	■ describing the experience of being in a particular situation	■ helping people ('empowering' them) to examine and improve their own practices

quantitative   qualitative

ACTIVITY

Which of the four approaches shown on the diagram best describes your research?

Which of the four research methods – experiment, questionnaires, interviews, observation – will you use to collect the data from primary sources? (Remember that you can use a combination of methods.)

Add another column to the table you made earlier and note down which collection method(s) you will use.

Stress support: data requirements

data needed	P/S	sources	practical difficulties
expectations of groups	P	members of support groups	questionnaire
whether expectations met	P	as above	questionnaire
advantages/disadvantages	P	as above	questionnaire
role of facilitator	P	as above	? interviews

Sample size

One of the limitations of the research described in the case study on page 448 was the sample size. The counsellor who carried out the study recognised that although there was a high response rate to his questionnaire (62%), the small number of people who were sent the questionnaire (34 people in total) made it difficult to draw firm conclusions.

Some research requires large amounts of data. For example, an analysis of how people acquire HIV infection would need data from several regions (preferably the whole country) and over a period of time to provide meaningful information. Demographic and epidemiological research usually requires large data sets.

Other forms of research do not require large samples. For example, a study into the effects of stomata on patients' sexual activity can produce good results from just a few participants, as long as the data is obtained in a sensitive way.

DISCUSSION POINT

Who might be interested in this information about acquiring HIV infection? Why might they be interested in the results of research in this area? How might they use the information?

ACTIVITY

Who are the participants in your research? What sample size do you need to make the results meaningful? Write the sample size in the third column of your table.

Effect on participants

Participants can be affected by the process of taking part in research and by the outcomes. The effects can be positive (beneficial) or negative.

STRESS SUPPORT

This is how the counsellor who carried out an evaluation of the effect of support groups on staff stress levels summarised the positive and negative effects of his research on the participants.

		PROCESS	OUTCOMES
Positive	1.	made group members think about what they were getting from the groups	1. justified the existence of the groups and helped to maintain funding
	2	encouraged some members to attend meetings more regularly	2 provided ideas for improving how the groups work
Negative	1.	emphasised the negative feelings some members had about the group	None – yet!
	2	took a long time to complete the questionnaire	

A researcher carrying out interviews with women who have recently been diagnosed with ovarian cancer emphasises the need to avoid possible negative effects of the process where possible:

66 *My study is investigating the psychosexual effects of the diagnosis, so the subject matter is especially sensitive. Some people find it very difficult to talk about their feelings, especially feelings about sex. You have to be very sensitive and not push people to talk if they appear to be getting upset. However, some people welcome the opportunity to talk about difficult things even if it does make them upset. The important thing is to let them make the choices all the time, whether to go on talking or turn to another subject.* 99

ACTIVITY

What possible effects are there on the participants in your research? Make a table like the one in the case study above to show the possible positive and negative effects of:

■ the process of taking part

■ the outcomes of the research.

If you are working in a group, discuss the possible effects together first.

Data analysis

In the planning stage, researchers decide what methods they will use to analyse the data collected. The main analytical techniques for both quantitative and qualitative data are described below. Most research produces at least some data which can be analysed using quantitative methods, even if the main purpose is to generate qualitative data.

Quantitative data analysis

Large amounts of quantitative data are usually analysed using computers, which do the job quickly and accurately. Software packages are available specifically for analysing quantitative data. The most important thing is to collect the data in a way which makes it easy to enter on to the computer. This normally means using codes (see page 454). Spreadsheets can also be used to analyse data. Small amounts of numerical data can be analysed by hand, using tally charts and calculators.

Data are normally arranged into rows and columns, as in a table of results from an experiment:

■ rows correspond to records – such as all the data obtained from one respondent

■ columns contain the data for a single variable.

Data sets

The table below shows the data obtained from four respondents who completed a questionnaire. The first three questions asked them to give a score from 1 to 5. The fourth question was a simple Yes or No answer. The fifth question asked respondents to specify a range from an option of six ranges, coded a, b, c, etc.

respondent	Q1 score	Q2 score	Q3 score	Q4	Q5
A	3	4	3	Y	e
B	1	0	2	Y	b
C	2	5	3	N	d
D	4	4	1	Y	c

Once the data have been analysed in this way, they form a data set. The data set can then be analysed further. Examples of further analysis include:

- frequency distribution – the number of times certain things happen, e.g. the number of respondents who answered Yes to a Yes or No question
- graphical displays – histograms, bar charts, pie charts
- summary statistics – such as the level and spread of distribution (range, interquartile range, variance, standard deviation); these can also be shown on graphs and scatter diagrams.

Data can also be manipulated or transformed` in various ways. For example, they can be:

- rescaled, by multiplying by a constant – for example, when imperial weights (lbs and ozs) are converted into metric equivalents
- standardised – for example to gain a standardised score from a set of individual scores.

Quantitative analysis often looks at the relationship between variables. For example, the link between smoking and lung cancer is shown quantitatively by the fact that the distribution of scores on one variable (smoker as opposed to non-smoker) links to the distribution of scores on another variable (lung cancer, no lung cancer). The strength of relationships between variables can be measured using correlation coefficients.

DISCUSSION POINT

Most of the methods described here are included in the Application of number key skills unit at level 3. What is the use of being able to analyse data in these ways? See if you can think of examples from health and social care where each of the quantitative methods described above has been used.

ACTIVITY

What sort of numerical data will your research produce? Describe the data you expect to get and how you will turn them into a usable data set. If you intend to do this on a computer, specify the package you will use.

You may want to analyse the data further using quantitative methods. If so, why? Which methods will you use? How will you expect to present the data?

If you are not sure about which quantitative methods to use or not confident about your ability to use them, now is a good time to practise. Keep a record of all the work you do as evidence for the Application of number unit in your GNVQ.

Three tips for analysing qualitative data

Tip 1

Start analysing as soon as you collect data – don't leave all the analysis to the end. This is because you may see more categories, or groupings of categories, once you start, which could make the process easier from then on.

Tip 2

Index the data as you go along – for example, if you are analysing interview notes or written comments on a questionnaire, you could use a highlighter pen to index different categories. File the data by categories. It is much easier to do this if the data are on computer, as you can use the cut and paste functions.

Tip 3

Remember that there isn't a single right way of doing the analysis. Follow your own rules, for example for categorising data. But don't let that stop you thinking of new, perhaps better ways of categorising it. Keep thinking about what the data are saying to you.

Qualitative data analysis

Qualitative data usually consist of words: transcripts or notes of interviews with other people, written comments on questionnaires, the researcher's own field notes. It may also include images, such as video recordings and visual records of observation (sketches, diagrams).

This can all be very rich – and quite tricky to analyse systematically if the analysis is left to the end. At the planning stage, researchers normally identify themes, patterns or other categories they are looking for. They may also have decided on a system for coding the data. Coded data can be analysed to form a data set (see page 454).

Analysing qualitative data means taking something complete – interview notes or a completed questionnaire – and rearranging bits of it according to a pattern or plan. It is, sometimes literally, a scissors and paste job. The important things to remember are;

- what are you analysing the data for?
- what categories are you looking out for?
- where do you put the data you 'cut out' of the complete thing?

ACTIVITY

What sort of qualitative data will your research produce? Describe the data you expect to get. Then describe:

- the categories you intend to use for sorting the data (remember these may change once you start the analysis)
- the method you will use to index the data by categories
- how you intend to file the data – if you are doing this on a computer, specify the package you will use.

If you are not confident about your ability to analyse written and visual data in the ways described above, now is a good time to practise. Keep a record of all the work you do as evidence for the Communication key skills unit in your GNVQ.

Handling ethical issues

At the planning stage, researchers should plan how to:

- tell participants about the potential benefits of the research and make sure they have access to these benefits

- anticipate negative effects of the research on participants and take steps to avoid or reduce them

- keep information confidential

- tell participants about their rights

- avoid any sort of cultural bias.

ACTIVITY

How do you intend to inform the people involved in your research about the benefits:

- in advance?

- afterwards?

DISCUSSION POINT

A student on a Science GNVQ course plans to research the effects of exercise on the heart rate of ten people in his year at college. He wants to relate the results to physical factors such as height and weight, so he plans to select people who are overweight and do not take much exercise as well as those who are more athletic. He is thinking of giving them all the same ten-minute exercise routine.

In what ways might this student's plan be unethical? How would you advise him to change the design of his research?

An ethical approach should be built in to health and social care research projects at all stages. Ethical considerations inform the research question and the methods chosen. For example, it would not be ethical for a researcher who knows very little about family relations in Asian communities to carry out comparative research into the influence of family and peer-group pressure on the health or lifestyle choices of teenage Asian girls.

Information obtained from research which is unethical in any way is not normally seen as useful or reliable.

Benefits

Research aims to benefit the person doing the research and other people as well. To behave ethically, researchers should make sure that all participants:
- know what the potential benefits are to them
- are able to benefit, e.g. by having access to the outcomes.

Making sure that people can benefit from research means informing them of:
- the aims of the study and any benefits they might get from taking part – this could be done in a letter inviting them to participate, or at the top of a questionnaire
- the outcomes – this could be done by giving them a copy of the report.

Effects on participants

People who take part in research might feel negative effects. In health and social care research, the main risks are to:
- their psychological wellbeing – if research is intrusive or insensitive
- their health – the clear rule here is that participants should not be exposed to any risks greater than they face in their normal lifestyles
- their values – the risk of causing offence is greater if researchers come from a different culture or social background from the participants
- their dignity – with people who have conditions which make them feel uncomfortable, the research process could make them feel worse.

How do researchers handle negative effects of the research process?

The best way is to avoid them in the first place. A good research design which follows the ethical principles discussed above and in section 8.1.2 will reduce the risk of negative effects. Interviews are the most risky from this point of view, because of the close contact between two people and the exploratory nature of the conversation. Two ways of reducing the risk are:
- being sensitive to how the person being interviewed is feeling – this helps to steer the conversation away from difficult issues
- regular, frequent debriefing – this helps to identify any issues which may cause a problem if they are explored further.

If the negative effects are too strong, there are two options:
- participants can withdraw from the research
- the researcher should reconsider the design and discuss the problem with a colleague or supervisor.

Confidentiality

The simple rule about confidentiality is that any information obtained about a participant during an investigation is confidential unless agreed with the person in advance. Any published information should not reveal the identity of participants. The rule of confidentiality applies to:

■ how the information is kept
■ how it is used in the report or other outcomes
■ what other use is made of it.

Participants' rights

Apart from confidentiality, participants have the right to:

■ take part only if they have given their informed consent – patients admitted to hospital for surgery are required to sign an informed consent form before surgery can go ahead
■ withdraw from the research at any time
■ comment on the outcomes of the research before it is published.

Culture

The ethical principles developed by the British Psychological Society for conducting research with human participants say that: 'in our multicultural and multi-ethnic society . . . the investigators may not have sufficient knowledge of the implications of any investigation for the participants.' This is also true if a study involves people of different ages, sex or social background from the researcher.

How to avoid culture shock

Choose participants from groups that you know about at first hand, in terms of age, sex, social background and ethnic background.

Be aware of any bias or prejudice in yourself and guard against it. Remember that bias is often unconscious, so:

■ keep your eyes open for it

■ look for signals in others, like being offended or shutting down

■ check it out with participants – ask them openly if anything you do or say is causing offence.

Collecting data

ACTIVITY

Many schools and colleges have a policy defining how students should send out questionnaires. For example, they may require a covering letter to go out with the questionnaires. Find out what the policy is in your own school or college.

The first four sections in this element describe the stages of planning a research study. If you have done all the activities, you should be almost ready to start collecting the data for your own project. Before you start, there are three more things you should do:

- prepare your research instruments and try them out
- agree a timescale, including review points
- agree a contingency strategy, including an escape route if things go badly.

Prepare and test research instruments

The research instruments are the things you will use to collect the data:

- questionnaires
- interview questions and record sheets
- observation sheets
- equipment for experiments.

Remember that a research instrument, like any other tool, should be fit for its purpose. Ask yourself: what do I need it to do? It makes sense to test your instruments with two or three people before you start the research. You may need to make some final adjustments to the wording or layout. Always test them with people from a similar group to the population you are researching.

Preparing instruments

Questionnaires should be produced on a wordprocessor or desktop-publishing package. They should give clear instructions and be easy to read, with enough space for respondents to write in their comments. There should be a short statement at the top saying:

- what the aim of the research is
- when the completed form should be returned
- who it should be returned to (name and address).

Interview questions should be clear, unambiguous and not too long – the aim is to get other people to do the talking. It is always useful to have another way of putting the same question, in case people don't understand at first. For example, you could ask either of these because they amount to the same thing:

- 'Is the length of handover between shifts adequate?'
- 'Do you usually have enough time to hand over to new staff at the end of your shift?'

Interview record sheets are for you to fill in. They may contain quantitative or qualitative data. If you have identified categories to look out for (such as the number of times people mention a particular issue), the sheet should list the categories and give space for recording how often they occur. If you are taking notes, leave plenty of space to write in between each question. There should be space at the top to write down:

- the name of the person doing the interview
- the codename of the person being interviewed
- the place where the interview was conducted
- the date of the interview, the time it started and the time it ended.

Observation sheets are like interview record sheets. They may have space for recording quantitative data or written notes.

ACTIVITY

Prepare a final version of all the instruments you need. Then test them. Note down what changes, if any, are needed. Then make the changes. Produce as many copies as you need, keeping one clean copy for your report.

Timescale and review points

Set a realistic timescale for collecting the data. Bear in mind that:

- people need time to complete and return a questionnaire – if you are sending them by post, allow at least three weeks before they are due to be returned and an extra week to do any chasing necessary
- it takes time to set up interviews – allow three to four weeks between contacting participants and interviewing them
- it also takes time to listen to recordings and write up notes – allow three or four times as long for this as for the interview itself.

Build in times to review progress. This is especially important if you are working in a group.

ACTIVITY

Prepare a timetable for doing the research. If you are working in a group, make sure that everyone can stick to it. Keep a copy of the timetable for yourself and check your own progress regularly.

Contingency strategy

What if the process of collecting data doesn't go to plan? Possible problems include:

- a low response rate to questionnaires
- people are not available for interview in the timescale
- the instruments don't seem to be producing the sort of data required
- too many participants withdraw.

There are really only two options. You could start again with a new timetable, a different sample and a revised set of instruments. Or you could carry on, analyse the data that you do manage to obtain and review the problems in your report. A report that is open and honest about the problems and identifies flaws in the design is more useful than one that hides them: it may help other researchers in future to avoid the problems and redesign the research.

And now it's time to start gathering the data. Good luck.

ACTIVITY

Agree with the person supervising your research and your research colleagues (if you are working in a group) what you will do if things go wrong.

Key questions

1 What is the rationale for your research?
2 Who is your research aimed at (the target group)?
3 How does your research question relate to previous research?
4 How specific is your research question and to what extent do you think the results of the research can be generalised?
5 What are your primary sources of data?
6 What are your secondary sources of data?
7 What method(s) will you use to obtain primary data? secondary data?
8 What quantitative methods will you use to analyse the data?
9 What qualitative methods will you use to analyse the data?
10 What ethical issues have you identified that may arise in your research?
11 How do you plan to handle those issues?
12 Have you prepared and tested the instruments for collecting data?
13 Do you have a realistic timescale for carrying out the data collection process?
14 What will you do if things don't go according to plan?

Assignment

This assignment is in two parts.

Part 1

Collect together all the working papers you produced by doing the activities in this element. Organise them in a folder under the four headings:
- rationale for the research
- sources of data
- research method(s)
- ethical issues.

Code each item and produce a list of contents showing what papers are contained under each heading. Remember to include a clean copy of all the research instruments you prepared. If you are working in a group, attach a note to each working paper describing your personal contribution to that particular stage.

Part 2

Collect together all the data you have gathered. Sort it into a sensible order so that it is ready for analysing. When you have done that, make a full list of all the data you have. Keep the list with the working papers from Part 1 of the assignment. Keep the data in a safe place until you are ready to analyse it.

Reflect on the process of collecting the data. You could do this on your own or with others if you are working in a group. Ask questions like these:
- Did it go according to plan?
- What problems were there?
- How did you feel about the process?
- How do you think the participants felt?
- How well did the instruments work?
- What would you do differently next time?

Write down your reflections. They will be a valuable addition to the working papers you collected in Part 1.

> **"** *I was involved in a highly practical research project which looked at particular categories of equipment for the disabled, including toilet and bathing aids for disabled children. The rationale was rather like that of a consumer report: to gather the views of patients and therapists on the equipment and evaluate it. The resulting data helps therapists provide an effective service. For those in isolated communities it is an essential reference.* **"**

occupational therapy services manager

> **"** *If we know about how child abuse happens, we should be able to formulate procedures on how to avoid it. So I hope the conclusions and recommendations from my research will be of use to other professionals in working more effectively with clients.* **"**

child protection adviser

> **"** *Research is vital within psychological services. There is very little evidence-based medicine for it. It is difficult to check outcomes – how do you measure quality of life? Effective psychological services could save the health service money on other care. What we are aiming to show as a result of our research is that access to counselling does work.* **"**

head of medical counselling and family support

> **"** *It's essential to read the results of research in places like the Pharmaceutical Journal.* **"**

pharmacist

ELEMENT **8.3**

Presenting the findings of research

This element continues the research project started in element 8.2. You will be analysing the data you have collected and producing conclusions based on your interpretation of the analysed data. Then you will write a final report containing all the relevant information about the process as well as the outcomes of your research. The report will include recommendations for further research. Finally, you will present your conclusions to a small group of people who know something about the area of health and social care you studied, and answer their questions.

Analysing data and producing conclusions

Quantitative analysis

create a data set

analyse the data set
frequency distribution
graphic displays
summary statistics

manipulate/transform the data
rescale
standardise

look at the relationship
between variables

Qualitative analysis

identify themes, patterns
and categories

decide on a coding system

index the data

file the data by categories

group categories

Methods of analysing data are described in section 8.1.4 and section 8.2.3. You may want to read those sections again before you start analysing the data from your own research.

Quantitative and qualitative analysis

Both primary and secondary data should be analysed. Quantitative methods should be used for numerical data, qualitative methods for other forms of data. The process of analysing the two types of data is summarised in the two flow charts on this page.

COMPARING SHIFTS: DATA ANALYSIS

A clinical nurse manager at a hospital trust carried out a comparative study of staff working twelve-hour and eight-hour shifts to evaluate the effect of the two shift systems on staff and the quality of care. Data was collected through:

- questionnaires sent to 100 staff on four wards (two working each shift system)
- semi-structured interviews with 20 staff.

Data from the questionnaires was used to create a data set which compared variables between the twelve-hour and eight-hour wards. An example of a variable was the level of sickness reported in the two types of ward in two different eight-week periods. The figures are expressed in whole-time equivalents.

Ward	twelve-hour shifts		eight-hour shifts	
	A	B	C	D
Period 1	12.89	2.67	6.47	12.22
Period 2	5.36	8.92	11.83	5.5

The semi-structured interviews also generated numerical data in relation to how staff felt about working 8-hour and 12-hour shifts. Some staff had worked both shifts.

	12-hour shifts	8-hour shifts
Number of staff interviewed	10	10
Tiredness reported working eight-hour shift	8	10
Tiredness reported working twelve-hour shift	2	–
Enough time for handover	6	10
Communication between staff could be better	6	8

The person who carried out the research described above called it a 'descriptive study'. This explains why she did not analyse the data set using any of the quantitative methods listed in the flow chart. If she had called the study analytical rather than descriptive, what sort of analysis of the figures would you expect to see?

In the assignment at the end of element 8.2, you gathered together all the data collected in your research and made a full list. Look back at the list. If you haven't already done this, group the data into two types:

■ numerical data

■ data in other forms (words, images).

Which methods of analysis will you use to analyse the data? Attach a note to each type of data. The note should:

■ describe which method(s) of analysis you intend to use

■ explain why you chose these methods.

Now use the methods you have chosen to analyse the data. Gather the results of your analysis in a folder. Keep all your working papers in a separate folder.

Valid conclusions

To be valid, conclusions should be:

■ consistent with the data

■ based on evidence collected during the research

■ closely related to the research question

■ relevant to the purpose of the research

■ within confidence limits.

Other units in this book have reported research findings or referred you to them (see especially units 4, 5 and 6). Look at some of those reports now and see how they present their conclusions.

Producing valid conclusions

After the data is analysed, researchers should be ready to:

■ summarise the results

■ provide an interpretation of what they mean

■ draw conclusions from the study

■ make recommendations based upon these conclusions.

A research supervisor advises how to draw valid conclusions:

❝ *All conclusions should derive from the data you have collected, whether they are from primary or secondary sources or a combination of both. You have to be able to justify everything you say on the basis of your analysis and interpretation of the data. That's the first thing. The second is to draw conclusions that relate to your research question and the purpose of the research. Any conclusions that don't do that are irrelevant. Lastly, you have to state the limits of confidence: how reliable and valid are the outcomes of your research?* ❞

Conclusions from quantitative analysis

A summary of results from quantitative analysis should start with a general outline of the findings. Where possible, this should be illustrated with:

■ tables of results

■ statistics derived from the tables, such as averages or standard deviations (see pages 435–437) – these can be in graphical form.

Further quantitative analysis can be used to interpret the data in more detail. If the analysis shows a correlation between the variables in a hypothesis, this may indicate a link. If there are doubts about this – for example, because of other factors – the recommendations can suggest further work that could be done to investigate the relationship between variables.

COMPARING SHIFTS: CONCLUSIONS

After analysing all the data from her questionnaires and interviews, the clinical nurse manager concluded that staff on twelve-hour shifts:

- spend more time on patient care than staff on eight-hour shifts
- make better use of their free time during the shifts
- provide better continuity of care for patients
- get less tired than their colleagues on eight-hour shifts

On the negative side, she concluded that staff on the longer shifts:

- needed more time for handover between shifts
- want better communication amongst themselves.

The researcher then cross-checked her conclusions with findings from other studies. She noted some important differences – for example, previous research had found that twelve-hour shifts reduced rather than increased direct patient care. She explained these differences by the attitude of staff to change: a positive attitude resulted in positive changes and vice versa.

Conclusions from qualitative analysis

When reporting a qualitative study, the aim is to capture and convey a sense of the particular reality the research was looking at. Conclusions should 'stay close to the data'. In particular, it is important not to draw conclusions that are not supported by the study. It's often not easy to generalise qualitative research to other situations, so avoid the temptation of suggesting that the findings have wider implications than in fact they have.

A qualitative study may not produce definite recommendations. It may be more likely to produce:
- insights which other people may find helpful in their practice
- a theory which could be developed further
- better understanding of how an existing theory applies in a particular context
- a hypothesis which could be tested out in further research.

One way to guard against over-interpreting the results is to discuss them with friends and colleagues. Different people may give different explanations based on analysis of the same data.

Confidence limits

How confident can researchers be that their conclusions are valid? It's only possible to be really confident if the results confirm several previous research studies and none of the data points in any other direction. The conclusion that most people benefit from regular, moderate exercise is an example.

Confidence can be reduced by:
- sample size and selection – is the sample big enough to support the conclusions? is it representative of the population being studied?
- research question or hypothesis – is the question exact and clear? does the hypothesis make sense?
- methods of collecting and analysing data – are they appropriate? have they been carried out consistently?
- bias and error – what bias is there in the interpretation? how has the researcher tried to avoid errors in observation?

ACTIVITY

Look carefully at the results of your analysis. If you are working in a group, discuss the results with others. What conclusions do they suggest? How do the conclusions relate to your research question? How confident do you feel about them?

Write down your conclusions. Make sure they can all be backed up by the evidence. Add a note explaining any factors that limit the confidence of your results.

Producing a final report

Research reports are special pieces of writing. They are easier to write if you follow guidelines for:

- structure
- writing style
- graphs and tables
- the writing process.

Structure

Most reports follow a structure like the one shown in the table below. Long reports may be divided into sections, with a contents list at the start. Shorter reports may not have separate sections, but they often use headings to show where a new part of the report starts.

Part of report	What's in it
title	says what kind of study it is, what topic is being studied and the population
summary (abstract)	a brief summary of the aims, methods, results and conclusions
introduction	explains why the study was done
methods	describes methods of collecting and analysing data, giving details of research instruments, sample size, place and dates when data was collected
results	summarises the analysis of data, using tables, charts and graphs where appropriate
discussion	presents the interpretation of data and discusses limitations
conclusion	summarises conclusions and discusses the implications for practice and/or theory
recommendations	presents suggestions for actions and/or further research
references	lists the books and articles you have consulted for the research
appendices	includes research instruments and any relevant data such as selection of data

Writing style

Keep the writing simple and direct. Try to express the meaning as clearly and concisely as possible. Don't use colloquial or emotive language, but don't be too formal either. Use technical terms where they are needed, but don't use jargon.

Quantitative studies usually avoid the first person singular or plural ('I' or 'we'). In qualitative research, where the actions and reactions of the researcher are often central to the study, first person sentences are used more often.

When you refer to studies in the text of your report, include the surname of the author(s) and the date of the book or article in brackets, like this:

> Critics argue that there has been a serious decline in local accountability of NHS organisations (Hunter 1992).

List all the references at the end of the report, before the appendices, like this:

> Hunter, D. (1992) Accountability and the NHS. In: Smith, R. (ed.) *The Future of Health Care*. London: BMJ Publishing

DISCUSSION POINT

Have a look at three or four research reports from a range of journals. Concentrate on the writing style. Which of the points mentioned above can you spot in the writing?

465

Graphs and tables

Use computer software wherever possible to produce graphs and tables. Many wordprocessing and spreadsheet packages include this facility.

Keep them simple and straightforward. It's easy to produce 3-D effects or multi-coloured pie charts but they are rarely useful. Readers are interested in what the data shows, not in fancy ways of presenting it. Take care not to mislead readers, for example by using different types of scale on two graphs you want them to compare. All graphs, tables and diagrams should be numbered and given a title.

plan what to put in – and what to leave out

write a draft

edit and rewrite the draft

check the grammar, spelling, etc.

make a final version

The writing process

Writing is easier if you do it in stages.

Start by doing a plan of what you are going to write about. You already have an overall structure of the report (see page 465). Think about the points you want to cover in each section.

Write a first draft. Don't worry if it's rough and ready. It is much better to get something down on paper, even if it's not exactly what you want to say. Write the whole of your report in draft before you go to the next stage. There is no need to write it in order – some bits that go near the beginning, like the introduction and abstract, should be written last. Some people start by writing about the methods because they feel confident about describing them. When you have finished the first draft, check it over to see if you have missed out anything important and whether your argument makes sense. Don't worry about spelling or grammar yet.

Now edit the draft. Read the whole draft over with a pen in your hand and write notes to yourself about what to do. For example, you might want to move bits around or make a point more clearly. Then do any rewriting that's needed. All this is much easier if the draft is on a wordprocessor.

Check the draft for grammar, style, punctuation and spelling. Put it through a spell-check, if you are using a wordprocessor. Then check that you have listed all the references, numbered the tables and figures and given them all a title.

A researcher who has just finished writing her report gives some last-minute advice:

66 *If you can, leave a day or so between finishing the report and the date you have scheduled for making a final version. Before you produce the final version, reread it all. You may find last-minute improvements you can make.* 99

ACTIVITY

Go through the stages listed above to produce your report. When you have edited the draft, but before making the final version, go through this checklist. It lists the things your report should describe. Tick off each item if you are sure your report contains it. If there isn't a tick, something is missing and you need to add it in.

Report checklist

Make sure your report describes everything on this list.

- the research process ☐

- methods you used to obtain the data ☐

- methods you used to analyse the data ☐

- any ethical issues raised by the research ☐

- how you handled ethical issues ☐

- the impact of the research process on participants ☐

- limitations of the research ☐

- the extent to which your conclusions can be generalised ☐

Presenting conclusions and recommendations

aim of research

⌄

research question

⌄

research methods:
collecting data
analysing data

⌄

description of findings

⌄

conclusions

Sometimes researchers are asked to present the results of their research to others at a meeting or conference. The order of a presentation is similar to that of a report, as the diagram shows. The aim of a presentation is to:

■ state the conclusions and show how they relate to the data
■ summarise the content of the report and its main messages
■ communicate in a style and at a level appropriate to the audience.

Presentations should be prepared in advance. A university researcher who studied the psychosocial impact of ovarian cancer diagnosis explains:

66 *I had worked closely with a consultant oncologist during this research. I gave him a copy of my paper and a few days later he rang and asked me if I would present the results at a study day at the hospital. We agreed that he would introduce the study and I would present the outcomes. I produced three overhead projector slides which introduced the presentation and summarised the method and findings. I also wrote a page of clear notes – just the headings of what I wanted to say so I would get them in the right order.* 99

Relate conclusions to the data

A researcher's work doesn't end when the research report is made available to others. An important part of the research process is critical review by a peer group, including other researchers and practitioners with a first-hand knowledge of the area of study.

The conclusions are one of the most interesting bits of a research report for anyone who knows the area of study. They will want to see whether the research has revealed anything new or different from earlier research. They will look closely at how the data was obtained and analysed, to check that:

■ the methods used are reliable and valid, and demonstrate good practice
■ the data justifies the conclusions.

A well-informed audience is likely to ask questions about these things in a presentation as well. You can't predict their questions, but you can be well prepared by being confident about the purpose of the research, how it was done and the conclusions .

Content and messages

When a research report or an article based on research is published, readers can look at it several times. They have a chance to focus on the bits that interest or worry them. In a presentation, they – and you – only have one chance, and there isn't usually a lot of time. So:

■ restrict what the presentation contains – its content – to the essentials
■ get the messages across clearly and concisely.

One of the dangers in a presentation is trying to say too much. Speaking always takes a lot longer than reading. It takes about a minute to speak aloud 150 words, at moderate speed. So a ten-minute presentation should not be

Preparing for a presentation (1)

Make clear, short notes to help you:

■ describe the methods used for collecting and analysing data
■ explain why these methods were chosen – especially the choice of quantitative and/or qualitative methods
■ state the conclusions clearly
■ show how the conclusions are justified by the data
■ explain the limitations of your research.

Preparing for a presentation (2)

Select what to say – and what to leave out. Then prepare OHP slides outlining:

- what's in the presentation (OHP slide 1)
- the aim of the research and research question (OHP slide 2)
- the research methods
- the findings
- the conclusions.

DISCUSSION POINT

Read the transcript on the right carefully. How is the style different from what you would expect in a written report? What do you think the extract says about the level of knowledge of the audience? How would you change the level for a different audience?

longer than 1,500 words. If time is added in for showing overhead projector slides or other images, the number of words goes down to 1,000 or less – that's between two and three pages of typescript.

OHP slides give the audience something to look at apart from the presenter and help to fix the main points in their minds. They also remind the presenter what to say. Sometimes OHP slides are photocopied and given out either before or just after a presentation. In a ten-minute presentation, the number of slides should be restricted to four or five. Each one should only contain three or four points and a maximum of 20 words.

Style and level

A presentation is a formal event and should follow a clear structure. The style of communication should also be formal, but not too distant – it's not a lecture. The aim is to present the findings as clearly a possible, not to convince the audience. If the audience knows about the area of study, technical terms can be used. They should be explained briefly the first time they are used. If the audience is not well-informed, technical terms should be avoided.

This is a transcript of a short extract from the research student's presentation on the effects of a diagnosis of ovarian cancer:

66 *The effects of the diagnosis on sexual functioning seem to be unrelated to the stage of the disease, the age of the patient or the treatment phase. Of the seven patients I studied, one was sexually inactive before diagnosis, one was more active after the diagnosis, three were less active and two told me there was no change in their sexual activity. The patient who reported increased activity and registered highest on the SAQ [sexual activity questionnaire] was 44 years old, at stage 3 and in treatment. The patient who had the lowest SAQ was aged 26, at stage 1c and in remission.* 99

When the formal presentation is over, people normally want to ask questions. Answers may need to go into more detail than was possible in the presentation – for example, people might want you to describe the sample more fully or justify an aspect of your conclusions.

ACTIVITY

Prepare to present the conclusions of your research to a small group of three to five people. They will know something about the area of study and will want to ask questions. If you have been working in a group, agree with the others who should do which part of the presentation – make sure you all do a roughly equal amount.

Prepare for the presentation by:

- making a small number of overhead projector slides
- writing a page of notes showing the main headings
- practising the presentation – check the timing (aim to spend between ten and fifteen minutes making your presentation).

Make a final check that you are able to:

- relate your conclusions to the data you obtained
- present the messages clearly and concisely
- address your audience in an appropriate style – neither too informal, nor too formal – and at a level appropriate to their knowledge of the subject.

Recommendations

If the purpose of the research is to inform policy or practice, recommendations can be in the form of actions justified in relation to the outcomes. For example, one of the outcomes of the research into the differences between eight-hour and twelve-hour shifts (see page 464) was that the benefits of the twelve-hour shift are greater if the transition from one type of shift to the other is undertaken by staff themselves. The recommendation could be:

66 *Any decision to change from an eight-hour to a twelve-hour shift should be taken on the basis of full consultation with staff and the process of transition should involve staff at all stages.* 99

If the purpose is to test a hypothesis or contribute to knowledge, recommendations often say what further research could be done to:
- check the results – with a different sample or using other methods
- extend knowledge and understanding of the subject further.

One recommendation from the study of patients with ovarian cancer was:

66 *A more detailed investigation is needed into the effects of diagnosis on younger patients, looking at their anxieties about fertility and ageing and focusing on how they deal with problems to do with their sexuality.* 99

Recommendations are the actions that can be taken arising from the outcomes of research. All recommendations should be:
- derived from the research
- practical.

ACTIVITY

What recommendations can be made, based on the outcomes of your report? Do they recommend:
- changes to policy or practice?
- further research?

Think carefully about the recommendations you can make. If you are working in a group, discuss them with others. Try writing them down, using the formal language of the recommendations quoted above. You may need several goes before you are sure that the recommendations:
- arise from the research outcomes
- are practical.

Key questions

1 What quantitative methods did you use to analyse the data from your research?
2 Why do you choose these methods?
3 What qualitative methods did you use to analyse the data from your research?
4 Why do you choose these methods?
5 What conclusions did you draw from the analysis of data?
6 How did you check that your conclusions are related to the purpose of your research and consistent with the data?
7 What are the limits of confidence of your conclusions?
8 What do the diagrams and charts in your report illustrate?
9 How did you check that your report contains all the relevant information?
10 What were the content and main messages of your presentation?
11 What visual material did you prepare for the presentation?
12 What feedback did you get on the quality of your presentation?
13 What recommendations did you make, based on the outcomes of your research?

Assignment

This assignment is in two parts.

Part 1

Analyse the data collected in element 8.2. Follow the process for analysing quantitative and/or qualitative data outlined on page 462. When you have completed the analysis, draw conclusions.

Now write a report of your research, following the guidelines in section 8.3.2. Go through all the stages of the writing process until you have a final version.

Reflect on the process of analysing the data and producing your report. You could do this on your own or with others if you are working in a group. Ask questions like these:

■ Did you use the analytical methods identified in the activity on page 463?
■ What problems were there with the analysis?
■ How did you overcome the problems?
■ What problems were there with writing the report?
■ How would you do it differently next time?

Write down your reflections. They will contribute to the grading of your GNVQ.

Part 2

Prepare for and give a presentation of your research to a small group of three to five people who know about your area of study. Your tutor and/or assessor will help to get the group together. It could include:

■ other students on your GNVQ course (not counting students in your group, if you did the research as a group activity)
■ tutors in your school or college
■ people who work in an area of health or social care related to the area you studied in the research
■ anyone else who supervised the research process.

Keep copies of presentation notes and any visual material, such as overhead projector slides. You should also keep a record of how the audience reacted to your presentation. This could be in the form of:

■ a video recording of the presentation and the question and answer session afterwards
■ an observation sheet completed by an observer
■ signed statements by members of the audience commenting on the quality of your presentation.

Index